She-Wolves

ALSO BY PAULINA BREN

The Barbizon:
The Hotel That Set Women Free

The Greengrocer and His TV:
The Culture of Communism after the 1968 Prague Spring

Communism Unwrapped:
Consumption in Cold War Eastern Europe (coeditor)

She-Wolves

THE UNTOLD HISTORY OF WOMEN ON WALL STREET

Paulina Bren

W. W. NORTON & COMPANY

Independent Publishers Since 1923

For information about special discounts for bulk purchases,
please contact W. W. Norton Special Sales at
specialsales@wwnorton.com or 800-233-4830

Manufacturing by Lake Book Manufacturing
Book design by Daniel Lagin
Production manager: Lauren Abbate

ISBN 978-1-324-03515-2

W. W. Norton & Company, Inc.
500 Fifth Avenue, New York, N.Y. 10110
www.wwnorton.com

W. W. Norton & Company Ltd.
15 Carlisle Street, London W1D 3BS

1 2 3 4 5 6 7 8 9 0

Contents

She-Wolves

Prologue

efore one even asks what Wall Street has become, one has to know what Wall Street was. The Wall Street that the women here experienced is long gone. It was a time when the New York Stock Exchange was still teeming with brokers, clerks, and runners, the clamor punctuated by the metallic flap of a badge number on the call board, paper flying in all directions, swept up into enormous piles, sometimes weighing up to three tons and carted off at night long after the closing bell. It was a time when a veritable army of secretaries and teletypists and data-entry clerks poured out of the subways in the mornings, the ambitious ones staying on after hours to attend night classes at New York University's business school or the Institute of Finance, both near Wall Street's Trinity Church. It was a time when the big-name firms were certainly there—JP Morgan, Goldman Sachs, Lehman Brothers, Merrill Lynch, Bear Stearns—but smaller firms had a presence, too, giving Wall Street a distinct character and feel. It was at these small brokerage houses that the women who dared enter this male bastion, this old-boys' club, could find a foothold, however precarious.

The female pioneers of Wall Street, its original She-Wolves, pushed into uncharted territory not knowing what awaited them there other than men, lots of men, few of whom were going to roll out a welcome mat. As one of the specialists, those at the very top of the New York Stock Exchange hierarchy, whispered to Alice Jarcho, the first woman to trade full-time on the floor: ". . . you do not belong here."

The She-Wolves arrived on Wall Street at the same moment as the women's movement was starting. In 1968, the tobacco company Philip Morris came out with a cigarette, Virginia Slims, specifically targeted at women. Its tagline was: "You've Come a Long Way, Baby!" The phrase, used up until the 1990s, caught on quickly, entering pop culture, where it was repackaged and coopted in all sorts of ways. The timeline for this book runs parallel with the life-span of their tagline, while also asking: *Have* you come a long way, baby?

Billionaire Paul Tudor Jones, of the hedge fund Tudor Investment Corporation, was called out on his response during a panel at the University of Virginia in 2013 when he was asked by an audience member why the panel only featured "rich, white, middle-aged men." He replied: "You will never see as many great women investors or traders as men. Period. End of story. . . . Take a girl that was my age . . . back in the '70s. I can think of two that actually started at E. F. Hutton with me. Within four years, by 1980, right when I was getting ready to launch my company, they both got married. And then they both had . . . children. As soon as that baby's lips touched that girl's bosom, forget it. . . . And I've just seen it happen over and over . . ."

The story told in the following pages challenges everything he said.

1

Jamming a Foot in the Door

The "go-go years" had finally come to Wall Street. In 1960, a good day on the floor of the New York Stock Exchange meant 4 million shares traded, but by 1967 it would be closer to 10 million. "Glamour stocks" with futuristic names (think Xerox!) were snapped up by investors. The "Nifty Fifty" stocks (much like today's FAANG—Facebook, Apple, Amazon, Netflix, and Google) included the technology innovators of the day: Polaroid, Texas Instruments, Telex, Kodak. "Gunslingers"—brash, young men helming aggressive new investment funds—were the new celebrities. In 1967, the brokerage firm Harris, Upham, Inc. claimed in its newsletter that markets were moving in the same direction as hemlines. They included an amateurish pencil graph of women's skirt lengths over time alongside stock-market gains: "From the days of street-sweeping skirts in 1897 to the days of Twiggy in 1967 the market is up 2100% in value," Harris, Upham declared. But the women wearing the Twiggy miniskirt, or any length of skirt for that matter, were not welcome on Wall Street. This half square mile of lower Manhattan was a world of men: some gathering for drinks at the private club India House, while others stopped to have their shoes shined, and still others rolled carts through the streets full of stock certificates—beautifully ornate artworks—to basement depositories for safekeeping.

When Alice Jarcho left home, dropping out of Queens College to start afresh in Manhattan, she did not intend to go to Wall Street. Neither she, nor anyone else for that matter, would have imagined she would become the first woman to fully trade on the floor of the New York Stock Exchange. Nineteen-year-old Alice just needed to pay her rent. She took a job as a receptionist at Hirsch & Company—one of the many small brokerage firms that proliferated on Wall Street in those days—coming home after work to an apartment on a sketchy, underpopulated block near the recently defunct Jacob Ruppert Brewery in Yorkville. The one-bedroom apartment she shared with a nursing student cost $157.60 per month and was so small that if you opened the Murphy bed, you had to climb over it to get to the bathroom. Even so, Alice's salary at Hirsch & Company could not cover her bills, and as red-inked overdue notices stacked up, she found a better paying job elsewhere.

Her only goal was liberation. Growing up in a row house in Forest Hills, Queens, Alice had a mother who was a card-carrying Communist (until Khrushchev's revelations about Stalin's crimes in 1956). She did not play canasta or visit the beauty parlor like the other mothers. Instead, she worked at the American Labor Party offices day and night, and if there was free time, she'd either be on a picket line or in front of the Macy's department store, with a seven-year-old Alice in tow, handing out copies of the Communist newspaper, the *Daily Worker*. The Forest Hills house, littered with books, the site of political meetings in the basement, was not a safe zone; the FBI "came often."

Alice had already bid goodbye to Wall Street when she bumped into Jane Larkin while standing in line for movie tickets for an Ingmar Bergman film. The daughter of a Manhattan detective, Larkin was a rarity on Wall Street, an exception that proved the rule: a successful woman in finance, a research analyst and partner at Hirsch & Company, the brokerage firm Alice had left for a better paycheck. Later, when the women's movement kicked into high gear, Larkin would insist, "A feminist I am not." In that sense, she was very much a woman of her time. Larkin pulled Alice aside and asked her to return to Hirsch & Company: they were opening a new branch office, and would she consider coming to work there as a secretary? Alice agreed as long as this time she'd be paid enough to cover her bills.

The branch was, as Larkin had promised, brand-new, with glassed-in offices and a wide-open room in the center where the so-called moneymakers, the big producers, sat. The ticker board ran across one wall, but if you thought you'd missed something, you could still get up and walk over to the old ticker-tape machine to check the seemingly infinite strip of narrow white paper with printed stock symbols and prices that the machine spewed out all day. If a stock suddenly showed movement, up or down, someone in the room would shout it out.

Hirsch & Company was on the retail side of the business, meaning their clients were individual investors rather than institutions, and a large part of a broker's job was to cold-call customers. For the brokers doing the cold-calling, however, these were easy times; the economy was booming, and trade commissions were fixed, nonnegotiable, so that investors paid brokers per trade, based on the volume of stock bought or sold. As a broker, you didn't have to hustle; you didn't even have to know the intricate ins and outs of the market, really, you just had to churn out trades, encouraging your clients to buy and sell. The hustle would come later, as would the serious money.

Alice had just about settled in at her new job when the manager walked in one morning, opened his desk drawer, and pulled out a gun. Everyone could see right through into his glassed office as he stood there, waving the gun about. People shouted at him to stop, pleading with him to put it down. When the police arrived, and then the ambulance, he was taken away in a stretcher under police custody. That same day, Alice Jarcho, the secretary, became Alice Jarcho, the de facto office manager. The number-two guy, the next in line, was a successful money producer, sitting prominently in the very center of the room, and he was not about to compromise his profits to manage the office. Instead, Alice was put in charge of office operations: hiring teletype workers, opening client accounts, and fixing stock errors (when buys and sells were hurriedly written out on pieces of paper amidst the rush of the New York Stock Exchange floor, sometimes the two tickets did not match).

But some of what she was doing—namely, opening client accounts, talking to customers—was illegal. Only a Registered Representative, otherwise known as a broker, someone who had passed the necessary exams, could legally do these things. The firm was liable, but all that had to be done was for her to take the licensing exam (as of 1974, it would be known as the Series 7) and everything would be above-board. She approached the firm's partners, asking for them to sponsor her, but they refused to pay the $300 exam fee: because she was a woman. The very firm that had made Jane Larkin a partner refused to invest $300 in Alice Jarcho to operate within the rules.

But the only reason slim, auburn-haired Jane Larkin was made a partner without ruffling feathers was because she was a research analyst, not a stockbroker. Typing and answering phones were reserved for women, as in all industries. Research, which took place behind the scenes and had the power to influence but not the power to execute trades, could tolerate a few women. Selling and trading, where profit was generated, was for men. *That* was the rule that was sacrosanct.

Alice had been brought up questioning capitalism, but that was not what drove her. What drove her was something else entirely: with a mother always "overthrowing the government," Alice had inherited very little fear of authority. And she was not about to stick around at Hirsch & Company if this is what they thought of her, of women, in 1969. She left and took a job at Oppenheimer, in the institutional investing division, working for an arbitrageur. Oppenheimer was a successful firm that focused on institutional trading, trading not for individuals but for large funds—insurance companies, retirement plans, unions—and unlike at Hirsch & Company, they agreed to get Alice registered.

Hired as a clerk on the trading desk, she was now in the bull pen, alongside the men. There was no training. Every day she asked what arbitrage was, and every day her boss would "slam on the desk" when she said she didn't understand (later she would explain it as "the simultaneous purchase and sale of equivalent securities which, due to market variations, are not selling at equivalent value"). One day it suddenly clicked.

Her job included doing her boss's paperwork, putting in orders, checking for errors, finding research for an analysis, following through with the orders on the trading floor. As trading volumes increased, the job of clerk was becoming ever more vital. Before computers, every trade was ultimately an exercise in trust between buyers and sellers, and the person to ensure it went smoothly was the clerk. Data on prices and shares traded needed to be recorded accurately, then reconciled before a trade was settled to avoid incorrect transfers of shares and cash. It was painstaking work that called for diligence, while offering zero glory but inevitable blame when things went wrong. Unsurprisingly, it was a way for women to get a foot in the door.

Alice's boss was extraordinarily smart but "a maniac," "a screamer." Once, when she missed something, he picked up the telephone, a clunky, corded, plastic-and-metal contraption that weighed close to five pounds, and lobbed it at her, narrowly missing her head.

She stood there, blinking, trying to process it. Her first thought was that he was the one who looked like a complete idiot; her second was that as a top producer for Oppenheimer, he would face no consequences. She then turned on her heel and made a beeline for the bathroom, where another woman tried to comfort her, but once she was over the shock, Alice found it so absurd as to be funny.

Besides her boss, there was another clerk on the trading desk with Alice, although much higher up on the ladder, who "bragged about the size of his member all the time." He would draw pictures of it for her to admire. Just as Alice appraised the head arbitrageur with a cold eye and thought how absurd it was for a grown man to have public temper tantrums, she would look at this other man, married with two small daughters—photographs of his wife and girls prominently displayed on his desk—and wonder what could possibly be going on inside his head.

Then one day it came to her: these men were having fun yanking her chain. She was catnip to them! Slim, pretty, five-foot-two, she was "a new toy, a shiny new object." But what they did not know is that she had spent a childhood fending off two brothers who had turned torturing their little sister into a sport—choking her with a curtain rod, mugging her on Halloween. She knew how to disassociate herself from the perpetrator. Like so many women who would come to Wall Street in the early days via the circuitous route, Alice was someone whom life had already taught how to navigate dysfunction. One could even say that she thrived on dysfunction, was its connoisseur. She was now in the perfect place—Wall Street—to hone this particular skill set.

———

AND THEN THERE WAS THE MORE DIRECT ROUTE TO WALL STREET: business school, B-school. Harvard Business School was the most prestigious, and in the late summer of 1963, a few years before Alice found herself on Wall Street, reporters descended on Cambridge, Massachusetts, because America's best B-school was about to let *them* in. *The women.*

Eight women had been officially admitted into the two-year MBA program. Elaine Luthy, a twenty-year-old English major at Stanford, opened up a telegram to find that she had been designated "the first woman" at HBS. *The Boston Herald* dubbed her the "Blond Bomb." Official Harvard photographs of her first day show her hair in a side-swept bouffant, wearing a black turtleneck, a tweed pencil skirt, and a matching jacket. Altogether very Jackie Kennedy.

Elaine Luthy registering for classes on her first day at Harvard Business School, 1963.

Luthy was joining 7 other women and 624 men in the HBS class of 1965. Despite the fanfare over the incoming class, some women had in fact already had a taste of what was in store. Since 1959, four years earlier, HBS had been offering the women who graduated from Radcliffe's one-year program in business administration (established in 1938 for women at Radcliffe, Harvard's sister school) the opportunity to sign up for the second year of the men's far more prestigious two-year MBA. In the first year of that experiment, three women— one married to a PhD student at the business school; another the daughter of a banker in the Midwest; and the third the only daughter of a single mother who worked as a janitor—had experienced firsthand the tiered classrooms and discussion-based pedagogy on which HBS prided itself. They had also weathered the male students' disdain, as well as that of the professors. But all the Radcliffe Program women got a taste of it too. Ann Leven recalled a professor fulminating: "I taught the same material to the boys—men this morning, and *they* understood it. What's wrong with you? Are you guys stupid?" Ann walked out in protest, the whole class followed, refusing to return until the professor was removed.

The Radcliffe women were also invited occasionally to join the men across the river, where their role seemed to be that of consumer "guinea pigs." One recalled how a classmate was asked to model her Dior gown for a class discussing the advantages of couture over mass-market knockoffs. Another time, the Radcliffe women were brought in to join a class discussion about whether women's hats would sell in a supermarket.

For a long time, Ann Leven believed that "we didn't need Gloria Steinem," that she and her classmates could take care of themselves without a women's movement to back them up. But looking back, she realized just how naïve they all had been about discrimination, seeing it clearly only when they were literally being screamed at.

They were not the only women during the '60s blind to the realities of what was around them. In 1961, 95 percent of American women said they saw themselves having careers once they'd finished school. Yet Betty Friedan's book *The Feminine Mystique*, which came out in 1963, documented how after the war, in a backlash against Rosie the Riveter's triumphs, educated women were expected to find fulfillment not in work but in a mythologized ideal of four children, two cars, one white picket fence, and weekly PTA meetings. The first female vice president of a Chicago department store, when asked about the odds for women like herself, sarcastically remarked, "A woman who is determined to play a game so fixed, had better be prepared to look like a girl, act like a lady, think like a man, and work like a dog." In 1966, *Newsweek* referred to a recent survey of businessmen who'd been asked if they would work for a woman: almost all found the idea "flatly repellent."

This attitude was largely shared at HBS. Even so, there were "good guys" among the male student body—"allies" in today's vernacular—as there were professors who were more awkward than antagonistic. One exasperated female student finally took her professor aside and asked why he wouldn't call on her. He replied that he wasn't sure she wanted to be called on, to which she replied that if she had her hand up, and was waving it frantically, it meant she did. Another professor asked a married woman with several children to leave the classroom because he was about to show photographs (presumably of naked women) related to their discussion about the Playboy Club. One finance professor unfailingly referred to a female student as "Mr."—and could never meet her eye.

Most of the women's living arrangements made their distance from the professors and male classmates more than metaphoric, sequestered as they were with other female graduate students at the Radcliffe Graduate Center, situated far from the business school campus. The distance mattered, especially on cold winter nights when, having to cross the bridge, the wind off the Charles River felt like an angry slap to the face.

No one, not in the Dean's Office or anywhere else, considered the HBS women's safety or comfort as they commuted between the two campuses, often late at night. No shuttle bus was offered. Dressed for class in business attire, wool dresses, they carried their stockings and heels to the HBS campus, where there was only one ladies' room in which to change.

The men's proximity to the school's amenities and to one another meant they could form study groups to lighten their workload. Presented with two to three case studies a night, students were expected to formulate strategies and solutions they'd be called on to discuss in class the following day. It was an impossible task unless divvied up. The women, absent from campus, were excluded and foolishly took the advice of the administration, which warned against students from different learning cohorts creating study groups.

The isolation could be as numbing as the blasts from the Charles River: Jane Lack walked into class on her first day and sat down, but as the men streamed in, she noticed that none of them were willing to sit next to her—nor beside her or even in front or behind her. She sat there like a pariah, never having felt such aloneness. Looking back on her section, Roberta Lasley, the daughter of the single mother who worked as a janitor, concluded that "some of them were nice, and some of them were jerks, and some of them were smarter than I was, and a lot of them were dumber than I was. And like really arrogant."

One of the major features of the Harvard Business School experience was the WAC—the written analysis of cases. On Fridays, students received an extra case study for which they had to submit an extensive written analysis, alongside charts and graphs, to be deposited on Saturday into a special door slot by a fixed time, after which the bin below the slot was removed and late WACs would merely thump to the floor and be marked as zero. With no calculators in those days, the analysis was painstakingly computed with the help of slide rules and typed up on old-fashioned typewriters with finicky, spooled-ink ribbons. The women on the other side of the river not only had to get theirs to the chute on time but factor in the travel there, sometimes with traffic and crowds streaming across the bridge for a Saturday football game. It was literally as if they were pushing against the current.

If the isolation were not enough, the women were constantly being told they were taking a man's place. Their classmates told them, unabashedly, that men, as breadwinners, as family providers, were more deserving of a spot at HBS. Even as some of the men got to know their female classmates, and liked them, they could not wrap their minds around why these women were there. The 1950s had come to an end, yet the decade's cultural tentacles were still tightly curled around them. After World War II, the American business-*man* had become a new kind of symbol for America's postwar success. Unlike before the war, he was now more likely to hold a college degree, and his "rough" work schedule (fifty-three to sixty-two hours per week— downright leisurely by today's standards) was equated with a sort of virile endurance. A 1955 *Fortune* article described a typical day for the businessman: he got up at 7 a.m., ate a large breakfast, arrived at work at 9 a.m., left the office at 6 p.m., rushed home, and ate dinner before settling into bed with work he'd brought home.

As fundamental as the pressed suit, the starched shirt, and the briefcase, however, was the executive wife. Single men were viewed with suspicion. It was far better to have been married and divorced than never married at all. A successful corporate wife was usually also college-educated, like her husband, if only to keep the proper intellectual balance between them and avoid her becoming what was then known as "the wife he left behind." It was also considered advantageous if the wife had briefly worked before marriage so she could relate to her husband's life.

Corporations, seeing wives as the weathervanes of a man's potential, had much to say about them. The ideal executive wife was "highly adaptable, highly gregarious, and realizes that her husband belongs to the corporation." Guidelines for executive wives included never talking shop with "the Girls" (other wives); never turning up at the office unannounced; remaining attractive (because there was a high correlation between "executive success and the wife's appearance"); becoming phone buddies with a husband's secretary; and "never—repeat, never—get[ting] tight at a company party." Corporate wives were also tasked with providing a calm, distracting environment for their pent-up, exhausted husbands working their fifty-three-hour workweeks. The wives themselves often bought into these ideals, as well as the surveillance necessary to keep the status quo: a 1957 survey of 4,000 executive wives found that 55 percent thought a company hiring a man should also interview his wife to check on how she behaved toward him (too much nagging, perhaps?) and how she handled her alcohol. But this happened anyway in less formal ways; it was not unusual for prospective hires and their wives to be invited to the local country club, for example. In one case, a man lost his job because his wife had dared to wear a strapless dress to a company picnic.

The perfect executive wife was also the shadow that trailed the female HBS students. She was the ideal dreamed of by the bachelors tucked away in their redbrick dormitory suites at night. The female students across the river at the Radcliffe Graduate Center were the un-ideal, the executive wife's polar opposite, the ones daring to steal a man's place instead of fluffing up his seat pillows.

THE EIGHT "FIRST WOMEN" POSING IN 1963 FOR THE PHOTOGRApher in Harvard's Baker Library were all white.

Four years later, in 1967, Lillian Novella Hobson arrived after a ten-hour train ride from Washington, DC. In one hand she carried a suitcase, and with the other she dragged a large trunk. When the cab dropped her off at her dorm at 6 Ash Street, she was disappointed to find that the Radcliffe Graduate Center, this "nondescript

Group photo at the Baker Library of the official first women at HBS, 1963:
Elaine F. Luthy (MBA 1965); Elizabeth F. Trotman (MBA 1965); Cecilia B.
Rauch MBA (1965); Caryl Maclaughlin Brackenridge (MBA 1965); Susan
Lauer Holt (MBA 1965); Lynne Sherwood (MBA 1965), Michelle Roos
Turnovsky (MBA 1965); Dixie Marchant (MBA 1965).

brick building" built less than a decade earlier, was not on the Harvard Business School campus, or anywhere near it. The housemother
answered the door, and if she was surprised to see a young Black
woman standing there, she didn't show it, but neither did she go out
of her way to welcome Lillian. She crossed off her name on a list and
said that her room wouldn't be ready until 3 p.m., but there was a
park nearby where Lillian could wait.

Sitting down on a park bench, she looked around, and said to no
one but herself: "Why am I here?" W.E.B. Du Bois, Harvard's first
Black PhD student, graduating in 1895, wrote, "I was in Harvard, but
not of it." Seventy-two years later, Lillian felt much the same as she
sat on that bench, missing her family down south, where her father
was a subsistence tobacco farmer and her mother a former teacher.

In Ballsville, Virginia, with barely more than two hundred residents, if you didn't have land to farm, and you were Black, you worked as a farmhand or domestic. Growing up, Lillian wore hand-me-down dresses or, worse, dresses made by her mother from fifty-pound burlap feed bags. At the school cafeteria, she was the one with a sandwich made from home-baked bread instead of the superior store-bought Wonder Bread. The schools were segregated, but when that ended in 1954, Lillian in fact felt a loss. She had found the all-Black environment empowering, and now many of her favorite teachers were forced to leave the profession. The only upside to high school was that Lillian's cousin was working as a maid for a Richmond family who owned a chain of jewelry stores. They gave her their daughters' hand-me-downs, and suddenly Lillian was a lot better dressed.

Graduating third in her high school class, she assumed that the scholarships traditionally allotted to the top two students were the only path to college. She had missed that opportunity by a hair. She took the next best route—leaving for New York—convinced there was something better "outside of the segregation system," if only because New York relatives who came to visit arrived "driving nice cars." Through one of them, she secured a job as a maid—the only kind of job going for a young Black woman—in an exclusive Hamptons resort. But one summer stuck out on Long Island without a car or public transport was more than she could bear, and after it was over, she moved into a tiny apartment in Harlem with two cousins, sharing a bed with one while the other slept on the living-room sofa. Cockroaches ruled the tiny kitchen. Looking for a job as a young Black woman, her options were limited, and swallowing her pride, she took work as a domestic for a family on Fifth Avenue.

It was here that she saw real wealth for the first time. The apartment closets were full, the kitchen appliances sparkled, and the family's whims were catered to by the servants—herself included. She wanted it, too, but if she was ever going to live like this, she would have to get away from domestic work. She tried to apply to Macy's, but when she admitted she had no office-work experience, the woman sent her away. When Lillian returned asking about seasonal work, she was again turned away. Third time around it was not so much luck as a lesson learned: Lillian replied yes to the question about previous work experience, listed three fake companies she had prepared in advance, and presented herself calmly as she had practiced in front of the mirror. When her typing test was over, the employment officer looked concerned, and Lillian's heart stopped. But she had done so well that the woman's only concern was whether they could afford her. Lillian tried not to laugh and accepted the position of clerk in the comparison-shopping department for $45 a week.

But New York City was expensive, even if you lived without extravagance, and Lillian was existing paycheck to paycheck. Understanding that this, too, was a dead end, no less so than domestic work, she left for Washington, DC, and eventually enrolled as a student at Howard University, where she met Professor H. Naylor Fitzhugh, one of the first Black men to graduate with a Harvard MBA. In 1933, he had found that even a Harvard degree offered no job security for a Black man: "Indeed, even if I'd wanted it, I couldn't have obtained a job as a grocery clerk in a chain store unit in an all-black neighborhood in Washington." As a teacher, Fitzhugh made it his mission to change the experience of Black people in business. It was he who turned to Lillian during her junior year and suggested she apply to business graduate school. One eyebrow raised, he added, hardly missing a beat: "Why not Harvard?"

It was better that she didn't know what she was getting into, that she walked in blind. That year, among 800 incoming students, still only 18 were women. Moreover, the Charles River, as Lillian would soon learn, "symbolized the Great Divide, separating Harvard's liberals from its conservative counterparts." Harvard students called the Business School "the West Point of American capitalism" and saw its students as "capitalist pigs."

Cambridge itself was a counterculture hub during the 1960s. The same year that Lillian arrived at HBS, Patricia Chadwick, who had recently freed herself from a heretical Catholic community, and who would eventually end up on Wall Street, was studying for a secretarial certificate. Never having so much as heard of the Beatles until she left the Feeneyites, she was now reveling in her liberation, wearing a "black leather miniskirt, a form-fitting red turtleneck sweater, and platform shoes that made me a full four inches taller than my true five-foot-five height." Even as she'd voted for Richard Nixon, she embraced Cambridge: "Hippies, unkempt and unwashed, roamed the square in sandals, tie-dyed T-shirts, and long hair, in arm with intellectuals and students and bands of saffron-robed Hare Krishna monks."

Lillian was less enthralled, but as she dashed across the river to get to class, feeling like a freak dressed in her business suit, nylons, and heels, she saw the irony: the female MBA students, dressed as conservatively as the men in "their gray flannel suits," were in fact "trailblazers," preparing themselves like warriors for battle.

———

IT WAS NOT UNTIL THE INCOMING STUDENTS, THE HBS CLASS OF 1969, had filed into the arena for their orientation, the only space that could hold them all, their ranks swelled by an influx of returning veterans, that Lillian grasped the enormity of her situation. She searched the crowd for another Black face. Eventually she counted five, all men.

Her section-D cohort included 97 white men, 2 white women, and Lillian. There was not even a Black female administrator on campus. The professors and HBS staff preferred to ignore her. If she were about to pass a professor in the hall, she would often hear him speed up "as if he were running down a ramp to catch the next flight out of town."

With eyes down, a grunt, a smile directed at the floor if she were lucky, he'd scuttle by without so much as a hello or a how-are-you.

But Lillian's white female classmates were not having an easy time of it either. "Never before," had they "been in such a testosterone-fueled classroom, with some of the most aggressive men on earth." The moment a professor asked a question, before he had even finished, "hands shot up in the air like rockets . . . and they started shouting out the answer like falling bombs."

Most of the women chose to keep quiet, to just survive the bombardment, even though class participation counted significantly toward their final grade. One of Lillian's female classmates, Robin Foote, who would also make it to the list of firsts, becoming the first female Baker Scholar—the highest academic achievement—was also the only one who competed with the men on their own terms. She shot her hand up in the air and made sure her voice was heard, which "pissed off" lots of the men; some, she knew, "hated my guts."

While Robin and one other woman had managed to join an informal study group, Lillian and the remaining women studied alone, Lillian in her small room with its single bed, narrow closet, and simple desk, listening to "the Temptations, Gladys Knight and the Pips, the Four Tops, and the Platters," for company. Sometimes Nancy Pelz would stop by her room to chat. Nancy had decided the only way to cope was to never speak up in class, ever.

There was some equality at least in the Saturday "brain-hazing" WAC assignments that everyone had to do. As the campus bells rang out the hour, students stuffed their WACs down the chute while a crowd gathered, applauding and hollering. The so-called WAC readers who graded these assignments were typically young graduates of women's colleges, especially Smith College. Lillian and her classmates were indignant: "To think that these women of privilege, with their fancy liberal arts degrees, were qualified to grade our knowledge of business was absurd. They may have known a thing or two about grammar and

punctuation, which was evident from all the red marks strewn throughout the blue booklets, but they were hardly able to grade us on our ana-
lytical and problem-solving abilities." There, Lillian was wrong.

Ever since the 1920s, HBS male students had been miffed that
women were grading their work, believing that "their painful lit-
erary efforts deserved male consideration." But the truth was that
while some men had initially tried to work as WAC readers, HBS had
found that "competent young ladies could be employed and trained
to do a more careful, dependable job than most of the men willing to
accept such employment." Any new hire was not allowed anywhere
near the students' case analyses with her red pen until she had first
completed a series of classes focusing on accounting, case management, and other business subjects. The pay was "paltry—$57 a week
after taxes," but the spots were competitive because, as one professor
observed, "We were the only employer in Boston at the time that was
hiring young women to use their minds."

The WAC readers were denigrated from all sides. John Loeb Jr.,
a true scion of Wall Street, whose mother came from the Lehmans
of Lehman Brothers and his father from the Loebs of Loeb, Rhoades
& Co., was a 1954 HBS graduate. He believed, with a wink and a
chuckle, that the men looking to do well intentionally dated the WAC
readers. But as to the question of who these young women might be?
"I have no idea," he said.

Almost twenty years later, the class of 1972 women agreed with
him. They insisted the WAC readers buttered up the male students
by giving them better grades. For proof, they pointed to the woman
among them who was "significantly older" and "therefore not a
social threat to the WAC readers' hopes and marriage intentions."
She received the best grades of all the women.

Yet the truth was that for many years the competition to become
a WAC reader had been stiffer than admission into the Harvard Business School. In fact, WAC reader applications at one point had a 1

percent acceptance rate—so desperate were educated young women for a job where they could use their brains. If anything, the HBS female students and the WAC female readers shared a similar conundrum in seeking a meaningful professional life despite the odds.

———

LIKE LILLIAN, PRISCILLA RABB WAS IN THE HBS CLASS OF 1969 BUT she came from a starkly different background. Her father, Maxwell Rabb, had been a senior advisor to President Eisenhower. While Priscilla's family was Jewish, her father was close with Sen. Henry Cabot Lodge Jr., scion of the prominent WASP Republican family. When the Rabb family moved to Manhattan, Priscilla was enrolled in Miss Hewitt's Classes, a finishing school of sorts, and arrived as the new girl looking "cool," with a Shetland crewneck sweater "turned backwards," a straight skirt, knee socks, and sneakers, all finished off with a chained medallion hanging from her neck. After a more rigorous high school, in 1963 she was accepted into Smith College.

Through her father, who knew John Loeb Sr., she got a summer job at Loeb, Rhoades & Co., working in utilities research. It was not what most young women would have considered exciting, but Priscilla could not get enough of it, coming in on Saturdays and Sundays even when she didn't need to. She was soon envisioning a future in investment banking. When Harvard Business School recruiters came to the Smith College campus, Priscilla was among the first to sign up. She walked into the meeting thinking she was there to apply to the MBA program, but the recruiters were in fact trawling for WAC readers. Priscilla told them she wasn't interested; it was the B-school experience she was after.

Yet even Priscilla's upper-class background and worldly outlook did not make her feel any less unmoored once she was there. Trying to make herself invisible on her first day in the Human Behavior class, she climbed up to the highest row in the tiered classroom, finding herself squeezed in between two large men: the professor's eye fell on her immediately.

"If you're walking in the halls, and a stranger comes up to you, what are you going to tell him about yourself?" he asked.

At a complete loss, paralyzed, she blurted out: "I wouldn't tell him anything, because my parents told me not to talk to strangers."

The class must have laughed—Priscilla was too distraught to hear anything in that moment—but the professor most definitely did not. He turned away, as if she had been making fun of him, and ignored her for the rest of the semester.

Then there was the daily onslaught of remarks from the men about how she did not belong at HBS. One student declared he would eat his hat if ten years down the road Priscilla didn't have kids and had ever worked a day in her life (Priscilla to this day attends reunions in the hopes of seeing him there, to eat his hat.)

Priscilla was fortunate to have various forms of protection that Lillian did not; not only was she white, and of a privileged background, but she had a large diamond engagement ring on her finger. It worked, back in those days, as a protective armor, a way to avoid certain social expectations. But since her fiancé never visited campus, rumors soon began to swirl: was she a closeted lesbian? Did she belong to the Rabbs of the Stop & Shop empire? Did she already have a thriving business in New York that she tended to on weekends? The truth—that she was a well-off girl from Smith College who had refused to be a WAC reader because she wanted to be an investment banker—seemed too improbable to believe.

And yet these ambitious women, who felt like they'd been set adrift alone on the open seas, had predecessors who might have served as role models, or at least as guiding beacons. Except that Priscilla and Lillian, like most people, had most likely never heard of them.

2

Breaching a Wall

In 1792—it is said—twenty-four brokers met under a buttonwood tree at 68 Wall Street. In what became known as the Buttonwood Agreement, they gathered under the sycamore and agreed to trade exclusively with one another and abide by a fixed set of rules, with a fixed commission rate on trades. By creating an exclusive club, they were ensuring a guaranteed level of trust amongst themselves, but that club was also in many ways a cartel—one that would eventually be known as the New York Stock Exchange, the beating heart of American capitalism.

Wall Street was named after a wooden wall built by Dutch governor Peter Stuyvesant to protect settlers from local Native American tribes. But it was the Buttonwood Agreement that gave shape to "Wall Street" as a recognizable space: all twenty-four signatories posted addresses in the area—Wall Street, Broad Street, Pearl Street, Hanover Square, Nassau Street, Broadway. Those streets would become New York's trading center, and "Wall Street" would be shorthand for it all. The very first New York Stock Exchange was in a room on the second floor of the Tontine Coffee House on Wall and

Water Streets. Across the street stood the market where, until 1762, enslaved Africans as well as Native Americans were auctioned off on the docks while coffee, tea, sugar, molasses, and cloth were unloaded.

Until 1817, the NYSE would operate out of the coffeehouse, which an early-nineteenth-century visitor from England described vividly:

> The Tontine coffee-house was filled with underwriters, bro-kers, merchants, traders, and politicians; selling, purchasing, trafficking, or insuring; some reading, others eagerly inquiring the news. The steps and balcony of the coffee-house crowded with people bidding, or listening to several auctioneers, who had elevated themselves upon a hogshead of sugar, a puncheon of rum, or a bale of cotton; and with Stentorian voices were exclaiming: "*Once, Twice.*" "*Once, Twice.*" "*Another cent.*" "*Thank ye gentlemen,*" or were knocking down the goods which took up one side of the street, to the best purchaser. The coffee-house slip, and the corners of Wall and Pearl Streets . . . were jammed up with carts, drays, and wheel-barrows: horses and men huddled promiscuously together, leaving little or no room for passengers to pass.

The first women to make a significant appearance on Wall Street were the sisters Tennessee Claflin and Victoria Woodhull, who arrived in the second half of the 1800s. Working first as clairvoy-ants and fortune-tellers, they became public personalities, opening a spiritualist salon in New York City. When it was time to ratchet up their operation, they turned to railroad and shipping tycoon Cor-nelius Vanderbilt, who had a soft spot for both women as well as for clairvoyance. Tennessee Claflin became his lover, and he became their silent investor. With a $7,000 check, he financed the opening of their Wall Street brokerage house at 44 Broad Street—Woodhull, Claflin & Co.

The press was all over it, as were eager customers, especially women for whom the firm had a back-door entrance so they could arrive clandestinely to deposit their funds. Poet Walt Whitman visited, calling the sisters' brokerage "a prophecy of the future." Susan B. Anthony, writing in the suffragist press, applauded them: "These two ladies (for they are ladies) are determined to use their brains, energy, and their knowledge of business to earn them a livelihood. . . . The advent of this woman firm in Wall Street marks a new era." The sisters began wearing men's business suits. At the famous Wall Street restaurant Delmonico's, women were not allowed to dine without a male escort; the sisters cleared this hurdle by inviting a coachman in off the street to sit with them.

But Tennessee Claflin and Victoria Woodhull were less investors than women with enormous ambition who wanted to be seen, and ultimately the first women's Wall Street firm was a way to garner attention for their evolving interests. Victoria had her sights on a political career and largely saw Wall Street as a way to elevate her profile. In 1870, she announced she was running for president, and the sisters' focus shifted to publishing their own newspaper, *Woodhull and Claflin's Weekly*, where they expressed their uninhibited views. Even Cornelius "Commodore" Vanderbilt, their secret (and not so secret) funder, found he was not exempt from Victoria's progressive punch: in an 1872 speech, she singled him out, along with other industrialists, for the visibly inequitable distribution of wealth. As her views on marriage, free love, and economics became ever more radical, she slowly lost support. At the same time, the sisters' brokerage firm began to falter, having been overly reliant on gold speculation. Eventually, both women moved to England and on to financially advantageous marriages. Yet the sisters had made a mark; often written off as amateurs, psychics playing at investment, they in fact understood well the power and allure of Wall Street, and how to use it to their advantage.

Henrietta "Hetty" Green, nicknamed "The Witch of Wall

Street," once listed in the Guinness Book of World Records as the "greatest miser" that ever lived, was the best-known female financier on Wall Street during the Gilded Age. Inheriting a fortune, and familiar with finance (as a child, Hetty had had to read the financial pages to her father, whose eyesight was failing), she invested cleverly, buying low and playing the long game, eventually becoming the richest woman in America. Unlike the Claflin-Woodhull sisters, Henrietta shied away from publicity, although her litigious, penny-pinching, and fashion-challenged ways seemed to invite attention (she inhabited dingy apartments in poor neighborhoods to evade taxes and wore the same black dress each day stuffed with crumpled newspaper to keep her warm and save on heating). Her infamous appearances in court, and her dragged-out lawsuits, were all centered on protecting her wealth and remaining in control of it. As individuals and institutions came asking for loans, Hetty Green became a "private bank." Each day she sat at a desk loaned out to her by the Chemical National Bank and oversaw her expansive portfolio. In a backhanded compliment, the press commended her for having "a masculine instinct for finance."

Hetty Green was hard to ignore, but there were in fact other women trying their hand at stockbroking in the late 1800s, including Mary Gage, daughter of the famous suffragist Frances Dana Gage. Mary opened a ladies-only exchange at 71 Broadway after one too many unpleasant experiences using male brokers. Unlike most of these women, Maggie Walker, born to a former slave and a white abolitionist writer, was treated surprisingly well as America's first Black female bank president, but that was in part because she was far from Wall Street. At the time, Black-owned businesses were being championed by African American leaders, yet white-owned banks were unwilling to lend them capital. Walker was a board member of St. Luke's Mutual Benefit Society in Richmond, Virginia, and in

1901 she insisted on the formation of a bank, of which she became president, that would directly cater to the Black community.

While there were a handful of women who planted a flag in new financial territories, it was American women's presence and potential power as investors that was thought more likely to shift the needle. The United States emerged from World War I as an economic power-house, and women, no less than men, were getting in on the bull mar-ket: the Pennsylvania Railroad was nicknamed "the Petticoat Line" because women now owned more than half of its shares. With such a substantial female clientele, the door creaked open for women to become brokers catering directly to other women. In the boom years of the 1920s, brokerage firms across the United States introduced "women's departments"—women-friendly brokerage rooms.

Money, women's money, was speaking. Journalist Eunice Fuller Barnard was enthralled. Writing in the *North American Review*, she described one of these women's departments: "It might almost have been a club. The same discreet lighting, the cavernous davenports, an occasional bronze. In the deep Florentine armchairs a dozen women lounged and smoked. But at one end of the room their gaze was transfixed by a wide moving ribbon of light. 'PAK—3/4 . . . BDLA—1/2'—the cabalistic symbols glided across the magnified ticker tape." And while the pretty, young assistants, "turned out as so many man-nequins," would sneak into a trading booth to hurriedly gulp down a sandwich for lunch, the customers could barely remember to eat, so glued to the ticker were they. In the *New York Times*, too, Bar-nard waxed lyrical about the recent sea change in the investing land-scape: "Behind the scenes the expert eye that analyzes customers' lists of security holdings is as likely as not to be a feminine one. In the marble-halled solemnity of banks, where even five years ago women officials were undreamed of, they sit today as a matter of course as assistant secretaries, assistant cashiers and managers of women's

departments." These female professionals also began to do what their
male counterparts had done for decades—create professional organizations of their own, such as the National Association of Bank
Women and the Women's Bond Club. People spoke of "social change"
being activated inside these women's departments and argued that
harnessing women's investing power could do more "than all the
noisy suffrage campaigns."

But there was also a sobering reality: the women running these
women's departments had nowhere to go from there. This was their
glass ceiling, even as the phrase had yet to be coined, because into
"the men's board rooms, woman, whether as customer or clerk, rarely
penetrates. She may shop, vote, ride in the subway and work in business offices with men, but when it comes to stock trading she is rigidly
segregated." Selling stock, when women in the 1920s were clamoring
to spend their money on securities, was one thing; women trading
stock was quite another.

As for the New York Stock Exchange, which had relocated in
1903 to its current columned neoclassical building on the corner of
Broad and Wall Streets, it was said—although no one was certain—
that in 1927, shortly before the crash, a woman had planned to buy
a seat on the exchange. The NYSE's Board of Governors, looking
through its constitution, had discovered that women were technically
not barred. All that was required of a member was "responsibility,
character and citizenship."

In October 1929, the stock market crashed, and with it, women's
departments and all that they represented. With so many Americans
having gone full in on the stock market, and with their life savings
now wiped out, the country turned against Wall Street. Bankers were
renamed "banksters" by an angry public. Wall Street was accused of
having turned into a Wild West and the U.S. government was forced
to step in, promising to ensure this never happened again.

Until then, Wall Street's banks had played dual roles as both commercial and investment banks: a place for ordinary people to deposit their money and apply for loans, and also a place for the buying, selling, and underwriting of securities. These two roles were now seen as a conflict of interest that had put ordinary people's savings in jeopardy by allowing banks to use that capital for their own investments. In 1933, the Glass-Steagall Act was passed, and banks faced a fork in the road: they could no longer be both commercial and investment banks. The famous JP Morgan firm, for example, remained in commercial banking, while six of its partners soon peeled off to create the investment bank that would be known as Morgan Stanley. The idea was to stabilize the system, to separate Wall Street from Main Street. The Glass-Steagall Act would not be overturned until 1999, although banks would start to chip away at it beginning in the 1960s.

AFTER THE UNITED STATES ENTERED WORLD WAR II, AND MEN WERE called to military service, across all industries women took on jobs previously reserved for men—even on the floor of the New York Stock Exchange. Eighteen-year-old Helen Hanzelin from Queens was the "first woman to appear on the floor in trading hours"—if one didn't count "a girl musician in the band that played for the New Year's Eve celebration three years ago," the *New York Times* wryly noted. Hanzelin stepped out onto the floor as a telephone clerk for Merrill Lynch, Pierce, Fenner & Beane at 9:30 a.m. on April 28, 1943, to "a barrage of boos, catcalls, whistles and jeers." Described as "a slim, self-possessed young woman with a good figure, tip-tilted nose, brown eyes and curly—but not too curly—hair that might be either brown or deep auburn," the next day her photograph appeared in almost every newspaper. A month later, Helen Kowalski, or "Helen the Second" as she was quickly nicknamed, was sent onto the floor as a second female telephone clerk for Merrill Lynch.

On July 12, another five weeks later, the New York Stock

Women pages on the trading floor of the NYSE, 1943.

Exchange itself hired thirty-six women to work on the floor as support staff. Floor support included pages (later they would be called runners, the bottom of the NYSE hierarchy, those who ran messages and trades—literally pieces of paper—between brokers and clerks); reporters (those who stood at the specialist posts, and when a trade was made reported it at the point of sale); and clerks (answering the phones in the floor brokers' booths and taking stock orders). They wore NYSE uniforms designed specifically for them—worsted wool, the blouse "French blue, with 'NYSE' embroidered on the left pocket, and the skirt in royal blue."

For a moment it looked as if a path had finally been forged, making way for women, sixty-six of whom were working on the floor as the war came to an end. But Lucy Greenbaum, one of a handful of women reporters at the *New York Times*, felt less optimistic. She herself had been hired in 1940, but largely sidelined to the society pages, and so when she wrote in May 1945 about the involuntary female exodus from the NYSE, it must have felt personal. She pointed out that Wall Street was not like other industries where women were able to use their wartime jobs to create "bridgeheads that they are planning to exploit in peacetime." Wall Street's Rosie the Riveters faced a dogged male resistance, the entrenched belief that "women can handle the money in the home, if their husbands are willing, but that they should remain at least a silver dollar's throw away from the Street." The frustration was perhaps best summed up by a young "page girl" who, as Greenbaum described, had had enough, and cracked, announcing to the men on the floor: "You're all living in the days of the Buttonwood Tree. This is 1945." Greenbaum commented: "The market failed to react violently to this news."

The young page's cry indeed fell on deaf ears even as some of the female floor workers dug their heels in and made a last stand, turning to their unions, who negotiated at length with the NYSE but to no avail. With the war over, women were marched right back to the secretarial pool, stripped of their blue NYSE uniforms. They went back to buying their office outfits from the Wall Street branch of the Anson-Jones chain, where all the dresses were priced $29.95. They were once again consumers rather than producers or, as a newspaper report observed, "Men make the big money on Wall Street, but it is the women who work for them who spend a fortune there."

John Wanamaker, owner of the only department store in the area—Wanamaker's at 150 Broadway—could set his watch by his female customers. Noon lunch hour, the "first group floods this store," with the second wave of women rushing in a few minutes after 1 p.m., in search of "a sterling silver peanut dish for an office shower, a cocktail dress, a bathing cap, a spotted leopard toy or a pair of shoes in size 12AAA." On weekends, with Wall Street closed, Wanamaker's did not bother to open its doors either.

As Greenbaum concluded: "Wall Street has always been a man's world and not even the manpower shortage could weaken its determination to remain just that." Wall Street was transparent about this

fact. If you found yourself in an elevator with a woman, you didn't
bother to take off your hat. Such niceties, the traditional gestures
of respect in those days, were only practiced north of Canal Street.
Below Canal Street, it was defiantly a man's world.

––––––

BUT WOMEN STILL HAD MONEY TO INVEST. IN 1947, AT THE ANNUAL
stockholders' meeting of the United States Steel Corporation, Wilma
Porter Soss, a stockholder and public relations consultant—who of
all her epithets, including the Corporate Conscience, and the Most
Talked About Woman on Wall Street, liked "economic suffragette"
the most—announced that she was creating a "Federation of Woman
Shareholders in American Business." Its aim was to force businesses
to acknowledge the breadth and impact of female investing: more
than half of "Big Steel's" stockholders were women.

Two years later, Soss was back at the same meeting, donning "a
late Victorian costume—a two-piece gray suit, a lace blouse and a
large purple hat." She told reporters, "The costume represents management's thinking on stockholder relations." (In 1960, she arrived at
a stockholders' meeting at CBS with a bucket and mop to "clean out"
the recent scandals surrounding their quiz shows.) Soss's mission was
to rally stockholders, especially women, and help them understand
that they were part owners of the corporations in which they invested,
and that they consequently had a voice—a powerful one.

Wilma Soss recognized that the numbers were in her favor, and
conditions were ripe for a stockholders' movement. New York Stock
Exchange data from the early to mid-1950s showed "considerable and
increasing public participation in the market." A news article spot-
lighting these new postwar investors interviewed, among others, "an
ash-blond interior decorator with a copy of The Wall Street Journal
tucked firmly under her arm," who had only just dipped into the stock
market and admitted not knowing a thing, but with $5,000 invested,

she didn't mind the gamble. Another was a "plump, cheerful woman with a pearl choker," who had owned a clothing store in Miami but now lived off her stock-market investments: $200,000 in holdings, from which she took home gains as high as $40,000 in one year and a loss of $10,000 in another. "A slim honey blond, looking like a model fresh from the pages of *Vogue*," pointed out that a stock like General Motors—one of the Nifty Fifty—was tied to the country's economy, and so her stock would tank only if the country did too.

By 1958, an astonishing 52 percent of stockholders were women (up from 35 percent six years earlier). Their investments represented more than a $100 billion worth of securities. As in the 1920s, these numbers again translated to the hiring of a small number of women working as "customer's women" (a play on "customer's men," otherwise known as Registered Representatives, otherwise known as brokers), among them even a few Black women, "to explain to new female stockholders why it is impossible to buy shares of Dow-Jones or that there is nothing vulgar or unladylike about 'common' stocks." Mrs. Lilla "Lilly" St. John, the first African American woman to take the New York Stock Exchange licensing exam, became a registered stockbroker in 1953. Little is known about her other than that she was the host of her own music television show on a local Milwaukee station before moving to New York and working for Oppenheimer (where Alice Jarcho would go to work for the arbitrageur in 1969). She had "crammed" for two months for the broker exam, switching careers because she found investing to be "utterly fascinating."

In 1957, Special Markets, the first Black securities firm in the financial district, started a tradition of "Women's Day on Wall Street." Wilhelmina B. Drake, its director of Women Activities, included a tour of the New York Stock Exchange, lunch at the restaurant Antlers, and a lecture on how to invest in mutual funds. This event pulled in their most important client, the Alpha Kappa Alpha sorority for Black women.

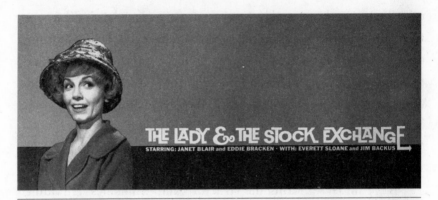

THE LADY & THE STOCK EXCHANGE
STARRING: JANET BLAIR and EDDIE BRACKEN · WITH: EVERETT SLOANE and JIM BACKUS

Poster for the NYSE film *The Lady and the Stock Exchange*, 1962.

The NYSE also started to actively search out female investors, placing advertisements in *The Saturday Evening Post, Collier's, Look*, and elsewhere. In 1962, the NYSE commissioned its own film to explain Wall Street to women. *The Lady and the Stock Exchange* premiered on the NYSE floor, turning it into a movie theater for the night, before traveling the country: in St. Louis, brokerage firms held a three-day event with a reception and film premiere at a local department store; in Rochester, brokerage firms organized free showings at the local shopping mall; in numerous cities, local television stations ran the film.

Only thirty-minutes long, it starred actress Janet Blair—who had played a dancer and friend of Rita Hayworth in the 1945 film *Tonight and Every Night*—as Mrs. Marge Jones, a pretty, smart, and loving suburban housewife, and the well-known comedian Eddie Bracken as her hapless husband. With Mr. Jones lured by get-rich-quick schemes and unwilling to invest for their teenage son's future, Marge secretly heads to New York City for an appointment at Brown, Smith & Co., a Wall Street brokerage firm.

Marge and her husband have $4,500 to invest, a recent windfall inheritance, and Mr. Huntley, the patient and attentive broker at Brown, Smith, offers her "a sound program" of investment. Marge takes home brochures and research reports, reads through them carefully, and eventually settles on two recommended stocks, returning to New York to put in the order. Mr. Huntley happens to be heading to a meeting at the NYSE and offers to show her around. Together they enter the visitors' gallery, and Marge leans over the railing to look down at the vast crowd of suited men moving around the floor. (While the floor scenes were shot during trading hours, the balcony scenes were filmed on a replicate balcony on a Hollywood set.)

Mr. Huntley explains the structure and mechanics of trading: While they were still at the brokerage house, he had called in Marge's order for the two stocks down to the firm's order room, which passed it via a direct line to their firm's booth on the exchange floor. While they watch, the telephone clerk picks up the line, writes Marge's order on a slip of paper, and then signals to the floor broker by pushing a button, which sets the broker's number flapping on a large metal board hoisted onto the wall of the NYSE. The flapping badge number tells the broker to return to his booth—or else to call for a runner—to pick up Marge's order.

Once the floor broker has the order in hand, he goes to the appropriate double-horseshoe-shaped counter, what's called a specialist post, where the specific stocks Marge picked are traded. She wants to buy, but the floor broker now needs to find someone who wants to sell, and at the best price at that moment. He first gauges the current bids and offers, and then determines which price he'll bid for Marge's stock. This is where "his skill" as a broker comes in: if there is more demand for the stock than supply, the price will go up, and vice versa.

The specialist at his post is responsible for creating "an open and fair" market for his specific stocks. This means that if someone wants to sell a stock at his post at $600 and someone wants to buy at $400, it is impossible to make a trade, and the market would come to a standstill. Specialists use their own capital to tighten up the difference; constantly monitoring demand and supply, they are the toll booth operators of the New York Stock Exchange. Marge's floor broker, who represents her brokerage house, and the seller's broker, will bargain, and their agreement is sealed not by a handshake, let alone a contract, but "their word is enough," Mr. Huntley notes. The NYSE only insists that it is done with "a loud, clear voice."

The deal closed, the information is jotted down—the stock symbol, the number of shares traded, the price per share, and the badge numbers of the buyer and seller—and sent in a small pneumatic tube to the ticker-tape room. In a couple of minutes, Mr. Huntley explains, her transaction will appear on tickers in thousands of brokerage houses across the country; in other words, not only is the transaction transparent but it brings Mrs. Jones into a much larger and exciting world of finance. She is now, officially, a part owner in the companies whose stock she has just bought; she will receive their company reports, as well as proxies with which to vote on company matters. "The exchange insists you get the right to vote and the important information that is needed to vote," he says. The film's message appeared to be: Capitalism and democracy are at work together on Wall Street! Or, as Wilma Soss would insist, there is potential power (waiting to be unlocked) in owning a stock.

Yet women's investment muscle did not include the power to work as floor brokers. When two *New York Times* reporters inquired in 1958 why there were no women with a seat on the exchange even as women were not explicitly barred, the NYSE's "official explanation" was that "No woman has ever seriously applied." Less officially "one Wall Streeter" told them, "It's not that women are prohibited. It's just that they're not allowed." Economist Sylvia Porter, syndicated *New York Post* columnist and Soss's liberal counterpart, said she was "confident" there would soon be a woman with a seat. But until that time, the excuses the reporters heard from Wall Street men ran the gamut:

"This isn't a business for amateurs. You don't learn to be a brain surgeon [or an exchange member] overnight."

"Charm and sex appeal don't mix with money."

"The exchange floor is too rough and physical an area for a lady."

"Women can't think or act decisively enough to keep up with the trading pace."

Women's presence might destroy the "genial, fraternal, man-to-man" floor vibe.

The only woman's voice to ring out from the New York Stock Exchange from the late 1950s into the 1960s was that of Jean Geiger, chief receptionist in the Exhibit Hall and Visitors' Gallery. When the brass gong signaled the end of the trading day, the reporters on the floor scrambled to get the closing prices on 350 NYSE-listed stocks into the pneumatic tubes up to the broadcasting booth. There, speaking quickly but enunciating carefully, Miss Geiger read out all the closing prices on the New York radio station WNYC. She received both fan letters and constructive criticism, including a letter from a ship's captain who offered this unsolicited advice: "for long reading, maybe . . . better stand, loosen the girdle, and breathe easier."

———

DID THE FIRST FEMALE GRADUATES OF THE HARVARD BUSINESS School know all this? Probably not, probably they had never heard of Victoria Woodhull, Tennessee Claflin, Hetty Green, Mary Gage, or Maggie Walker. But there was one woman who must have been on their radar. Muriel Siebert, known to everyone as "Mickie," had arrived in New York in 1954 in a seen-better-days Studebaker with $500 to her name. She had dropped out of Western Reserve University in Cleveland, instead playing bridge all day, when she learned her father was sick with cancer. After he died, she had no desire to stay on in Cleveland and follow in the footsteps of her mother, whose tread marks were filled with regret. Her mother "had a God-given voice, and she was offered a place on the stage, but nice Jewish girls didn't go on the stage in those days," which meant that Mickie "grew up with a woman who was frustrated her entire life." Mickie was determined not to feel the same when it was time to look back on her own life, and she left for New York, a city she had visited only recently as a tourist.

The previous summer of 1953, she'd taken a bus tour of New York City. At the New York Stock Exchange, she had stood on the balcony overlooking the trading floor—the very same where "Marge" and her broker would stand—and looked down onto a "sea of men in dark suits, punctuated by the occasional pastel jacket of a runner or clerk." Feeling electrified by "the clamorous human buzz of those thousands of deals," she saved the souvenir handed out at the end of the tour; a piece of personalized ticker tape that read "Welcome to the NYSE, Muriel Siebert."

In the 1950s, at around the same time, writer Martin Mayer was also on Wall Street, walking its streets, meeting its denizens, so he could reveal this world to his readers. He observed as the limousines rolled in at four o'clock in the afternoon, their uniformed chauffeurs congregating for a smoke while they waited for their bosses to exit

Floor of the New York Stock Exchange, 1969.

the banks and brokerages. The smell of fish wafted in from the Fulton
Fish Market a few blocks north, sometimes mixed in with the more
pleasant smell of coffee beans from the roasters, "the coffee men,"
who had not yet moved from their nineteenth-century hub on nearby
Front Street over to the Eastern Shoreline—today known as DUMBO
in Brooklyn. With setbacks on tall buildings not mandated until 1916,
Wall Street's narrow streets were dark, some parts seeing sunlight for
only twenty hours in total during a whole year. Looking up, one
found "brick bas-reliefs, brass sculptures, stone statues, gargoyles,"
with the architecture of Trinity Church, built by slaves, replicated in
nearby buildings that showed off ecclesiastic "vaulted arches."

Housed on the ground floors were the commercial banks, from
the largest to the smallest, both domestic and foreign, even private
ones with hidden entrances and backdoors. Intentionally located at
street level for easy access, they offered the basic services but also
functioned as stock transfer agents. The buying and selling of stocks
was still entirely based on the exchange of paper, and part of the
bank's job was to cancel sold stock certificates, issue certificates for
the new stocks bought, and write the checks to pay out the divi-
dends. The elaborate, oversized certificates moved between brokerage houses via handcarts rolled through the streets "or in smaller
amounts by gray-haired men carrying big wallets."

Many floors above the street-level banks sat the investment bankers, those in the business of underwriting companies, helping them
expand by selling shares through IPOs, "secondary sales," or corporate bonds. These underwriting institutions were among Wall Street's
most famous names: Morgan Stanley & Co., Lehman Brothers, Smith
Barney & Co., Goldman Sachs & Co., and Kuhn, Loeb & Co.

In the 1950s, the telephone was Wall Street's most advanced piece
of critical technology. Each stock trade meant at the very least six
phone calls, so that the monthly telephone bill for Wall Street ran
into several million dollars. The teletype was a useful and cheaper

adjunct to the telephone, and even less work than a telegram: punch in a company's TWX code, and their teletype machine would start tapping out your message.

Wall Street, Mayer explained, was loud. Only the executives, the C-suite, could find a modicum of peace and quiet in their closed-off offices; everyone else was unprotected from the unrelenting click and clatter of the ticker tape, the teletype, and the ringing phones. Without office printers, let alone computers, everything was printed by small, independent print shops nearby: from letterhead for the secretaries to type on to brochures and customer newsletters distributed by research departments. One print shop, the Ad Press, had a bowling alley for its customers waiting for their orders to be ready. Others offered luxury waiting rooms with free liquor, coffee, and "hideaway beds" for a quick nap.

Mickie Siebert thought she might be able to get a job at the United Nations through her cousin, but when that fell through, she tried Wall Street. At an interview with Merrill Lynch, Pierce, Fenner & Smith, Inc., she admitted she had dropped out of college—a mistake she was sure not to repeat the second time around. She was hired at Bache & Co. as a "college graduate," passing up a $75-a-week position in the accounting department for a $65-a-week job in the research department because the latter sounded more interesting. In the research department, they put her on the wire desk, where the telex machine spat out a litany of questions from brokers and clients around the country, as well as from "pension funds, mutual funds, bank trust funds, college endowments and foundations—wanting to know: What do you think of General Electric? Should we buy or sell General Motors?" Mickie's job was to collect the telex messages and bring them over to the senior research analysts.

Research, she began to see, was both a science and an art, with the financial data a science and "seeing a pattern in those numbers" the art. She discovered she "could look at a page of numbers, and they would light up like a Broadway marquee."

Only six weeks after she'd started, she got a $5 a week raise, from which she put aside an extra 20¢ for lunch, and the rest went toward renting a nicer apartment with her sister in what used to be the maids' quarters in a building on Park Avenue. (Mickie slept on the Foamland sofa in the living room.) But her real lucky break came when the senior analysts, rewarded for their work, were allowed to shift some of that workload onto the underlings, discarding the industries they considered the least lucrative. Mickie, now their trainee, got some of their castoffs. One senior analyst gave her coverage of the radio, TV, and film industries; another, a brilliant railroad analyst, gave her the airline industry in which he had little faith.

Yet commercial jets were just around the corner, and TV and film were about to explode, and it was sheer luck that Mickie was "saddled" with these industries. The railroad analyst also gave her some important advice: learn everything there is to know about an industry, and a company, and "let the numbers tell the story."

Companies, industries, and businesses had long produced "reports" for their investors and clients, but they were often mere fairy tales, musings, because there was little incentive to tell the full truth or impress with well-substantiated research. But a man by the name of Benjamin Graham changed that. Successful on Wall Street, when the 1929 market crash came, he lost a substantial amount, after which he turned his attention to research, studying companies and searching for those he considered undervalued (he would go on to teach Warren Buffett at Columbia University). When Mickie Siebert joined the New York Society of Security Analysts, an organization founded in the 1930s with only twenty members, it had close to three thousand members, and research analysis was a robust field using the modern concepts of securities analysis started by Graham.

Mickie was among the very first women to become a research analyst, but her start was typical because it was in these new research departments where women found a place for themselves beyond the secretarial pool or the occasional token hire as a salesperson or broker. Research, even when done by men, was considered the most feminized area of work on Wall Street. As one of the first female analysts herself noted: "I was with the geeks—they were a different breed who worked in wrinkled shirts."

By 1966, there were around sixty women on Wall Street who were neither receptionists nor secretaries nor data-entry clerks nor statisticians but research analysts. Alongside Mickie Siebert, there was Mary Wrenn, profiled in the *New York Times* in 1964, "a pert, attractive brunette to whom people are always coming up at parties and saying, 'What do you think of my XYZ stock?'" Mary Wrenn, like most female research analysts, focused on drugs, cosmetics, and merchandising—the areas seen as within a woman's natural expertise. That she was working for Merrill Lynch was no accident. Merrill Lynch (founded by Charles Merrill in 1914, joined later that year by Edmund Lynch) took a pragmatist view, insisting that the "mystery" be taken out of finance. In Charles Merrill's opinion there was no need for luxurious décor: you just needed telephones. He was an early adherent of Benjamin Graham and demanded that his brokers be informed by research and not speculation or wishful thinking. He not only built up a significant modern securities research department but trained the investing public, too, placing page-length newspaper advertisements that read like crash courses in stock-market investing. By 1960, Merrill Lynch's firm was practically four times the size of the second largest brokerage, Bache & Co., and almost equal to the next four combined. With 540,000 brokerage accounts, Merrill Lynch was referred to as "the thundering herd."

Mary Wrenn's reports on her particular industries were distributed to "153 offices and more than 500,000 customers," filled with the information she gathered by reading everything she could, traveling to visit with CEOs, as well as lunching with the representatives of large asset funds, pensions funds, insurance companies, and banks, who were all "scouting for investment ideas." She smoked a pack of filtered cigarettes a day, liked her coffee black, favored Welsh rarebit with a dash of Worcestershire sauce, and always removed a clip-on earring as she reached for the phone, which she did often. In the office, she was expected to pick up the phone for anyone—brokers and customers alike—calling her with questions. The day the *New York Times* interviewed Mary Wrenn, questions were pouring in about a trending product, Magic Secret, the Helene Curtis wrinkle cream.

————

SPRING WAS HIRING SEASON AT THE HARVARD BUSINESS SCHOOL, when corporate recruiters descended on campus and second-year students might field five to ten serious job offers by the end.

But for the women of HBS, despite the presence of Mickie Siebert and Mary Wrenn on Wall Street, there were not even five to ten bona-fide job interviews. Some of the women tried to sign up with recruiters using only their initials, but then there was still the "big reveal" awaiting them: that moment when they walked into the interview room, heels and skirt, not knowing if they'd be welcome.

Usually, they were told the firm was not hiring women. *Not yet. Maybe later down the road.* The process itself was humiliating. A 1962 graduate of the Radcliffe Program walked into an interview and was told point blank by the General Foods representative: "Why are you here? We'd never hire a woman."

Some recruiters encouraged the women to sign up for interviews, but only for kicks, so they could see what a female Harvard MBA looked like. One 1965 female graduate, disgusted, joked with her female classmates that with her degree, "at least when I go shopping I'll be able to figure out if I'm benefiting from the 10-cent sale."

Some companies were willing to hire women, or contemplate the possibility of doing so, but mostly for positions that were either in the so-called back office or in the research department, hidden from sight. Client-facing jobs were off-limits. In 1964, a major consulting firm did hire three female graduates as associates, meaning they were on the consultant track. But before the women even arrived, the three teams to which they'd been assigned received instructions that the new female hires, referred to as "the experiment," were not to be sent out to client sites.

And then there was the question of pay. Roberta Lasley, daughter of the single-mother janitor, was offered a job at the investment bank, Smith, Barney & Co. for $4,500 a year. When she asked why a male classmate with a lower GPA had been offered $5,500 just the day before, the recruiter seemed surprised: "You don't understand . . . You are a woman. You are going to be in research."

Elaine Luthy, the blond bomb, the "official" first woman at HBS, interviewed for what she hoped would be a job at the advertising agency Young & Rubicam. But they had only just hired a woman, and they wanted to give it a few years to see how it went. She was finally hired by another advertising agency, but while she was searching for the information she needed for a client's campaign, she was told she wouldn't be able to get her hands on it without having sex with the man who held the research. She informed her boss, and after some time had lapsed, word came back from upstairs that she should go ahead and have sex in exchange for the research. Luthy stopped coming to work and had a breakdown. (In 1991, a Wall Street investment banker would similarly tell *The Wall Street Journal* how she discovered she'd "been promised romantically to the principal in a deal her boss was hoping to snag.")

The limited or else degrading job prospects were hard to square with the eager and optimistic photo-op of the first eight official HBS women posing in Baker Library. It was fair to say that for many of the 1960s female graduates of the MBA program, the promises of Harvard Business School had fallen short. But different routes to Wall Street were just as pitted with landmines.

Patricia Chadwick had won her freedom from the Feeneyite sect by getting into Vassar College and thus helping them gain state accreditation. But once done, they made her turn down Vassar's offer, and with no college degree, her only option, now out on her own, was to pursue a secretarial certificate, which landed her a job at the brokerage firm Ladenburg, Thalmann & Co. Determined to get the college education she'd been denied, Patricia also enrolled in evening classes at Harvard, writing papers until the morning hours.

Ladenburg, Thalmann was thriving, and the following year the partners hired new brokers and more secretarial support staff. One of the new brokers was known as a hardcore producer; he arrived with a "long client list," a "rollicking sense of Irish humor," and photographs of "his third wife and their three children," which he displayed prominently in his office. An unattractive man, with thick glasses and a thick middle, he frequently invited Patricia and his British secretary for drinks at the 99 Club, a place popular with Boston's traders. Patricia would sometimes go along before heading off to her classes at Boston University, where she was now getting her undergraduate degree.

One afternoon he asked her if she wanted to grab a drink before classes. "Sure," she replied. When she arrived, her drink was already perched on the bar in front of the bartender. The next thing she remembered was waking up, "in the pitch black, naked, in pain and aware that a man was getting out of my bed." As he "slipped into his trousers," she caught sight of those familiar thick glasses.

3

Mickie and
the Gunslingers

W all Street was not new to the idea of keeping certain people out. Firms had historically segregated along ethnic
and religious lines. By the 1950s, a Jewish broker might,
just might, be hired by an Irish firm, or the other way around, but
if you were Irish American, and—better yet—with a military background, you had a significant advantage at Merrill Lynch, just as you
did at Goldman Sachs if you were Jewish, or at Morgan Stanley if
you'd been a member of Yale's elite secret fraternity, Skull and Bones.
Wall Street investment banks and brokerage houses were stamped
with their founders' backgrounds: White Protestant, or German
Jewish, or Eastern European Jewish, or Irish Catholic, or African
American.

Robert Bernhard, later a partner at Lehman Brothers and Salomon Brothers, was barely offended when at the end of an otherwise
pleasant interview with First Boston, he was advised that he "should
go to Lehman Brothers because, you know, we don't hire Jews." It
was 1953 and it was a matter-of-fact understanding that "if you were
young and Jewish and wanted to go into the investment-banking busi-

ness, you worked at Lehman Brothers, Loeb Rhoades, Kuhn Loeb, or Goldman Sachs. And if you were Gentile you went to First Boston, Morgan Stanley, Dillon Read, et cetera."

Morgan Stanley, a financial services company founded in 1935 after the Glass-Steagall Act, was a "white-shoe" firm, the most prestigious of all (the term "white-shoe" came from "white bucks," the nubuck Oxfords worn by Ivy League men in the 1950s). But "white-shoe" of course also signaled *not Jewish*. Morgan Stanley, like its clients, was predominantly WASP, with a heavy scent of Ivy League. The firm's signature look was "mahogany walls and stuffed leather sofas." In its early days, its partners sat together behind rolltop desks, charting "the course for corporate America's growth plans."

Goldman Sachs, an investment banking company founded in 1869, was of Jewish origin, as was Lehman Brothers and Bear Stearns. The Wall Street behemoth, Merrill Lynch, was the best known of the Irish firms. Apart from these big-name firms, each with its own particular hiring policy, there were also hundreds of much smaller firms, each similarly imprinted by the origins of its partners. But there was one point of view that they all shared: as the *New York Times* had observed, this "nebulous half-mile-square community known as Wall Street" constitutes "the nation's last great stronghold of masculine supremacy."

Yet when Mickie Siebert stepped onto Wall Street in 1954, New York's financial center was not only an all-male bastion but also surprisingly quaint, almost provincial. An ambitious Ivy League man looking to strike it rich in the 1950s was unlikely to buy himself a one-way ticket to Wall Street; rather, he dreamed of corporate life, of one day rising through the ranks to lead a company. On Wall Street, wages were decent but not spectacular, and competition felt phlegmatic at best. Firms each had their own client base that remained with them over generations. Morgan Stanley could readily tap into theirs and "a single phone call from one of those rolltop desks . . . could raise $100 million or $200 million." Investment bankers were largely hired based on kin and contacts; the right school, the right background, and then a tap on the shoulder inviting you to join the other gentlemen on Wall Street. As one Wall Street man recalled, "It really was like a secret society."

Public restaurants were scarce around Wall Street, in part because street-entry space was reserved for banks. Lunch instead was served inside the financial institutions' buildings, in a hierarchical assortment of dining halls; from employee cafeterias to executive dining rooms to private luncheon clubs with stunning views and masculine décor and men-only rules. The Bankers' Club, at the top of the forty-story Equitable Building, not only had breathtaking views but four dining rooms with thirty-foot ceilings, and a main lounge with standing ashtrays and one of the largest Oriental rugs in America. At the Stock Exchange Club, cigar holders were affixed to the walls of the bathroom stalls—at just the right height for taking care of all kinds of business simultaneously. The Downtown Association was known for "broad stairs, old tables and open fireplaces"; the Lunch Club at 63 Wall Street was nicknamed the "Boys' Club" because initiation fees were lower, making it a top choice for younger Wall Street men; while the vast Wall Street Club was an "infinite stretch of chairs and tables and carpets." The most exclusive, the Recess Club and the Broad Street Club, both had waitlists stretching out for years.

All the clubs, regardless of size or prestige, offered a well-priced lunch and a convenient spot for deal-making. These were men's clubs in what was already a "boys' club," as Martin Mayer observed in 1955: "What the food lacks is made up by the atmosphere, which is spacious and intensely masculine: women are admitted rarely if ever."

Mickie Siebert was an iconoclast precisely because she had forged ahead in this atmosphere and was now regularly attending the New York Society of Security Analysts' lunches, with food brought in from the nearby Coachman Restaurant, and where waiters could be found loitering, holding on to dirty dishes so they could eavesdrop for stock-market tips. It was 1957, and she was the up-and-coming expert on the new aviation industry, but she was also getting more and more frustrated by the day. Her salary had doubled in two years, now up to $130 a week, but it was significantly—egregiously!—below what the men were making.

The only way to negotiate for a higher salary was to leave for another job. One of her contacts, Eddie Rickenbacker, former fighter pilot and now CEO of Eastern Airlines, offered to help by introducing her to two of his banker friends—one at Kuhn, Loeb & Co. and the other at Smith Barney. Both top Wall Street firms, neither had ever hired a woman for anything other than secretarial work. But as a favor to Captain Eddie, they agreed to interview her. Mickie was ready to impress, to showcase what she could bring to the table, but at the first interview, the banker told her she would not be allowed to travel as a representative of the company (that would be client-facing!), and at the other, the interviewer told her that when she took the elevator, she'd be expected to wear a hat and white gloves "like the rest of the 'girls.' "

She thanked them and left. She went next to the placement department of the New York Society of Security Analysts and asked them to send out her résumé. But not one firm responded. OK, thought Muriel, the name would have to go; she asked them to send out a second batch of résumés, but this time with "M. F. Siebert" instead of Muriel Siebert. (A common practice: Mary Wrenn, the research analyst at Merrill Lynch who liked Welsh rarebit, did the same. Even earlier, Isabel Benham, who arrived on Wall Street in the 1930s and by the 1960s was a major railroad industry analyst as well as the first female partner of a major Wall Street firm, would sign off as I. Hamilton Benham.) Almost immediately, she had a job offer as a research analyst for $9,500 a year at the brokerage and investment banking firm of Shields & Co.

But soon she was faced with the very same situation: even as she was bringing in serious institutional funds, including National Aviation, her base salary remained stuck at $9,500, and when Shields & Co. hired two men fresh out of business school for $8,800 a year, she was furious. The firm's partners called her in and offered to increase her salary to $12,500.

"Would that make you happy?" they asked.

No, it wouldn't. A male colleague doing exactly the same job was being paid $20,000 a year, which was justified by the fact that he had a family to support—unlike Mickie.

YET BY THE 1960S, WALL STREET WAS STARTING TO CHANGE, IN PART because New York City was changing too. On Mayor John V. Lindsay's first day of work on January 1, 1966, the city came to a standstill as two unions forced a massive transit strike. A seven-month-long teachers' strike followed next, and in 1968, a nine-day sanitation workers' strike left 100,000 tons of trash strewn across New York's streets, garbage "piled chest-high. Egg shells, coffee grounds, milk cartons, orange rinds, and empty beer cans littered the sidewalk."

Amidst a background of growing unrest and urban breakdown, technology was accelerating and the volume of stocks changing hands soared. In 1965, the old-school ticker-tape machine started to be swapped out for the 900 ticker, which produced nine hundred characters per minute, capable of handling 10 million shares a day. (Once the ticker tape itself became obsolete, there were no more strips of paper to toss down on passing parades, and the City of New York Department of Sanitation would sometimes distribute scrap paper to the city's offices the day before a parade—only to sweep it up again the following day.)

A new kind of person was also emerging on Wall Street: the so-called gunslinger who practiced fast-paced trading, sometimes pulling large bundles of stock in and out of the market as quickly as

A young woman reading ticker tape from the new 900 ticker, 1960s.

yanking down on the lever of a slot machine (some say the term the "go-go years" came from this sped-up trading). John Brooks, writing about the 1960s, sees in the gunslingers, the new money managers, a radical takeover of Wall Street:

> Hardly anything else on Wall Street had remained the same since 1965. The most conspicuous change was the triumph of youth. . . . The late sixties became, for a shockingly brief moment, the heyday of the young prodigy, the sideburned gunslinger. What manner of young man was he? He came from a prospering middle-income background and often from a good business school; he was under thirty, often well under; he wore boldly striped shirts and broad, flowing ties; he radiated a confidence, a knowingness, that verged on insolence, and

he liberally tossed around the newest clichés, "performance," "concept," "innovative," and "synergy" . . .

The gunslingers were *all* about performance, until recently valued much less than having the right social contacts. One of the best-known gunslingers was Gerald Tsai, about whom *Newsweek* wrote that he "radiates total cool." Investing was suddenly a game, and those who could keep their "cool" were destined to come out on top.

Wall Street's gunslingers and '60s student protesters were flip sides of the same coin: both were driven to create change. When Harvard students occupied University Hall, one of their demands was that HBS, the cheerleader for American capitalism, be jettisoned. But for Lillian Hobson and the other Black students at HBS, they didn't so much want the business school to disappear as they wanted it to diversify.

Lillian and the other founders of Harvard Business School's African American Student Association (counterclockwise from Lillian: Clifford Darden, Theodore Lewis, and Leroy Willis).

In their first year at Harvard, they convinced the Business School dean that they themselves would help recruit Black students for the next year's incoming class if he would tap into corporate funding for scholarships. They managed to bring in twenty-seven Black students for the following year, most from historically Black colleges. They next lobbied the administration for an African American Student Union, arguing that it would ease the kind of loneliness they'd all experienced. It would mean companionship but also something as basic as help finding a local barber shop that knew how to cut Black hair. The first meeting of the new African American Student Union was held at the start of Lillian's second year. She and her three cofounders of the AASU stood up front and toasted their new classmates.

———

MICKIE SIEBERT WAS NOW AT STEARNS & CO., WHERE SHE'D BEEN made a partner, but more than anything, she wanted to play in the big leagues where the major deal-making took place. But it was impossible—as a woman—to become a partner at one of the major firms. The small brokerages were more open to women but they could also be suffocating. She was at a loss. She wanted more, but no one would give it to her.

She was saying all this over lunch with her friend Gerald Tsai, the superstar gunslinger of Wall Street, when he suggested she circumvent the system entirely: "Don't be ridiculous. . . . There's *nowhere* you can go. Buy a seat on the Stock Exchange and work for yourself."

"Don't *you* be ridiculous," she replied. "There are no women on the Exchange."

"I don't think there's a law against it."

That night, Mickie pored over the NYSE constitution, and saw he was right: nowhere was it written that she, as a woman, could not apply for a seat. Still, it was one thing to be legally free to apply and another to be allowed to buy a seat.

Nonetheless, Tsai had planted the idea in her head, and six months later, she approached an NYSE official: "Can I buy a seat, or is this just a country club?" she asked him. He intimated that if the NYSE were to ignore her request, they would make themselves legally liable. After all, there was now the federal Equal Pay Act of 1963 and the 1964 Civil Rights Act prohibiting employment discrimination based on race, color, religion, national origin, or sex. Not that employment discrimination had miraculously vanished, not by any stretch, but there was now a legal pathway for recourse.

There was another hurdle, however: a seat on the NYSE in 1967, with the bull market in full swing, was not cheap. The seat that had opened up was going for $445,000—more than $4 million today.

But on December 7, 1967, Mickie Siebert went ahead and signed a conditional sale contract and paid 20 percent of the seat price. She now needed two more things: two NYSE members to sponsor her application, and a bank to loan her the remaining 80 percent.

Men who had once promised to sponsor her suddenly made quick exits when they saw her coming. Nine men turned her down before she finally found two who would sponsor her. (One of them later said that he was asked by the NYSE Board of Governors about Siebert's personal life—something never under consideration when men were being vetted for a seat.) As for the bank loan, Mickie banked and did business with Morgan Guarantee, but although the bank said it was willing to give her a loan if she were to get the seat (betting that she would not), it refused to provide a letter saying as much. (A letter that had, as far as Mickie could tell, never been requested of any men purchasing their seats.)

Getting loans, be they large or small, was no easy matter if you were female. A woman recounted to *The Wall Street Journal* how in 1971, recently divorced and needing to secure a $500 loan to cover medical expenses for her daughter, she went from bank to bank until one credit manager agreed to give her a loan—if she slept with him. As the reporter obliquely noted: "Jan Eddins got her loan, but she vowed that she'd never be so desperate again." In 1974, the Equal Credit Opportunity Act would be passed precisely so women would have an equal right to a loan as well as to a credit card without needing a man's signature as a guarantor.

But this was still 1967, and Mickie's hurdles were significant. Eventually Chase Manhattan Bank guaranteed the loan, thanks to a friend for whom Mickie had once stuck her neck out, although she would later learn that Chase bank employees—like at JP Morgan— were wagering that they'd never in fact have to deliver on it.

But they did have to. On December 28, 1967, Mickie officially became a member of the New York Stock Exchange, the first ever woman. After she handed over the remaining balance due on the $445,000, plus a $7,515 initiation fee, she arrived at her office with three bottles of French Champagne to celebrate.

She would refer to her membership badge as "the most expensive piece of jewelry going." This close-to-a-half-a-million-dollar bling was not particularly attractive; it was a white metal badge with the number 2646 embossed in red. Since the entire NYSE institution was constructed for men by men, that meant the badge, too, which came with a clip for attaching to the breast pocket of a man's suit. Mickie took her badge to a jeweler to see if they could refashion it, but when they asked for $11.50 for the adjustment, Mickie—relentlessly middle-class—opted for a safety pin instead. Sometimes she fantasized about how her half-million-dollar badge would look on a full-length gown.

The press, much like the exchange, had reservations about Mickie's presence on the trading floor. One headline barked: "Now the Girls Want to Play, Too." Mickie's audacity was seen by many as outrageous. This was not only a man's world but a place where boys could be boys, where there were rites and rituals—like tossing talcum powder on newcomers and grooms-to-be. (When in 1969 pranks were banned, at least officially, it was because a clerk who'd been squirted with a water gun turned around and punched the man behind him, breaking his shoulder—except it was the wrong man.)

The *New York Times* put Mickie on its front page but also assured nervous readers that friends described her as "bubbly and ebullient and fortyish" (she was thirty-eight). They further reported that at "five feet four inches," she hoped to lose twenty pounds in the New Year, smoked "one pack a day of True cigarettes without inhaling," and "lives in an apartment on Manhattan's Upper East Side, talks with a slight Midwestern twang, likes to play bridge and golf, and is thinking about taking cooking lessons." In other words, she was a "girl." Harmless. (The same year, Ginny Clark arrived at Salomon Brothers as the first ever female trading trainee. She was repeatedly

A 1968 *New York Daily News* caption read, "In her Manhattan apartment, Muriel relaxes with a pot of coffee."

told she was there as "a token," and when her class finished the training, the men received gold watches while she got a rabbit [used at the time to determine a positive pregnancy]: the message was clear— you're done, now go get pregnant.)

Fears that Wall Street was going to change were allayed when Mickie revealed that her revolution was going to be only symbolic in nature. It was reported that "the petite blonde will not appear on the trading floor . . . but will start her own brokerage house . . . the actual floor transactions will be handled either by another member of her firm or by 'two-dollar' brokers who make their living by buying and selling stock for other houses." She had bought the seat to start her own NYSE-member firm so as to have greater control over the buying and selling of securities; she did not intend to become a trader on the floor, disrupting the "sea of men" that had so mesmerized her during her first visit to the NYSE as a teenager.

Mickie launched her firm, Muriel Siebert & Co., Inc., on the first workday of 1968, intending to advertise her new firm with a flyer describing herself as the "First Lady of the New York Stock Exchange." But when she submitted the ad piece to the NYSE for preapproval, the NYSE chairman demanded a rewrite. By definition, he insisted, it was his wife who was First Lady.

The following year, in 1969, author Martin Mayer, who had observed 1950s Wall Street and its "masculine air" up close, published a splashy coffee-table book profiling sixty-two of Wall Street's youngest and brightest traders, brokers, and investors: its gunslingers. Gerald Tsai was of course featured in the book, but Mickie Siebert was included too: the only woman in a book titled *New Breed on Wall Street: The Young Men Who Make the Money Go*. In her profile, she explained why she did not take to the floor "despite much urging from the women's magazines." It was because she "could afford to pay floor brokers to do her work, and she needed all the friends she could get. The only friends she would make by violating the masculinity of the trading floor are in the Lucy Stone League . . ." (The Lucy Stone League was an early feminist organization that advocated for women keeping their names after marriage.)

Mickie was always hedging her bets, however. She knew that as the owner of a small brokerage firm and a woman, she could easily fail. As a precaution, after purchasing her $445,000 badge, she had quietly taken the exam that would allow her to work on the floor of the NYSE, if push came to shove.

———

MOST OF THE 1,366 MEMBERS OF THE NEW YORK STOCK EXCHANGE worked within privately owned partnership firms. These were not publicly traded companies; there was no stockholder input, no board of directors. Decisions were made entirely by the partners, and most were small outfits. But as Americans after World War II again began to invest in the market, and trading volume rapidly grew, some of these smaller firms now struggled to survive. In 1952, 6.5 million Americans held stock but by 1970, that number would be 31 million. And stocks—the selling, buying, trading of them—were all based on the exchange and safekeeping of paper. The stocks were made of paper, the ownership transfers were written up on paper, the paperwork was, well, paper. There were no computers and software programs to convert the paper trail into an orderly digital database. Wall Street's back offices were responsible for recording it all, but they were failing to keep up under the growing deluge of paper.

The back office's primary role was to guarantee an orderly transfer of stock, which included matching buy and sell information. If the two did not match, if the selling broker or the buying broker had scribbled down a different sale price or quantity, then the trade was called a "fail" and had to be fixed. According to Alec Benn, by April 1968, the "value of shares not delivered within four days totaled $2.7 billion." As trading volume surged, the paperwork became yet more impossible, and unfiled stock certificates piled up. At one firm, a visitor who stopped by spied baskets wedged in under desks filled to the brim with stock certificates. There were rumors of criminal gangs who would pinpoint a troubled back-office employee, someone with an alcohol or gambling problem, or a messy divorce, and use them to get hold of the loose stock certificates the employee had yet to report.

A significant part of the problem was that the head and tail were not working together and more often than not, they could barely recognize one another: the firms' partners "were like deck officers on a cruise ship. They concentrated on keeping the customers happy." The back office was completely outside of their purview, let alone interest. This strict separation was bolstered by class difference. Those who worked behind the scenes lacked college degrees, sometimes even high school diplomas, and their accents gave them away as outer-borough New Yorkers. The brokers and bankers and other front-office staff tended to have four-year college or even graduate degrees and "spoke with broad a's even though they weren't from Boston." Most of them had never even seen the back office and could barely locate its whereabouts.

Yet it was up to the back offices to match the countless—and growing by the day—slips of paper between buyer and seller. In 1965, the NYSE had predicted that its average daily trading volume would reach 10 million shares in ten years; instead that happened just two years later, in 1967. And it was not just individual investors who were adding to the volume. Institutional money managers, who had once erred on the side of caution with high-grade bonds and blue-chip stocks with relatively reliable if slow growth, were now getting in on the action, vying to get the best possible returns by the year's end. More aggressive trading in more speculative "growth stocks" meant enormous turnover, and of course yet more paper to record and file.

Firms scrambled to hire more employees for the back office, but they found the pool of applicants ever smaller and less qualified. Their resources, as private partnerships, were also limited. With the paperwork piling up, and despite share trade volume soaring, the governors of the New York Stock Exchange voted to close on Wednesdays as of January 2, 1968, later opting for an early closing time of 2 p.m. on Wednesdays, which continued through much of 1969. Quickly renamed "golf day," on Wednesdays Wall Street's front office headed out to the golf course while the back office toiled, playing a game of catch-up that often felt like treading water.

As firms were drowning in paper, it started to become clear that the only way for many of the NYSE-member firms to survive the paper debacle was to take on more staff, and for that, they needed more capital. In fact, they needed the very kind of capital injection that they were in the business of drumming up for every other industry in America: capital acquired through publicly traded stock.

That is when a boutique investment banking and brokerage firm called Donaldson, Lufkin & Jenrette (DLJ) stepped in. Dan Lufkin, then thirty-nine years old, one of the gunslingers, quietly filed a request with the Securities and Exchange Commission asking for DLJ to go public.

Recently elected to the exchange's Board of Governors, Lufkin decided to spring the news on them at the first board meeting. It didn't go over so well: "Old men screaming, 'Who the hell do you think you are'?" They compared Lufkin to Judas Iscariot. At the dinner afterward, Lufkin stood alone with a drink in his hand, nibbling on canapés, no one speaking to him.

But they were swimming against the tide, and once DLJ successfully pushed through the constitutional amendment, on April 10, 1970, they became the very first NYSE-member firm to go public, immediately raising $12 million through their own IPO. Dan Lufkin's victory was little known outside of Wall Street, but on the Street, DLJ partners and employees were suddenly celebrities. The Associated Press compared the NYSE amendment with the landing on the moon, and when two DLJ floor brokers walked into a popular lunch club, they were given a standing ovation.

Gradually others followed DLJ in going public. In 1971, Merrill Lynch, Wall Street's juggernaut, saw its own stock listed on the exchange. A few months later, Bache & Co. went public too. In 1981, Salomon Brothers, the largest bond house, would merge with an already publicly traded firm. And after that, more mergers would follow, repositioning Loeb, Rhoades; Lehman Brothers; Bear Stearns; and Morgan Stanley as public, stockholding companies. Goldman Sachs, the most top-tier of them all, a firm that had more than enough capital, along with strict, well-established guidelines against partners pulling their money from the firm, only went public in 1999.

The gradual shift to publicly owned companies would change the look of Wall Street in fundamental ways. A 1960s study of Wall Street law firms found that they looked for employees "who are Nordic," "with pleasing personalities, clean-cut appearances, the 'right school and social backgrounds' and 'tremendous stamina.'" Only 17 percent of the lawyers interviewed for the study had not gone to "one of the 19 socially acceptable colleges or the three preferred law schools," and while most firms were increasingly willing to take on Jewish employees, they limited the number through a quota system. Discrimination against Catholics was viewed as a class issue rather than a religious slight, and as for Black employees, within the twenty law firms interviewed for the study, there were only three, two of whom were women with no client-facing responsibilities. Wall Street itself looked much like the lawyers they hired to represent their interests. But with firms going public, making themselves accountable to stockholders and to new rules and regulations, this would have to change.

4

W.I.T.C.H. on
Wall Street

There was fame, and then there was notoriety. There was progress, and then there was its speed: two steps forward, one step back. In 1967, the same year that Mickie Siebert bought her seat on the NYSE, Francine Gottfried was hired by Chemical Bank to operate an IBM 1260 machine at their data-processing center for $85 a week. Even as Wall Street was very much a man's world, legions of female support staff were needed to run it. Their arrival was heard each morning as the "click-click-clack-click" of heels resounding through "the narrow canyons of Wall Street."

Francine Gottfried had recently joined them. Five-foot-four, from Williamsburg, Brooklyn, one of six children of a postal worker, Francine had lived a sheltered life of Hebrew school, piano lessons, and parties. At the age of sixteen, she had already "matured," as it was called, into a full-figured teenager, rapidly drawing unwanted attention from men. She had learned to ignore the men, walking with her shoulders back, looking straight ahead, intentionally oblivious to their whistles and stares.

On May 27, her first day of work, she set out from Brooklyn on

Crowd waits patiently at Broad and Wall Street BMT subway station exit for "the Sweater Girl," Francine Gottfried, to arrive, 1967.

what would soon become a route well known by the men of the Financial District. Her data-processing shift began at 1:30 p.m., and she caught the subway about forty minutes before, arriving on Broad and Wall Street, right outside the New York Stock Exchange, at around 1:28 p.m. At first, it was just a few men who caught sight of her on the short walk to her office, her sweater clinging to her figure. But they told their friends, who told their friends, and soon enough brokers, bankers, and clerks were out there on the street trying to catch sight of "the Sweater Girl," as she was now being called.

Francine and her forty-three-inch chest were soon Wall Street's main attraction, its titillation, its sport. The number of men waiting for Francine Gottfried to emerge from the subway station at 1:28 p.m. grew exponentially. Toward the end of September, there were crowds, applause, and cheers when she appeared. Traffic stopped. Over five thousand men took up positions along the length of Wall Street, some climbing lampposts and even scaling the famous Buttonwood Tree. From the windows of the JP Morgan offices, executives had a good, unfettered view of Francine Gottfried.

The day the press showed up for what was now a major viewing event, Francine emerged from the subway in a yellow sweater and a red skirt, and all hell broke loose. Men swarmed around her, pushing others up against the walls, damaging three cars. Two plainclothes policemen, assigned to protect her, managed to pull her to safety through a back door into her office building. "There are thousands of girls on Wall Street and they act as though I'm the only one," Francine would later say. The media coverage made her famous: "A Bust Panics Wall Street as the Tape Says 43," read the *Daily News* headline; "10,000 Wait in Vain for Reappearance of Wall Street's Sweater Girl," the *New York Times* reported. The attention forced Francine to stay at home for a while and lie low, but the men didn't know that. The crowds that still waited for her swelled to fifteen thousand, making it impossible to move along Wall Street or Broad Street on any workday around 1:28 p.m. Francine's analysis went straight to the point: "These people in Wall Street have the responsibility of handling millions of dollars and they act like they're out of their minds."

A few months later, it was "witches" that descended on Wall Street. WITCH—the Women's International Terrorist Conspiracy from Hell—was an offshoot of New York's Second Wave feminist groups. WITCH members believed capitalism to be at the root of patriarchy, and sought the "destruction of passivity, consumerism and commodity fetishism." They believed that if capitalism remained untouched, even if women were to achieve liberation, that achievement would soon be coopted and absorbed by capitalism. WITCH called its guerrilla theater acts "zaps," and they liked to hex things, people, and places. In Washington, DC, they hexed the inauguration

On the steps of Federal Hall, costumed members of the feminist activist
group WITCH (Women's International Terrorist Conspiracy from Hell)
perform a Halloween Hex on Wall Street as onlookers watch from the
sidewalk below, 1968.

of Richard Nixon. In Chicago, after a female lecturer in sociology
at the University of Chicago was fired, they threw hair and nail clip-
pings at the department chair and shouted, "Beware of the curse, the
witch's curse."

In New York, on Halloween in 1968, the original founding members of WITCH descended on Wall Street, "the epicenter of corporate
America's persecution of women," they said, dressed up as witches
with brooms and wands. They "demanded an audience with Satan,
our superior, at the Stock Exchange," and stood with "a paper-maché
[*sic*] pig's head on a golden plate" on the Federal Hall stairs beside
the George Washington statue that looks directly onto the NYSE,
"a symbol of patriarchal, slave-holding power," they explained.
But it would take a lot of hexing to make Wall Street's rampant
sexism disappear.

———

THE NEXT YEAR, LILLIAN HOBSON AND PRISCILLA RABB WERE PRE-
paring to march in Harvard University's graduation ceremony as
members of the class of 1969. Priscilla wryly noted that the HBS
graduating class had been picked to lead the procession as a reward
for their conservatism, for being the only school within the university
that in 1968 had not shut down classes in political protest.

The recruiters had been descending on HBS in the months prior,
as they did each spring, but no one had been knocking on Lillian
Hobson's door. "What would corporate America do in 1969 with a
black woman, even if she did have a Harvard M.B.A.?" Lillian's professor of business at Howard University, the man who had urged her
to apply to his alma mater, had since been hired by PepsiCo to lead
early forays into the African American consumer market. Yet here
was Lillian in much the same position as when he had graduated in
the 1930s: unhirable. But it was not only Lillian. Robin Foote, the
most accomplished of all the women that year, who had stubbornly
refused to let the sexism and misogyny get to her, who had raised her
hand as often as the men, who had won the prestigious title of Baker
Scholar, would later write a ditty for their twenty-fifth reunion: "*Left
HBS eager, all full of hope,/ Terribly naïve, ill-prepared to cope./
Business was not ready for women in our day./ Limited our choices,
affecting our pay.*"

HBS student Margo, soon to be Margo Alexander, slated to graduate the following year in 1970 alongside the twenty-seven Black
students whom Lillian had helped recruit, had opted out of student
housing at the Radcliffe Graduate Center and moved into an apartment share in Cambridge. One of the other building's tenants was
a fellow HBS student who would become her husband. Like Robin
Foote, he also graduated as a Baker Scholar, and coming home, sort-
ing through the mail, there were so many job offers for him that he

barely bothered to open them all. Margo received mail too: credit card offers.

"Maybe, maybe, hmm, no," he would mutter, flipping through his job offers. "Oh, here's another credit card for you!"

When she finally received a dinner invitation from a consulting firm in Boston, she was over the moon, but midway through the meal in the fancy restaurant where they'd brought her, the two men asked, "Aren't you getting married to Bob Alexander?"

"Yeah, yeah, next month," Margo replied.

"Well, here's why we invited you to dinner. We've sent him several letters and been unable to set up an appointment, and we thought if we told you about our company, you would help us . . ."

Margo did no such thing.

Lillian's mother arrived for the graduation ceremony, dressed up and excited, but this wasn't enough to buoy Lillian's spirits. She was looking at a post-graduation future with no job prospects and with more questions than answers. From the 1950s to the 1960s, there had been a 600 percent increase in Black stockbrokers—but all that meant was that by the end of the 1960s, there were sixty at most. In 1965, Merrill Lynch had hired its first three Black stockbrokers. But even those hired could not count on being accepted. George King, one of the three Merrill Lynch hires, had established a good telephone relationship with a female client who asked if she might stop by the offices to say hello. When she walked in and asked for him, and the receptionist pointed to him, a Black man, she headed straight to the manager's office and demanded a new broker. (The manager, to his credit, instead pulled her account).

Black female brokers in the 1960s were rare but not entirely unheard-of. June Middleton was the first Black female stockbroker to work for an NYSE-affiliated firm. She had taken the circuitous route to Wall Street, working her way up from secretary while taking night classes at New York University's business school. She was comfortable in the language of finance because at her Manhattan public school, where she'd been the only Black student, the class had read the stock tables every morning and for half an hour discussed what they saw happening in the markets. Just as the *New York Times* financial reporter Vartanig G. Vartan—known on the Street as "Tonny"—had told readers a year earlier about research analyst Mary Wrenn, now he profiled Mrs. June Middleton, tall and twenty-seven, "who likes to cook chicken cacciatore flavored with wine and who wears a fashionable mink hat outdoors in the winter." Married to an architect, June was able to lean on family and friends as her first clients, circumventing the most common problem for African American brokers— the difficulty of finding customers, of having to turn to cold-calling instead of tapping into existing connections and networks.

Well-connected Priscilla Rabb had had much better luck during recruitment than Lillian, but what helped especially was her substantial business experience, which most of the other female graduates lacked. Throughout business school, Priscilla had continued to work summers at Loeb, Rhoades & Co., and now the firm offered her a full-time job. Yet she couldn't help but be curious what else might be out there for her. She landed interviews with Morgan Stanley and Lehman Brothers, and she was especially eager to work at Morgan Stanley, the top white-shoe firm. They called her back in for a series of follow-up interviews and were on the brink of making her an offer when suddenly they pulled back. Upon reflection, they told her, they just couldn't imagine Priscilla in the bullpen, exposed to loudmouthed traders who let four-letter-words fly (not that they had asked her if she minded). Lehman Brothers also invited her back for follow-up interviews, but when they finally made her an offer, the catch was that she would not be joining her male business school colleagues in the Lehman training program for the corporate finance

track. Instead, she would be joining the training program for women
straight out of college, preparing them to be the men's support staff.
It was as if her MBA had been erased, of no consequence. Humiliated,
she took the job offer from her old bosses at Loeb, Rhoades.

———

WITH DISCRIMINATION RAMPANT, AND THE CIVIL RIGHTS MOVEMENT
a blueprint for protest, the women's movement was growing. On
August 26, 1970, feminist Betty Friedan, founder of the National
Organization of Women (NOW), author of the bestseller *The Feminine Mystique*, was scheduled to speak in front of New York's city
hall, just a short walk north of the Financial District. Ten thousand
gathered as Friedan declared that what was coming was "not a bedroom war" but "a political movement . . . the women's movement is
going to be the biggest movement for social and political change in the
nineteen-seventies." Earlier that day, a much smaller group of women
had stood in front of the New York Stock Exchange, a world away—
despite the physical proximity—from the massive crowd that gathered
to hear Friedan. They hoisted placards and handed out flyers, deriding
Wall Street as "the most visible symbol of de facto sex discrimination."

Mickie Siebert, famously running her own NYSE-member firm
now, was asked by the press what she thought about it all. She was not
impressed, nor was Jane Larkin, the woman who had pulled Alice Jarcho out of the movie line and brought her back to Wall Street, and who,
fleetingly, was the second woman to become a member of the NYSE.
Mickie told reporters, "I just had lunch at 21 with four people—all
males," and, "If I complain to the boss," then I'll have to "complain to
myself." She thought the women's movement had started off "great,"
and she agreed with the argument, made by Friedan in *The Feminine
Mystique*, that "there's no reason to go to college, get married and then
stop thinking. People should be able to do what they're capable of doing
and there's no reason why a woman doing the same job as a man should

be paid less." But as for the rest? "I like men and I like brassieres," she said, buying into the cliché of feminists as bra-burning man-haters.

Two months later, many among the click-clack heeled army of women, "from rare vice president to bank teller," showed up for work on Wall Street wearing pantsuits as a coordinated silent protest. It was a serious statement at a time when women, without exception, were expected to wear dresses and skirts exclusively. But Marylin Bender in the *New York Times* was unimpressed, semi-joking that the women must first have received permission "from their male sovereigns." In her view, "In the financial community, women's liberation is an amoebic and poorly organized movement."

In the Doubleday Bookstore at 14 Wall Street, one could find the work of Robin Morgan, a poet and radical feminist, who insisted, "In the long run, we should bring it all down—with industrial sabotage and secretarial sabotage—because Wall Street is the essence of white male power gone mad." Until that time came, however, Morgan urged women on Wall Street to at least organize for their rights. But if you were a woman who had to punch in for her 9-to-5 job, Marylin Bender objected, industrial sabotage was unlikely to look like a productive option. The click-clack army, the Francine Gottfrieds, could not "afford inflammatory rhetoric."

But there *were* women on Wall Street who were organizing regardless. At work, they eyed one another, gauging who might be a feminist in hiding, and gathered after work in the cocktail lounge of the Coachman to talk.

Research analyst Mary Wrenn told Bender that despite her accomplishments, a recent slight had reminded her of her place in this world: "If I ever thought I'd want to join the women's liberation, it was the time I went to the Sky Club and had to go through a separate entrance. I was never really bothered by the downtown men's clubs, although I never liked to be left out of a meeting from a professional standpoint, but this was an uptown club." The Sky Club, perched on the fifty-sixth floor of the Pan Am Building, was a favored spot for the city's powerbrokers to eat and deal, and while Mary was eventually let in, it wasn't through the front door.

Indeed, coming across a sign that read NO LADIES ALLOWED was hardly a rarity in New York, even as late as 1970. Executives like Mary were frequently shut out of business meetings in this way. They experienced discrimination in other guises, too, from secretaries addressing them by their first names to being kept out of planning meetings because the men assumed they couldn't possibly understand what was being discussed to not being allowed to work as a broker even if registered as one to being treated like an office wife instead of an employee. Adding to the problem, Marylin Bender argued, was that despite the discrimination, these women were so steeped in "Wall Street's stag atmosphere," they thought it was best to "grin and bear the system" and on some level collude with the system, because it made no sense to distance themselves even more from the men.

Karla Jay, a young lesbian feminist in New York, later a prominent gender scholar, did not believe in discreet measures like pantsuits or NOW memberships. She had decided to launch the "First National Ogle-In" after hearing about Francine Gottfried, the Sweater Girl. Being whistled at, catcalled, and air-kissed was a daily occurrence for most women of a certain age, and an ogle-in would mean to "turn the tables on leering, lip-smacking men by giving them a taste of their own medicine."

Jay and her friends planted themselves on Wall Street during lunchtime in March 1970, months before Friedan's appearance at city hall, and waited for men to pass by so they could catcall them.

"I just looove those pants! They bring out your best!"

"Hey, how do you like that hat over there!" another woman shouted out.

"Oh, that *chapeau*!" Karla purred.

They were clearly amateurs when it came to sexual harassment, their catcalls G-rated. But Susan Brownmiller nevertheless found it "incredibly liberating to reverse the wolf whistles, animal noises, and body-parts appraisals that customarily flowed in our direction." Her favorite moment was when Wendy Wonderful, as she called herself, a "free-spirited hippie" standing beside Karla Jay, "sauntered up behind an unwitting passerby and grabbed his crotch." A group of women at Lehman Brothers got in on the fun and created a mock-up centerfold of a buck-naked man, called him "Mr. April," and circulated the centerfold around the office for women to ogle. The men were *not* amused.

5

Rukeyser's Elves

In 1970, the same year as Karla Jay's Ogle-In campaign, television producer Anne Truax Darlington came up with the idea of laying bare "the arcane world of Wall Street." As she saw it, a TV show about Wall Street would be about something everyone was interested in—money. The result, *Wall $treet Week with Louis Rukeyser*, became a surprise hit on public television, with even a higher viewership than the ever-popular children's show *Sesame Street*. Louis Rukeyser, the show's charismatic host, believed in "speaking English," as he called it, by which he meant scrubbing the conversation clean of Wall Street jargon. He saw his television program as educational in the best sense of the word: he wanted to let the viewing public in on Wall Street and to reveal to them the practices of trading and investing.

The show started on the Baltimore PBS station, but when it went national, an astounding 2 to 4 million viewers (rising to 6 to 8 million in the 1980s) tuned in every Friday night, after markets had closed for the week. Louis Rukeyser, a modern-day flaneur with a 1970s deep side-part in his wavy gray hair—a "snowy Edwardian hairdo" as described by one financial analyst—was key to the show's success.

He flew first-class (paid for by his extensive and lucrative lecture tours once the show took off), played blackjack, and insisted on the "best and gaudiest suites in the finest hotels." He was funny, irreverent, direct, and a brilliant if fastidious host, who would never let anybody off the hook, which made for good television. He also liked women, in the sense that he thought they had a place on his show, and since he favored bringing securities analysts on to give their stock predictions to the TV public, women in finance—still largely ghettoized in research departments—were suddenly making a weekly appearance in America's living rooms.

It was a revelation. *Wall $treet Week* introduced America's TV viewers to the very idea of women in finance and to the handful of women—besides Mickie Siebert—who had been there for decades and now qualified as experts in investing.

The show's popular theme song, "TWX in 12 Bars," sounded as if it were being played on taxi horns, with the rapid tapping of various office machines for percussion, along with the chimes of Wall Street's Trinity Church—the music stimulating a slight bump up in blood pressure in anticipation of the raw, rushed rhythms of New York. At the same time, a camera panned through lower Manhattan, moving to the entrance of the Stock Exchange, and then onto its trading floor as if viewers were being led into the inner sanctum.

The show always began with Rukeyser, perched on a sofa, speaking directly to his audience at home. His opening monologue about the week's market performance combined shtick and information. One time, with Easter two days away, he told viewers, "Indomitably hopping down the bunny trail was the U.S. economy." When the space shuttle was the big news, he used the term "uncertain orbits." When it was time for the Kentucky Derby: "Clearly, in most parts of the U.S. economy, there's life in the old nag yet."

The *New Yorker* described how after his monologue, he "lunges across the set to what appears to be a dining room," to meet up with that evening's three panelists, research analysts, chosen from a roster of regulars. He quizzed them one by one on their opinion of the state of the market, and then together they tackled some viewer letters, of which the show received about two thousand a week. Continuing the curious dance across the *Wall $treet Week* set, the three panelists and Rukeyser then maneuvered themselves toward two sofas in the living-room section, the wires to their mics hanging down to the floor, slithering behind them as they walked. (Without commercials, this being public television, there was no way to hide the awkward transitions around the set.) Once they'd made it over to the sofas without incident, they greeted their special guest of the week, and Rukeyser held court in a black leather swivel chair while the others sat themselves down on the sofas.

Humorist Russell Baker wrote about his fascination with the show: "Fridays at 8:30 find me—amply fed, digestive organs ruminating contentedly to the rhythmic sloshing of martini juice—sitting in my Louis Quinze armchair awaiting another installment of 'Wall Street Week.'" Rukeyser brought entertainment to finance. *Wall $treet Week* popularized the markets and investing in a way that the NYSE's earlier short film, *The Lady and the Stock Exchange*, could only have dreamed of doing.

Rukeyser had little tolerance for doomsday talk and was bullish about the market regardless of what was actually happening: an endearing optimism, considering that during the show's first decade on air, the market was often in freefall. It was reassuring to viewers that Rukeyser took it all in stride, quick to poke fun at financial losses: "There sure is news tonight, folks. If you're a closet masochist, you're going to love it." He named his 1973 year-end show the "Wall Street Wake" because the year had looked like "a sort of great national disaster area."

He was tolerantly kind to the special guests on the sofa but roasted his regulars mercilessly. Even with the special guests, when he saw a joke coming, he could not jump out of the way. When one guest stopped himself midsentence, noting they were now getting into semantics, Rukeyser quipped that it was OK, because they were not "anti-semantic" here on the show. To be invited as a guest was an enormous coup, so much so that the Wall Street crowd was willing to drag itself to Owings Mills, Baltimore, to appear on air for a laughable fee of around $200, and then stay on for forty-five minutes after the taping to watch the show broadcast across America.

Rukeyser, laughing out loud, liked to remind the show's regular panelists about their past fumbled forecasts. He favored so-called technical market analysts, technicians, also known as "chartists"— those who looked at charts and graphs as opposed to fundamental analysts, who focused on the particulars and the intrinsic value of a company. He nicknamed his analysts "the Elves," and the show compiled an Elf Index based on their market forecasts, which, although never fully explained, featured a "buy" or "sell" alert button for viewers to see. "Elf" was not a reference to the regulars' role as Rukeyser's helpers but to the "Gnomes of Zürich," a phrase coined by British politician Harold Wilson to describe the Swiss bankers known for their discretion.

When *Wall $treet Week* first ran as just a local production of Maryland Public Broadcasting, for budgetary and logistical reasons the first set of panelists were recruited from the Baltimore area: a business community "not previously noted for its telegenic possibilities." And even if they did OK in the screen test, the show's producer, Anne Truax Darlington, could never be certain that they wouldn't tense up once the cameras were rolling. For that reason, she created a set that looked like an apartment, with soft, comfortable sofas to keep guests at ease.

Julia Montgomery Walsh, located in Washington, DC, and within driving distance of Owings Mills, was the very first female panelist among a rotating roster of about two dozen men. When *Wall $treet*

Week ran its first episode on November 20, 1970, she was by then a finance veteran, yet the show turned her into a celebrity.

Julia was born Margaret "Peggy" Julia Curry in Akron, Ohio, where her father, like most of the men in town, spent his life on the assembly line of the Goodyear Tire and Rubber Company. Excelling in school, she won a scholarship to Smith College, but with wartime rationing, couldn't afford the travel. She went to nearby Kent State University instead, and on a student trip to Washington, DC, she met First Lady Eleanor Roosevelt, who asked if she was taking in the sights. Peggy explained that she and her friend could not afford their accommodation for another night, and next thing she knew, a limousine had pulled up to the dorm as they were packing to leave, and whisked them off to the White House, where they stayed overnight and enjoyed breakfast in bed, private chats with Mrs. Roosevelt, and dips in the presidential pool. So that her parents wouldn't worry, Peggy had sent them a telegram that she'd be staying at the White House. Thinking it was a joke, her father called the White House and the operator answered: "Is this an emergency, sir? Miss Curry is dining with Mrs. Roosevelt. Shall I interrupt them?"

Peggy Curry graduated from Kent State in June 1945, the first woman to graduate with a degree in business administration. Working for the Foreign Service in Munich soon after the war, she met tank officer John Montgomery, and in 1948 she became an army wife, moving to Washington, DC: "Like so many women of that era, I disliked giving up my own meaningful work, but decided that marriage was more important."

An army officer's paycheck was only $40 a week, no fortune, especially once Peggy Curry, now Julia Montgomery, had had her first son, then second, and third. She signed up for a correspondence course in investment and security analysis with the New York Institute of Finance, and when she heard the vice president of a local brokerage firm was going to teach a course on securities and investment at nearby George Washington University, she went. She impressed him as a student and he offered her a job as an apprentice broker. Six months later, Julia passed the exam and became a Registered Representative at his firm. She decided to make her first investment in the very company that had treated her father with decency over many decades, even as "the dust and dirt of the plant" had "filled my nose and eyes in early years." Her Goodyear stock tripled in value, and the Montgomery family was finally able to buy a new car. She gave birth to her fourth son in 1957, and when she and her husband did the weekly shopping on Thursday nights, the shopping cart included twenty-four quarts of milk.

When at the end of that year John broke the news that he was being transferred to Fort Riley, Kansas, Julia, "like any dutiful Army wife," " 'paid, packed and followed.' " She thought that was the end of her securities career. But on December 23, 1957, halfway to Kansas with the boys, she received news that John had died in field maneuvers. Julia suspected suicide, but the reality was that she was suddenly a single mother with four small boys. The brokerage firm in DC offered her her job back, and she in turn invited her mother-in-law to come work for her, looking after the boys, running the household, in return for 20 percent of everything Julia made after taxes.

Less than two years later, Julia was a partner at the firm, Ferris & Co., the only woman to make partner of an NYSE-member firm in the Washington, DC, area. In 1962, Ferris & Co. sent her on the semester-long Advanced Management Program at Harvard Business School. She was the first woman ever to attend the prestigious one-semester program for established businessmen. From Cambridge, she wrote to her parents, describing a fun-filled adventure: "I have delightful living quarters in the graduate dormitory with a small living room, a private bath, and a little kitchenette, lots of closet space, and a very nice bedroom. . . . Tomorrow night, I'm taking the six girls in the Graduate Business School to dinner and having the 130 men in my program here for coffee at the Radcliffe Graduate Center after dinner."

But the truth was very different, a foreshadowing of Lillian Hobson's and Priscilla Rabb's experiences several years later. Not wanting her parents to worry, Julia had intentionally left out the part about how "the comfortable apartment across the river with the 'Cliffies' was located as far as it could be from my classmates in Hamilton Hall," and that "at 39 I faced for the first time the full force of male chauvinism." Demoralized and feeling inadequate—all the men in the program had the answers in class when she did not—she planned not to return after spring break.

As Julia was packing up, the one man who'd been genuinely friendly let her in on the secret: the men had been divvying up the assignments the night before, and then meeting before classes to share and discuss their answers. He promised Julia that if she returned, he would bring her into the fold. She came back, and while the East Coast men remained unwilling to acknowledge her, she now fell in with the more easygoing Texans and Californians, who also happened to be leading the new industries in which she would soon be investing—Texas Instruments, Hewlett-Packard, Aerojet, and Xerox. These would become the glamour stocks and tech stocks of the go-go '60s just around the corner.

Those who resented her presence at HBS softened a little when they learned that she was a widow and the sole breadwinner for a family of six. After all, wasn't that the first thing that the women at Harvard Business School would hear, that they had no right to take a spot from a breadwinner? But it still wasn't enough. On the day of commencement, she brought her eleven-year-old son to the reception. He was drinking fruit punch when one of her HBS classmates bumped into him, making him spill his drink. Later, the man confessed to

Julia that he'd done it on purpose: he wanted to see her son's reaction because he was convinced that women who worked outside of the home for long hours must have "emotionally insecure" children.

Bernadette Bartels (later Bernadette Murphy) was another early female panelist on *Wall $treet Week*, a technical analyst who relied on charts and graphs to make her predictions. From City Island in the Bronx, Bernadette had traveled far to her first job interview on Wall Street in the late 1950s: it was a schlep, over an hour and a half to get there. She had emerged from the subway onto Broad and Wall Streets, and immediately "smelled the salt from the water . . . off the harbor." Wall Street smelled like home. Her interview at Ladenburg Thalmann, one of the venerable German-Jewish firms, was arranged by an uncle who'd worked on the NYSE floor. At 25 Broad Street, the firm had a prime spot from the days when the American Stock Exchange, known colloquially as the Amex, still traded out on the

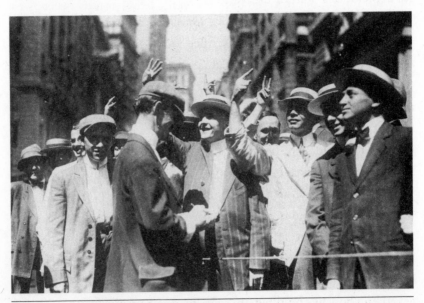

Stock trading on the New York Curb Association market (later the American Stock Exchange), c1916.

sidewalk, and Ladenburg Thalmann brokers would just lean out the windows and shout down their orders.

The interview went well, but Bernadette was certain she did not want the job. It was the late 1950s, and she'd be the only woman there assisting in the trading department of the firm.

She turned it down, but for whatever reason, the man who'd interviewed her refused to take no for an answer. He called her five more times until he eventually persuaded Bernadette to give it a go. She was presented with an electric typewriter, which she had no idea how to use. For practice, each morning she took the editorial page of the *New York Times* and typed it out. Bernadette's job in fact turned out to largely consist of writing letters on behalf of the partners who knew how to make money but not how to string words together. There was no air conditioning in the offices of Ladenburg Thalmann—there was only one firm on Wall Street that used a system of fans and ice blocks delivered daily—and so she had to open the windows wide and hope for some of that harbor breeze.

When the trading department moved to a larger office, Bernadette was seated in a glassed-in office looking out onto the trading floor: to the right was the municipal bond division, on the left the trading desk, and in the center were the brokers. Curses flew back and forth. There was a mechanical rhythm to the office: there was the ticker tape, and "a big cork board too, and, when the prices would change, it would slap, bang, slap, bang. Over in the corner was the Dow Jones news ticker—'ding, ding, ding'—when important things were coming on." One day during the "Flash Crash of 1962," the office erupted in mayhem, with people literally throwing stocks out the window. She thought: "There has got to be a way to anticipate this." As traders were desperately trying to unload their stock, there was one man standing in the middle of it all completely unruffled. She asked him how he could remain so calm, and he replied that he wasn't selling but buying at that moment. She wanted to be that person too:

the calm at the center of the storm. She began studying graphs and charts to better understand the market.

Then came the day Kennedy was shot. All those sounds suddenly stopped. The cork board wound down as if on a key: "clap—silence—clap." The Dow Jones news tape stopped printing. It was just silence, whereas down on the floor of the New York Stock Exchange, U.S. Steel was suddenly "selling for three different prices," and there was loud mayhem, complete chaos.

And then, in the midst of this silence that surrounded Bernadette, the phone rang. It was a client at an insurance company in Canada. "Ron, they killed our president," she said.

"I know, Bern, but I have an order for you."

And so she took the order, and executed it, and reported it, and doing those three actions calmed her down, because they were now a habit, a process that she understood when everything else in that moment seemed incomprehensible.

She was still living on City Island in the Bronx, with aunts, uncles, and cousins scattered across the island, less than one square mile looking out onto Long Island Sound. Everyone was sitting out on their porches when she'd get off the bus and her father would holler: "Ah, here she comes, Tillie the Toiler!" She had started at $75 a week, and after a couple of years, received a $3 raise. When she asked for another raise, the managing partner told her: "You are young, you are pretty, you are going to get married; you don't need any more money."

She was constantly fending off the men in the office. They didn't hesitate to offer her trips to Paris or a new wardrobe in return for sexual favors. One partner would return after lunch each day, having had his martinis, and proposition her. She would try to distract them with humor: "Oh, you are not being serious. I know your wife." For them it seemed to be a game on autopilot, the very same clumsy rituals of office seduction, day in and day out; for Bernadette, it was deeply depressing.

But watching the trading floor from her glassed-in post, Bernadette started to put the pieces together: how the economy impacted
the market, how investors responded, and how their emotions were
tied to the process. She pulled together charts until her eyesight
started to suffer. Being a technical analyst, which she was trying to
learn, was frowned upon then and she would hide her materials in her
desk drawer, hoping no one would see what she was up to.

Bernadette had initially shied away from Wall Street because of
the paucity of women. A friend of hers, a respected securities analyst, was once scheduled to speak at a corporate gathering held at
one of the private clubs that barred women. She literally was forced
to climb up the fire escape to give her presentation, helped through
the window by the men gathered there to hear her advice on stocks.
She gave her talk, then left again the way she came—via the window
and fire escape.

It was for reasons like this that in 1956 a handful of Wall Street
women founded the Financial Women's Association, the FWA. It
was originally called the Young Women's Investment Association
(renamed the FWA in 1971) because they'd been barred from the
"regular" all-male Investment Association of New York. Their need
for an organization was even more fundamental than discrimination:
"We had no one to have lunch with." Starting off, they were mostly
securities analysts. Bernadette joined in the early 1960s, when the
FWA still had only about eighty members at best. They would tell
their guest speakers they had two hundred and then beg every member to bring a friend or two to fill the empty seats in the dining room
one floor above the Bankers Club where women were allowed.

One of the women who attended FWA events regularly was Beth
Dater, a few years younger than Bernadette. Beth was a former airline stewardess who had previously worked a Pan Am flight to Puerto
Rico nicknamed the Vomit Comet because it was still using non-
pressurized DC-4s unable to fly above the weather systems and avoid

severe turbulence. The Vomit Comet left New York City around
noon, arriving in San Juan at 6 p.m., and then left again at 6 a.m.
the following morning, allowing for a solid straight twelve hours
of debauchery in Puerto Rico, thereby guaranteeing a planeload of
nauseated, hungover passengers on the return flight. Actress Joan
Crawford and PepsiCo CEO Donald Kendall would always board the
Vomit Comet with a cooler full of Pepsi (Pan Am served Coca-Cola,
Kendall's competitor), as well as gin and olives for martinis.

There was no assigned seating, chickens ran loose in the aisles,
and cockfights broke out. Almost always a group from the 21 Club
stumbled onboard, a few cocktails down the hatch already, thinking
it would be fun to hop a ride to San Juan for the night. Accustomed
to Pan Am's First-Class Clipper Service, with its sumptuous seven-
course meals and full carving boards, they were in for a rude awak-
ening. Beth would later swear that the Vomit Comet could not have
been a better training ground for Wall Street; that as she wrangled
the vast array of customers, she learned to read people, to understand
what made different people tick, to assemble an efficient team to get
the job done.

When Beth was not riding the Vomit Comet, she was living in
Manhattan in a one-bedroom apartment in Tudor City, on Midtown's east side, with seven other airline stewardesses—a rooming
situation that sounded like the makings of a 1960s screwball comedy
but worked because they were never all home at once. Not only was
the rent cheap, split seven ways, but the food was abundant, as each of
them made sure to deboard their flights with fruit baskets and leftover
delicacies from the first-class cabin. Sometimes Beth wondered how
they hadn't bankrupted the airline industry.

Beth started to date a pilot, Michael Dater, and when they married, she dutifully quit her job when he asked, finding temporary
work through an employment agency for retired stewardesses that
sent her to pass out chocolate-covered cherry bonbons in a parking

lot, dressed up in red as Miss Mon Cheri. Then one day, the agency sent her down to Wall Street, to Robert "Bobbie" Lehman's office at Lehman Brothers. She walked in and found herself staring at Monet originals that lined the walls.

Bobbie Lehman was dying, in and out of the hospital, and his staff was helping put together his voluminous art collection that also included Renoirs and Rembrandts to gift to the Metropolitan Museum of Art for what would be the Robert Lehman Wing. His assistant needed to be in Europe for the summer, and Beth was hired to sit in the office, to smile at everybody and answer the telephone. Once or twice a week, his lawyer, Eddie Weisel, would stop by to pick up some more paintings, and they would sit and chat. As the summer drew to a close, he told Beth he'd had an idea: "You seem like a pretty bright lady. Have you ever thought of a career on Wall Street?" Beth was startled by his suggestion. She insisted she was not fit for Wall Street because she could "hardly add two and two." Eddie ignored her excuses and said that they were hiring a very young salesman, full of promise, who needed an administrative assistant. Beth would be perfect.

Beth Dater's promising young boss turned out to be "very, very temperamental," with a propensity for "tantrums." He fired her three times, and she did him one better by quitting four times. But she tolerated him—the Vomit Comet had equipped her—because what she was learning at Lehman was invaluable. She observed the ticker tape and learned to read it, she talked to clients, she watched everyone's behavior, she noted what each man was in search of, what made him good at his job, or not. She was starting to see how trading, research, and client services fit together. And when she did, she was furious to realize that so many of the secretaries, most of them naïve young women straight out of Catholic high schools, were not registered as brokers and yet they were "trading big accounts" for Lehman Brothers, "being paid at a very sub-acceptable level." What they were doing was completely against the law. Moreover, the women were doing all the work while the men, the actual Registered Representatives, the brokers, "were running around making millions" while barely lifting a finger for their commissions. But it also made Beth realize something else: however unethical and unfair it was, "it could not be that difficult to be doing this."

When Beth had married Michael Dater, they'd agreed to no kids. But now he changed his mind, and he not only wanted a wife no longer flying but a pregnant one too. Beth had to choose, because "it was that in-between time when you were going to be either a mother or have a career; very few people really did both." She made a clean break from both her husband and the tantrum toddler boss at Lehman Brothers, joining Fiduciary Trust Company of New York as an assistant to client services. A short while after starting, she was approached about trying out as a research analyst. She was sent over to speak with Darley Randall, who ran the research department, and whom everyone called "Jolly," a nickname he'd picked up from a French nanny who'd thought him *joli* (cute).

"Well, give it a try," he said. "What do you want to do? Pick a company and do the work on it. Pick a company, any company."

Beth chose Gannett, a media company that owned strings of newspapers but was also starting to get into broadcasting. None of the research analysts wanted Gannett—it was there for the taking. And as for her not being able to "add two and two," the invention of the calculator, she later liked to say, was the "miracle" that changed the course of her life. She, too, would soon become an Elf panelist on Rukeyser's *Wall $treet Week*.

In the early days, one of the primary tasks of the Financial Women's Association was to cheerlead the women on Wall Street who found themselves isolated among men, cut off from other women. And while its founders had needed to find someone to have lunch with, now the FWA was a place to celebrate the small, incremental victories. If an FWA member received a promotion, a celebratory lunch or dinner always followed. The women made sure someone was on hand to say: "Hey, look what you've done!" When in 1967 research analyst Mary Wrenn was promoted to VP, vice president at Merrill Lynch, phones were ringing off the hook as women across various brokerage houses and investment banks called one another in disbelief, relaying the good news. Milestones never felt like merely individual accomplishments.

Mary Wrenn had maneuvered herself skillfully from cosmetics, branching out into pharmaceuticals. A 1965 Merrill Lynch print advertisement in the *Wall Street Journal* asked readers: "Why do so many pension funds do business with Merrill Lynch?" The answer? "When Art Warde has something to say about the automobile industry, or Mary Wrenn about drugs, or Len Reichhard about petroleum, or Arch Catapano about electronics, or any Merrill Lynch specialist about any industry—we think it makes good sense for any Pension Fund to listen. Don't you?" A 1969 advertisement similarly declared: "Ideas are a dime a dozen on Wall Street. Ideas with a solid perspective are harder to come by. . . . All this takes manpower. We have enough people in Research to follow more than 2,000 stocks, and to *stay close* to them. Take our pharmaceuticals unit. We can send Mary Wrenn out visiting managements in the field for a week, and still have three first-class men minding the store."

This kind of exposure for a woman on Wall Street was remarkable, and yet Mary Wrenn remained largely invisible. Her name was frequently featured in Merrill Lynch advertising, but pictured in the ads, those representing the firm pictorially, were still middle-aged white men, those whom the marketing department presumably believed Americans trusted more with their money. In contrast, Louis Rukeyser put faces to the women's names, turning Julia, Bernadette, and later Beth into recognizable market experts and letting the American public know that here were Wall Street's pioneering women, its female movers and shakers. On his show, the women were not asked to smile more, they were not asked if they'd make the coffee; they were asked for their opinion, and sat on the set facing the camera, speaking to America, explaining the numbers, explaining the market, offering their hard-earned expertise.

6

Zero Points for
"Intelligence"

Nina Hayes was working in the back office of Benj. D. Bartlett & Co., a small brokerage firm in Cincinnati, Ohio, as the women's movement was taking off. She had taken a job working for the firm's three elderly partners—she balanced Mr. Reynolds's checkbook, and listened to Mr. Bennett's tales of his trips to Europe and Mr. Snyder's counsel to "buy blue-chip stocks and hold on to them for the long term"—when she couldn't afford the Cincinnati Art Academy.

While at Bartlett, Nina quietly enrolled in a course for the broker exam. When she told the partners, they were supportive, and when she passed, they gave her the title of dividend manager. Although still seated in the back office, Nina could now make trades for clients and collect commissions. She only had one client, but a good one—the local restaurant association, run by a man who similarly encouraged Nina. With so much goodwill, sure she could conquer the financial world, she went to apply for a place in the trainee program at Merrill Lynch. But when she told the receptionist at the Cincinnati branch office that she was there to take the exam, she got a blank stare. Eventually an older woman emerged from the back, took one look at Nina, and declared: "No, we do not hire women as brokers."

Nina would not take no for an answer, however, and finally the woman handed her the exam booklet. Nina thought she'd done OK, but when she didn't hear back, she telephoned. "Oh, you failed the exam," the woman told her matter-of-factly.

Between that and the lackluster response to the women's movement that she was experiencing in Cincinnati, Nina decided it was time to move to New York.

She checked in to the Barbizon Hotel, the famous women's hotel on Manhattan's Upper East Side whose glory days were fast disappearing. The hotel bellhop took her belongings up to her tiny room, including a small television set she'd brought with her, and after placing them down on the carpeted floor, he said with a leer: "I'll be back tonight to watch with you."

It took Nina a moment to register, but then she jumped up and shouted down the hallway after him: "No way!"

The encounter made her feel uneasy, especially walking from her room to the shared hallway bathrooms late at night when everything was quiet and dark, and only once in a while one might hear the rumble of the elevator.

Nina quickly found a job with a boutique investment firm, Epstein, Parker, Carmel & Gaer, hired as a syndicate manager. Her job was to ferret out upcoming IPOs, talk to the Wall Street investment banks that were underwriting them, and see how many of the shares she could get for her firm's clients. Her salary was enough to rent an apartment with a window seat at 2 Fifth Avenue; a chic location but only a short walk out of the lobby to Washington Square Park.

That same year, in September 1970, the New York City Commission on Human Rights held a series of hearings on sex discrimination in the workplace. In his opening remarks, Mayor Lindsay spoke of "a total environment of inequality in which half the population is systematically denied rights and opportunities taken for granted by the other half, and in which the community's desperate need for the fullest use of all its human resources is foolishly sacrificed in the name of custom." Anthropologist Margaret Mead—who recalled how she'd marched alongside her suffragist mother and as a child believed anti-suffragists were "wicked, rich women with poodle dogs"—testified about these "customs" that kept women locked out of the workplace or else in low-paying positions. She argued that societies had always been geared toward women making babies and men providing for them, but there was no longer a need for an expanded population, quite the opposite, and yet society remained mired in the "customs" of a time that had outlived its purpose.

When a representative for Merrill Lynch testified, he was asked about the low female enrollment in the firm's broker trainee program. His answer was that there were few female applicants and "even fewer of those who can qualify with the combination of finance education, and/or financial sales experience." When challenged—there were countless women working in business, he was told, and so "Why wouldn't more of these women . . . be inclined to come over and apply for your program?"—he replied: "I don't really have an answer to it except that the net effect is that they do not." He further defended his position by insisting that women were not allowed to work as brokers on the floor of the New York Stock Exchange or the American Stock Exchange because there it "would become an occupational disability to be female." (It was pointed out to him that if women were actually barred from trading on the NYSE or Amex floor, given equal rights legislation passed in the 1960s, that would be illegal. Moreover, he had clearly never heard of Muriel Siebert.)

At the hearings, women recounted their experiences of how they'd received training and promotions reluctantly, if at all. To be considered for the Registered Representative examination, they needed a sponsor, and while their firm might even offer their sponsorship—

especially to "ambitious secretaries or sales assistants"—it then refused to give them the title or the income of a broker, even as they were now licensed and making trades for the company.

The Bankers Trust revealed at the hearings that while 54 percent of its employees were women, only 1.5 percent occupied what might be considered top jobs, meaning non-support staff jobs, and no women at all were executives. Merrill Lynch had 40 percent female employees, but only 2 out of 70 were officers; and while they had 499 brokers, only 15 were women; there were no female traders. Its Research Department had an impressive 7 women out of 26 industry specialists, but as Mary Wrenn, one of those seven, explained: "Financial analysis is probably the one area where women are equal to men because we don't deal directly with them. For a long time, those who read my reports didn't know whether I was Miss or Mr. Wrenn."

In December 1970, three months after the New York City Human Rights Commission hearings, the NYSE finally let women back on the floor . . . as pages.

BACK AT THE HARVARD BUSINESS SCHOOL, ROBIN WIGGER, CLASS OF 1970, wrote to the women in the next incoming class with some tips on how to survive their HBS experience. First, have a well-rehearsed answer to the inevitable question: "What's a nice girl like you doing in business school?" The men, especially the first-years, believed that women were only there to find themselves "rich husbands."

There'd been one significant change since Priscilla and Lillian had graduated the year before; Robin Wigger was one of four women who'd participated in the "Experimental Residence Project," which had her living on the Harvard Business School campus so the administration could gauge "whether there were any major problems for the women living in the men's dorms," or if they might suffer from "a possible loss of our (feminine) identity." There were not, and they did not, and now in her letter to the incoming female students, Wigger strongly advised them to take up the offer to live among the men in accommodations that "are far superior to the Radcliffe Graduate Center."

Two years later, in a 1972 editorial in the *Harbus News*, the student paper for HBS, Ilene Lang wrote on the "progress" achieved in the MBA program: "Now several years and two lavatories in Aldrich later, we notice that the old stereotypes have hardly budged. HBS clings to its old attitudes about women. . . ." These attitudes she laid out as *incredulity* ("What are *you* doing here?"); *condescension* ("I don't care if my wife works—I want her to—but I want my dinner ready at six, and of course, she'll stay home and take care of my children."); and *derision* ("I'm a male chauvinist pig, always have been and guess I always will be . . . and that's that.")

The daily reminders of a woman's place did not stop there. There were the jokes: "about women's work, women's liberation, and women's physical, mental, and emotional frailties." Those who wrote the WACs, the real-world business case studies, referred to women workers as girls; the name tags and name cards handed out by the school—that Lillian Hobson, too, was given on her first day; a rectangular piece of white cardboard, eighteen inches by four, with her name printed in black—included the title of Miss or Mrs., thereby distinguishing "the available bodies from the unavailable ones."

———

ALSO IN 1972, TWO YEARS AFTER THE MERRILL LYNCH REPRESENTATIVE had testified that the low female enrollment in their broker trainee program was due to the lack of qualified women applicants, thirty-three-year-old Helen O'Bannon applied for a spot. She was an honors graduate from Wellesley College with a master's degree in economics from Stanford University; she had job experience in the House Banking and Currency Committee and the Treasury Department. She had even taught college-level economics. None of this prepared her for an exam that asked: "When you fight with your wife, which of you usually wins?" and "When you meet a woman, what interests you the most about her?"

The Merrill Lynch exam was multiple choice. For the question "what interests you most about a woman you meet," the possible answers were Beauty, Intelligence, Dependency, Independence, or Affectionateness. Helen picked "Intelligence." (Wrong!) There were zero points for Intelligence, and zero points for Independence. But there were two points for Dependency and for Affectionateness. Beauty offered one point.

Helen was told she'd failed, just as Nina Hayes had, but her antennae went up when she saw that her rejection letter was addressed to "Mr." O'Bannon and expressed the firm's regret at not being able to accept all the "young men" who applied. Although by all accounts Helen had a great sense of humor, she didn't find this funny.

Priscilla Rabb was feeling similarly unamused. Life at Loeb, Rhoades was like business school in that there were the predictable bullies, the skirt-chasers, the women-haters, the inappropriate jokesters. One partner, entering the elevator with senior associates, thought it funny to shout: "Let's get Priscilla in there. . . . !" But there were also the good guys, the allies: another partner took her under his wing. Once, when they were meeting with a client at the Harvard Club, the doorman jammed his arm in front of Priscilla and wouldn't let her pass. "You have to go in through the Ladies' Door," he said. He didn't care when Priscilla told him she was a Harvard alumna.

"Come on, we're all going," the partner announced, and off they all went to the Ladies' Door.

That day, Priscilla vowed that she would never become a member of a club that did not want her. And just as she waits for the man to return for a reunion to eat his hat, so she has never joined the Harvard Club.

Priscilla was now a full associate in the Loeb, Rhoades corporate finance division, and the rules were clearly set out: if you brought in business, the firm owed you a finder's fee based on the size of the business you brought in. Yet when she scored a major client for the firm, there was no mention of the finder's fee. She waited, and waited, and when there was still nothing, she finally asked. A small sum was grudgingly handed over. She asked again for what she was actually owed. Her boss refused. Pulling together her courage, she decided to go over his head and talk to the formidable John Loeb Sr. himself.

Priscilla was nervous, but she hoped for a positive reception because her father and John Loeb Sr. knew each other. They were two successful, well-connected Jewish men who had dealt with their own share of prejudice.

As she hoped, Loeb smiled up at Priscilla as she walked in. She sat down and laid out the situation, explaining that the deal she'd brought to the firm was already vetted and approved, and the consensus was that it would generate significant profit. As she spoke, Loeb's expression began to change, and it was as if he'd "turned to stone."

When she was done, he fired her.

She telephoned her husband, her fiancé when she was at the Harvard Business School, her protective armor, her excuse for leaving HBS every weekend for New York. He met her downstairs; she took his arm to steady herself, and then promptly threw up on Wall Street.

———

OVER AT THE PBS HIT SHOW *WALL $TREET WEEK*, A CONTROVERSY WAS brewing. Louis Rukeyser was the show's star, its emcee, but there was one other person who figured in every episode: a young woman referred to as "Miss Smythe," but who never spoke. She escorted Rukeyser onto the set to do his opening bit. As soon as she'd sat him down, she left, wordlessly, only to reappear to escort that week's special guest over to the sofa. After that, she would disappear again, returning briefly as the credits rolled and TV viewers watched that week's participants—including Miss Smythe—gather around on-set, as if at a cocktail party, their mouths moving but microphones off.

Miss Smythe now became a lightning rod for viewers who saw her as a silent "anonymous handmaiden who seems to be treated as a piece of furniture." Letters referred to her as "that innocuous and wraithlike creature who flits in and out," "the coffee-tea-or-milk type," and a "sop to women's lib." In 1973, Rukeyser was forced to address the controversy of Miss Smythe:

> For some reason her presence in our midst seems to offend the
> occasional feminist viewer. . . . Well, enough already. As any-
> one will discover, this program needs no sop to women's lib.
> If you disagree, then take it up with the woman producer. But
> as the father of three daughters . . . I don't want to seem any
> worse of a chauvinist pig than absolutely necessary. And so
> tonight let's let Miss Smythe emerge from anonymity. The role
> of Miss Smythe is played by Natalie Seltz, a professional tele-
> vision technician . . . So, you see, she really is essential around
> here, and not just decorative.

Anne Truax Darlington, the show's originator and producer, had come up with the idea of a "Miss Smythe" as a way to help with technical issues, to help Rukeyser as well as the guests from tripping on the labyrinth of floor cables. She penned an angry form letter that was routinely sent out to any viewers who wrote in objecting to Miss Smythe and her obsequious role.

Rukeyser's unveiling of Miss Smythe, and the brouhaha over her inexplicable role, came along in the same year as the episode "Women on the Street." Rukeyser, perched on the sofa, looking straight into the camera, told viewers they would be meeting an "extremely attractive young woman"—Mimi Green, one of only a dozen women who had made it in the high-powered world of institutional sales. He pointed out that there were now around 5,000 women with the title of Registered Representative (out of approximately 205,000 brokers). Female securities analysts complained, Rukeyser said, that men liked to give them "sissy stocks" for their portfolios—household products, cosmetics, and the like.

All three male Elf panelists got up from the table, along with Rukeyser, and smiling broadly, they made their way over to that week's special guest, Mimi Green, already seated on the sofa. Rukeyser, by way of introduction, explained that Mimi had arrived on Wall Street four years before, at age twenty-two, with a junior degree and "some advanced studies" in Switzerland. She'd initially had a job as secretary, but after getting fired, she'd managed to secure a spot in the company's training program instead. She had a flair for institutional sales and focused on leisure-related stock. *BusinessWeek* had written that she often got through to company CEOs by calling and saying, "Tell him it's Mimi, and it's personal." It was a call, said Rukeyser, that "few secretaries would dare to block."

Mimi nodded along, looking, by today's fashion standards, older than twenty-six, her dark hair past her shoulders and swept to one side in a hair-sprayed blow-out, big gold and jade earrings, red lipstick, and red nails. Even as she drank her water nervously, she was full of bravado. As she answered Rukeyser's questions, she leaned in, almost seductively, but Rukeyser had something else in mind; he wanted her to admit that there were serious disadvantages to being a woman on Wall Street. She refused.

"All the men have been helpful," she insisted.

"Then why the complaints [from other Wall Street women]?" Rukeyser asked.

"Well, women love to complain," she drawled.

As to the problem of women being handed "sissy stocks," instead of U.S. Steel stock, for example, Mimi replied: "Frankly, I don't know why she'd want steel stock."

When Rukeyser brought up feminist activists, Mimi replied, sounding as if she had a martini in one hand and a cigarette in the other: "Frankly, I find them a bore." She added that she'd told the women libbers as much when they called her asking why she said such inflammatory things in the press.

Like Mickie Siebert, Mimi Green strutted her anti-feminism in the most contradictory ways. Speaking a year earlier to the *New York Times*, Mimi had insisted she had a significant advantage in being young, female, and attractive but even so, she remained "shocked at the number of people who listen to a man just because he has position and reputation." Then, two years after appearing as a special guest on Rukeyser's show, Mimi was hired by the New York brokerage house White, Weld & Co. to head a five-woman women's department created "to attract more female customers." Mimi Green told the *Wall Street Journal* that women "are no longer content to accept paternal advice dealt out to them by patronizing male advisers." Just a few months later, she moved over to Oppenheimer to become the director of its "Women's Financial Services Department." Mimi, if anything, knew how to capitalize on being a woman on Wall Street even as she turned her back on the "women libbers."

As the Human Rights Hearings in New York had shown, research analysis remained the most favorable area for women to work, a place where their gender identity could be masked while their skills appreciated and compensated. Beth Dater, now a well-known analyst at Fiduciary Trust, was "thundering around the country visiting companies and going to conferences." When Rukeyser approached Gannett, scouting for more women, Beth's name was put forward. She had already made a splash at Fiduciary Trust, and not only as an analyst;

one day she'd dared to show up wearing pants. Until very recently, women in pants was considered so scandalous that they were barred from most of New York's upscale restaurants. When she'd walked into the office, she heard an audible gasp. Later that afternoon, Larry Huntington, the president of Fiduciary, had made a point of coming down to her office: "I just want to tell you right here and now that I think you look stunning."

Beth was invited on the Rukeyser show first as a guest, to test her out, and a couple of weeks later, she received a call asking if she would join the panelists. She was now an Elf, but whenever she would say, "We think this . . ." Rukeyser would interrupt her to ask: "Is that the royal 'we'?"

Unlike Mimi Green, Beth believed both in women's liberation and in the power of women coming together to help one another. A member of the Financial Women's Association from early on, she counselled other women entering Wall Street or looking to get ahead, and frequently attended FWA events, such as talks by Katherine Graham, the publisher of the *Washington Post*, and Mary Wells, the advertising executive who famously put the Braniff International Airways stewardesses in their designer Emilio Pucci uniforms.

But there was no getting away from the fact that Wall Street rules had been created by men, for men, and women had to follow an established rulebook if they wanted to succeed. Beth Dater was typical in this sense. Even as she fully identified as a feminist, even as she worked weekends on behalf of NOW, canvassing Connecticut, trying to convince suburban women to start their own local NOW chapters, she rejected the idea of any special accommodations or considerations for women. She clung to the dream of a neutral and unfettered meritocracy, and despite evidence against it, believed she had found that place on Wall Street. And yet: if a well-above-average salary, even if significantly below that of the men, equaled success and inclusion, then she was perhaps right.

After Priscilla Rabb got fired, she found another job in corporate finance, but she could not shake the sense of injustice over what had happened at Loeb, Rhoades. She was advised to let it go; if she sued, it would ruin her career, possibly make her a social outcast. But Priscilla could not stop thinking about it. It ate at her. She finally hired a reputable lawyer and sued Loeb, Rhoades, but exactly as everyone warned her would happen, Priscilla lost. As another Wall Street woman of the 1970s remembered: "Sure, there were women who sued. And they were gone the next day, vanished, disappeared."

Helen O'Bannon was also going to court, in her case to sue Merrill Lynch for supposedly "failing" her broker trainee exam. She had learned something about the four men who *were* accepted when she was rejected: not one of them had an advanced degree as she did, and in fact one of them had even dropped out of college because he couldn't keep up. Two of the four had not even passed the aptitude section of the exam. But what they had passed, which Helen (and Nina) had not, was the so-called psychological section, which might as well have been called the female tripwire.

Helen's drawn-out legal battle would finally end in 1976, when Merrill Lynch settled with a cash payment of $10,000 for Helen O'Bannon and $182,000 for her lawyers to cover their extensive fees. Her payout was small, certainly, but that was not the point (just as it was not for Priscilla). Helen's case had not only generated publicity but also the attention of the Equal Employment Opportunity Commission (EEOC), which in 1972 was granted permission to initiate its own legal suits. They decided to throw their hat in the ring with Helen by filing a parallel case against Merrill Lynch. As part of that separate settlement, Merrill Lynch now had to use $1.3 million of its money toward recruiting more women and people of color to train as brokers. In addition, women and minorities at Merrill Lynch, many working in sales, who felt they had lost out on income since 1972 because of their gender or race, could submit a claim for backpay out of a $1.9 million fund set up for that purpose.

1976, the year that Helen O'Bannon finally won her case, was also the year that the FWA, the Financial Women's Association, held their twentieth anniversary dinner at Windows on the World at the top of the World Trade Center. A hundred and thirty-five women, no longer only research analysts, ate a dinner of "spinach pâté, chicken Véronique, mashed broccoli, anisette ice cream"—as the *New Yorker* detailed—while listening to the secretary of the treasury offer them, as most seemed to agree, a bunch of empty platitudes. At a table where Bernadette Bartels, one of Rukeyser's very first female Elves, sat, one of the women told the *New Yorker* reporter they were thrilled to see both Mickie Siebert and Julia Walsh have seats on the stock exchange, but they had yet to see a woman become a partner at a major Wall Street firm. One woman explained that "the early titles come quickly, so there are plenty of assistant treasurers and assistant corporate secretaries." After that, it was like trying to climb Everest.

Helen O'Bannon left Wall Street and went on to become the vice president of the University of Pennsylvania, before succumbing to cancer while still in her forties, leaving behind a husband and four children. But she also left a legacy on Wall Street; her case forced doors open that would otherwise have remained shut. Nina Hayes would meet Helen O'Bannon in the late 1970s at a small gathering at the University of Cincinnati, organized by the Women's Studies Department chair, and they would swap stories of their "failed exam."

During her years in New York, Nina immersed herself in NOW, attending protests, marches, and gatherings in Central Park. She went to hear speakers from Gloria Steinem to Bella Abzug to Kate Millett. She was an original member of the National Gay Task Force, marched in the Gay Pride parades, and sometimes attended Sunday-afternoon meetings at the Firehouse on Wooster in SoHo, where the Gay Activists Alliance gathered (until an arson fire in 1974 destroyed it). After the meetings, Nina would go over to Bonnie & Clyde, a lesbian nightclub and disco where "the tabletops were covered in laminated photos of women."

Every weekday morning Nina would take the bus down Broadway to Wall Street, preferring to avoid the filthy, graffitied subway that New Yorkers in the 1970s had taken to calling "the mugger's express." The World Trade towers were going up, and as she sat on the bus, staring out the window, and those looming towers would suddenly come into view, unease would wash over her. New York's radio row filled with electronics stores had been razed to make room for the World Trade Center, and now those hulking towers of metal and concrete looked like interlopers in the historic Financial District. Finished in 1973, for a time the tallest buildings in the world, initially they stood largely empty. They were meant to herald the future at the moment that New York City was falling apart. In Harlem and the Bronx especially, fires set by arsonists hired by landlords to collect on the insurance of their empty, rat-ridden buildings were an almost daily occurrence.

When the partners at Epstein, Parker, Carmel & Gaer decided to retire, Nina moved over to Mack, Bushnell & Edelman at 5 Hanover Square. At five o'clock, there was a mad rush for the door as people grabbed their coats, jostling to get out of the building to be among the first to put in their order at everyone's favorite Wall Street restaurant Delmonico's for one—or two—of their classic vodka gimlets, and reach for the hors d'oeuvres that might, possibly, take away the bad taste of an all-round disappointing stock market: it was the early 1970s, and the bull had turned into a bear.

In fact, at the very moment that more women were starting to come to Wall Street, as the feminist movement was making it politically and culturally imperative that women be included on the Street, the market was starting to slump. From a peak in 1968, it was down throughout 1969 and into 1970, rallying in 1970, and shaky in 1971 and 1972. With a decline in stock trading and profit, brokerage firms were closing or, if they could, merging with others to stave off bankruptcy. Richard Nixon's administration tried to keep the economy from collapsing, but the fixes proved to be temporary.

In 1973, Nixon's bear market officially arrived. Inflation was back on the rise, and in April of that same year, the Watergate scandal broke. In October, the Yom Kippur War triggered the oil crisis, when OPEC, composed of oil-rich Arab states, retaliated against Israel and its ally with an oil embargo on the United States, sending gas prices soaring. Across the country, gas lines snaked for miles. The Dow Jones continued to tumble, as did the most haloed stocks, the so-called Nifty Fifty—the top fifty stocks held by major institutions and considered to be guaranteed safeguards against any economic downturn. Not anymore.

Nina Hayes had gotten exactly what she'd come for. She'd been a part of the women's movement in the city where it felt like it mattered. But no longer seeing the returns she wanted, she left.

7

"Dress for Success"

The go-go years were gone, and as Nina experienced, so too were the returns, but even as the economy slowed significantly, Wall Street still had something to offer the women taking the circuitous route there. On weekday mornings, seventeen-year-old Maria Marsala rode the subway from Dyker Heights in Brooklyn, an Italian American neighborhood known for its over-the-top Christmas-light displays, and got off at the first stop in Manhattan. For two weeks, she followed the same routine: pounding the pavement in her new pastel matching tops and bottoms purchased on Orchard Street in Little Italy, deciding which office building to enter based on whether she thought it was "pretty." Inside, she asked for directions to the personnel department to fill out employment forms. She didn't especially want to work, but she wanted to get out of her parents' house. She didn't want to be a nurse, and her grades weren't good enough for her to work as a teacher, and so office work it would have to be. She knew enough to skip Goldman Sachs and Salomon Brothers; that's where the college kids went.

One day, Maria got off at the second stop into Manhattan because

Century 21, the designer discount clothing store, was there and she wanted to browse the racks. That's when she saw the building: black, beautiful, and with a small park to one side. It was Merrill Lynch at 250 Vesey Street, from where she could also see the Twin Towers. Merrill Lynch had a back-office job opening in the unexciting sounding non-resident-alien tax division of the dividend department. Her job was to fix trades, rewrite wrong tax numbers, which she would mark off in tiny little boxes on sheets of paper and, at the end of the day, walk over to the computer room for the technicians to process overnight. Maria was fascinated by the computer room, by the efficiency and order of it. When she asked to take a look inside, they had her put on white protective clothing so that not a single speck of dust could fall into the machines. Standing there, dressed like a doctor on call, she stared in wonder at the enormous reels that reminded her of outsized cassette-tape spools.

She was still old-fashioned at heart, a romantic, and only three months after she'd started at Merrill Lynch, she quit to marry, turning her attention to creating a cheery new home in Brooklyn with her husband. She took a job locally at a greeting-card company.

And then the unexpected happened; the cruel and inhuman treatment began.* She took one look around her and decided she was not going to accept this. She left the marriage, even as she was ostracized and criticized in her Dyker Heights community for refusing to look the other way, to forgive and forget like other women did. She returned to Wall Street, to a firm called Reynolds Securities (which would later merge with Dean Witter to become Dean Witter Reynolds), an institutional house, one of the best. Maria was put to work in the Municipals Department—in "munis"—and she set about putting that house in order even as hers had crumbled. Instead of painting walls and making curtains, she spent her time finding the mismatches between what a

---

* This is from her divorce papers.

trader had written and what the ASR teletype machine had spat out. She organized the matched trades alphabetically; she learned what a coupon was, as well as a maturity, and created filing systems for both.

In those days, it seemed almost everyone on Wall Street was smoking marijuana. A lunch jaunt out to the park for Maria and her friends to smoke a joint before returning to work was par for the course.

When in 1968, Blackie, an undercover cop in the narcotics squad who'd been working tough New York City neighborhoods for years, was assigned the Wall Street beat, he'd thought he was in for a relaxing stint. Sitting on the steps of the subtreasury, dressed to blend in in "bellbottoms, a neat shirt, maybe even a jacket—like a securities runner, or a clerk," he could not believe what he was seeing: "It was wild. It was like nothing I'd ever seen. Kids were just sitting there and smoking pot openly, as if they were smoking Chesterfields."

At first, he'd assumed the drugs were being brought in from the outside, but then he realized dealers were everywhere, and unlike in the rest of the city, they were not necessarily users trying to pay for their own addiction but sometimes "just businessmen making a buck."

And it wasn't only marijuana; it was pills and hash and skag (heroin). A favorite dealing spot was a hidden area "right in Trinity churchyard." But for Blackie, what was the worst was seeing the "young office girls on pills—Tuinal, Seconal, Blue Angels." You could pick them out because they looked like office girls, but also not. They were slightly off, "disheveled," constantly "scratching at themselves." (And it wasn't just the office girls; a 1966 story in the *Atlantic Monthly* described the writer attending a "white-collar pill party," where a five-pound box of Dexedrine, the over-the-counter diet pill that was speed, sat there for the taking while "colorful pills were being politely passed around like canapes and discussed with all the elements of connoisseurship." The drug scene was commonplace enough that the gunslingers stood out for not doing drugs, and some wondered out loud whether the back-office meltdown might have been related to the rampant drug use by those working in operations.)

Maria Marsala was no innocent; she liked a whiskey sour, and didn't say no to a joint. She was having more fun than she imagined could be had at work. But when she visited Studio 54, that was too much! The drugs were hardcore, and she was pretty sure she saw a couple copulating right out there on the dance floor.

Alice Jarcho, although a teetotaler, was also having fun. She'd left her first firm, Hirsch & Co., when they refused to pay the minuscule sum of $300 to get her registered as a broker. She was now a clerk on the risk arbitrage desk at Oppenheimer, focusing on the short sell: borrowing shares from a brokerage to sell them on the open market, betting the price would fall and they could buy them back—"return" them—for less, and pocket the difference. The stress of the job was significant, but the bump in her salary had meant she could leave her Yorkville apartment share for a place of her own on Seventy-Fifth Street between West End Avenue and Riverside Drive. When her Oppenheimer boss moved over to the firm Cogan, Berlind, Weill & Levitt (CBWL), a young investment banking and brokerage house, Alice went with him. But when he then left CBWL, unable to handle a sudden downturn in risk arbitrage, Alice stayed.

CBWL had a vibe more typical of the gunslinger firms. The rules were loose, the employees were young, and everyone went by first names. There was no time for titles or hierarchies even as CBWL would be the incubator for some of Wall Street's future financial titans: Marshall Cogan, Roger Berlind, Sanford "Sandy" Weill, and Arthur Levitt. Peter Cohen, who ten years later in 1981 would become CEO of Shearson, Lehman, was then carrying Sandy Weill's luggage for him as his assistant.

CBWL was primarily a Jewish firm, and when the partners first "unveiled" it in 1960, it was quickly dubbed "Corned Beef With Lettuce" by some on Wall Street. Marshall Cogan saw it as an "anti-

Semitic slur," but to him the backlash was also telling, an indication of how they'd triggered Wall Street by "shaking the roots of Morgan Stanley, Dillon Read, and First Boston. We were challenging Goldman Sachs, Lehman, and Salomon."

Even as she was an anomaly, a woman sitting at a trading desk as a clerk, there were now many other women around her at CBWL, even if primarily support staff. Like her, they were all young, and there was a constant merry-go-round of office affairs. The single women found it convenient to date the men who were in the office, and available, even if most of them were married. One unattractive but very important man in the firm was having a thing with his secretary; they would close the door and keep it closed for hours at a time. The annual Christmas Party was interesting—that's when the female employees at CBWL met the wives of the men with whom they'd slept or were sleeping.

Marshall Cogan, who at thirty-four was just nine years older than Alice, was her supervisor. When he'd started out, he'd wanted to join one of the famous German-Jewish investment banks. With an undergraduate degree from Harvard, and an MBA from its business school, he should have been a shoo-in, but he claimed the personality tests they gave him showed him to be resistant to authority, and neither Goldman Sachs nor Lehman Brothers wanted that in a new hire.

Roger Berlind found Cogan to be difficult, certainly, exactly as those tests had predicted, but also "a hell of a salesman." Even before Cogan was made partner, he switched the firm from retail (individual clients) to institutional, befriending CEOs and going wherever necessary to make a sales pitch. What made him a great salesman also gave him a big personality. He was, to Alice, "the personification of the Wild West," as she called Wall Street in these days when everyone knew everyone, and no holds barred was the reigning policy. Cogan was "big" about everything, "with no boundaries": "a big mouth, big ideas, big lies, big, big everything." He would "crow about his accom-

plishments and also be willing to admit what a schmuck he was . . .
very endearing." He liked to tell the story of the time he was trying
so hard to pitch an idea for an enormous deal to General Motors that
he took a plane to Detroit only to be told their meeting was in New
York at the GM building. He found it hilarious.

Cogan was as generous as he was fallible, fond of making grand
gestures; one time he went over to T. Anthony, a famous luggage
store inside the GM building, and bought each member of his trading
team a set of monogrammed luggage after they'd landed a big sale.
Another time, he hired a limousine—until then, Alice thought limousines were only for caskets—to take them all to one of the famous
steakhouses, and then to the celebrity-studded Ali vs. Frazier fight at
Madison Square Garden. Cogan was constantly at Alice about her
dressing like a girl from Queens. One day he slipped her a credit card
to go buy herself some proper clothes at Denoyer, the only New York
store with European prêt-a-porter, to make herself look like someone
who belonged. She was "like Julia Roberts" in *Pretty Woman*, with
no idea "what my budget was."

But in September 1970, CBWL purchased Hayden, Stone, which
was on its last unsteady legs even as it was one of the largest firms on
Wall Street. The Street could not afford for Hayden, Stone to fail, and
at the same time Cogan realized that CBWL would do well to buy
them up. The institutional side of the business was starting to dry up
now, but since CBWL had built its own back office from scratch, the
firm, unlike most, could handle the significant spike in business that
buying Hayden, Stone would mean. In terms of cultures, however,
the two firms were a total mismatch. Hayden, Stone was Catholic,
straightlaced, old-school, retail; CBWL was jostling cowboys. Sandy
Weill was sure that the Hayden, Stone employees objected to being
"taken over by a bunch of New York City Jews." A former partner at
Hayden, Stone, and great-grandson of one of its founders, admitted
that the CBWL crew were "smarter than we were," but also thought

they lacked the kind of traditions he valued: "They were members of no lunch clubs, members of no syndicates, and very much on the outside looking in at the securities business, whereas Hayden Stone had been on the inside, even though in many ways its people were less capable than those of Cogan, Berlind, Weill and Levitt."

Alice had liked CBWL for all the reasons that marked it as an outsider looking in, and she now wanted out. Others were also jumping ship, and when Alice heard the investor Laurence "Larry" A. Tisch, co-chairman with his brother of the Loews Corporation, and co-owners of the Loews movie theaters, was looking for a trader to run his money, Marshall Cogan encouraged her to apply.

Cogan, like everyone, considered Larry Tisch an investing god, and he insisted she try. She went in "shaking," but they hit it off, and when he offered her the job at $25,000 a year, she was "thrilled," even as she knew of at least three men who had interviewed and were asking for twice that much. But $25,000 was enough for her to stop worrying about paying her bills. It was enough to take her friends on vacation, including one friend she took to Florida for an abortion pre–*Roe v. Wade*.

Working for Larry Tisch, Alice was now handing out large stock orders to brokers because as the market started to fall in the early 1970s, Larry, who "liked bargains," was taking up ever bigger positions. She was suddenly the person everyone needed to court.

After eighteen months performing well at her job, Alice asked Larry for a raise. He came over to her office, sat down, and started negotiating with her: "How much do you pay in rent . . . what's your electric bill?"

"What does that have to do with anything?" she asked. She pointed out that this was not how a raise was evaluated.

But in this case it was not about Alice not being a family breadwinner: it was about Larry, who was just "cheap." When she finally pried from him a much smaller raise than she deserved, she moved into a one-bedroom apartment with bay windows that looked right onto the Metropolitan Museum, and an enormous living room that included a working fireplace, perfect for parties.

But Tisch was generous to her in other ways, including her in his inner circle, introducing her to the financial big shots who stopped by his office regularly—Huntington Hartford, Gus Levy, Saul Steinberg, Gerry Tsai. She was also on the exclusive invite list for Saturday-night movies at his house in Westchester. Since Tisch owned movie theaters, the films he showed on Saturday nights were pre-release and the dinner guest list was made up of Wall Street's titans. But Larry's stinginess remained on full display: Alice's boyfriend, imagining a lavish spread awaiting them, did not eat all day and then ended up with pretzels for dinner at the Tisch house. Some of the stars of finance that Alice met were also less spectacular up close. One time, the financier Saul Steinberg, sitting next to his sixteen-year-old daughter, spoke luridly about his sex life. (In 1989, his fiftieth birthday party would include live models posing, in some cases naked, as Old Masters paintings.) Another time, following a dinner there, Michael Bloomberg invited Alice to his office for lunch, where he ate his food off china and crystal and she had hers served on a plastic plate while he mansplained about the difference between an A trader and a B trader. "And which are you?!" he demanded to know.

Not that Alice didn't have attitude either. She knew that Wall Street had changed her, and she didn't feel particularly proud of it. She wasn't the one drinking scotch or snorting cocaine or lighting up a joint but, she realized, if she were to appraise herself honestly, she did now "act like a man." She did what she wanted, as she wanted, unbothered by the idea of consensus. She had also became a serial curser, a lover of expletives and four-letter words. While working as Tisch's trader, an out-of-town broker came to see her expecting to find someone else entirely, not this "tiny" young woman, because "I had a reputation as being a bitch." She was "not a yeller," like so many of the men around her; instead, sarcastic put-downs were her weapon of choice, and she could not care less if someone was hurt by them. But neither did she ever really feel hurt because she didn't get hurt, she wasn't a people-pleaser. Only one time was she truly stopped in her tracks. It was when a man called her the "c word." She shut him down. There were limits to what she was willing to tolerate.

Or so she thought.

———

MARIA MARSALA FROM DYKER HEIGHTS HAD BEEN PROMOTED ON the trading desk and was now making $105 a week. Her new boss told her she needed to look managerial, to dress appropriately for her new position. *But what did that even mean?* He pointed to her miniskirt and her "hooker boots," as she called them, the kind that tied to the top of the knee (the demure pastel outfits were long gone). "Go to Wanamaker's!" he insisted.

But all the clothes at Wanamaker's make you look like a guy, thought Maria.

She went instead to the library to find books on how to dress in a "managerial" style, but all the manuals and advice books were for men. She eventually capitulated and made the trip to Wanamaker's, as most Wall Street women did, where she bought a beige-colored suit, a white blouse with one of the floppy bowties so popular in the 1970s, beige stockings, and closed-toe shoes. She definitely looked like a man, she thought—moreover, the ugly suit camouflaged her best assets.

Like Maria, most of the early generation of women on Wall Street lived in "cramped studio apartments," and came from backgrounds where, as anthropologist Melissa Fisher found, their "fathers tended to be salesmen in insurance and business," while their mothers were "stay-at-home moms." They were clueless about "what kind of dress to wear to a business dinner party, what kind of wine to order at such

an event, or even what fork to use for the salad." When the Financial Women's Association started, the guest speakers who drew the
largest crowds not only elucidated the world of finance but also the
cultural codes necessary to succeed there.

The 1977 publication of John T. Molloy's *The Woman's Dress for
Success Book* was for this "growing breed" of women now coming
to Wall Street from working- and middle-class backgrounds. They
were women like Peggy Schulder, profiled in the *New York Times*:
"Schulder . . . does not fit the Wall Street stereotype. For one thing,
she does not come from one of those moneyed families whose names
have been identified with the brokerage business for decades." Peggy
was a gifted mathematician, "the daughter of a post office clerk"
who "grew up in Queens." Peggy did not "fit the Wall Street stereotype" only because that specific stereotype was for men. In the
case of Wall Street's *women*, Peggy Schulder's background was very
much the norm.

John Molloy, who called himself a "wardrobe engineer," wrote
The Woman's Dress for Success Book in response to the lack of
guidance Maria Marsala had found on the bookshelves of her local
library. It became a runaway bestseller. Issues of class were among
the central themes that Molloy tackled head-on: "Today hundreds of
thousands of women whose parents never went to college are going
to college themselves. They're getting training and degrees that will
point them toward the power ranks of American society. But in order
to move in, they must do more than arm themselves with degrees and
training. They must learn the manners and mores of the inner circle.
And the inner circle is most emphatically upper middle class." Molloy's plan for rescuing working women by showing them the right and
wrong ways to dress was to create for them a "business uniform." The
right uniform would protect and legitimize them.

There was "nothing morally wrong with a polyester pantsuit" he
wrote, but it was going to tell the world that you were not of the upper

middle class. The "imitation man look," he noted, merely made you look like "a small boy." A jacket was always to be full cut so as not to outline the bust. Materials were to be wool and linen; patterns, solids, tweeds, and plaid. A designer's name visibly displayed on a piece of clothing made you look like a "lightweight," "more interested in form than substance."

The ideal business uniform was a skirted suit with a blouse in a contrasting color from the suit. Even as Molloy saw himself a champion for this new breed of women, he stumbled on his own sexism: "despite the rhetoric of the feminist movement," he declared, "many women, including businesswomen, continue to view themselves as sex objects." He wanted to see women cover up, to hide not only their backgrounds but also their bodies; just as Maria Marsala had been told to cover up. Florence Graves, writing in the *New York Times*, quipped: "OK. So you've made it to the boardroom with your no frill suits and it's lonely at the top. If you've paid close attention to the dictates of John Molloy . . . you may have found, as he so pointedly warns, that 'dressing to succeed in business and dressing to be sexually attractive are almost mutually exclusive.' Alas, a choice between the bedroom and the boardroom." A piece in the *Wall Street Journal* was even more insistent that Molloy was wrong as well as offensive: "Molloy seeks to neuterize women, trading sex appeal for authority. He strips them of color (he outlaws purple and gold because they symbolize the middle class), of sweaters (they 'spell secretary') and skirts without jackets (it's a 'flag of failure' for the businesswoman). Molloy even advises women to 'hang neuter art' in their offices."

Yet while some were up in arms over his advice, 1970s working women were heeding it in droves, rushing out to buy suits in understated colors and accessories that simulated upper-class tastes such as "pumps, gold or silver pen (no Bics!), leather attaché case (with a dial lock, preferably), plain wrist watch (try a tank watch) and canvas and belting leather luggage." He received the most pushback for his rule that women never wear boots to the office, but he insisted that the research bore this out: "if two women walk into an office, one wearing boots and the other plain pumps the one with pumps will always be judged more efficient and businesslike."

Molloy was willing to admit that clothes could not single-handedly destroy presumptions and prejudices about women. Women, by existing as women, automatically received second-class treatment everywhere and from everyone, from "hotel employees, store clerks, receptionists, telephone operators, doctors, and bureaucrats." He confessed to his readers about the time he was to meet a group of executives at a hotel bar, and became impatient thinking they were late when all along they'd been sitting right there: "three of the best and most conservatively dressed women I had ever met." But he had made the error of thinking they could never be executives even as they dressed exactly as he counseled women in business to dress. The women shrugged it off. That always happened, they told him; one of them sometimes wondered whether she shouldn't just carry around her desk plaque that read: VP SALES.

In 1977, the same year that Molloy's guidebook came out, Marilyn Loden coined the term "glass ceiling." She was working in human resources in the telecom industry, where she was routinely told by her boss to "smile more," and where she'd been passed up for a promotion more than once because it needed to go to a "family man." She first uttered the phrase "glass ceiling" while sitting on a conference panel listening to the other women attempt to find reasons, including their own fault, for why they were not getting past the middle-management level. Unable to continue listening to the self-flagellation, she spoke up and said she believed there was an "invisible glass ceiling" that was largely cultural and "not personal."

Yet Molloy's advice *was* personal: you could only have a chance of breaking through the glass ceiling by disguising your modest class background. Even in a chapter devoted to time off called "Dressing to Attract Men," Molloy insisted that in his researchers' tests, when men saw a woman for only a split second, a fleeting reflection in a shop window or a revolving glass door, they had no idea what the woman looked like but they were sure they could identify her socio-economic status.

But hiding or compensating for one's modest background was a lot more complex than Molloy's book suggested, especially when you added race, which he did not address. Julia Walsh, *Wall $treet Week* superstar and partner at Ferris & Co., hired Lillian Hobson in 1971. Ferris & Co. was, as Lillian observed, "an anomaly" because it had more women employees than any other brokerage firm at the time. But still, they were all white women. Lillian was just two years out of HBS, living in Maryland. She and her husband—she had returned to her second year at Harvard with an engagement ring like Priscilla—had just bought a house in what was, until their arrival, a completely white neighborhood. As she searched for work, she should have tapped into the extensive HBS alumni network, but she'd never shaken the feeling from that first day in Cambridge, sitting on the park bench while she waited for her room at the Radcliffe Graduate Center, that she was at Harvard "but not of it." And so instead she was going through the classifieds in the local papers, which is when an advertisement for an investment seminar being offered by Ferris & Co. caught her eye. She signed up, thinking this might fill a gap in her knowledge, not being from a family that had invested in the stock market.

On her first day in the seminar, she was thrilled to see that a woman, Gail Winslow, was leading it. When it was over, Lillian thanked Gail, and as they chatted, Gail suggested that she try her hand working as a broker.

Before long, Lillian was sitting in an interview with George M. Ferris Jr., the owner and president of the brokerage firm. But even a progressive firm that was committed to hiring women, where Julia

Walsh was a partner, was myopic when it came to race. During the interview, Ferris commented that he thought white clients would welcome working with Lillian because they "could relate it to my being a servant to them." This, to Lillian, was absurd at best, but she gladly took the job he offered her as an account executive.

What Lillian hadn't realized was that being a retail broker was much like the hated magazine-subscription job she'd once had, forced to go door to door, trying to convince housewives to buy magazines. Now she was behind a desk, a phone to her ear, cold-calling people to sell them stocks just as the bull market was starting to turn into a bear. When she asked Gail and Julia for advice, they told her how they'd started off, how they'd found their first clients: both had built their client base through their circles of friends, family, and business associates. But no one in Ballsville, Virginia, where Lillian was from, was looking to get into the stock market.

Molloy's *The Woman's Dress for Success Book* was in many ways a manual for "passing," a guide on how to come off as if you'd been born with a silver spoon in your mouth. But there was just so much a beige suit fitted correctly around the bust line could do if you were Black.

8

The Pinto Decade

The 1970s had come to feel a lot like the infamous Pinto, the subcompact car introduced by the Ford Motor Company on September 11, 1970. The Pinto, "The Little Carefree Car," was supposed to be zippy and fun; a cute, mechanized pony to get you where you needed to go. Instead, it proved to be unreliable and prone to exploding. Jokes followed it like exhaust fumes. Its failure matched the prevalent mood in America: it spoke to things not being what they seemed, of disillusionment, of decline in American manufacturing power, technological prowess, and ingenuity. And as the markets wilted, so too did the confidence of American manhood.

In spring 1970, when construction workers, many from the nearby World Trade Center construction site, descended on Wall Street, violently attacking students demonstrating against the recent deaths at Kent State University, they singled out the hippies with long hair. The attack was in part a reaction to a growing crisis of masculinity. In their construction helmets and orange-and-brown overalls, these working men saw themselves as representing not only a much-needed patriotism but also a manliness that the hippies appeared to scorn.

Newsweek described a bygone era, a nostalgic past, when men were defined "by their advantages: physically superior to women, psychically more stalwart, men seemed to be predestined for dominance. They were the hunters and warriors, the bridge builders and lawgivers, the natural autocrats of the breakfast table and oligarchs of the bedroom. They worked and earned for their families, came home to hot meals and compliant wives, took their ease in the privileged fellowship of the locker room and the all-male club." But even the men who accepted that that time was now over could not dodge the national male identity crisis. Sociologist Mirra Komarovsky had found that only 10 percent of the men she interviewed were genuinely behind the women's movement, with the rest expressing contradictory feelings: "Typically, they would endorse the idea of working wives, then add the proviso that a wife's career should not rival her husband's or interfere with the smooth functioning of the home. They approved of women entering the professions, then disapproved of 'aggressive, ambitious' women. . . ."

These very contradictions were articulated by Bob Amore, a music and drama major at Northwestern University who would go on to star in the first touring production of the musical *Cats*. He professed an alliance with the women's movement and believed his parents had recently divorced precisely because of his father's overbearing manner yet confessed to his own discomfort if his date paid for dinner or if she drove them there. As much as he believed in women's equal pay, Bob Amore knew that once married, he would need to be the boss: "I don't think my family would work if I wasn't the head of it in a domineering way. I think I need it, and I think my wife would have to know I need it."

In the workplace, this masculinity crisis was acutely felt. The *Saturday Evening Post* ran a piece in 1974 titled "Why Men Fear Women in Business." The article, written by a woman, poked fun at how federally mandated equality, policed by the Equal Employment

Opportunity Commission, had upset the apple cart: "Uncle Sam, traitor to his sex, has ordered that the hunt be opened to women, that there be equal opportunity, that the Man's World hang out both 'his' and 'her' signs."

But while Uncle Sam might have been trying to do his bit—the 1963 Equal Pay Act, Title VII of the 1964 Civil Rights Act, the 1965 establishment of the Equal Employment Opportunity Commission, the 1972 authorization for the EEOC to file lawsuits against private companies—the 1970s recession meant that all such efforts were diluted by current economic circumstances. As the *Wall Street Journal* reported, the hopes for a "great leap forward to job equality has slowed to a sluggish shuffle." Between the recession and "spotty federal enforcement," it didn't look like women were that much better off than they had been before. Women, even if more of them were now entering the workforce, were being herded into the usual female jobs. As Barbara Bergmann, director of the University of Maryland's Project on the Economics of Discrimination, observed: "More women are clerks than ever before, and more women are underpaid than ever before."

The Labor Department reported that in 1975 the median income of a woman was 57 percent of that of a man, whereas in 1955 it had been actually higher, at 64 percent. The EEOC calculated that 20 percent of college-educated women were working in a clerical job that required few skills and no college degree because they were unable to find other work. The number of jobs for women was growing, but the quality of those jobs was not: the chance of finding a management job in the 1970s was the same as in the 1960s. Government-mandated affirmative-action programs focused on race more than gender because racial discrimination was easier to prove. Moreover, in white-collar jobs where output was often subjective, it was much more difficult to prove that women did not get hired or promoted because of their gender.

Yet with the markets in steep decline, men were not exactly clamoring to be on Wall Street. The bull had "stopped rampaging in Wall Street in December, 1968," the *New York Times* reported, and even gunslinger Gerald Tsai's Manhattan Fund was performing so poorly that in 1973 he resigned from it. While Mickie Siebert's NYSE seat had cost $445,000 in 1967, by 1970, one could buy a seat for $130,000. By 1974, the bottom of the bear market, a seat was going for $65,000.

Unemployment was up, development was down. Times Square was such a den of iniquity that in 1973 Mayor Lindsay had a "Vice Map" drawn up to pinpoint everything on Forty-Second Street that was a contaminating stain in need of removal: massage parlors, prostitution hotels, peep shows, live burlesque entertainment, and adult bookstores. In 1977, even the serial killer Son of Sam would write to *Daily News* columnist Jimmy Breslin: "Hello from the gutters of N.Y.C. which are filled with dog manure, vomit, stale wine, urine and blood. Hello from the sewers of N.Y.C. which swallow up these delicacies when they are washed away by the sweeper trucks. Hello from the cracks in the sidewalks of N.Y.C. and from the ants that dwell in these cracks and feed in the dried blood of the dead that has settled into the cracks." In 1978 the director of compliance at a commodities firm, who had taught jujitsu at the New York City police academy, offered a free course to the women of Wall Street after hearing that muggings and assaults increased during the summer months.

Patricia Chadwick, the former Feeneyite, arrived from Boston in January 1975 at age twenty-six. It was a terrible time to make her New York debut. Just a few days after, a terrorist bomb went off at the historic Fraunces Tavern, a Wall Street landmark where in 1783 George Washington had bid farewell to his soldiers. The bomb was detonated by a Puerto Rican nationalist group at 1:25 p.m., just as the dining rooms were filled with the lunch-hour crowd, killing four, one of whom was decapitated by the blast. Dozens of others were injured, fleeing into the streets. In October, President Gerald Ford, in meetings with New York officials about the city's dire financial straits, publicly wiped his hands clean of the problem that was New York City. Then, just four days after Christmas, a bomb went off at LaGuardia Airport, killing 11 and injuring 70. At first the same Puerto Rican nationalist group was suspected, but when that trail went cold, it remained an unsolved crime, adding to an atmosphere of uncertainty and fear.

For Maria Marsala, back on Wall Street after leaving her husband despite her family's resistance, the hardest part was the commute back and forth from Brooklyn. A born-and-bred New Yorker, she was inured to seeing men with their pants down urinating in the subway. But after she moved to Bensonhurst, her commute became a battlefield. "Stuffed" into the train car "like a sardine" she searched out other women so they could stand together for protection, but on the rush-hour B train, women were relatively scarce. Inevitably she felt the hands moving up under her skirt, and at least twice a week she was kicking and screaming at her assailants, shouting at them to get the hell off her.

Not that it was much easier at work. The work area was tight in the municipal bonds department at Reynolds Securities, as trading desks were, and her boss was always accidentally brushing up against her. After he'd had his cocktails at lunch, the "accidents" were more overt: he started to touch her legs, or he massaged her shoulders and then would suddenly dip in low to feel up her breasts.

"Stop that!" she would tell him loudly, but he'd only laugh and insist that she liked it.

When it was clear he wouldn't stop, she knew she'd have to make an official complaint. "I didn't want to stay with my ex-husband because of not being treated right . . . I didn't want to stay at home because of not being treated right, and I was not going to stay at work not being treated right."

To cover her bases, just in case she was shown the door once she'd initiated the complaint, Maria started to reach out to other brokerage firms, and also, so she wouldn't be left hanging without a paycheck for even a week, she took on an extra, after-work job at a hardware store back in Brooklyn. All the while, she carefully collected the evidence of her boss's harassment: dates, remarks, physical touches. And then she readied herself to fight.

When it came time, Maria went to his superiors to tell them what was going on; they did not fire her, as she feared, but neither did they fire him. They did nothing. And nothing was the equivalent of a green light. The touching and groping continued.

Next, Maria approached one of the firm's managing partners to ask that at least her seat be switched so she wouldn't be sitting directly next to him. But he, too, refused to help. (When the trader was eventually fired, it had nothing to do with his behavior or Maria calling him out for it. She heard he'd lost money for the firm—the only punishable crime a man on Wall Street could commit.)

Trying to figure out who to tell—if anyone—was often impossible. Mary Farrell came to Wall Street in 1971, only twenty-one years old, fresh out of college, answering a want ad in the *New York Times*: a small firm, Pershing & Co., was looking for a securities analyst trainee with a major in economics. She didn't know what a security was, and she thought the firm's Broadway address meant it was something theatrical, but she *had* been an economics major. The director of research, known for bragging that he'd figured out how to hire cheap talent (that is, he hired women), gave her the job. From there, she hopscotched in the late 1970s to a job as a research analyst at Smith Barney, the only woman among thirty-five analysts. After she found herself in an elevator with an executive who pushed her up against the wall, she shoved him off and ran out, then went to see her friend in human resources. If there were repercussions, if it became a "he said/she said" situation, she wanted her version on record. But when she got there, her friend in HR was crying: she herself was leaving the firm that very Friday because something similar had happened to her. "There was no one to go to in that era," Mary observed.

Mary arrived to work the following Monday to find her usually neat desk in disarray. Under a pile of documents, she discovered a single computer printout: the names were cut off but a list of salaries, bonuses, and dates of hire remained intact. It seemed to be a parting gift from her friend in HR. Studying it, she saw she was being paid exactly half of what the lowest paid male analyst was making.

MARLENE JUPITER, QUEENS RESIDENT AND PROUD GRADUATE OF New York's "nerdy but prestigious" Stuyvesant High School, arrived at 17 Battery Park Place in a beige pantsuit holding a briefcase with "a TI-30 calculator, a couple of copies of my résumé on beige bonded paper and *The Wall Street Journal*." She was interviewed at Paine Webber by a man whose office was crowded with bulls and bears and who explained the market symbols to her: the bull fought with its horns up, while the bear fought by reaching down. Up or down, one fought.

He warned her that this would very much be an entry-level position. Starting at 7:30 a.m., she would be expected to make copies of *Trading Week* and distribute them, fetch lunches, coffees, sodas, and generally run errands on demand while xeroxing endlessly. She had a degree from Cornell University, but she took the job anyway. To celebrate, she met with a friend who had landed a similar entry-level position elsewhere a few weeks earlier. They agreed to treat themselves to drinks at Windows on the World. Taking the elevator up to the 106th floor of the World Trade Center felt like a rocket ship to a new life, and taking up positions at the bar, the two of them watched the sun set and the bridges light up. It took a while, and a friendly word from a man at the bar, before they learned that they were being mistaken for prostitutes on the prowl for customers.

When they explained to him that they were in fact celebrating their new jobs on Wall Street, he bought them a round of drinks: "Welcome to Wall Street! . . . Watch out for the wolves, they like their prey young and innocent." Marlene would later wish she'd heeded that warning.

Marlene as the "new girl" got the jobs no one wanted, including making sure that one of the strategists, who smoked three packs of cigarettes a day, always had a Tab diet cola on his desk. He never asked for the next one—he just grunted. Marlene would have to figure out which flavor he'd like next: regular, root beer, or cherry? She also had to ask if anyone else wanted something, then feed endless quarters into the vending machine one floor down from the options desk and stumble back up with an armload of cans.

The secretaries stuck together, helping one another coordinate their slow rise to trading assistant. One of them told Marlene to sit for the Series 7 broker exam. She herself had just passed it and would lend Marlene her notes. Even as they helped one another, the consensus was that if you were a woman who advanced further up the ladder, past trading assistant, you would become almost as bad as the men, and you would certainly dress like them.

Marlene passed the Series 7, got her license, and was soon being wooed by the institutional trading desk to be their assistant. It wasn't so much that she now had the Series 7, it was because of her computer skills—unusual at the time. Once, when no one could get the trading software to run, Marlene had offered to help. The men rolled their eyes. She sat down in front of the computer screen, and out of the corner of her eye could see they were placing bets on whether she'd fix it. Even after she'd quickly found the problem—it was a simple syntax error—she pretended she was still looking for it. Once $500 was in play, she "suddenly" fixed the program and set it whirring happily.

"How?!"

"Cornell."

"What? I couldn't even get into Cornell, and you're my secretary!"

If any of the traders had asked, they'd know that the other two office "girls" were, like Marlene, also college educated and overqualified. And although the institutional trading desk wanted her, the head of the options department refused to move her up from secretary to trading assistant. He was forty years old, three times married, and had his eye on Marlene, whereas she was twenty-one, too young and naïve to think that a forty-year-old man could have ulterior motives.

One day after work the whole options team headed out for a night on the town, starting at Harry's at Hanover, then moving on to one of the nightclubs—Leviticus, Ipanema, or Copacabana—where tableside backgammon boards were all the rage. When the group finally hit a dance club, her boss made his move. He shimmied up to Marlene and started dancing with her, but before she knew what was happening, he was trying to push her up against a pole, his hands sliding all over her body, reaching under her clothes, and she was in complete shock, stunned. The traders, who'd been keeping watch all night, pulled him off and put him in the limousine he had waiting outside. The charming head of institutional trading, who put flowers and chocolates on every woman's desk for Valentine's Day, gave Marlene cab fare to get home.

———

SHORT OF OUTRIGHT HARASSMENT, THERE WAS HARMFUL GOSSIP. Alice Jarcho, still in her twenties, was always being gossiped about. It was an inevitable catch-22: as a woman, you needed a mentor to rise through the ranks, and with only men in positions of power, your mentor was a man. And then the presumption, almost always, was that you were sleeping with him. That is certainly what had trailed behind Alice like the slithering cables that followed the guests on Louis Rukeyser's *Wall $treet Week*. At CBWL, everyone assumed that Alice was having an affair with Marshall Cogan (she was actually "involved with a best friend of his"). Now that she was working for Larry Tisch, everyone assumed she was sleeping with *him*, including his daughters-in-law, who told anyone who would listen that Alice was their father-in-law's lover. And then there were the targeted lies that brokers spread about how she would routinely go to bars after work to pick up men. Never mind that she did not even drink.

It was all the more complicated by the fact that men often slept with women for strategic reasons. Brokers would try to date women who had any influence whatsoever at an institutional trading desk— they would wine, dine, and charm them into buying stock from them for their funds. Alice Jarcho and the handful of other female traders were prime targets, but they also knowingly participated, charmed by the flattery, ignoring that these men, being married, always had the upper hand. There was one broker at Salomon Brothers sleeping with two different women that he was trying to "charm" in this way. But there was no denying it could be fun. They'd all go out, in big, raucous groups, to the big-name restaurants trendy at the time, especially the steakhouses like Peter Luger in Brooklyn and Christ Cella in Midtown, tables laden down with food and drink, and someone would always pick up the check.

But after four years with Larry Tisch, Alice was getting bored—he had bought all those stocks at rock-bottom prices, and once they went up, he sold them off, leaving her little to do. She now had experience on both the sell side, from when she'd worked at CBWL, and the buy side, as Tisch's trader. In 1976, a "very iconoclastic" friend at Oppenheimer, where she'd first worked on the arbitrage desk, suggested that she go work on the New York Stock Exchange floor, the "Big Board," as a floor broker for Oppenheimer.

"Are you crazy? I'm not going on the floor."

As she saw it, they were all animals down there, and she was a woman, and they were going to eat her alive. At the same time, she knew the floor could be a crucial stepping-stone to the job she really wanted: to be the number-two person—as a woman, she couldn't hope for number one—on an institutional trading desk.

It was well known that Mickie Siebert was the first woman to buy a seat on the exchange, but that did not mean she worked on the floor. No woman had yet done that full-time as a trader. But Alice had a crush on her friend at Oppenheimer, which made her more susceptible to his insistence.

But just because he thought it was a good idea did not mean she could count on the support of anyone else at Oppenheimer. The guys on the firm's trading desk knew Alice Jarcho, and they knew she was up to the job, but they did not want her—a woman—down on the floor executing their trades. They'd be a laughingstock. Jack Nash, a good friend of Tisch, who ran Oppenheimer, who had escaped Nazi Germany with his family at age twelve, also couldn't see any upside to sending her down there. But Gus Levy, the trader who also ran Goldman Sachs, was her sponsor, and that prestige was hard to resist.

Her friend wouldn't let it go, until finally everyone at Oppenheimer agreed and Alice was hired. But a few weeks later he was fired, and she was now stuck with the job of NYSE floor broker for Oppenheimer with no one to go to bat for her.

Alice was assigned nine days on the floor as a trainee, learning to execute orders under the supervision of another member.

The noise of the floor hit you first: "a roar that sounds like pounding surf," interspersed with shouts of "buy," hurriedly penciled onto slips of paper as "bot," and the call for a runner to pick up the piece of paper and "run it" over to the floor broker's booth. Then there was the whooshing sound of the pneumatic tubes that transported stock trades to the ticker department, and the constant thump of the stock tickers, "mounted on balconies like movie projectors," so you could see the stock symbols and prices from anywhere. A good "print" on the ticker tape meant a stock had risen sharply, which elicited cheers across the floor, while the opposite sent off a round of boos.

Until 1971, when floor brokers began to carry pagers, "pocket-sized radio receivers" as the *New York Times* referred to them then, there had been a constant clacking from the annunciator board paging system that summoned brokers back to their booths. The NYSE's gold-leaf ceiling soared five stories high, expanding rather than dampening the noise. Long after the closing bell, late at night, carpenters arrived on site to redo sections of the two-inch-thick maple wood floor of the exchange, regularly worn away by the foot traffic.

The stock exchange, the size of Grand Central terminal, looked at from the visitors' balcony above, was an ant nest of brokers, clerks, and runners milling around, covering miles a day. The floor brokers traded, the clerks took orders, the runners ran—in theory only, because in practice running was not allowed—the slips of paper with

Trash being swept off the floor of the NYSE after a day of trading, 1975.

orders and trades from brokers to clerks and back. Paper, "pink, yellow, white and blue," was strewn everywhere like confetti. As were "soft-drink lids, husks of gum." Not a single trash can could be found on the "grimy wooden floor" because there was no room for them. There was so much paper that up to three tons of it would have to be swept up and removed each night.

The specialist posts, horseshoe-shaped semicircles facing one another, a figure eight in walnut, was where the action was. Stock prices were displayed in oak boxes, the numbers moved using a thumbwheel (until 1980, when these original specialist posts were removed). Here the brokers needing to buy or sell specific stocks gathered, clustered around the "specialist" in charge of that stock. If you wanted to buy, you might call out: "Three-eighths for a thousand." If you wanted to sell, it would be: "A thousand at three-eighths." "Sold!" the taker would have to shout, and then buyer and seller quickly jotted down their badge numbers, firm, price, and number of shares. A "reporter" would simultaneously write down the same information and send it out to a clerk, who would send the information on to the ticker tape.

There were time-honored initiation rites for first-timers, already confused enough as it was by the seeming chaos of the floor. One ritual was so stress-inducing that it had been brought to a halt, considered too cruel and potentially hazardous: it revolved around sending a newbie into the throng to buy a fake stock. Other brokers, in on the prank, would jostle him out of the way, shouting over him as they pretended to bid on the fake stock, pushing its price up and up, the specialists playing along, trying to keep a straight face, until they finally let the newbie get in on the action, by which time the stock price had shot up so high that he would have to buy it at an absurdly inflated price. The coup de grace was when they all watched him as the price of the stock then rapidly fell, sweat visibly soaking through his new suit.

But Alice would get worse.

When her training was over, she sat for the floor broker test, not particularly taxing, especially since she was a good test-taker. Only later did she learn that the sabotage had already begun; someone who worked on the floor—she never learned who—had tried to pay a thousand dollars, perhaps more, to have her exam marked as failed.

Alice was thirty years old now, attractive, a woman who had already seen and done more than most, but the photograph that ran in the *New York Times* marking her first day working on the floor was not exactly flattering; she looked like a bewildered young boy with short, curly black hair. When she left her booth to execute her first order—ten thousand shares of Franklin Mint—her hand was shaking. As she strode forward, trying to look confident and determined, she stepped on a piece of carbon paper, her foot gave way, and she landed "on [her] ass." When she walked past one of the specialists, seated near her Oppenheimer booth, he said to her: "I want you to know I have daughters. I have nothing against women . . . you do not belong here." (He was one of the few men on the floor who would actually become her friend.)

Like Mickie Siebert and Jane Larkin, Alice Jarcho refused to publicly acknowledge the revolution, and counterrevolution, that her presence on the floor had triggered: "I have all the fears and trepidation of any person who first comes on the floor. But I have these feelings as a person, not a woman. That's just an accident of birth," she told the press. She meant it, too—she had always referred to herself as a person, not a woman. But the reactions to her had *everything* to do with being a woman.

Furthermore, Alice knew there were very clearly demarcated class differences on the trading floor of the NYSE. There were the outerborough people, like herself, from Brooklyn, Queens, Staten Island, and the Bronx. Then there were the Ivy Leaguers, the Harvard MBAs, the specialists whose seats had been passed down for generations within a family. She thought it was going to be the outer-borough set who ate her alive, but at first it was the well-heeled, well-dressed specialists—like the one who told her she had no right to be there—as well as other floor brokers.

Alice was technically an outer-borough girl, but she was, in her own words, "a snob." She had grown up in an intense environment and prided herself on her intellectual prowess. Except that here it was meaningless; it held no currency. Nobody was interested that Alice cared about ballet, Proust, and antiwar demonstrations, or that she was a political liberal on Wall Street. In part, it was because of the way that the Big Board practiced a meritocracy quite different from that at the investment banks and brokerage houses. If a young man's skills as a runner got noticed, he would get promoted to clerk, and then, possibly, to floor broker. The brokers had their own hierarchy: the top dogs were the institutional brokers because their order sizes were significant whereas the retail brokers executed smaller trades for individual clients. The so-called two-dollar brokers took up the slack when a firm's floor broker was too busy to attend to a trade right away. Then there were the independent traders, the small floor outfits, who bought or leased a seat to trade their own accounts. But despite a certain kind of floor meritocracy that was present, none of it took women into account.

The attacks on Alice were immediate and relentless: dildoes—instead of stock orders—delivered to her through the pneumatic tube system; tampons left in her booth covered in ketchup, and condoms filled with mayonnaise. If she left a can of Tab soda in her booth, she'd find spit on it when she got back. It was easy to plant things in her booth because it was in the back, perfect for a prankster to get in and out. If she was able to catch and confront him, she would say out loud: "Oh yeah? Let's call your wife and tell her all about it!"

The comments to her were uncensored and constant.

"Oh, you must have your period. I can smell it."

"You're walking funny today. You must have had sex with a big dick last night."

Her reactions were carefully gauged. Everyone within sight would be watching to see how she responded. The trick was to deflect, never to show offense, always to hide her hurt. Sarcasm was the best.

Then there were the anonymous calls she got at her booth, one so threatening that even Jack Nash, president of Oppenheimer, had her call the police. After that, she had to have a plainclothes policeman drive her to work every morning for several days.

Perhaps the worst, however, were the traders who wouldn't talk to her, even when she needed to negotiate a stock sale with them. Instead, they made her talk to their clerks, who had to act as an intermediary, like a child with quarreling parents. A three-hundred-pound Polish American guy called Mike worked in the Oppenheimer floor booth with her. When she arrived, he made it clear how much he hated working with the first woman ever to trade on the floor. He found it humiliating; he could not believe his bad luck. But as he watched how Alice was treated, he came around and became her floor protector and friend (he would also dispose of the dildoes that arrived for her through the pneumatic tubes).

She consoled herself that surely the jokes, the pranks, the stomach-churning remarks would eventually let up, but they did not. In fact, it only got worse once she started doing the bigger orders, because now she was a real and not only symbolic threat. Some specialists started to respect her, certainly, but they were at the top of the pecking order, and they could hardly continue to look down on a trader who was responsible for such orders. But now those below her within the floor's caste system became irate, wanting her gone, and the crude jokes were accompanied by schoolyard sneers: "O-oh, watch out! Here she comes. Ooo, big shot!" It didn't help when she reported the clerks in the Neuberger Berman booth to the NYSE governors: they'd been leafing through an S&M porn magazine and laughing. "There were women with their legs spread apart and they had dog collars on them and whips and stuff like that." She told them to "put it away," that she didn't "want to see it." But instead they blocked her and shoved it in her face.

If only she had not walked in blind, she told herself later, or if she had been less naïve about the enormity of what she was about to do, or if there had been one other woman, just one, to counsel her, she might have known how to adjust her behavior from the start. She would have been less sarcastic for sure, less of a wise guy, less aggressive perhaps. But by the time she realized this, it was too late. When you walked onto that floor, you set your personality in a particular way and there was no changing it. Another specialist said to her: "You're not understanding. We were brought up down here. Our fathers were here. Our grandfathers were here. We've never dealt with a woman." She was disrupting almost two hundred years of sedimented testosterone culture.

Not that the floor was quick to welcome a Black man either. In 1970, Joseph L. Searles III, a partner at the brokerage firm of Newburger, Loeb & Co., a former football player with the New York Giants who had worked with city government to promote minority businesses, became the first African American floor broker. His firm worried, among other things, where Searle would sit in the NYSE Luncheon Club. As if to compound the problem, the Luncheon Club was "pure Teddy Roosevelt," the entryway walls "lined with heads of moose, elk, buffalo and white-tail deer." Ultimately, so as not to upset sensibilities, Searles was given his own table: "a lone black man at a table." He left less than a year later.

Alice stuck it out, but she couldn't seem to get a break. Shortly after getting the job, after becoming the first full-time woman trader on the floor, after appearing on CBS News and in the *New York Times*, her father came to visit her at her apartment that faced the Metropolitan Museum. He looked around, taking it all in, and then said: "When are you going to do something useful with your life?"

9

Floor Queens
and an Arb King

T here was another stock exchange on Wall Street, the American Stock Exchange, adjacent to New York University's Graduate School of Business Administration, just a five-minute walk away from the NYSE via a pleasant route around Trinity Church. The American Stock Exchange, called the "Amex," was founded in 1911 to handle stocks that did not yet qualify for the NYSE. Less prestigious but also less culturally conservative, in 1965 the American Stock Exchange had admitted its first two women: one of them was Julia Walsh, Rukeyser's first female Elf on *Wall $treet Week*. But both Julia and the other woman were partners at Washington, DC, brokerage firms, and—like Mickie Siebert at the NYSE—would never actually trade on the Amex floor.

On May 1, 1975, a young woman named Doreen arrived at the American Stock Exchange to work as a wire clerk. On that very same day, fixed trading commissions officially came to an end. Doreen's stepfather, who worked on the floor and had found her the job, joked about her phenomenally bad timing. Someone at Morgan Stanley called that ill-fated day "Mayday" and the name stuck. Fixed com-

missions had been in place since the Buttonwood Agreement back in
the late 1700s. For almost two centuries, every investor in the market,
anyone buying or selling stock, paid the same commission, the exact
same transaction fee, regardless of whom they had as their broker.
Brokers did not, could not, compete against one another by offering
better rates. They competed by having more clients or more clients
who actively traded—because a trade, any trade, meant a commission. The day Doreen stepped out onto the Amex floor was the day
that these previously fixed commissions would steadily start to drop.

Even as many were unhappy about the change, it was inevitable. The so-called "third market"—for example, the Midwest Stock
Exchange and the Pacific Coast Stock Exchange—had started to offer
lower commissions. What then was the incentive to make the trade
at the NYSE or Amex, especially for institutional traders who were
buying in bulk and thereby paying commissions in bulk? In 1970,
five years before Mayday hit, the president of the NYSE had already
admitted as much to the Economic Club of New York: "I am concerned lest we bask solely in the glory of the past, and in the process become oblivious to emerging trends . . . The New York Stock
Exchange, to put it crassly, no longer has the only game in town."

No one was happy to lose their "financial Camelot," but within
minutes of the opening bell on May 1, 1975, word spread that some
brokerage firms were already slashing their commissions.

Mickie Siebert was one of those who pivoted. Her firm became
a discount brokerage, offering bargain-rate commission fees, under-
cutting brokers still wedded to the luxuries of the pre-Mayday era.
A year later, in September 1976, she called a press conference at the
iconic 21 Club to announce that she was extending her discount rates
to the public, to retail clients. Individuals with small stock holdings
would be charged as little as institutions with blocks of stock. The
ensuing advertising campaign showed a smiling Mickie cutting a
hundred-dollar bill in half.

Others weren't smiling, and there were some on Wall Street who stopped talking to her.

The difference between pre- and post-Mayday was significant. The fixed rate commission on large trades had come out to 26 cents per share, but by the end of 1977, with negotiated rates, it was 12 cents. After 1975, if you wanted to make money, you had to hustle. Fortunately, Doreen loved to hustle. Despite what her stepfather said, she had in fact arrived at just the right time.

No one loved a trading floor quite like Doreen. Her father had died when she was seven, and her mother had then married William Earle, who worked on the Amex. Trying to bond with his new step-daughter, he taught Doreen the Amex sign language for trades, practicing with her at the dinner table. The American Stock Exchange, originally known as the New York Curb Exchange, had started out at some point in the 1800s—no one is exactly sure when—and eventually clustered around Broad Street. According to one account, curb brokers blocked traffic and when cars attempted to pass, "husky traders occasionally applied their brawn to front bumpers and sent them rolling backward." To communicate orders with the clerks up in their offices hanging out the windows (it was not unheard of for a clerk to fall out if overly excited), the traders down on the street, who wore hats in various colors so clerks could recognize them, created a sign language unique to the Amex.

Doreen learned to spell out stock names with her hands, and she memorized the slew of special hand gestures to indicate whether to sell, buy, hold, at what price, and how much. Even as the Amex went indoors to 86 Trinity Place in 1921, some curbside trading continued until well into the 1950s. But even inside the Amex Building, tiered booths ringed the trading floor and hand signals remained in use: there was no time to leave your booth and make your way down to the floor to find your broker and tell him what order had just come in. It was much faster to stand up, shout for him, and then lift your hands and start to signal. The faster your hands moved, the faster you made your trade. Seconds counted.

When her stepfather was made a partner at W. E. Hutton & Co., Doreen's family had moved to Scarborough in Westchester, to a large house where he would often host his Wall Street colleagues. But in 1972, the fun had abruptly ended. The back-office paper debacle had hit the firm hard. At W. E. Hutton, a back-office employee had not been filing the stock order tickets. He had been hiding them, stuffing them into a drawer, which meant those orders were never officially executed, even as the clients thought they had been. There was a name for this: "fail to deliver." W. E. Hutton & Co., of which William Earle was a senior partner, owed the money their clients would have made. As a private firm, the partners, Doreen's stepfather included, carried the liability. The family went bankrupt. Sotheby's arrived and carted off their furniture for auction. The house went next. They moved to a three-room apartment in Ossining, New York, a town perhaps best known for its maximum-security prison, Sing Sing. Doreen slept on the sofa.

She was glad she had by then started college and at least didn't have to face the humiliation of living through this as a high school student. While many of her friends were attending Katharine Gibbs, the famous secretarial school, she was hoping for a college degree and then a job in retail, possibly as a department-store buyer. But that came to an end when her stepfather broke the news; there was no more money for college. Instead, she had to get out there and earn a living. He found her a job on the Amex floor as a clerk for the new firm at which he was working.

The locker room was the first stop at the Amex, lined with cubbyholes "into which traders and other floor personnel stuff their hard-soled Florsheims and Bally street shoes, to slip into soft-bottomed trading shoes." The Amex trading floor was an enormous square, each side approximately 150 feet long, with "twenty octagonal trading posts" out on the floor and "three tiers of booths" ascending "bleacherlike along three sides of the floor," where the clerks, including Doreen, sat.

Doreen had not put much thought to the fact that she was stepping into a man's world. The American Stock Exchange was for her like home, a place of comfort. It was where her mother and she, back when they still had the grand house, would meet her stepfather after work; it was where she would come visit on a day off from school; it was where she would take her friends to show off what her stepfather did for a living. Men might be everywhere, but she knew some of them from when they used to visit the house in Scarborough. There was only one other female wire clerk, Maureen Cunningham, who took Doreen under her wing.

Doreen was petite yet her voice was piercing, and a female voice was so unexpected that when Doreen shouted for a broker from her tiered post above the floor, the sound easily traveled to the other end of the room. Her job was to take down the orders that were phoned into the booth, and then relay them to a broker out on the floor. She would stand up, holler the broker's name, and once she had their attention, her hands would start to fly. Most often she shouted out for her stepfather, but if he was busy on other orders, Doreen would use one of the two-dollar brokers to execute the order.

That first day, Mayday, her stepfather told her that she must never wear pants to the Amex; only a skirt or a dress were appropriate. Later she would switch over to suits, just as *Dress for Success* suggested, with a jacket, a skirt, and a blouse of a different color, but this was still the era of carbon paper copies, which came off the teletype machines and turned your fingertips black. God forbid you ever touched your face. Almost everyone found it easier to change into a set of old clothes as soon as they got to work—seen-better-days suit jackets, old green sports jackets, frayed golf jackets. Later, everyone would come around to wearing a "smock," a loose-fitting jacket in the team colors of one's firm, with pockets for the essentials, most importantly the pencil and paper that were the tools of the trade. Doreen accessorized with bright-red nails, and if she wanted to switch it up, she did a French manicure.

At most, there were twenty women on the floor of the Amex; a few clerks, a few runners, but all support staff, and most of them teletype operators. Doreen secretly hoped to be the first female floor broker but Lynne Greenberg would beat her to it, buying a membership for $52,000 in 1977, at the age of twenty-one, with the help of her father, Alan "Ace" Greenberg, soon to be CEO of Bear Stearns. When Doreen arrived on the Amex floor in 1975, Lynne Greenberg was still in college, and had started dating her brother's math tutor, the notorious late Jeffrey Epstein, then a teacher at Dalton, a prestigious New York City private school. Ace Greenberg took a shine to him, seeing in Epstein what he always said were the most important qualifications for Wall Street—not an MBA (he hated those) but a "PSD" (poor, smart, and desperate [to be rich]). He gave Epstein his first job in finance.

Doreen was still living at home, and it was becoming overwhelming. Her stepfather had been a captain in the Army Corps of Engineers, and now that Doreen was on the Amex floor with him, commuting to Wall Street with him, living under the same roof with him, he trained her 24/7. He quizzed her nonstop on the various stock symbols and made her practice her hand signals daily, starting at 4 a.m., when he quizzed her during the one-hour drive into the city.

Arriving at 5 a.m. on Wall Street, Doreen would have breakfast at Harry's, in the basement of India House on Hanover Square, with her stepfather and other brokers. Opened in 1972 by the Poulakakos husband-and-wife team, Harry's doors were open only Monday through Friday, like the market. Surrounded by all the major Wall Street firms, Harry's served eight hundred lunches a day; the larger brokerage houses even had private lines connected to a bank of telephones that lined the wall of the restaurant's enormous bar room.

Long before the opening bell—a small hammer against a gong at 10 a.m.—Doreen had to ensure the firm could start the day with a clean slate. After she'd finished her breakfast, she headed upstairs to the Amex, 6 a.m. at the very latest, where the clerks gathered in a room to sort out the mismatches recorded on the out sheets delivered from the back office that morning (the mismatches were called DK's, don't knows, on the Amex; and QT's, questionable trades, on the NYSE).

On the way back home, her stepfather would again grill her. Once home, he did not think twice about picking up a telephone extension in another room and blasting orders at Doreen to see how fast she could write them down and how accurate she could be. *It was time to move out.*

Doreen found an apartment in the oddly named West New York, New Jersey, which sits on the Hudson River right across from the 79th Street Boat Basin in Manhattan. She had a car—she drove through the Holland Tunnel to get to Wall Street each day—a studio apartment, a weekly salary of $120, and a monthly rent of $150. Her best friend lived in Jersey City, and many a night, they met up at the Irish pub Narrowbacks. Having untethered herself from her stepfather, she went a step further and left his firm to go work for Robert "Bobby" Galardi, one of the two-dollar brokers, as a clerk in his booth. Bobby was as fast with the signals as Doreen, and their hands flying, they covered the buying and selling for various firms that phoned in, needing quick representation on the floor.

It was hard not to take notice of Doreen: she was hustling. Great clerks were like gold. Only a year into her stint with Bobby Galardi, brokers working for investor and arbitrageur Ivan Boesky approached her.

In 1975, the same year she had started on the Amex floor, Boesky had founded his brokerage firm, Ivan F. Boesky & Company, with a start-up fund of $700,000 (around $4 million today) from his wife's family, who owned the Beverly Hills Hotel. The son of Russian immigrants, an outsider, not particularly talented as a student, never having stood out at the various Wall Street firms where he'd worked, he'd decided to open his own firm, which quickly became an enormous success.

Boesky's particular specialty was risk arbitrage, which, in its simplest form, meant betting on whether a merger would go through or not. When buyouts were publicly announced, the target company stock would move closer to the deal price but there was always a gap that reflected the uncertainty of whether the deal would in fact go through. A superstar arbitrageur like Boesky had to act quickly to size up the risk that the offer would be rejected or rescinded. It meant anticipating the news of mergers before the public announcement, a murky area in securities law and one that required delicate, discreet trading to avoid other traders suspecting something was brewing.

Boesky was famous for working with a 300-line telephone bank (used to call multiple investment bankers, trying to confirm or deny rumors of deals), barely sleeping, and subsisting largely on coffee. To be talent-spotted by Boesky's people meant something. Doreen was brought in for a series of interviews, the final one with Boesky himself. She found him to be "an extremely, extremely nice man." He would be, according to Doreen, "the best boss a person could have." If you did your job right, she noted, you became part of the close-knit Boesky team.

From the moment she started as a clerk for Ivan F. Boesky & Company, Doreen made it clear to him and anyone else who would listen that she did not plan to remain a clerk. She planned to be a floor broker.

Boesky listened. When the New York Stock Exchange opened the New York Futures Exchange, hoping to compete with the dominant

futures exchange in Chicago, Boesky decided to open a floor operation there. He bought a seat, offered it to Doreen, and then sent her to
Chicago to train for a month, where she worked as a runner for men
trading bonds and bills on the floor of the Chicago Board of Trade.

It was a total culture shock; the Chicago futures exchange was
like a commodity exchange, with a pit and ring, and it was bedlam,
or at least that's how it felt to Doreen. There was paper everywhere,
tossed on the floor all day long until the place looked like a trash
heap that you'd have to wade through. Half the time, when someone
handed her an order, it fell to the floor, and she'd have to get down on
all fours to find it amidst all the other bits of strewn paper.

The pit and ring of commodity trading was especially difficult
for women, in part because it was so brutally physical, with tightly
packed "rings" "where traders cluster[ed] six and eight deep to shout
out bids." Being physically "pummeled" was nothing out of the ordinary. Athletes—basketball, football, hockey players—were intentionally hired because they were comfortable using their size and
strength to make themselves stand out in the crowd and be heard. In
1977, Sherry Collins had been trading potatoes on the floor of the
New York Mercantile Exchange for just a short while when her boss
asked if she'd like to be the first woman to trade coffee. To test the
waters, she went to speak to a trader at the Coffee, Sugar & Cocoa
Exchange, who told her it was a great idea because "I can't wait. I'll
rip you up." She decided against it. When Kazia Sperling, two years
later, in 1979, took on the challenge of coffee trading at forty years
old, not only did she get the usual taunts ("You're in a man's world—
take it like a man") but the men would pretend not to hear her bids,
which was even worse. She was having none of it, however, and even
men in the sugar trading ring would sometimes stop their jostling to
watch her lash out at the coffee ring, demanding to be heard.

With the month of training in Chicago over, Doreen returned to
New York as Boesky's futures trader. She was just twenty-four years

old and trading T-bonds, T-bills, and currencies. It gave her a chance
to strut her stuff, and a year later, Ivan Boesky moved her over to the
NYSE as a floor broker for his firm. She had not managed to become
the first female broker on the Amex, but she was among the first on
the New York Stock Exchange. Alice Jarcho had just left the NYSE,
but between Alice's arrival there in 1976 and Doreen's in 1980, some
more women had found a way in.

On her first day at the NYSE, Doreen carried a copy of the floor
map so that when someone said, "Get me a quote on IBM," she
wouldn't have to think, "Where the hell is IBM?" The only way to
move quickly was to memorize the layout, where each specialist post
was, and which stocks were being traded where. The NYSE itself was
composed of three rooms: the original room at 11 Wall Street, known
as the Main Room; the Garage, a second room that functioned as
an extension; and the Extended Blue Room (the EBR), located in an
adjoining building—although if you didn't know this, it was impossible to tell. Still, no one relished the idea of having to hike all the
way out to the EBR.

Doreen loved the physicality of the trading floor, and the way
in which every day was different, but there was no denying that the
power of her position was exciting too. Wall Street was still centered physically and symbolically on the floor of the New York Stock
Exchange. That power had not quite yet shifted, as it would start
to in the 1980s, to the raucous trading rooms inside Wall Street's
brokerage houses and investment banks. For now, the action was
still here.

These days, you could even catch sight of Mickie Siebert on the
floor, deep in conversation, wearing her favorite multicolored patch-
work fur jacket. She was there not as a trader but as the Superinten-
dent of Banks. In 1977, New York's Democratic governor, feeling
pressure to appoint a woman to the job, had offered her the post
even though Siebert was a Republican (a fiscally conservative one, but

Muriel Siebert and Donald Stott on the NYSE floor during her tenure as New York Superintendant of Banks, 1977–1982.

very much a liberal when it came to social issues and human rights). During his search for a candidate, Mickie's name kept coming up, over and over. To accept the job, she grudgingly put on hold her most recent hobby: solo flying. But it was worth it. Speaking at a conference for women in business, she would say: "It gives me great pleasure that I now regulate the bank that refused my loan application."

Doreen was not nearly as alone on the NYSE floor as Alice had been. There were now a few other female brokers alongside her—out of 1,366 members and around 2,000 support staff. But it still could get lonely. She didn't like the slow moments; you could choose not to see, not to hear certain things, when the pace was fast, when you were hustling, but it was more difficult to shut out the remarks or cold shoulders or worse in the moments of quiet. She'd gotten used to most of it, but what really got to her, just as it had gotten to Alice, were the men who refused to do business with her. They told her outright that they were not going to work with a woman, as if they had nothing to be ashamed of as long as they confessed to their prejudice. It was these men that ensured, through their actions—or inaction, that Doreen was never playing on a level field, not even when she was the hotshot Boesky broker.

Ivan Boesky eventually bought Doreen her very own NYSE seat. On Christmas Eve 1980, a message was relayed down to her that she should come up to sign the book after the closing bell. The swearing-in ceremony was a time-honored ritual; Doreen would be signing the leatherbound membership book that went back to the very start of the NYSE, its constitution penned just a few years after the American Constitution. She was going to add her signature to the same book as the Gilded Age railroad magnate Jay Gould, and "Black Jack" Bouvier, Jackie Kennedy's father.

She called her husband—Doreen had finally become a "first" when she married Achille Mogavero, another NYSE floor broker, becoming the first married couple to work on the floor—but he said he was too busy. She called her stepfather, but he also couldn't get over there. She finally called Kathy, her best friend in Jersey City.

"I'll be right there!"

Kathy arrived with flowers, and out came the venerable membership book, stashed in the closet, and Doreen signed. Kathy headed home right after, and when Doreen's husband later saw the flowers, he asked where she got them.

"Oh, that was nice," he said.

———

TWO YEARS LATER, LOUISE JONES, ONLY A HIGH SCHOOL JUNIOR, walked out onto the floor of the New York Stock Exchange for the very first time. It was a revelation for her: "I felt like I could breathe." To be somewhere that felt right, where she could breathe, was not something Louise took lightly. She did not know (still does not: "I can't even get a proper astrology reading!") which day she was born, and had settled on July 17, 1965, because that was the day she was found, a newborn abandoned in a telephone booth on the corner of Columbus Avenue and West Eighty-Eighth Street in Manhattan.

Discovered by a Pedro Martinez, Louise was lying there wrapped in a white blanket with a Saint Jude medal pinned to it, wearing a cloth diaper and rubber leakproof underpants. Pedro Martinez picked her up and carried her to the nearest police station. From there, she was moved to the Metropolitan Hospital in East Harlem, where she remained for three months while the authorities waited to see if someone would come forward. No one did. Her next stop was the New York Foundling Hospital, followed by a foster home on Staten Island where most of the kids brought in were Hispanic, picked up again by their parents once the family's luck had improved.

Three years later, now a toddler, her case was finally closed, her biological mother never found, and Louise was put up for adoption. The foster couple, a cement mixer originally from Virginia and an off-the-boat Italian woman from Naples, had first dibs on Louise, but they said no. Fostering children brought money into the household, and an adoption would mean the opposite, they feared. But a nun at the Foundling Hospital assured them there would be monthly subsidies and clothing allowances. They finally agreed to keep Louise, and she became an official permanent resident of the Stapleton housing project on Staten Island, oblivious to ever having been adopted (although she would soon wonder why she was the only one with blue eyes and blond hair).

Her adoptive mother spoke broken English, and so everything was *the thing*: "put the thing in the thing with the thing." When Louise turned ten, they moved out of the projects—technically. Her parents bought the only house they could afford, right between two projects, the Stapleton Houses and the Park Hill Apartments. It was

like living in "a parallel reality." During the day it was a typical suburban street with kids out playing, but at night bullets whizzed by,
fired off by rival gangs in the projects on either side.

Louise loved the other foster kids who'd arrive at the house, and
by the time she left home, she saw herself as the sister to about forty
New York–based Hispanic siblings. (Years later, walking with friends
near Hell's Kitchen, they turned a corner to find five men shooting
the breeze. Louise could feel her friends tense up, and she decided to
have some fun with it. "Yo, you mother fucka!" she started hollering.
Her friends, alarmed, tried to shush her, and the men glared at her,
until one of them broke free and ran at her, laughing hard. It was
her brother John, a Puerto Rican "no holds barred" mixed martial
arts fighter.)

Even as a child, Louise had unstoppable drive. She took on three
paper routes and hired kids on the block to deliver on her behalf. She
was always washing cars, mowing lawns, flogging things at flea markets, and making sandwiches at the deli. Snow was like falling dollar
signs to her. She didn't even have a proper snow shovel; she used a
regular, giant, impossibly heavy metal shovel for snow removal. The
mania for working wasn't about the money, it was about independence, it was about a sense of self-worth, it was about momentum.
She felt like she had uncovered some hidden secret: she could make
money, put it in the bank, and watch it grow.

In tenth grade at Curtis High School, Louise enrolled in a program in which students alternated one week of school with one week
of work experience. The program sent students into Manhattan to
interview for jobs, and Louise started working alongside her sister-in-
law April in the typing pool of a life-insurance company, First Investors. The pace was intense because suddenly so many young men's
annuities and life insurance policies were being cashed in. Policy after
policy, Louise found herself typing out: male, 28, dead, complica-
tions, GRID. "I kept saying to the boss, what is GRID?" GRID stood

for gay-related immune deficiency. AIDS—as it was renamed by the Centers for Disease Control in 1982—was hitting New York hard.

A year later, April took a job at the New York Stock Exchange as a teletype operator, and once again pulled Louise along with her.

"Weez," she whispered into the phone to Louise during a break, "there's an opening at the stock exchange. Tell the school!"

The job was for a teletype operator for Pershing Donaldson, a division of DLJ, and it paid a lot more than the typing pool at First Investors. Louise got the job and the next week, when she walked onto the trading floor, she looked around and thought to herself: "*I'm going to make so much money here!*"

If the pace of the typing pool was exhilarating, this was like a roller coaster on continuous loop. "People were screaming, papers were flying," and Louise was in her "glory." She was shown to her "rickety old wooden booth" in the Blue Room, with stools that pulled out although you never had time to sit. Recently, the old specialist posts had been updated, adding millions of dollars' worth of electronic equipment to speed up trading, as well as small overhanging TV sets to broadcast financial news, but the booths, vintage 1930s, had remained untouched. Phones were everywhere, and in the very back of each booth a terminal, with stock quotes on its screen, so you didn't have to always look up at the ticker tape, as well as an input data station—the pneumatic tubes had been retired—where Louise would type in the information the brokers bought back to the booth: 10k General Motors for 45 and 1/4, from Goldman badge #27. On the other end, in another booth, Goldman's teletype operator was doing the same. If they didn't match, the ticket got kicked out and became a QT—a questionable trade. That was the NYSE's matching system. The system was archaic, quaint even, but it worked, especially if, like Louise, you were good at numbers and had an elephant's memory for them.

She was in week two when she discovered that the hardest thing

about the job was deciphering everyone's awful handwriting. Louise
was squinting at one particular ticket, trying to make out the stock
symbol, but it was impossible to read. She could, however, read the
price, and so she punched those numbers into the Quotron to figure out which stocks were going at that price—a simple process of
elimination working backwards. She was a perfectionist who wanted
nothing to do with the Questionable Trade room.

One of the head brokers for Pershing Donaldson saw her punching in the price and suddenly started yelling. It was Achille "Arcky"
Mogavero, Doreen's husband, notorious for screaming at everyone, always, perpetually furious with the underlings. "What are
you doing?!"

Louise looked up. "I can't read the symbol. I'm just checking
the price."

A beat passed and then he turned to everyone in the Pershing
booth and started screaming more: "You see how effing stupid you
are! You've never once looked at the Quotron!"

He calmed down for a moment and then turned back to her.
"What's your name?"

"Louise Jones."

"You're going places!"

Louise grabbed that small moment in the spotlight to jumpstart
her career on the floor. After that, every week without fail, she went
up to Arcky and asked to be promoted to clerk. To be a telephone
clerk was the next step up after teletype operator: it would mean picking up the phones, taking the orders to buy and sell. Each time, every
time, Arcky Mogavero turned her down. Pershing had booths all over
the floor, among the various rooms, because if something were happening to a stock, if there was breaking news that was going to affect
its price, and the specialist post—the only physical space where you
could trade that particular stock—was two rooms away, there was
no time to fast-walk the distance and make it there among the first

arrivals. And so Louise started to circulate, doing the rounds, visiting one Pershing booth after another, meeting the brokers at each, and asking if there was a clerk position available. Louise was seventeen years old, and she didn't care that all she received was a string of no's.

When she finally heard about a position at Charles Schwab for a hybrid typist-clerk, she sought out Miriam Weinberg Buraccio, a Schwab floor broker. Even as hundreds of people were milling around, Louise stopped her in the middle of the floor: "I heard you're looking for a clerk typist? I'd really like to apply."

"Can you type?"

"Yeah."

"You've got the job."

(Years later, Miriam would tell Louise it was impossible not to give her the job, this "adorable, wide-eyed" teenager in an orange shirt that made her stand out like a traffic cone.)

Her new job, she told anyone who would listen, was "fucking great" because she was now on the phone with the traders upstairs on the Charles Schwab trading desk, who were yelling at her all day, and she couldn't get enough of it: she "loved it." Nothing this cool had ever happened to her. She could only think: "*When I start screaming at people, then I know what I'm talking about.*" At one point, she was even sent out to San Francisco, where she met "Chuck" Schwab, who was like a guru to her, and she swore she could hear music in her head as she sat in his presence.

The booth next to her Schwab booth had a "crazy, older guy," a floor trader in his late forties, who had bought his own seat and ran his own show. But he did it without the help of a clerk, which meant he'd charge into his booth to pick up his own phone, take down the order, and then charge out again to make the trade. His name was Mike Cassidy, and Louise started picking up his phone when it rang and he was out in the crowd trading. She was picking up his phone so often—pork-chopping is what they called it on the floor for reasons no one could remember—that she started to have a rapport with those who regularly phoned Cassidy. There was one guy especially who called each morning and gave Cassidy "the same stupid order." "Sell 1k of Permian Basin [Royalty] Trust at 6 and 1/8."

That really got her goat. The price he gave was nowhere near market price, which was 5 and 1/2; it wasn't even in the range. The trade could never get executed, and Cassidy would never get paid, but he was being sent out there to try. One day, picking up the phone, hearing the same order, Louise had had enough: "Why do you always give him this shitty order? Why don't you give him a real order? He's busting his ass, he's running back and forth," she said.

One morning, in early at 7 a.m. as she always was, even as the market didn't open until 9:30 a.m., as she was reading the newspapers to stay ahead of the market, the phone rang in Cassidy's booth. It was that guy again.

"What are you doing in so early?" he asked Louise.

"I'm trying to get you to give this man a nice order," she said without skipping a beat.

He laughed. "OK, fine, sell 50k of Permian Basin at 6 and 1/8."

This was a real order. It wasn't in the price range, but it was the size that counted. It showed liquidity, meaning there could be enough stock circulating to create a market. Maybe there was a buyer out there who wanted a big chunk of Permian Basin and was willing to pay for it?

"Now you're talking!" she said, writing down the order.

When Mike Cassidy walked in, Louise handed it to him. "What's this?" he asked, looking at it in disbelief. "Why did he give you a fifty-thousand-share order?!"

"Because I've been busting his balls for weeks."

Mike picked up the phone and called to check it was real. Not only was it real, but suddenly it was moving. Even as Louise was manning the Charles Schwab phones, and passing on the trades coming in, she was in the thick of it with Cassidy, who had shown his cards to buyers, revealing he had lots to sell, and the 50k was snatched up at 6 and 1/8.

Was there more? they wanted to know.

Yes. There was a customer with a lot to sell and a buyer who was buying, and when it was all over the 50k order had turned into a 250k order. It was one of the biggest orders that Mike Cassidy had ever had.

Soon after, Cassidy was flying out to Texas to try to land an account that he'd been after for a while. "If I get this, I'll need a full-time clerk, just keep it in mind," he said to Louise as he was leaving.

But a day or two later, a fast-paced arbitrage firm run by Johnny French out of the same booth offered her a job at $75k a year—in 1985. Louise was twenty years old. To clerk for an arbitrage house, you had to be on your toes, sharper than most. "Wow, that's really good," Louise said, "but, you know, Cassidy wants to offer me a job . . ."

"Look, I'm offering you a job now. Are you in or not?" Johnny French insisted.

"I'm in."

10

Power Play

Barbara Moakler was sitting in her political science class at Mount Holyoke College when the word "elite" came up. She had never heard it before. She asked, mispronouncing it: "What's an eee-light?" It turned out to be a useful word to have as she, a working-class "townie" dressed in "corduroy slacks" and "a green-and-white striped button-down shirt," washed dishes in the dining hall to help cover her tuition.

In her senior year, the Mobil Corporation offered Barbara a place in their training program—the first ever undergraduate hire—which included the promise to cover tuition for an MBA at New York University's business school. Barbara was put on the fast track at Mobil, but as she socialized on weekends at the city's various college clubs, she realized the action was shifting to Wall Street, and to investment banking especially. Ronald Reagan was not yet president, but he'd just been elected, and late 1980, Barbara lined up interviews not knowing—no one really knew—that this was the very moment that Wall Street would truly take off.

Interviewing at Salomon Brothers, Drexel Burnham, Lehman

Brothers Kuhn Loeb (following a 1977 merger), all the big ones, Barbara did not fit the usual profile for their first-year program. Investment banks had for a while now hired recent MBA graduates as "associates," and evaluated each year's new "class" in terms of how they performed in comparison with one another—the best could then begin to climb the ladder. Typically, the first-year associates at these top Wall Street firms almost all came from the same five or six business schools. Barbara had an MBA—well, almost, she was two courses shy of one after four years of taking night classes—but from New York University, which, if she were being honest, was "a journeyman's school." It was where the ambitious secretaries and trading assistants went to work their way up.

At Lehman, a small group of partners sat around a table to interview her, but it felt more like an interrogation

"Who are you? Who's your father?"

She answered that her father was a mailman who'd died when she was seven.

They kept firing questions at her, trying to place her within a schema that they understood. But she had one thing going for her even as her background was lacking: four years at the Mobil Corporation, which effectively made her an energy expert.

For her final vetting, she was brought in to see William Morris, head of the investment banking division, who said to this twenty-six-year-old woman: "How much money do you think is a lot of money? . . . We're a little concerned. You're a young woman. We train people, they get married, they get pregnant, they leave."

He continued to needle her. (Only later did she learn that what he was doing was subjecting her to a so-called stress interview to see if she'd hold up.)

"How much money do you think is a lot of money? Because we have to work with people who understand the economics," he continued.

She looked at the framed photographs behind him and asked, "Mr. Morris, is that your home?"

He nodded.

"Well, I'd say whatever you're making would probably work for me," she replied.

He laughed.

She had passed.

Barbara was hired as a first-year associate in energy, natural resources, working on underwriting—debt underwriting, equity underwriting, mergers and acquisitions—for companies in gas, oil, and energy that needed to raise capital. It was November 1980, and blazers were de rigeur, blouses with ruffles down the front were the epitome of sophistication, and skirts now landed just below the knee. Just like in the film *9 to 5* that came out that year, the women who sported actress Lily Tomlin's layered hair, her fire-alarm lipstick and belted silk blouses, could sense something in the air. Change was afoot.

Jane Fonda, Lily Tomlin, and Dolly Parton on the set of the movie *9 to 5*, 1980.

Lehman Brothers Kuhn Loeb at the time had around 700 employees, most of them men, advising CEOs and CFOs on how to strategize and position themselves in the market. Barbara's first assignment was handed to her by managing partner and former CIA operative Henry Breck. He needed spreadsheets of comparable data and analysis for a coal company, Holland Carbon Fuels, about how much these companies traded for.

Acquiring such data today would take little time, but with no digitized databases or search engines, research was done the old-fashioned way; the kind of research one learned in college, where you had to hunt down information. All financial institutions had their own library, where records and data were stored, typed out on "Jacquard typewriters." But Henry Breck needed it the next day. He told Barbara there *was* a guy at another firm who already had the spreadsheets that Lehman needed, who had done the research, but there was no way to get hold of them.

If there was "an advantage to being female," Barbara sensed it was now: she called up the man, introduced herself, confessed she was a first-year associate who had literarily started her job the previous day, and also the one and only woman in the energy division at Lehman. She could do the spreadsheets, she told him, but she needed the data: would he know where to find it?

These were still the days when the Street was genuinely concentrated around the Wall Street area and to invite someone over meant only a three- or four-block walk at most. He offered that she come by. When she arrived, the man, much older than Barbara, handed her his spreadsheets. "Look, Barbara, this is market data," he said, playing it down. "You could pull it together, it'll take you a while, here's what you need . . . And tell him where you got them."

The next day Barbara Moakler arrived at work and handed over the spreadsheets. "Where did you get these?!" Breck asked in astonishment.

"I called him up . . . we had some coffee . . . and he gave them to me."

"Kid, you're going to make it! You figured out how to get the work done without actually doing the work!"

Unfortunately, getting the work done without putting in the hours proved to be illusory. During her first year as an associate, the workload was eighty to a hundred hours a week, which required working every single day, all-nighters the norm. She had to prove that she belonged. There were two other women who started with her, and with political correctness a long way off, "they would call you names," and nothing was considered out of bounds. The energy sector was "beyond macho," more so than investment banking generally, and everyone was of the same mind: Barbara Moakler couldn't hack it.

At the end of her first year, a well-known Lehman partner who hadn't thought she should be there in the first place because she hadn't entered the class through the usual channels of a prestigious B-school, started showing up with a little notebook to jot down observations. He was in charge of ranking the seven associates from Barbara's class of 1980. One by one they were brought in to hear where they stood. When it was Barbara's turn, she entered a room filled with cigar smoke, rings of pungent gray-blue emanating from the Lehman partner. Sitting beside him was Barbara's boss, who was clearly uncomfortable, leaning back in his chair, staring fixedly at the ceiling as he puffed on his own cigar. The partner opened the notebook and proceeded to break down her performance. He then announced her ranking: she had come seventh out of the seven associates.

"I don't understand," Barbara said. "You just told me that my work is considered to be technically quite good."

"Yes, but we just don't think you're very comfortable here."

"What do you mean?"

"We've noticed when you come in in the morning, you seem to be coming in with Bob, and then you're having lunch with Steve." *What did that mean? These were her classmates, her buddies.* "You're quiet," he went on. "You don't say very much, you're always taking notes . . . you don't seem to have a presence, you're more subdued. You do all the work, your work is excellent, everyone thinks your work is excellent. You're very good at numbers."

She felt like pointing out that she was also good at making coffee—which she was often asked to do, and which she did, because she wasn't going to fight every battle.

She looked at her boss, who was still leaning back, staring blankly, and asked, "Do you agree with this?!"

He murmured something unintelligible, taking another inhale of cigar smoke, still mesmerized by the ceiling.

Exasperated, Barbara asked: "So is there anything positive other than that I do great numbers and I'm quiet?"

He looked down at his notes. "People think you dress well. You're not wearing those bowties and masculine kind of clothes."

When she got home that night, she called her stepfather for advice. He told her to be herself, to go back in the next day and tell her boss that he should have stood by her.

So that's what she did. She asked her boss point-blank if he agreed with the assessment of her. "Do you really think I'm seventh out of seven?"

He parroted the company line: "I don't think you're comfortable here."

"I don't think you're comfortable with me being here," she replied. "Do you think this is fair? Do you think I'm being treated fairly?"

He finally shook his head. "I don't."

But they weren't wrong that she knew how to dress. When she received her first bonus, she went out and bought herself a mink coat in a white-amber shade. It was a showstopper even if "so ridiculously tacky." But she loved it. She arrived at the office with the coat draped over her shoulders, and immediately the questions started up from the men: "Where did you get it?"

"My boyfriend gave it to me," she said without skipping a beat. "He's a partner at Goldman Sachs."

Goldman Sachs was Lehman's archrival, and there was no boyfriend, and certainly not a Goldman Sachs boyfriend. But Barbara had them hooked now.

They wanted to know his name.

But she wasn't telling. No, she explained patiently, he did not want to put Barbara in an awkward position and because of that, it had to remain hush-hush.

"Oh, and by the way, we're going to Paris this weekend," she announced. "So I'm going to need Friday off. We're leaving Thursday."

There, she had said it, and now there was nothing to do but spend her sudden windfall of a long weekend lying on her couch in her studio apartment eating Häagen-Dazs ice-cream, the latest New York craze, and catching up on her favorite television show, *The Paper Chase*. (Never mind that John Houseman's starring character was modeled on Harvard law professor A. James Casner, who put aside only one day a year when he was willing to call on female students. He called it "Ladies' Day.")

But it wasn't just about gifting herself a long weekend, courtesy of her male colleagues' gullibility; it was about strategy. Everyone expected Barbara—young, good-looking, gregarious (despite the partner's claim that she was quiet and timid)—to leave Lehman sooner than later, to fall for the inevitable offer of a plush marriage, to abandon her nascent career for a wealthy man she would meet on Wall Street. And if that's what they thought, why not get the wheels turning in their heads? Why not have the men around her think twice about how they treated her? Because if there was a chance, even the slimmest of chances, that she might marry this mystery partner at Goldman Sachs, the man who was already gifting her mink coats and taking her to Paris for the weekend, there was also a chance that one day in the foreseeable future, one of these Lehman men would be sitting across from her Goldman Sachs husband, at a dinner party, or in a conference room, or playing doubles on the court, hoping to close a deal, and Barbara's husband might turn to him and say, *Explain to me why I would give you this deal after the way you treated my wife?*

She had just given herself not only a mink coat but a superpower.

Barbara understood it was a chess game; and that she had to think several moves ahead. It would have been easier to have left, to have stormed out after being placed seventh out of seven, but where would that have gotten her other than further away from money, and the power that came with it?

Moreover, invisible boyfriends were sometimes necessary on Wall Street for other reasons too. Carolyn "Cali" Cole, a Vassar College graduate, folk singer, and Janis Joplin groupie, had run out of money by 1966 and landed a job at Standard & Poor, the ratings firm for bonds and companies, before moving over to Paine Webber. Despite her hippie past, Cali eventually donned a quintessential WASP look with circle pins, expensive jewelry, and preppy clothes. But she was also gay, and had watched enough people be fired for their sexuality that she was not about to risk the same. It was much easier to say, when she was asked, that she didn't have a boyfriend at the time ("which is true"!). Others opted to have "boyfriends" who were conveniently out of town, traveling for work.

AROUND THE TIME THAT BARBARA BOUGHT HERSELF THE WHITE-amber mink coat, Marianne Spraggins had decided that she, too, needed to be on Wall Street. The daughter of a prominent lawyer and activist in New York, Marianne had grown up in a historic Harlem brownstone once owned by the wealthy, well-connected racketeer Madame St. Clair. Marianne had been adventurous in her twenties, marrying a jazz musician and moving to Los Angeles, working as an airline stewardess and then on the NBC television shows *Speaking Freely* and *Positively Black*. After her adored father died in 1971, she decided to honor him by becoming a third-generation Spraggins lawyer.

Marianne now had a law degree from New York Law School, an additional LLM degree in international law from Harvard Law, and was an associate professor at New York Law School—she did not need Wall Street. Yet she could not forget a seminar she'd taken on international business transactions, taught by Nicholas Deak, "a very suave . . . mysterious" Transylvanian-born American Hungarian who would arrive for class in a different vintage car each time, his chauffeur behind the wheel. When she learned that Deak owned a Swiss bank, as well as the New York financial group Deak-Perera, she practically swooned. (Deak had in fact worked as an operative for the OSS, the precursor to the CIA, during World War II, and just five years after Marianne's seminar, his firm would be accused of laundering money for Latin American drug traffickers. Soon after, Deak was shot dead alongside his receptionist by a homeless woman in a suspected assassination.)

Marianne, already attuned to the finer things in life because her father had believed giving her luxury as a child would ensure she'd work hard to keep it within reach as an adult, immediately understood that Deak represented a level of power she had not yet experienced. Growing up, she had "understood political power from this Harlem vantage point of getting people in jobs and knowing city hall and getting people in judgeships. But I always knew there was something more. And when I took that course, and we went down into those bowels of Wall Street, I didn't know what they did, but there was a different energy, and just a, kind of like a veil being lifted for me. I didn't know what it was, but I knew it was really important and it was kind of a magnet." She realized that *this* "was the real seat of power."

The money was certainly an allure for Marianne, "but that wasn't the driving force." Instead, it was the dawning recognition that Wall Street represented power and "knowing that this is a table that we did not sit at. And that we had to." And so she set her sights on Wall Street, to be one of the first Black women to sit at the table with a full place setting in front of her. But it was one thing to decide to go to Wall Street and quite another to figure out how to get there, or even figure out what Wall Street was. She had heard of Merrill Lynch and the term "bull market," but that was the sum of it. Marianne took to calling herself an Alice in Wonderland because she was about to fall down a rabbit hole and had no idea what she'd find at the other end.

Looking for a way in, Marianne was introduced to Russell L. Goings Jr., the founder of one of the first Black brokerage firms, First Harlem Securities Corporation, on 125th Street. Goings had started out as a shoeshine boy at a brokerage house. A former professional football player with an intellectual bent, he warned her that Wall Street was rough, "brutal for Black people," and told her the story of when he and a friend were invited to someone's mansion in Connecticut, where fancy food they'd never seen was being served on trays, including what must have seemed very sophisticated then, the mini Babybel red-wax-covered rounds of bite-sized cheese. His friend reached for one, not knowing what it was, and popped it in his mouth, including the indigestible fire-engine-red wax.

But Russell L. Goings did not put Marianne off. "I called up every single black person on the Street at firms and said, 'Hi, I'm Marianne Spraggins, let's get together.'" Few of them were willing to meet with her, and she should have understood right then that the game of survival on Wall Street was so cutthroat that the ideas of kinship to which she was accustomed might be meaningless there. But she did manage to rustle up some meetings, and slowly started to figure out who was who, what each firm did, who their clientele was, what part

of the financial world they represented, and what you were expected
to do once you entered their world.

The journalist and civil rights activist Evelyn Cunningham introduced her to a friend at JP Morgan with whom she was serving on a
board. As they had dinner, making small talk, Marianne asked: "Oh,
how long have you been there at JP Morgan?"

He looked at her and replied with all seriousness: "Seven years
of four generations."

She was starting to get a sense of what she might be up against.

She was still searching for a way in when she happened to arrive
at a friend's housewarming party and saw her friend's boyfriend
standing there, looking, to Marianne's eyes, "very bankerly," in a
pinstriped suit and a shirt with a white collar.

He noticed Marianne too: "You know, I know you."

"You do?"

"You get off the train at Franklin Street. I see you in the morning."

The stop after Franklin was Wall Street—and, indeed, it turned
out he worked for Salomon Brothers.

She got right to the point; she wanted to get onto Wall Street.
Could he help?

The next day he called her: "Can you get me your résumé?"

He managed to get her an interview but warned her not to get her
hopes up: Salomon Brothers were putting together a "class" of incoming analysts (the analysts program worked much like the associates
program, except it was targeted at recent college graduates instead
of B-school graduates). That was the good news. The bad news was
that they'd already picked four Black people for it—two men and two
women—and this was itself revolutionary. It was hard to imagine
they'd bring in a fifth Black analyst. To complicate things, Marianne
was not a recent college graduate but a law professor.

On Monday, she arrived at her interview on the forty-second floor
of Salomon Brothers, all rich wood paneling and Persian rugs. (Years

later she would call it the "false front.") The imposing reception area was filled with paintings and art objects, and the interview room with white men. While she'd sat waiting to be called in, she'd observed the other interviewees and was unimpressed. "Average," she thought to herself. "They were average." When it was her turn, she went in, determined to act herself because she needed to be sure she'd fit in.

It worked. She got a callback for a second interview, this one held in a large meeting room that overlooked the trading floor. Marianne decided to take the lead. She walked in first, chose where to sit, and followed the same advice that she gave her students at NYLS: "If you believe you are excellent . . . the world will be persuaded to accept your view of yourself." But part of her confidence stemmed from her ignorance: it was all still a game to her—she still "had no idea what they did" on Wall Street. When she was asked what she wanted, she didn't say money or power, she said: "I don't see anyone here who looks like me and I want to be here for that reason." On Friday, they told her she had a spot in the training program. She had found a seat at the table.

Each analyst class started off with basic training: one week they learned about treasuries, another week about securities. Half the time Marianne had no idea what they were talking about, but she had faith in what she'd learned at law school; if push came to shove, she could always lock herself in a room, read everything she needed to on a given subject, and figure it out. Department heads arrived to give lectures about their specific financial sectors with a binder tucked under their arms with each analyst's profile, including background and photograph. As far as Marianne could see, these weren't so much training sessions as they were "beauty contests," a chance for department heads to come and have a look-see and decide who they wanted to snatch up for themselves.

Who did they want? The pressure to conform was intense. One

of the other two Black women had arrived sporting an Afro and a hippie vest. Within a week she had entirely changed her appearance, her clothes, and her persona. Women especially, Marianne noticed, felt the pressure to blend in, to show up wearing a pinstriped lady-suit and a "little yellow tie thing." But Marianne was having none of that. She told the woman there was no point in trying to blend in; that for Black women, blending in wasn't even a possibility, and so why pretend? A Black woman needed her clothing to say: "So this is who I am, and this is who I'm going to be here." For Marianne, that meant a blazing red suit and high heels.

As the weeks passed, department heads stopped by to recruit their top picks. The white men were the first to be hired into a department. Most of them had arrived knowing someone and had all along planned to join their friend's department at "Solly." Among the five Black trainees, one of the women was immediately shipped off to a branch office. No way was Marianne going to be removed from New York, where the action was. One of the two Black men had barely spoken to the other four African Americans in the class; he had a plan just like his white counterparts, and he, too, was placed quickly. Now there were three Black trainees left, and time was ticking. The remaining man, who had a military demeanor and might have gone to West Point, suddenly vanished and Marianne heard he'd been found dead in Central Park.

Now there were two. Two Black women—Marianne Spraggins and a super-smart math major, who was not from New York. No one invited either of them to join a department at Solly. With nothing to do, they languished. They watched and rewatched the training tapes. During a twelve-day subway strike in April 1980, the two of them had to take cabs to and from work, all paid for by Salomon Brothers, only to do nothing once they arrived at the office. They attended social events where they were asked what they did at the much-revered firm. The power of their imaginations was tested; they had to pretend they were doing something, they couldn't say, *We sit and stare at the wall all day.*

The holding pattern was awkward, excruciating, deeply humiliating. It was like a nightmare version of being the last to be picked for a team in middle school. They had nothing to do. No one spoke to them. They were like pariahs. An Irish security guard would stop by Marianne's desk and ask how she was doing. *Not well.* She felt "like Hester Prynne with her scarlet letter." Worse, it was almost time for the next class of trainees to arrive, to assume their place in the lecture rooms. The other Black woman in the meantime had started to date a white man at the firm, not a partner but someone high up in the pecking order. It was "a fatal error," in Marianne's assessment. Sure enough, she disappeared all of a sudden, presumably removed by either the Salomon partners or an angry spouse, and Marianne heard the men calling out to one another, laughing: "Guess who's gone?!"

Now it was just Marianne.

One thing she knew for certain; she had to keep her game face on no matter what she felt inside. Much of the time she was doing what she could just to hold back the tears: to show any vulnerability, any pain, was out of the question. How did she go from being a law professor to this? She never told her family what was going on; she didn't want them to make it worse by asking her if she was OK, like the Irish security guard did daily whether out of genuine concern or some perverse delight.

One day she was walking down a long hallway when she heard a wolf whistle. Not thinking it was for her, she kept walking. When she realized that the wolf-whistler was coming up behind her, she did not flinch. She was a New Yorker—a young, very good-looking one, a woman who had heard her fair share of whistles. It was a guy from her analyst "class."

"Marianne, I can't believe you didn't turn around!"

Without breaking her stride, without even turning her head, side-eye only, she said: "No. And I won't until your name gets to be John Gutfreund." *Take* that *back to Gutfreund*, she thought to herself, let the Salomon Brothers CEO know that she was still there.

But there was another time when it was much harder to keep her composure, when the humiliation cut her to the core. Because she had nothing to do, and everyone knew it, sometimes she was sent out onto the trading floor—a place populated, to her mind, by "uncouth, ill-bred, uneducated people making boohoo money"—to get a quote. The traders would make the women (and anyone else they wanted to torment) stand there for fifteen, twenty minutes before they even acknowledged them. She was on the floor being yelled at by one of the traders after having already done her time waiting for his attention when suddenly she heard: "Oh, Professor Spraggins!"

Marianne turned around. Standing there was one of her former law students, who turned out to be the sister-in-law of one of the senior partners. Marianne excused herself after a bit and went to the bathroom, where she broke down in tears. She had been reduced to nothing by these people, and now her former student had been a witness to her humiliation.

What made it worse was that she was having to answer to a man who was "a total racist" with "steel-blue eyes, like a beetle." One day he sent her to interview at one of the departments, and when she got there, she saw that here were the people of color. They were working in either money markets or municipal bonds. It didn't take having an MBA to work it out. Money markets were the sector in which you made the least money. As for municipals, Black mayors were starting to be elected all around the country, and it was in every firm's interest now to have minorities sitting at the table representing them in meetings with these newly elected Black officials in charge of investing large sums of public money.

Marianne made a quick calculation: these Black employees were going to be pitted against other Black people hired at the other firms for the same reason, all of them chasing after Black business. This is where he thought she belonged. She did the interview, saying everything she was supposed to say about how she wanted to make bundles of money. The man then looked up, pointed to the secretary's desk, and said that she'd have to sit "there," with the secretary, because there was no desk space "here." She thanked him politely and left, her anger building.

By the time she reached her supervisor, she was yelling, screaming, crying. "Let me tell you one thing," she said, planting herself in front of his desk. "You can subject me to anything you subject everybody else around here to. That, and no more. Because you don't understand who I am. I am Roy Spraggins's daughter. That means nothing to you, but it means everything to me, and it means everything to everybody who ever put anything into trying to make something out of me in this life. I will do that and no more, and do you understand?"

He stood up, apoplectic, turning various shades of purple.

"And everybody tells me I'm not supposed to cry," she continued. "Well, I don't care. This is what I do. I see those people out there [on the trading floor], and they cuss and swear and go to strip clubs, and I cry. And if you don't like it, it's tough."

He pointed to a desk outside his office as if he were putting her in detention, shouting that if she hadn't liked it "up there" then she was just going to have to sit down here in that chair.

She sat down. She did what he ordered. She tried to compose herself. And as she sat out the rest of the day on that chair outside his office, she made up her mind that either she'd be a huge success or else she'd be "carried out feet first." There were no other options left at this point.

The next day, she gathered up her things and moved herself to the cafeteria.

Salomon Brothers had private dining rooms, where partners

invited clients and guests, but the company cafeteria was where everyone usually went to grab some food, even the partners, especially in the mornings. Marianne parked herself at a table right near the cash register so that everyone who came in would have to see her. She sat there from the time she came in until it was time to go home, reading the financial papers, busying herself. She made it her office because "one day, somebody is going to have to say, 'Who is that Black woman? Why is she sitting there every day reading the papers,' right?"

Deciding it was better to be glaringly visible than conveniently invisible, to put herself on view, to make a spectacle of herself no matter how awkward it was for her or anyone else, brought its own kind of liberation. Glass walls were everywhere—an investment banking specialty, as if promising transparency—and there was literally no place to hide, so why not be seen instead? Sometimes she would get up from her cafeteria table and ride the escalator that went down to the trading floor. CEO John Gutfreund notoriously sat right on the trading floor, instead of in his office in the back, perched "like the captain of a ship." Marianne, dressed vividly in her bright-colored suits and high heels, shoulders back, would ride up and down that elevator. She wanted him to see her. He had famously said that to make it on the Salomon Brothers trading floor, you had to get up each morning and be "ready to bite the ass off a bear." This was Marianne's way of saying she was ready to bite.

Sitting at her cafeteria table, if anyone so much as made eye contact with her, she found out who they were, went to their office, and introduced herself: "My name is Marianne Spraggins, and I was in the last class." A new "class" of analysts had since started up, and she did not hesitate putting that out there: "I was in the class and I didn't get placed. Do you have any work you need done?" Some, taking pity on her, or feeling so awkward that they just wanted to make her disappear, gave her work. She was handed small tasks here and there, and after she was asked to write a paper on European floating rates, she eventually got an interview in the newly emerging field of mortgage finance. A man named Lewis S. Ranieri handed her a prospectus on a Friday and said they'd talk on Monday.

Lew Ranieri was not yet a familiar name outside of Salomon Brothers, although he would become well known after the publication of *Liar's Poker*, Michael Lewis's autobiographical account of life at Salomon Brothers in the late 1980s. Ranieri had started in the mailroom at Salomon Brothers while a college student in Queens, alighted on the trading floor as a college dropout, and then blew past everyone when he created an entirely new market in mortgage-backed bonds. He would be known for coining the term "securitization," and be among the first to practice "financial alchemy," in his case packaging together home loans and selling them to institutional investors. He was also known as loudmouthed, "uncouth," and prone to orchestrating inappropriate practical jokes.

When Marianne arrived for her interview in the early 1980s, however, the mortgage trading department on the forty-first floor was not yet filled with what Michael Lewis would call "the firm's Biggest Swinging Dicks." Ranieri's department would eventually be the golden goose laying the firm's most monumental golden eggs, outpacing all other departments at Solly; it was where every analyst trainee would want to be assigned, desperate to play alongside the "baddest dudes," the mortgage traders who made a sport of throwing corded phones at one another.

But for now, there was no sign of this future. That Ranieri handed Marianne a prospectus explaining what his department did, what it was they were selling, suggested that no one yet understood mortgage bonds. Mortgages as a possible source of Wall Street trading was, in hindsight, obvious. Yet mortgages had not been recognized as a potential source of seemingly endless revenue until Salomon Brothers started Wall Street's first mortgage securities department in 1978.

At the center of it all was the small-town savings-and-loan bank, known as a thrift, which doled out most of America's mortgages, and benefitted from government protections and tax breaks. Outstanding mortgage loans were at $55 billion in 1950, rising to $700 billion in 1976, and becoming a whopping $1.2 trillion by January 1980. Debt, selling and buying it, meant money, serious money.

Marianne, even after she'd read the prospectus cover to cover and her friends had quizzed her until she could recite it in her sleep, still wasn't sure what these mortgage-backed securities were, but on Monday morning she took a deep breath and knocked on Ranieri's office door. She was ready, or as ready as she could be, to answer any questions he could possibly throw at her, but after a short while he simply said that she sounded like everyone else at the firm so she might as well have the job.

It had taken Marianne over a year, but she finally had a position at Salomon Brothers.

Marianne set about making cold calls, trying to sell this product—the mortgage-backed security—that was still then an unknown. She started by calling insurance companies, but she was clearly stepping on toes: after she hung up with the Thrift Insurance Corporation, a Salomon partner called and started yelling at her never to call Thrift Insurance again. When she tried calling Prudential Insurance, she received another incensed call telling her to stay away. So now what? Marianne decided to use her common sense—"women have it"—and thought: this is a long-term asset, and what does that mean in terms of who wants to buy it? Pension funds was the obvious answer. She switched gears, and started calling pension funds, and this time no one at Solly was calling to chew her out: "So I knew I was on to something." Public, government pension funds proved to be the most receptive, and as soon as she did her first deal, she was on to the next state to do another. Soon she was selling not one but a whole series of mortgage bonds to various state and city pensions.

Marianne had lucked out. It could not have been predicted that Ranieri's department would become the top earner at Salomon Brothers. When the department finally took off, it was because of a single tax decision. In October 1979, the Federal Reserve, under Paul Volcker, appointed by President Carter in a desperate attempt to stanch inflation, had significantly raised interest rates. The S&Ls, the thrifts, were hit hard. Until then, the joke had been that they operated under a system of 3–6–2: pay depositors 3 percent, lend their money out as mortgages at 6 percent, and hit the golf course at 2 p.m. But with Volcker now trying to tighten up money to lower inflation, the reliable formula imploded. Volcker cooled the economy, as intended, but he also brought the housing market to a screeching halt, and the S&Ls to the brink of collapse. Congress, unwilling to give up on the mom-and-pop banks of middle America, agreed to help them out.

Starting in October 1981, these small thrifts were given the right to sell off their mortgages to pay off their depositors. To make it yet more advantageous for them, they were also able to turn their loss on these mortgages into refunds on taxes they'd paid in previous years. With such a profitable tax break dangled in front of them, S&Ls were suddenly extremely eager to unload their mortgages, and Salomon Brothers was the only brokerage house with a fully established mortgage trading department. Overnight Ranieri found himself, even if briefly, with a Wall Street monopoly.

At first, he bought mortgages from one S&L and sold them to another at a markup. But to make them more tradeable for institutional investors, he came up with what became called the mortgage-backed security, the MBS. These securities were pooled, turned into baskets filled with anonymous mortgages that the buyer and trader only saw as paper, and that the mortgage-owner only saw as a monthly mortgage reminder from their local, friendly S&L, the kind of community-based bank at the center of the Christmas movie classic *It's a Wonderful Life.* In 1982, Ranieri's department made $150 million for Salomon Brothers.

In 1984, about three years after joining the department, Marianne was called on to testify before Congress about the mortgage-backed securities market in relation to a proposed bill to increase the ability of pension funds, both public and private, to participate in this new market. Marianne, representing Salomon Brothers, explained, "We are pioneers in developing mortgage securities and, indeed, I think we could go so far as to say that we have been missionaries, in that field. We have learned a lot of lessons." She was asked why other firms were so slow in getting in on the MBS, and she countered, "I would love to say that that was true, that other firms haven't tried, but they have. . . . We were willing to come into this market at an early stage in time," and as a result are "now trading about $15 billion in mortgage securities a month." That same year, Marianne would herself do four Connecticut transactions that totaled $500 million.

Even as Marianne was now thriving, she recognized that on Wall Street, as a Black woman, the worst of it was actually being a woman—even as Black women hires were cruelly referred to as "two-fers" because a firm could tick off two minority hires in one go. But being a woman in a male culture seemed to her to be the greatest disadvantage. She wasn't surrounded just by men but by men with military and professional sports backgrounds. They were all trained to respond to commands: move left, move right; say X, and I'll say Y. There was a discipline and hierarchy built into the Wall Street system that appealed to these men. One time, when a partner yelled at Marianne for something, he literally finished with: "And that's a direct order!"

But Marianne "always did whatever I wanted to do, period, always. Part of the fun was circumventing all this, and then looking at them like I had no idea what they were talking about: what are you so upset about?" Said with an innocent voice, of course. Women wanted context; men wanted rules. Bosses, male bosses, when asked "why," why did this need to be done in *this way*, were at first flabbergasted and then infuriated.

Marianne also came to understand that inside these organizations there were three levels of people: the people at the top, who, for the most part, were not a threat; the people at her own level, in the middle; and the people at the bottom, who were invisible, ignored, and if you offered them even the slightest bit of respect, they would help you. She had a lot of friends at the bottom, and she had recognition from the top. Her problems all stemmed from the middle, where she was blocked at every turn even as she would eventually find her way around the obstructions they set up. She had also grasped the importance of "external constituencies," meaning mayors, state treasurers, and the elected officials she worked with in making the deals. In part, she saw them as her protection, as a second set of eyes: "There are people who know I am here, and they are watching, so you can mess with me just so much."

Marianne was extravagant and reveled in being so. When she closed on her first big deal, she invited her friends, most of them from outside the finance world, to the Palace on East Fifty-Ninth Street, "known as the city's most expensive restaurant." She jubilantly announced to the waiters at the start of the dinner to put the glasses on the bill "because we're going to break them!" Marianne had not only found a seat at the table but had guaranteed herself a full place setting.

11

Yuppiedom

Louise, Barbara, and Marianne all took a stab at Wall Street, sensing something was afoot, at the very moment that Ronald Reagan took up residence in the White House. Reagan was inaugurated as the fortieth president of the United States in January 1981, and the celebrations in Washington, DC, could not have looked more different from four years earlier when Rosalynn Carter arrived at the Kennedy Center Ball wearing the same blue chiffon gown she'd worn at her husband's inauguration as governor of Georgia back in 1971. Her choice had said it all: austerity and thrift were the name of the game. Rosalynn's reused gown had spoken directly to the 1970s, to the Pinto Decade.

Nancy Reagan's gown in 1981 was a study in contrasts—a hand-beaded sheath of lace over silk satin designed by James Galanos. It, too, sent a clear message as she "came glittering down the staircase to the bejeweled, waiting throng." Her shimmering sheath announced that the 1980s had arrived, and that they were going to be starkly different from the 1970s. It would be a decade of excess: towering

hair-sprayed hairdos, beefy shoulder pads, big payouts. The Reagan
era would unapologetically embrace opulence.

Friends and donors who joined "Ronnie" and Nancy at the inauguration balls expressed their shared belief that money and the desire
to show it off were the rightful rewards of achieving the American
dream through hard work, as they saw it. Bonnie Swearingen, wife
of the board chairman of the Standard Oil Company of Indiana, got
to the point: "All of the women here have husbands who have worked
hard for what they have. . . . What have we worked for if we can't
enjoy it? It's getting a little tiresome to always have to apologize for
ourselves." Pointing to herself in a satin gown of "tucked sleeves" and
much jewelry, she added, "If a little girl from Alabama whose father
was a minister can appear in public wearing beautiful jewels and
gowns, it should be a symbol to everyone that they can do it, too."

Ronald Reagan, believing like his hero Calvin Coolidge that "the
chief business of the American people is business," set about freeing
up the practice of doing business. His initial tax cut took the top
rate down by 20 percentage points, from 70 percent to 50 percent
in August 1981—an enormous boon to those in the upper income
brackets, who now had cash galore for a rampage of conspicuous
consumption and political influencing. The thrift characterized by
Rosalynn Carter's recycled gown was cast aside, and not just by those
who benefitted most from the tax cuts. Everyone wanted to be a part
of the gold rush, especially when saving and scrimping had started to
feel passé: at Reagan's inauguration, household debt was at around
60 percent of a family's income; by 2007, it would be almost double.

Nancy Reagan and Bonnie Swearingen were not the only ones
itching to dress up and forget the '70s, the decade of long gas lines and
tenuous manhood. The hugely popular television series *Dynasty* premiered just a week before the Reagans did, and both would legitimize
and elevate the desire to be lavishly rich. The TV series, revolving
around a fictional family named the Carringtons living in a forty-

eight-room house with $200 million in the bank, had been in production for over a year and a half, its creators clearly tapping into an already burgeoning sense that New Deal values and social protest had become tiresome. Esther Shapiro, co-creator of *Dynasty*, felt as much: "I wore granny dresses in the 1960s. I baked bread. I marched in peace marches, I made speeches. . . . I felt like dressing up again." All of America seemed ready to dress up again.

In 1982, Merrill Lynch took out full-page newspaper advertisements declaring the "Dawn of a Bull Market." Many on Wall Street balked at the bold optimism, seeing it as premature. Yet on August 12, 1982, the contrarian Peter Vermilye over at Citibank decided that, yes, the Dow Jones Industrial Average had in fact finally bottomed out. He turned to his team of portfolio managers, which now included Patricia Chadwick, the former Feeneyite, and instructed them to buy, buy, buy. He even did the unthinkable and had them take over the portfolio of someone out on vacation—Vermilye was adamant that everyone that day ride the wave that he could finally see coming. Five days later, on August 17, Salomon Brothers' chief economist, Henry Kaufman, known ominously on the Street as "Dr. Doom," announced that he believed the recent fall in interest rates would continue. His unusual optimism sent stocks soaring. By August 20, at the close of the week, the Dow Jones was up 10 percent. It didn't hurt that in Reagan Wall Street felt it had found a like-minded soul. Not only was the bull back, but 1982 would turn out to be the beginning of a new era on Wall Street.

It was also the beginning of a new era for New York City. In SoHo, dilapidated warehouses only recently converted into artists' studios were now being turned into trendy lofts for the young Wall Street crowd who liked to mingle with the downtown artists— Warhol, Madonna, Basquiat, Run-D.M.C., Keith Haring, Cyndi Lauper—at New York's hot spots. While The Police sang "Every Breath You Take," yuppies showed off their Swatches and turned their socks inside out before putting on their Reeboks and designer denim jeans. MTV arrived in August 1981—"*I want my MTV*" went the jingle—showcasing all the touchstones of the decade: lip gloss, hair spray, Spandex, Reagan, and the ever-present Cold War threat of nuclear mushrooms. MTV, with its studios on West Fifty-Seventh Street, also showed America a transforming and transformational New York City. Suddenly New York was the place to be.

Donald Trump from Queens was erecting a bronze-encrusted Trump Tower on Fifth Avenue, a luxury apartment building partially financed by tax abatements that were originally earmarked to boost the city's housing construction, although not for the super-rich until Trump sued the city and won. His female doppelgänger and publicity-seeking rival was Leona Helmsley, the owner, by way of marriage, of many of New York's showcase buildings. Trump's famed hotel was the Grand Hyatt next to Grand Central station, and nine blocks north was Leona Helmsley's more upscale Helmsley Palace, over which she reigned like an outraged, unhinged queen. The behavior of the "Queen of Mean," as the press dubbed her, was cleverly incorporated into the Helmsley television commercials and print ads, where her unpleasant demeanor was recast as perfectionism for the sake of the Helmsley hotels' guests.

Both greed and debt were becoming fashionable, and those who felt unshackled from earlier standards of humility and fair play were elevated in the public eye, photographed for magazine covers, emulated. Doreen Mogavero's boss, Ivan Boesky, the King of Arbitrage, was among them.

If it felt like a gold rush, then the MBA was like the mining pan, and now almost every Ivy League graduating senior wanted to grab their shovel and pickaxe and head to Wall Street. When, in October 1981, Princeton University career services arranged for a panel of alumni to discuss their experiences getting an MBA, there was so much interest that the event had to be moved to one of the university's largest lecture halls. At Yale University, 20 percent of the graduating class of 1980 planned to go to business school, and by 1987, as historian Dylan Gottlieb writes, more students were going off to graduate school for business than for law, medicine, and education combined. *Wall $treet Week*'s Louis Rukeyser, employing his usual hyperbole while also managing to say something pertinent, claimed, "The M.B.A degree is in the same position as the high school diploma was two decades ago." Nor was the gold rush limited to men this time around. Gone were the days when Lillian Hobson and Priscilla Rabb cast their eyes around their HBS sections and could barely if at all find another woman there. In 1971, women still made up only 4 percent of MBA students, but by 1980, over one-third were female.

The investment banks and brokerage houses—the gold mines—were ready for the deluge. Investment banks now had their associate and analyst programs in place, which is how Barbara Moakler and Marianne Spraggins had found a way in. It was no longer a circuitous path, a rickety ladder from secretary to assistant to research analyst or broker, with extended pit stops along the way. It was a straight if competitive path from Ivy League graduation to a prestigious analyst program, or from a highly rated B-school to a top-notch associate program.

The landscape had changed in other ways, too, since the 1970s. For the longest time, bonds had remained lackluster and unexciting because interest rates were stable, or as one Salomon Brothers trader opined, "At cocktail parties lovely ladies would corner me and ask my opinion of the market, but alas, when they learned I was a bond man, they would quietly drift away." But in 1979, because of Federal Reserve Chairman Paul Volcker's efforts to slow inflation, interest rates began to oscillate, which led to bond prices fluctuating too. Movement meant money. Suddenly "bonds became," in the words of

Michael Lewis, "a means of creating wealth rather than merely stor-
ing it. Overnight the bond market was transformed from a backwater
into a casino."

The boom could be felt everywhere. Mary Farrell, whose friend
in HR, years before, had gifted her with a list of her male colleagues'
salaries, received for the first time a significant bonus. She was struck
by the overwhelming sense of relief that flooded through her knowing she no longer needed to worry about money. As someone who
had worked throughout college, who had struggled for many years
in New York to make ends meet, she could now walk into the swank
department store Saks Fifth Avenue and buy whatever she wanted.
She had never wanted a fur coat, she still did not want one, but she
walked past the rack and *knew* she could have one.

Wall Street recruiters descended onto Ivy League campuses, and
students lined up to interview. The head of Princeton's career services,
looking on, called it "a herd mentality." College curricula changed,
too, as students tried to get into oversubscribed economics courses,
and university resources shifted away from the humanities to economics and related fields. The ripple effect was profound. Even if
one did not want to work in finance, other options seemed to shrink.
Gottlieb describes a Columbia University graduating senior flipping
through the list of firms recruiting on campus: Goldman Sachs, Salomon Brothers, Shearson Lehman, Bear Stearns, Kidder Peabody—
"No, no, no. I turned the pages faster. The never ending stream of
big bucks jobs became a dizzying blur, and before I knew it I had
reached the last page without circling a single firm." In 1986, over
30 percent of Yale's graduating class (Yale later claimed that was an
overestimate, but the statistic lives on) applied to work at First Boston, a major Wall Street investment bank that specialized in mergers
and acquisitions.

———

PHYLLIS STRONG, YALE CLASS OF 1983, WAS ONE OF THOSE WHO GOT caught up in this ideological swoon taking place on college campuses. Phyllis, the daughter of Holocaust refugees, felt the weight of obligation to make her future meaningful. Wanting to be in the entertainment industry, but feeling that was perhaps too frivolous, she had settled on entertainment law, applied to law schools, and was accepted to Stanford. Yet when the various Wall Street firms arrived on Yale's campus to begin recruitment, she decided to go ahead and sign up—"but only for the interview practice," she told herself.

Although Phyllis knew nothing whatsoever about Wall Street, she was in fact a double major in American studies and economics, having picked up economics in her junior year when she started worrying about her future. This made her recruitable—never mind that most of the economics courses she'd taken focused not on finance but on the history of economics. She interviewed on campus with Lehman Brothers Kuhn Loeb, who then invited her to a series of six follow-up interviews with various executives and vice presidents, the last of whom was Ira Sokolow, head of M&A, mergers and acquisitions. She spent her interview arguing with him about pricing. He said there was no right or fair price to anything because no matter what, the price was what the market could bear. Phyllis, young, idealistic, and not yet of Wall Street, insisted that there was such a thing as a fair price. That didn't go over so well, she thought. Yet when the job candidates were seated at dinner, she found herself next to Sokolow, and they continued the debate. Perhaps more accustomed to "yes men," and charmed by Phyllis's idealism, he became her so-called closer, the person who calls to invite a job candidate to join the firm.

As soon as she arrived at Lehman Brothers, it was clear to Phyllis that if there was ever a time to be a woman, it was at this moment. Wall Street was trying to make up for its earlier track record of discrimination, and for once women had an advantage, at least when it came to climbing the first few rungs of the ladder. Of the twenty-

four analysts in Lehman's class of 1983, there were fourteen women
and ten men. (Phyllis had secretly hoped she'd be surrounded by
more eligible young men.) Lehman had grown so much that the new
class could no longer fit in the original bull pen, lined with beautiful
mahogany cubicles with tall, well-spaced dividers. The new bull pen,
filled with drab-looking desks pushed right up against one another,
looked to Phyllis like it might well have been a cafeteria in a previous
life. As a crossing space between other departments, it was ideally
situated for the Lehman men to wander through, checking out the
new crop of female analysts.

Yet even as it constituted a significant step forward, this influx of
women on the trainee track was also creating a new division between
the women now being trained as future bankers and traders, and the
female support staff. Ambitious secretaries and clerks could no longer use those jobs as stepping-stones the way that so many—Mickie
Siebert, Alice Jarcho, Beth Dater, and many others—had done in the
1960s and '70s. In 1980, a group calling itself the Working Office
Women (WOW) held a noon mock trial in the Financial District,
charging four banks with paying them low wages. The women hid
their faces behind their banks' logos, with the Chemical Bank "plain-
tiff" telling reporters that as a key-punch operator for fourteen years,
with four children, and a salary of $11,000, she was forced to use
food stamps. As for rising in the ranks, the Bankers Trust "plain-
tiff" said that she was never told of any training programs she could
apply for, and only knew that training existed "because I open my
boss's mail."

The first IBM PCs hit the market in August 1981, arriving in
offices at the same time as the young female college graduates now
on the fast track. The computers were too expensive for everyone to
have on their desk, and instead one was placed in a corner of the room
to be shared by Lehman's analysts. The white, boxy PC was about
to do away with the tiresome spreadsheets of the 1970s. In the first

few months, Phyllis's class learned to use the Hewlett Packard 12c calculator with reverse function—which no one outside of finance could possibly operate. Transitioning from the previous decade, Lehman still had a department full of secretaries available to type out handwritten notes and take dictation, but the class of 1983 was also being trained on the word-processing program WordPerfect, and the computer spreadsheet program Lotus 1-2-3. They had arrived on the cusp of the computer revolution.

The transition from paper to screen would in fact run parallel with Mickie Siebert's entire career. When she bought her seat and created her firm, she recalled, "if someone gave me an order, I wrote out the order ticket. I either called the order down to the floor of the New York Stock Exchange or I took it to an order clerk, who called it down to the floor." Each handover was called in or delivered—from stockbroker, to clerk, to floor broker, to specialist, and then back again. By the 1990s, the process would look entirely different: her brokers would "take a telephone call from a customer . . . type it on the screen . . . It automatically goes down to the post electronically, where that stock is traded, the order is filled, and it is back within two or three seconds—totally untouched."

As a first-year analyst, Phyllis could choose to start in June or August, and with all the eagerness of a first-generation American, she signed up for June even though she'd have to live with family friends in the suburbs while she waited for her friend from Yale, Joanne Lipman, an aspiring financial journalist, to arrive in the city to room with her. The first days of the six-week training were dedicated to going through the basics—finance, accounting, stocks, bonds, debt equity—during which time the analysts were assigned to temporary desks. For her first assignment, she was put onto a savings-and-loan financing deal. The partner in charge was "deadly boring," and Phyllis's job consisted of doing spreadsheets and going to meetings in the "exotic" city of Hartford, Connecticut, accompanied by old white

men. The analysts were the ones who put together the paperwork for
the deals: they xeroxed, they edited, they ran scenarios, they barely
slept. It was as boring as it was exhausting. Phyllis thought to herself:
If this is what it's about, I'm quitting. She still had Stanford Law
School in her back pocket.

But she found an escape hatch when she was temporarily assigned
to a small deal that was tangentially related to communications, run
by investment banker Steven Rattner, in whom she could finally see
a little of herself. He wasn't just a number cruncher but a former economics correspondent for the *New York Times*. Smart and charming,
Rattner had just recently joined Lehman in late 1982. Phyllis was put
on the project with him to help with the numbers, and after it was
over, the deal done, she asked Rattner if she could join his team. The
next deal, selling Puerto Rico's largest newspaper, had them flying to
meetings in balmy San Juan, a significant improvement over Hartford, America's insurance capital.

She and her friend Joanne were now sharing a one-bedroom
apartment—Phyllis getting the bedroom because she could pay a
larger share of the rent, and Joanne sleeping on a pullout sofa. After
her freshman year at Yale, Joanne had interviewed for an internship
at a magazine in New York. She'd sat down, carefully crossing her
legs and yanking the front slit of her skirt closed. But her interviewer
was having none of it. "If you want the job, you'll leave that open," he
"barked" at her. She was no longer naïve about how things worked.
She'd landed a full-time job at the *Wall Street Journal* for much the
same reason that fourteen out of the twenty-four analysts at Lehman
were women that year; employers were nervous about getting called
out for discrimination or, worse, sued, and were hoping a quick hiring of women might help insulate them.

But no equal rights act was going to stop Joanne's part of
the newsroom from being dubbed the "Valley of the Dolls." Like
Wall Street, the *Wall Street Journal* was literally built for a male

staff and a male readership, with the women's bathroom an after-thought intended for the occasional female visitor. And like the women on Wall Street learning to read and play by the men's playbook, Joanne and the other women in the newsroom quickly learned to "curse like truck drivers" and dress like mini versions of men in suits.

That was one way of trying to break through the glass ceiling, but for some there was an additional ceiling: the so-called lavender ceiling against which queer women, and men, were constantly bang-ing their heads. In 1978, the first official gay student organization at Harvard Business School had been founded, called Alternative Exec-utive Lifestyles Club. In 1984, LGBTQ Stanford alumni and gradu-ating students quietly began to build professional networks even as they remained closeted to the outside world. The question of whether or not to come out lingered throughout the 1980s, not helped by the growing fear over AIDS. But being gay on Wall Street brought other unique challenges. Gay culture largely identified as politically liberal, yet many gay women on Wall Street did not necessarily feel their views aligned with the trope of the left-leaning, lesbian-feminist.

Role models generally were hard to come by. Phyllis was certainly unimpressed with what was on offer. She found the older women, the original pioneers, to be very "male," not just dressing conserva-tively, without any femininity, but imitating the men's management style too. Years later, in an op-ed for the *New York Times*, Joanne Lipman would reconsider the point of view that she and Phyllis had held so firmly in those days fresh out of college: "My generation of professional women took equality for granted. When I was in college in the 1980s, many of us looked derisively at the women's libera-tion movement. That was something that strident, humorless, shrill women had done before us. We were sure we were beyond it. We were post-feminists." Barbara Moakler also had little time for the previous generation. In her opinion, "Being an analyst in the 1970s was the functional equivalent of making coffee and sandwiches; you could make the spreadsheets."

There was a certain non-reflective self-satisfaction at play. Joanne and Phyllis, as Joanne would write many years later, mistakenly confused their being hired into prestigious entry-level jobs with the arrival of workplace equality. And while they had little good to say about the pioneers who came before them, the pioneers did not think much of this next generation either. Beth Dater, now a partner at Warburg Pincus, had a one-eyebrow-raised kind of skepticism about this new breed of Wall Street women, even as she now started to feel insecure about not having an MBA. They seemed to think they belonged, and they failed to understand, let alone appreciate, what Beth and her friends had had to do for that to happen.

But as far as Phyllis Strong was concerned, the only thing she had in common with these earlier Wall Street women was that they, like she, were now victims of the 1980s scourge, the shoulder pad. The television show *Dynasty*, running parallel with the Reagans' residency in the White House, "was putting linebacker shoulder pads on the map." Men carried black rectangular briefcases, like mini suitcases, while the new female power suit came with padded shoulder inserts, indicating the women were ready to play like the men.

But Phyllis did not want to "look like a man." She wanted to look like a woman, and she defiantly bought her power suits in peach and dusty pink.

Ultimately, however, the color didn't matter. What mattered was the suit itself, which signaled that you were *not* one of the female support staff. In *Dress for Success*, John Molloy might have gotten some things wrong, but he understood how people, women especially, signaled, both consciously and unconsciously, their socioeconomic class and their professional status through their clothes. If one could afford it, Giorgio Armani and Calvin Klein were the go-to for the 1980s power suit, but more moderately priced versions were to be found on clothing racks everywhere.

Westina Matthews, a member of a prominent civil rights activist family, had arrived on Wall Street later in life. She had come by way of Chicago following a career as an elementary schoolteacher and then a PhD in education. Deciding between two job offers, one at the Ford Foundation and the other at Merrill Lynch, she sought the advice of James A. Joseph, later the ambassador to South Africa under the Clinton administration, who told her, "You can go to Ford and give away money, or go to Merrill Lynch and *be* civil rights." Westina decided to be civil rights on Wall Street, heading up the firm's philanthropy initiatives, working like the others from 7 a.m. until 9 p.m. on weekdays and coming in on Saturdays too. She took to wearing green—the color of money and power, she liked to say—and acquired an entire wardrobe of expensive St. John suits. (There was a senior woman at Merrill Lynch known for luring young associates out under the pretense of lunch only to shepherd them into a St. John store.) This particular executive-level uniform further demanded manicured nails and perfectly coiffed hair, along with the right shoes—preferably Ferragamo heels.

But before the heels were slipped on at the office, there were the sneakers, which Beth Dater, always elegantly dressed, could not abide; young women traversed Broad Street, Wall Street, Broadway, Trinity Place in their power suits incongruously paired with sneakers, their high-heeled pumps snug inside preppy Land's End canvas bags. Like all the analysts, Phyllis Strong worked around the clock, sometimes doing two back-to-back all-nighters, and when that happened, when she stepped off the subway half-asleep, often she'd leave her heels on the seat beside her. She measured her workload by how many shoes she'd lost to the Bronx.

When Phyllis did have time to go out on the town, she was ready

to spend some of her hard-earned cash. That was one of the iro-
nies: all this money but little free time to spend it. Studio 54 had
reopened, but under new ownership it had lost its glamour and glitter.
But there was no lack of new nightclubs where the finance warriors
could party. Area, on Hudson Street, had an entryway that was a
"habitat diorama," and unlike the famous dioramas of taxidermized
animals at the Natural History Museum, Area's was a themed tab-
leau of live, still humans. Every six weeks, Serge Becker, the club's
art director, staged a different habitat diorama with a new theme;
one time Joanne and Phyllis found themselves walking through an
ode to suburbia, an exhibition of humans in pajamas, sitting around
watching television, eating cereal and TV dinners. Area's dance floors
were also themed (one included a shark tank), and the bathrooms
were unisex. Old-fashioned "cigarette girls" in short, tight uniforms wandered the floors selling cigarettes and makeup and, Phyllis guessed, probably drugs. Andy Warhol and Jean-Michel Basquiat
were sometimes sighted.

Limelight was another popular club, a deconsecrated church.
There was also the preppy Surf Club on the Upper East Side, where
out on the sidewalk, as the *New York Times* described it, "limousines
lined up for a block . . . and supplicants waved $100 bills at the door-
man." Both Area and Limelight had opened in 1983, the same year
that Phyllis and Joanne arrived in Manhattan; the Surf Club opened
the following year. Living in New York on a Wall Street income in the
1980s, you could think you were at the center of the universe.

That you wanted to be there—that in fact you *had* to be there,
in New York City, working on "the Street"—was a relatively new
idea. In 1970 almost 73,000 abandoned cars had been towed away,
rotten metal carcasses scattered in burnt-out lots and under bridges.
Typical then was a 1973 Harvard Business School graduate's feeling
that "New York is too dirty and grubby" to work in, a feeling further
underscored by the 1977 blackout that shrouded the city in dark-

ness and set off large-scale looting. Soon after, on Valentine's Day in 1978, the city launched a marketing campaign, backed by desperate private investors and others who had a keen interest in seeing a revived New York. The campaign's most successful result, alongside the city's renaissance, was the catchy "I ♥ NY" slogan, splayed across countless tourist T-shirts and turned into an earworm of a TV jingle.

By the early 1980s, red-bereted Guardian Angels, a volunteer vigilante civic group, was patrolling the subways. The Urban Park Rangers, hired by the city, took on the parks, pleading with people to throw their garbage in the trash cans. New York's no-man's-land of drugs and hookers was fast transforming into a landscape of artist lofts and penthouse apartments. In 1982, as Gottlieb writes, a Harvard Business School graduate was reporting to his classmates that, "contrary to popular rumor, a summer job in New York is not the equivalent of a three-month sentence in some steamy, lurid urban jail." In fact, New York was now "one of the most highly-favored locations for adventuresome MBA's," who congregated in the "yuppie-dominated dating scene" concentrated in the Financial District (an area previously abandoned after 5 p.m.), Murray Hill, and the Upper West Side's Columbus Avenue. On a weekend morning, you might find them in their sneakers taking a run around the Central Park Reservoir. In 1984, developers, creators, architects, and artists were called on to submit reenvisioning concepts for Times Square, the first step of what would be a radical makeover.

In 1984, Ronald Reagan ran for reelection with a powerful television campaign: "Morning in America." It was a seductive lullaby, featuring a story of nostalgia for an uncomplicated past. The images flashed on the screen, one after another, like a satisfying dream sequence: A family moving into a new home . . . Boy Scouts raising an American flag . . . a paperboy on his bicycle in the early morning. The voiceover, calm and soothing, put words to the pictures: *It's morning again in America. Today more men and women will go to work than ever before in our country's history. With interest rates at about half the record highs of 1980, nearly 2,000 families today will buy new homes, more than at any time in the past four years. This afternoon 6,500 young men and women will be married, and with inflation at less than half of what it was just four years ago, they can look forward with confidence to the future.*

The wildly successful advertising campaign was the work of a team of advertising executives who worked on "Morning in America" out of a windowless suite above Radio City Music Hall. They had turned down free offices in the newly built Trump Tower for fear it was "a little showy."

MARLENE JUPITER, THE CORNELL GRADUATE WHO HAD SHOCKED her male bosses by fixing the computer-trading software, was now living the Yuppie dream. After being manhandled by her boss on the hunt for his fourth wife, she'd left that firm and taken a job at DLJ, the company that had brought about the end of mandatory private partnerships for NYSE-member firms. She started as a trading assistant on the options desk, the department head "dressed elegantly in Brooks Brothers suits, custom-tailored and initialed shirts, wingtip shoes, Princeton pinkie ring, and a Gold Rolex Diamond Studded Presidential watch." Twelve years older than Marlene, he was on the fast track, already making about $250,000 and sporting "a year-long tan." The DLJ trading floor was on the thirty-fourth floor at 140 Broadway, the red steel cube balanced on its axis out front, a sculpture by Isamu Noguchi. The options desk, where Marlene sat, was relatively small and quiet. Nearby, the block trading desk had about fifty people and was all noise: they fought, they cursed each other out, and at 2 p.m., they'd light up cigars, so that the "entire room would look as if a smoke bomb went off."

She was loving her work, however, and had moved to the newly

built Gateway Plaza in Battery Park, into a studio apartment that
looked out onto the Statue of Liberty. The building was yuppie central. From there, she could walk to work, dash home for a workout,
and easily meet up with clients after hours. As the *New York Times*
reported, "For the first time in decades, the narrow streets of Manhattan's financial district—once empty, lonely, even spooky after
dark—are coming alive with people, lights, food and music." If you
bumped into a work friend, it was par for the course to buy them and
the people they were with a round of drinks. It would be reciprocated
the next time. Generosity, like dollars, was flowing, she observed.
Like Phyllis and Joanne, on weekends Marlene was going to the Limelight, Area, Palladium, Heartbreak Disco, Roxy, Surf Club, as well as
the more subdued Régine's and Au Bar. When the out-of-town portfolio managers came to New York to meet with their various brokers
(it could easily be five different brokers at five different firms with
whom a portfolio manager was working regularly), the team would
take them out. There was one portfolio manager who, when she visited, insisted on lunch at the Four Seasons, but only in the famous
Pool Room. It did not matter if you were already spending $500 on
dinner and your client asked to choose the wine and doubled your
bill. You just let it be. Expense accounts were plump. In fact, as Beth
Dater noticed, "if you were blowing up the expense account, it meant
you were seeing clients."

Phyllis Strong at Lehman, now working on media deals, made
sure to have dinner at all the hot spots, if only to say that she'd been
there: Le Cirque and Lutèce, where everyone went to see and be seen;
the Regency Hotel for power breakfasts; and the 21 Club for what
everyone knew were just overpriced burgers. When Phyllis was working on the sale of the *Houston Post*, she was flown down to Washington, DC, for a party at the exclusive F Street Club. It felt more like
a Hollywood premiere than an investment-bank deal, but that was
the point: finance was now glamour. In 1984, the popular television

show *Lifestyles of the Rich and Famous*, the first of its kind, went on air. Robin Leach, its British host who shouted his lines as if he were declaring hard truths, led television audiences through the lives and homes of the famous and super wealthy. He signed off by wishing his viewers "Champagne wishes and caviar dreams." The show was an instant hit, and by the following year, viewing clubs had sprung up, including one in California where its members dressed up in tuxedos to watch the week's latest episode while they drank Champagne served by maids hired for the evening. The message had been delivered and received: ostentatious consumption was in.

On Wall Street, sometimes all the freebies—the radio cabs, take-out deliveries, expensive restaurants—were not enough to keep everyone running at the speed necessary for the all-nighters. Phyllis's boss drove a Porsche 911 with a car phone, and when he stepped on the gas, she was thrown back into her seat as if she were on a plane taking off. Once, coming back from a meeting, he told her they'd need to make a stop on Central Park West to see his dealer. He left her double parked on the street in front, when she didn't even know how to drive a manual shift, and she sat there, sweating, terrified she'd be asked to move the car or, worse, the cops would ask her to move it at the very moment her boss came out with the bag of coke. He wasn't even getting the cocaine for himself; he was getting it for his team, Phyllis included, for the double all-nighters they were going to have to do that week. (In 1987, fifteen Wall Street employees, including brokers and one senior partner of a brokerage firm, were arrested for selling and trading cocaine in return for stocks and information. In what was a three-year federal undercover operation, police had found "a subculture in which cocaine is widely accepted, purchased at well-known neighborhood bars, snorted in bathrooms, stairways and board rooms, and occasionally used to help make financial deals.")

Phyllis was soon off on yet another IPO roadshow, this time to

Geneva, first class on Swissair, where she was served "real black Russian caviar" in her fully reclining seat. From Geneva, a private jet took the team to London, Edinburgh, and Zürich, before returning them to Geneva for their commercial flight back to New York. Any free time she'd had in Europe, she'd spent shopping, but as they waited for their flight home, she went to take a peek at the Swiss watches in the duty-free shop. There was one that caught her eye, that beckoned her: a $3,000 gold Ebel watch.

Staring at it, all she could think was: "How beautiful, I want it, I can have it." She whipped out her credit card, put the gold watch on her wrist, and walked through customs. From that day on, she called her watch her "golden handcuff," because that is exactly what it was—a physical manifestation of the cliché: you might well be a prisoner to your endless work hours, but at least the prison was a gilded cage.

In 1984, *Newsweek* declared in its year-end issue that it had been "The Year of the Yuppie," of the young, upwardly mobile professionals "barely looking up from the massed gray columns of *The Wall Street Journal* as they speed toward the airport, advancing on the 1980s in the back seat of a limousine." The magazine's cover was a *Doonesbury* cartoon by Garry Trudeau, best known for his renditions of America's hippies. He'd drawn two young finance professionals, a man and woman, walking side by side, crossing Central Park on their way to work. She is carrying a briefcase, striding forward in her New Balance sneakers, a Walkman strapped across one shoulder, the trendy, orange-foam-covered dinky headphones over her ears. Yuppie obsessions, *Newsweek* wrote, include physical fitness, Cuisinart food processors, Perrier sparkling water, and real estate.

The Yuppie Handbook, published that same year, described "a couple so far ahead on the fast track that they take their cordless telephone with them to walk their Akita." Except that "cordless"

then meant a hefty off-white Motorola DynaTAC, weighing in at
two and a half pounds, that cost $4,000, the equivalent of almost
$12,000 today.

But whether yuppies were admired or derided, they signaled a
larger cultural shift that would remain long after the yuppie was out
of fashion. As Barbara Ehrenreich, the preeminent observer of class
in America, noted: "In the eighties, the class contours of American
society were undergoing a seismic shift. The extremes of wealth and
poverty moved further apart."

LOUISE JONES WAS ON THE FLOOR OF THE NEW YORK STOCK EXCHANGE
when President Ronald Reagan appeared on the visitors' balcony
in March 1985 to offer Wall Street a pep rally, to announce that
his economic policies were "driving the bears back into permanent
hibernation."

"We're going to turn the bull loose!" he shouted.

The trading floor chanted back at him: "Ronnie, Ronnie, Ronnie!" And then he triumphantly rang the opening bell.

Louise thought it "magical," and not because the floor was some
kind of haven for Republican Party members—from what she could
tell, if anything, there might have been more Democrats—but Reagan
was so "electrifying with his movie-star good looks and charisma"
that Louise down on the floor could feel her blood pumping. Everyone was cheering not so much for a politician as for his promise to
unlock Wall Street's wild potential. It was like an amplification of
what Louise had felt the moment she'd first stepped out onto the floor
at age seventeen: she could breathe, she could make more money than
she'd ever imagined, and for Louise, the two went hand-in-hand.

When Mike Cassidy had returned to the floor of the NYSE, he
arrived in a good mood: he had landed the client he'd flown out to see,
and he was ready to hire Louise. But when he offered her the job, she

broke the news to him that she'd taken an offer to clerk for Johnny French, the arbitrage outfit running out of the same booth.

"They're giving me $78K," she told Cassidy, adding an extra three thousand just in case.

"I'll match it," he replied.

"I told him yes . . ."

"I'll get you out of it. If you want to work with me. It's going to be a better career. It's just going to be you and me, we're going to build this business, and you really should take it. I'll match him. I'll talk to Johnny French. . . ."

Mike Cassidy, "this old curmudgeon," as Louise liked to say, and she, barely in her twenties, were now an official team. It was "good cop, bad cop"; an eager young thing, lapping up information, and an old man screaming his head off every minute of every day. It worked because it was pure "yin yang."

Cassidy arrived early each morning to call his clients one by one and give them a quick morning market commentary. He taught Louise how to do it, how to formulate a market call. With no computers to show them the market trends, they would go upstairs to the NYSE Luncheon Club, where Doreen was, too, and pull information off the Reuters machine to look at the overseas markets: *Are they following us or are they creating a new pattern for the day?* The futures market also had all sorts of indicators about which way the market was going to go, what might be the flavor of the day. They spliced up the information and then put it back together into a coherent and often funny three-minute call. The dialing started at 7:30 a.m. and ended at 8:30 a.m. They called one number after another, giving their morning spiel over and over in quick succession.

At the other end, their morning call reverberated across various trading rooms from a squawk box, "like the *Charlie's Angels* speaker on the table." Cassidy and Louise would try to get everyone pumped up for the day: *"These are the numbers, and this is the thing to watch!*" Their morning calls were enough of a draw that when brokers on the calls moved on to another company, they usually continued to do their business through Cassidy. In this way, over the following five years, Cassidy and Louise would grow the firm to forty accounts, which meant playing in a different league, and hiring more staff. Cassidy in fact hired another broker before he made Louise a broker; she was "invaluable" where she was.

The '80s felt like boundless wealth with minimal effort. The bull market, which had taken off in August 1982, seemed to have no end in sight. But while the time was ripe for making buckets of money, not everyone took advantage, and Louise marveled at those who failed to grab this opportunity. From where she stood at the center of the trading floor, it felt like money was raining down on them, and all she had to do was run around the floor of the NYSE with a bucket, catching those dollars. But there were lots of people around who didn't do the same, and she just couldn't understand it. There were the timid guys from small regional firms who weren't getting any of the New York money flooding in. She got that. But there were also those who could have done better, like a friend who worked for five firms while on the floor of the exchange and never made more than $150,000 a year, which she thought "stupid." He was more interested in partying and hanging out than grabbing the bucket.

But making money was hard work. As a clerk in the booth, manning the phones, taking the orders, talking to clients, Louise was standing eight hours straight a day. There was a stool, but you couldn't do the job sitting. You needed the energy, the alertness. "It would be like a rock star sitting down on a stool and rocking it out—it doesn't make any sense." Her back was in agony much of the time. She wore tennis shoes with arch support and the men all wore "ugly orthotic Frankenstein shoes, custom made." Anything to ease the physical pain. On most days, you might not eat, or else you'd pull a sandwich out of your pocket and take a bite as you were running to do a trade. Even if there was a lull and you contemplated taking that bathroom break you needed, it wasn't easy to get to a ladies' room. When Mickie had purchased her seat in 1967, she'd hear brokers on the floor whisper that she bought her stock exchange seat for $445,000 but now they'd have to build a bathroom for her for $500,000. The building, like all of Wall Street, had been designed for men.

Louise wasn't a drinker, but almost everyone "got tanked" every night. She knew if she did, she wouldn't survive her days on the floor, or get to where she planned to be. The men, in their bright-colored '80s fashion suspenders, didn't bother to travel far for their after-hours booze, preferring the Irish pub right across from the exchange. And then there were the drugs.

Her sister-in-law, April, who'd called up Louise when that first fateful teletype job at the NYSE opened, now charged over to her, shaking a finger in her face: "Weez, if I ever see you doing cocaine . . ."

"Are you kidding me? Have we met?!" Louise laughed.

Cocaine was of no use to her; it was the buckets of cash she wanted.

12

Mamma Mia!

Barbara Moakler at Lehman, who had paraded around in her new mink pretending it was a gift from a boyfriend at Goldman Sachs, understood the 1980s as a "a tough world" even as women were now arriving in numbers unimaginable a decade earlier. But old habits die hard, and it was almost as if more women meant more prey. Once, when a very high-level senior partner offered her a ride home, he had the driver stop at a bar. She tried to insist she was tired and wanted to go home, but as a first-year associate there were just so many ways you could say no. As he reached for her hand across the table, she was so taken aback that she jerked her hand away and sent the bottle of red wine flying, spilling it all over him. She stood up and mumbled that she had to leave. He leaned in close: "If anyone ever hears about this, I will see to it that you lose your job at Lehman and you won't get another on the Street." She knew he wasn't bluffing.

Maria Marsala, back on Wall Street after leaving her marriage, was interviewing at Bear Stearns. She'd spent the whole weekend putting together her résumé and prepping for any questions they

might throw at her. But during the interview, no one seemed interested in her well-crafted résumé, and she was hardly asked anything
that might be pertinent to the job. Instead, she was shown around
the trading room and introduced to the bond traders. At one point,
she heard something fall and turned to see that a pile of the large red
Moody's bond-rating books had tumbled to the floor. By the time she
was back at the elevator bank pressing the button for the lobby, she'd
been offered the position. It was only once she was working at Bear
Stearns that she noticed the Moody's books had a habit of falling
off desks, and when she finally asked about it, she learned it was a
"smoke signal" to let the other traders know a good-looking woman
was on the premises.

If anything, the women's movement had taught Wall Street's men
to be more careful, less obvious. Phyllis Strong, at Lehman, noticed
that the blatant comments about a woman's breasts, commonplace in
the 1970s, had turned into a less easily litigated "looking good!"—
said loudly whilst staring at her chest. When Chippendales, the male
revue, opened in the city, some of the men at work would talk about
how they waited outside for the women to come out after the show,
"like lemmings, hot for it." Barbara, also at Lehman, knew a banker
who kept a list of call girls to keep his clients happy, and when on
business trips her own team would go out to a strip bar to entertain
clients, they'd tell her to stay behind in her hotel room.

Alice Jarcho, the first woman to work as a broker on the floor of
the New York Stock Exchange, was now the number-two person on
the Shearson American Express institutional trading desk. Her ultimate dream job was to be the number-one, but she knew that was
still out of the question for a woman; number two was as good as it
got for now. Tommy Gallagher, who interviewed her for the job, had
been at a dinner years before at the Christ Cella steakhouse when the
guy who ran an important Wall Street desk, skunk drunk, had said to
her out loud at the table: "Not only do we have to deal with the Jews,

now we have to deal with women too." But she had at least made it to number two at the trading desk, and as the market took off, the trading rooms became "wild." It was her birthday one time and when she looked up, a muscled "cop" was there, moving across the floor in her direction, blowing his whistle and hollering her name. The men around her were doubled over laughing. Alice hated what was about to happen, but she had to play along.

She stood up from her desk and beckoned him into her office. As soon as the door was shut, she gave the stripper his instructions: "I'm not going to look, I will not look, take your underpants off, I give you my word I won't look."

With her back to him, she waited for him to hand over his briefs, and when she had them in her hand, she opened her office door a crack, and waved them like a victory flag. The trading floor exploded with cheers and hoots. (It wasn't a case of playing along: it was, as Alice said, "You think you're going to embarrass me? Well, fuck you!")

Humor was the women's best weapon, their most successful deflection, resistance that read as if you were being one of the guys. Another Lehman employee, Karen Valenstein, was having a client dinner with "some polyester people from Florida," when she felt a hand on her knee. She leaned over to inform the owner of the hand, "I think your hand is lost," even though what she really wanted to do was "punch him in the face." Another time, after being propositioned by a senior colleague at an office cocktail party, she decided to deal with it head-on. The following day she showed up at his office door, leaning against the door frame, wearing what was clearly a maternity dress. She was three months pregnant, and while no one had guessed, and she had not planned to tell anyone just yet, and certainly not in this way, she had to make her point. He looked up and laughed when he put two and two together: "touché!"

But senior partners propositioning young female associates wasn't always just about the sex. Second marriages now proliferated—Alice, arriving at Shearson American Express at the start of the 1980s, married Tommy Gallagher in 1983, her boss and the number-one guy on the desk. No one had suspected they'd been dating for two years.

But often feelings were not reciprocal. Senior men would become infatuated, obsessed with young female associates, which in many ways posed a greater threat than a sexual proposition. Alice, who had been on Wall Street since the late 1960s, had seen how the men had first married airline stewardesses and secretaries, but now suddenly for the first time they were surrounded by young women who shared the same interests, who understood the world in which they operated, who spoke the same language, and it was "intoxicating" to them.

Phyllis Strong experienced it when a man several significant rungs above her, a very powerful man, fell for her, and even as she liked him and admired him, it was excruciating watching him clumsily show off for her in meetings. One time they were pitching to a client, and the moment the meeting was over and he had left, the other associate in the room turned to her: "*What the hell was that all about?*" In Wall Street's office politics, where the power imbalance almost always favored the men, Phyllis found that this was the one exception. These infatuated senior colleagues were reduced to weak-kneed supplicants. Yet the women were often disadvantaged by their pursuer's crush because they were having to accommodate it while trying to do their job. One of her friends had no option but to continue to work with a powerful private-equity banker who was utterly enamored with her, despite her having a boyfriend whom she would intentionally and frequently mention. But it did not stop the banker from relentlessly declaring his love.

Of course, there were also the women who took advantage of the weak-kneed men, "the teases" who used their appearance to further their careers, who slept their way to the top, who used men's overblown sense of themselves to their own advantage.

And for the men, if it wasn't about sex, or pining for a younger woman, it was about babies. Beth Dater, the Rukeyser Elf, like most women of her generation on Wall Street had simply decided not to have children (or had been too busy to think about it much). She and her friends had collectively understood a basic formula: career and children did not go together, one could seldom have both, a woman inevitably had to choose. That is certainly the way Beth felt, leaving her first husband, the airline pilot, when he wanted to have children— that you couldn't do both. Her second husband, Mitch Jennings at Bear Stearns, whom she married in 1977, was less bothered about children. It was a second marriage for both, and while Beth was only thirty-two, the question of children did not come up.

By the 1980s it was becoming less a question of either/or, as Beth had experienced it, but of mixed messages. Lewis L. Glucksman, the head of Lehman, proud of hiring outside of the typical white male applicant pool, told Karen Valenstein when he hired her: "I'm not going to pay you like a broad, and I'm not going to treat you like a broad, so don't act like a broad." She kept her word and didn't "act like a broad." In fact, she found it liberating because "Glucksman rewarded aggressive behavior that I was penalized for my whole life. I saw I could be myself, make money and be respected." She learned to "trade locker-room vulgarities, belt back stingers until dawn and recite National Football League scores on Monday morning." All this despite having a husband and two children. She was promoted meteorically, only for Glucksman to ponder, while speaking to a journalist, if Karen's "sense of priorities is sensible on a long-term basis." Glucksman added that perhaps by acting like the men, Karen "may have chosen a way of life that 'is clearly not good for family relationships.'"

The media, too, began to get worked up over working mothers, the handwringing unsurprisingly coinciding with the first serious surge of professional women as well as the growing number of

women over thirty who were having babies. *Working Woman* magazine joked, "The over-30 mother, it seems, is America's own Prin-
cess Di. There was 35-year-old Jaclyn Smith on the cover of *Time*
magazine, wearing a maternity dress over her obviously plural body,
and an equally expansive expression of delight. And there was the
New York magazine cover story, 'Mommy's 39, Daddy's 58—and
Baby Was Just Born.' " Its author, feminist writer Mary Kay Blakely,
warned women to ignore the advice being meted out by experts about
the vital importance of a child's first five years of life and their need
for a stay-at-home mom. In her opinion, while a child mostly ate
and slept in those first five years, it was the relationship between the
mother and father that was being formed—a relationship of inevitable unevenness if the woman quit her job for the sake of the children.

But many failed to take heed. Young, educated women were soon
swearing they would never sacrifice their future children's well-being
for their careers. Mary Anne Citrino, a senior at Princeton University, who was planning on attending business school, had decided
that upon having a child, she would quit her job for eight years to
become a full-time mother. She hoped that she'd return to her job
after those eight years. (The seasoned women on Wall Street must
have had a good laugh when they read that.) "If I can't give my children 100 percent," she told the *New York Times*, "I'd rather not be
a mother at all."

A study of college students at Barnard, Brown, Dartmouth, Princeton, Wellesley, and the State University of New York at Stony Brook
found that 77 percent of female students felt that "mothers should
either not work at all or work only part-time until their children were
5 years old. Some 84 percent of the men agree." The young women
who imagined careers on Wall Street were especially haunted by "the
large number of professionally successful women who had remained
unmarried." (A recent Gallup poll had showed that 42 percent of
female business executives were single, divorced, or separated.)

Janet Tiebout at Goldman Sachs was among that statistic, and understood the pressure, the panic, of the "ticking clock." She had graduated from Columbia Business School at twenty-four and gone straight to Goldman Sachs as an associate in the Fixed Income Division. She was the second woman there when she arrived in the late 1970s, five years after the first. Janet as the new girl was told to cold-call a client list referred to as "the dogs"—those who had no money or else hated Goldman Sachs. "Dialing for dollars," Janet called it. Meanwhile she watched the senior saleswoman, a brilliant math geek from Trinity College, with a graduate degree from Wharton, spend her days on the phone with her curated list of heavy-hitting institutional clients, having already paid her dues fending for herself in a crowded room full of men, abandoned crusty leftover food, eye-stinging cigar smoke, and a complete lack of privacy.

There was someone else on that desk who also made lucrative trades all day: John Bottrell. He and Janet started dating almost immediately, although they kept it under wraps so successfully that when, three years later, they announced their engagement, everyone was caught off-guard. Four years after, they divorced, but amicably so, and continued to sit opposite one another. John Bottrell was reaping the benefits of the era, a man about town with money burning a hole in his pocket, on a perpetual dating spree. Janet bore witness to the bouquets of red roses delivered to his desk on Valentine's Day while hers remained empty. With no prospects in sight and unlikely to meet someone considering the hours she kept, she stepped on the accelerator some more: "having no dates allowed me to work longer hours." The following year, she was promoted to co-manager of the Money Market Sales Group and was now her ex-husband's boss. He found it "amusing," and to celebrate her promotion, they went out to dinner "for old time's sake," and as they got tipsy on margaritas "the size of soup bowls," the idea of getting back together started to look good—to her.

"No f'ing way," was John's response.

Why?

"Because you're too old."

Janet was thirty-two.

Just a few years younger at twenty-eight, Lisa Wolfson was profiled in a 1984 in-depth feature in *Esquire* magazine called "The $100,000 a Year Woman." According to the Census Bureau, the article noted, there were now a hundred thousand women making over a hundred thousand a year, but in fact on Wall Street, women like Lisa made a lot more than that. She had passed the $100,000 salary mark early on while at Goldman Sachs, before she moved on to Odyssey Partners, a small private firm that invested only its own money.

Lisa was the first to admit, "Thirty years ago I'd have been the greatest corporate wife you ever saw. Thank God it's not thirty years ago." Married once and now divorced, she couldn't seem to keep a boyfriend because as soon as she had out-salaried him, he was done with her. One man had broken up with her when she passed the $150,000 salary mark because he was still trying to get to $40,000 at the time. Her assessment of the dating pool was eviscerating: "The single men I meet are wimps; the married ones just use me like the Nautilus at their gyms, for calisthenics." No less gutting was her ex-husband's take on her when asked what happened that they divorced: "I didn't know if she could share enough of herself to have children, or to raise them lovingly." His new wife was, in contrast, "completely uncompetitive, she seems born to share, and she doesn't use her smartness to punish you." Lisa and her ex-husband had met as undergraduates at Harvard, when her smartness and ambition had been attractive to him.

Lisa Wolfson's honesty, coupled with a seeming tendency toward navel-gazing (she allowed the reporter to live with her and even read and reproduce parts of her diary), led to some harsh conclusions about what it meant to be a young, successful woman on Wall Street.

In trying to explain her bad dating streak since divorcing, Lisa said: "You begin to feel it's very difficult to get involved with men not as successful as you are. So you see older people, you get a little cynical. Success eliminates men you would like to care about."

Lisa, described as a short brunette with "the high forehead and cheekbones of a taller woman; she is pretty but doesn't think so," was a bond trader "bounded by five monitors," including the Quotron and the Telerate. She was the only female trader in the office; the two other women were assistants. All three were single while all three men sitting at the same set of blinking monitors were married.

Even as far more than a handful of American women were now making over a hundred thousand dollars a year, Lisa's role as a trader was still relatively rare. To be a broker was to sell stock, or buy stock, to get paid for that regardless of how that stock then performed. As a trader, you were buying and selling, trying to reap significant profit and stave off losses; it was high-stakes gambling and until very recently, almost entirely off-limits to women. Sounding like she might suffer from ADHD, with a diet Tab soda permanently on hand while she stared intently at the monitors, Lisa quipped with the men, throwing barbs and bad jokes.

Her boss, when interviewed, did not hold back, even as he nursed, according to the *Esquire* reporter, an "avuncular crush on her." His assessment of Lisa was downright cruel: "We joke about it . . . but Lisa's personal life is nothing short of disaster. The men are either too old, too poor, or too neurotic . . . I gather she was as aggressive with her husband as she is in the rest of her life. What serves beautifully in her business becomes a tragedy at home. She's in a masculine business, so she becomes a take-charge guy like the rest of us. What man wants to be married to that? . . . Almost no woman in our business is happily married."

He went on to explain that the market's ups and downs led to his having erratic mood swings, so much so his wife would have to cau-

tion their children to stay away from him: "Now just think if I were
a woman. I have my shortcomings as a father, but as a mother I'd be
a disaster *and* a criminal. And what kind of man wants to be married
to that kind of woman?"

Perhaps he did have a crush on Lisa, and perhaps it was a case
of he "doth protest too much," but his assessment of her was like a
gut-punch. Lisa was of the generation that was being pushed by various forces—her ambition honed at top colleges and business schools,
her being told she could do anything in the wake of the women's
movement a decade earlier, yet this was coupled with continuous
male judgment of her high-status position and outdated expectations
of women as nurturers and baby-makers. When she first moved in
with her now ex-husband, her mother advised her to place an empty
notebook on his nightstand because, as Lisa's friend explained, her
mother believed "men have these profound thoughts at night, which
they need to put down on paper, but women don't." Ultimately, Lisa
put her finger on the problem: "I'm still enough of a product of the
1950s, or maybe I mean traditionally, inescapably female, to want a
man who is more successful than I am."

But for those women who had found that man or else didn't have
such rigid requirements, the question was whether to have children,
and if they agreed with writer Mary Kay Blakely not to give up their
careers, how then to juggle the two? That was the dilemma tackled by
the working mothers' group of the Financial Women's Association,
whose members met regularly for lunch "dressed in suits, silk shirts
or cashmere sweaters, and high-heeled shoes," to eat "boneless breast
of chicken" and discuss how to juggle it all.

The group had started informally in the late 1970s, the outcome
of a fortuitous breakfast meeting between a research analyst, Elaine
Rees, and Wall Street portfolio manager Betty Frank. Elaine had a
small son for whom she'd arranged childcare, but was feeling anxious
about it, and a friend put her in touch with Betty, who had two sons,

slightly older. Over breakfast, Betty regaled Elaine with tales of her parenting fails as a career woman, and when it was over, Elaine felt significantly better. She decided this sort of exchange would be good for all working mothers, and she started the group. In 1979, when she noticed everyone was especially confused about questions of childcare, she sent around a survey asking for specifics on nanny salaries and duties. With so many research analysts in the FWA, the survey results were quickly and expertly tabulated and shared.

Often, the working mothers' group invited guest speakers to their luncheons. Once, four professional men married to Lisa Wolfson–type women were brought in to discuss how they coped with their dual-career marriages and shared childcare responsibilities. But in some ways, the most popular meetings were when there was no guest speaker and instead just the women, usually about forty of them, around a lunch table, letting off steam and offering advice and useful tips—how to "have disposable diapers delivered to your house, find a baby-sitter at the last minute when your regular housekeeper gets sick, or mail-order a smoked turkey to make weekend entertaining easier . . ." Questions and debates also emerged: "How much . . . can you be away from your child to travel or socialize for business, or stay late at the office? Is it OK to have help for the children seven days a week, or is it important to be with them yourself on weekends? Can you let the housekeeper take the child to the doctor or help him or her with homework, or must you do these things yourself?" No one pretended that they were not in a unique position of being able to pay for what was needed, but that didn't mean the emotional burden felt lighter.

Mary Farrell, who was both Beth Dater's friend and also Cali Cole's—who was still simply saying she didn't have a boyfriend "at this time"—came to her first meeting of the working mothers' group while still pregnant. Growing up, she had watched her mother take care of six children, and the "drudgery" of it weighed on her. When she was a teenager, her mother bought Betty Friedan's *The Feminine Mystique* and Mary, thinking it was some sort of murder mystery, picked it up. "It was an eye-opener" because "what Betty Friedan was describing was kind of what I saw my mother" as.

It stayed with her, and at that first working mothers' meeting, Mary managed to get the name of a woman who went on to be her daughter's childcare-giver. At another meeting, Mary discovered that a woman at the NYSE, whom she knew professionally, had a son close to her daughter's age and lived nearby. Not only were weekly playdates arranged but the two Wall Street women created a backup plan should one of their housekeepers need time off—the other would then take both children.

Vitally, the working mothers' group was about having likeminded women around who helped stave off the incessant feeling of guilt that was coming at them from many directions. Mary was "hooked on the stock market, and I wanted very much to keep on working after my child was born. But many of our mothers and mothers-in-law who did it differently still questioned that choice." It just felt reassuring for her to be with women who didn't question the choice—even as she would divorce in 1987, in part because of her husband's expectations of a traditional family life.

The FWA contained many different views on feminism and its place on Wall Street, however. One member saw the organization as more of "a downtown Junior League, sort of a Republican conservative group" that would not let supporters of the Equal Rights Amendment canvas anywhere near their meetings—even getting a court order to ensure it. Yet, in 1981, the same year the working mothers' group became an official committee of the FWA, the association celebrated its twenty-fifth anniversary, purposefully choosing the august Federal Hall, where George Washington was inaugurated as president in 1789, a place very much built for men.

A former FWA president recounted how in the following year, the

FWA started to invite CEOs to their annual dinner. It was clear to them all that most of the men did not take the organization seriously. When Peter Cohen, formerly Sandy Weill's luggage-carrier and now CEO of Shearson American Express, arrived, he tried to charm them with condescending talk, including that he was so nervous to be there that he'd had to turn to his wife for help on how to dress for the occasion. Behind these closed doors, there was surely many a meaningful eye roll. A far more useful guest was Edwin Locke, president of the prestigious Economic Club of New York, who brought FWA women in and even onto the board. He also advised them on how to go about building their presence on corporate boards, starting with nonprofits and working toward corporate.

Like Beth Dater, Mary Farrell also appeared regularly on *Wall Street Week* as a Rukeyser Elf. Visibly pregnant with her second child, Rukeyser joked that she was "analyzing for two and should have a particularly clear view of the future." What surprised her was the amount of mail her pregnancy generated; viewers were fascinated by her having a high-powered job and a baby on the way. But Mary timed the birth of her two children so they wouldn't come when company earnings were reported—she had clients who were relying on her judgment calls at that crucial time. (Well into the late 1990s, women were timing their births, often using scheduled C-sections, around the financial world's schedules.) She understood it was career suicide to be unavailable.

When Mary moved over to Paine Webber in 1982, it was in part because the director of research was a woman, "probably the most prominent woman on Wall Street" at that time; in fact, she was Margo Alexander, Harvard Business School class of 1970, whose first offers after graduation were credit-card applications arriving in the mail. Margo had started out on Wall Street thinking she could enact change through business, and while she had abandoned that idea since, she did still strive to help other women. A mother herself,

Margo understood the costs of work versus family, and when Mary gave birth to her second child, for the following few years Margo quietly left her name off the business-trip rosters. (In the late 1980s, when firms were called on to account for their unequal hiring practices, Paine Webber noticed that any division Margo took over saw a significant increase in female hires.) It further helped that Paine Webber was run by Donald "Don" B. Marron, a man known on Wall Street for supporting women, in part because his first wife, Gloria Swope, had been one of the original eight founders of the FWA.

In 1985, the *Stanford Daily* reported on recent campus recruitment interviews with a Goldman Sachs representative, Michael Werner. One student was asked by him "whether I would have an abortion to save my job." Werner, who had himself graduated from Stanford just three years earlier, had met with around fifty seniors for the position of financial analyst. He defended himself by arguing that all he wanted to do was see if the interviewee would "go to the end of the world to be a professional." (In the early 1970s, Goldman Sachs was briefly banned from recruiting at Stanford after a recruiter told a Black job candidate that he "wouldn't fit in at the company.") A seasoned interviewer was quickly sent in to re-interview the students.

But Wall Street women rallied in anger. At Goldman Sachs, some women organized, calling themselves the Antidiscriminatory Underground, and sent letters out to business school deans informing them that, as women, they were there to say that they were not in fact allowed into Goldman Sachs' inner sanctum, regardless of what the firm might publicly claim. A partner at Goldman Sachs later told Mickie Siebert that the scandal had forced at least a couple of the partners to realize that when they interviewed women, "they tended to look for the qualities they admired in their mothers, sisters or wives—totally different qualities from those they sought in men."

According to Janet Tiebout, also at Goldman Sachs, this was a "moment of introspection," and countless women on Wall Street hoped it might be a "watershed moment," the one that would finally lead to "a level playing field." The hope was that as women started to occupy offices in the C suites of Wall Street's firms, they would demand to see a woman on every deal team. But that presumed that women were going to be promoted quickly. It also ignored the fact that being on the deal team usually meant hours too brutal for many women contemplating a life outside of work. Women were found more often in the less lucrative world of municipal finance because the hours were more humane, the pace slower, and at the end of the phone line, the pension- and insurance-fund managers were themselves often women.

Alice Jarcho, however, the only female trader on the Shearson American Express institutional trading desk, was now also in charge of it. Her husband, Tommy, had left to be a partner at Oppenheimer, and from being the second on the desk, she was promoted to number one: "That was it. That was where I had always wanted to be." She was in charge of two hundred people scattered across various offices, including London. "I was in heaven. I loved it. . . . I really had power."

She was still predominantly surrounded by men, but now there were some high-flying women retail brokers with her on the trading floor on the 104th floor of the World Trade Center. She could hear the men talking about them, and it made her stomach turn: "One of them was really large-breasted—endless conversations about her tits. . . . That was the word. . . ."

If someone had made a mistake on Tommy's watch, he would yell at the desk, whereas Alice, now in charge, reverted to her old friend, sarcasm. Her desk was profitable, she was well respected, and when in 1984, Shearson American Express bought Lehman Brothers Kuhn Loeb, it was assumed she'd continue to lead when the desks merged. The Lehman desk had more people on it but was far less profitable. The numbers couldn't lie: her desk was the better one. Peter Cohen, the CEO of Shearson, said as much to her.

But then suddenly she heard that "the Lehman guys wouldn't work with me." Because she was a woman. They threatened to walk out if they had to work for Alice Jarcho.

Alice had overcome so many obstacles, but this one really got to her. She went through "the five phases of grief, and, frankly, I never got to acceptance. I was just heartbroken." She would later wonder if she shouldn't have stayed on as head of the merged trading desk, feelings be damned. But instead, Alice Jarcho, even after—or perhaps because of—everything that had been thrown in her path, left. Gutted, she enrolled at Marymount Manhattan College to finish her college degree, and in 1986, she had a son. She had been placed in a situation where she did not have to choose between work or children. It had been chosen for her.

13

What Goes Up
Must Come Down

Wall Street had discovered junk bonds, and Michael Milken, the Junk Bond King, was now the ruler of the markets. Back in the 1970s, working on the research desk of Drexel Burnham Lambert in "an ill-fitting toupee" and "clothes that looked to be straight off the rack," he had come up with the idea of repurposing the junk bond. Junk bonds were bonds issued by corporations considered financially shaky. Because their rating (in terms of creditworthiness) was low (a BB, B, CC or worse)—as determined by the ratings agencies Standard & Poor's, Moody's, or Fitch—these bonds came with much higher risk, and the pot to entice investors was sweetened in the form of a very high coupon return for the investor—10 percent or 12 percent. The return was alluring enough that, as Dylan Gottlieb shows, while in 1980 banks issued $5.35 billion worth of such bonds, in 1986 they issued $46 billion.

Junk bonds were initially derived from "fallen angels," companies once considered stars but whose investment grade had fallen dramatically, leaving few investors willing to touch them. But Milken found that the problem often was that these companies had overdiversified, whether into new companies or new products, which led to a lowered rating when in fact they contained value well above their investment grade.

Yet even as Milken's junk bonds took off, there were just so many companies whose ratings were low even as the company held high value, and thus he needed to come up with something more in order to create a real market in junk bonds. His answer was to tap into the vast number of medium-size firms in need of capital that had been unable to convince investment banks to underwrite their IPOs. Milken's team found that they could raise capital for these firms by creating entirely new junk bonds.

Milken's department was soon producing 35 percent of Drexel's profits. Leveraging his power, he not only got to distribute his department's profit share as he saw fit—taking a substantial portion for himself—but also moved his team away from Wall Street and out to sunny Southern California. According to his tax returns, in 1983 Milken took home a whopping $47.5 million, an extraordinary sum for the time, but it reflected his role as the creator of an entire market that generated both enormous deal fees and trading profits for his firm. When for his thirty-eighth birthday his colleagues called in a stripper, he hid under his desk, pulling his phone down with him, and continued to trade while the stripper did what she was hired to do.

The junk bond was now a gushing spigot of capital that powered the financing behind leveraged buyouts (LBOs) and mergers and acquisitions (M&As). As Gottlieb writes, "In 1975, the total value of U.S. merger transactions had been $11.8 billion. By 1983, that figure surged to $73.1 billion. Merger values hit $122 billion in 1984, $180 billion in 1985, and $248 billion in 1988—twenty times the 1975 baseline." Junk bonds were changing the landscape of American finance, while the investment banks and bankers, the puppet masters orchestrating the M&As and LBOs, were collecting million-dollar-plus fees for their services.

There were those who argued, like Milken, that these takeovers were good for corporations, and therefore good for America. Louis Rukeyser agreed, believing that "many U.S. corporate managements had grown stagnant and complacent and contemptuous of their own stockholders, the ultimate owners of the corporation," and that they had bought into the idea that they were "major figures in our society" and not just men doing the "vulgar" job of making money for stockholders. As a result, they overpaid themselves and "lived the lives of 19th Century maharajas." Corporate raider T. Boone Pickens told Rukeyser privately after a taping of *Wall $treet Week* that he used to be invited to hunting lodges and parties, wined and dined by "the corporate oil club," until one day he was asked what he would do if he were running one of the oil companies. He said he'd "go to work for the *shareholders* for a change." He was not invited back. Asked about the fallout when the corporate raiders like Pickens arrived, about the auto workers who might well lose their jobs, Rukeyser answered: "Certainly, there is pruning that is inevitable."

———

JOLYNE CARUSO, LIKE RUKEYSER, WOULD BECOME FASCINATED BY these new cowboys, these 1980s-era gunslingers. She had started off wanting to be a young Barbara Walters, the pioneering TV journalist, and planned to take that route as a Barnard College student. The summer before her freshman year, needing a summer job, her father, who worked on Wall Street, secured her a position with Bear Stearns working in "the cage." Every brokerage firm had "the cage," the room where the physical stock and bond certificates were received, transferred, and distributed. Most often it was a windowless room down in the basement of a building. The following summer, now on the masthead of Barnard's student paper, Jolyne was back doing cold calls for Bear Stearns' retail sales department. Each morning she was handed a stack of index cards with names, addresses, and phone numbers (there was a company from which brokers would buy these nuggets of private information printed out on index cards with holes punched in to fit into the Rolodex) and she would dial.

By her junior year at Barnard, she was working Christmas vacation and spring break at Bear Stearns, and when they asked if she'd come in regularly on Fridays, Jolyne arranged her class schedule so she'd have Fridays clear. While everyone else started partying on Thursday night, she was in bed and then up early on Friday, catching the subway from 116th Street down to Water Street. Graduating in 1981, she still wanted to be Barbara Walters, and landed an interview at the *New York Times*, where they offered her $10,000 a year as a "copy girl." Ace Greenberg, the head of Bear Stearns, counter offered with a hard-to-resist $25,000, plus an end-of-year bonus.

Hired as a sales associate, Jolyne was soon promoted to the institutional equities sales desk. Bear Stearns was, in Jolyne's words, a "commission shop," a "Jewish scrappy firm, and I loved it there" but it was also "the worst place for women." There was one man who would rent out an enormous limousine to ferry clients to games and events, and Jolyne, barely twenty-one, would be sitting in the car surrounded by women, not knowing if they were wives or mistresses or hookers. A typical week on the trading floor meant the air was so thick with cigar smoke that it was "like walking into a bar." For birthdays, the traders would pool their money and hire strippers with tasseled pasties to jump out of cakes. The *Wall Street Journal* described the Bear Stearns trading floor in 1982, the very year that Jolyne arrived there as a full-time, entry-level junior salesperson, as "jammed with some 250 people. The traders buy and sell stocks, options, corporate and municipal bonds, government securities and other financial instruments. Tiny green numbers glitter across computer terminals sitting on traders' desks amid baskets of paper, empty Styrofoam cups and brown-bag lunches lugged from home to enable traders to stay wired to the market's pulse all day long."

The Bear Stearns trading floor was notorious as one of the wildest on Wall Street. Jolyne attributed it to the jock culture that had started to invade the Street in the early 1980s, turning the trading floor into a locker room. The Ivy League and B-school graduates most often went into investment banking and research, they were the pinstriped M&A crowd, but out on the trading floor, it was different. Hiring policy for the floor leaned heavily toward athletes in the same way that before it had favored war veterans. All of Bear Stearns equity traders seemed to be former ice-hockey players, including former NY Rangers Dave Maloney and André Doré. It didn't hurt that star-struck clients wanted to have dinner with them.

Jolyne's boss was Mitch Jennings, Beth Dater's second husband. He was "very fit, handsome—he used to play squash—always a pin-striped suit, shirt and tie, white shirt, very starched, very WASPy, very buttoned-up." Jolyne was completely intimidated by him, but he proved to be a "champion of women," and Jolyne credited Beth for that. Mitch took Jolyne to sales meetings, portfolio manager dinners, to lunches at the India House, the private luncheon club above Harry's at Hanover Square, where wine was always served, everyone smoked, and a vodka on the rocks was there for the asking. Sometimes he'd ask her to take notes and write them up as minutes, and when he thought she was ready, Mitch asked her what she thought, asked her in a room full of mostly men seated around tables with dirty dishes, half-empty glasses, and overflowing ashtrays. She was the junior salesperson, and he gave her accounts she could work on, where she could test her mettle.

The first time she met Beth in the flesh was at the annual Bear Stearns summer barbeque. In walked Beth, this iconic portfolio manager, a Rukeyser Elf (Jolyne watched *Wall $treet Week* with an addict's attention). She was "whip-smart" with "a strong voice" that was impossible to ignore. She walked into the backyard barbeque "polished," just like her husband, with not a hair out of place. But it was her engagement ring, an enormous sapphire, that Jolyne could not stop staring at. She wanted to be Beth, but she also wanted children, and like so many women around her, she was trying to figure out how to do it all, wondering if it was even possible for her, even as it hadn't been for Beth and her generation.

Jolyne was also fascinated by the corporate raiders, the "big deal kings," and the "sophisticated financing techniques" that used debt as it had never been used before. It was an entirely new form of financial engineering, the creation of new products, and a rethinking of capital, as she saw it. In 1987, when Mitch Jennings handed her an early version of the laptop, she would "schlep" this impossibly heavy computer that "felt like it was two hundred pounds" home to Brooklyn, its enormous charger and the four-by-four rigid plastic disks that one slid into a slot to feed it information, also stuffed into the cumbersome shoulder bag. Bear Stearns's risk arbitrage department, soon to become the largest on the Street, courted the corporate raiders as clients and invested in their takeover targets. When Mitch handed Jolyne this computer, he said he wanted her to be the risk-arbitrage liaison for their institutional salespeople.

Jolyne loved it all, the takeovers, the leveraged buyouts, and she avidly followed what Michael Milken, Carl Icahn, and Ivan Boesky were doing, fascinated by "the deal." She watched it up close, sitting at the center of the takeover mania: "I loved going to work, I used to run to work." Everyone now wanted to work on Wall Street, and the Street seemed to have an insatiable hunger for new hires. Jolyne watched young men—still mostly men—get recruited right out college, "plopped down" at a trading desk, and made over into traders within a matter of weeks.

Milken argued that leveraged buyouts, fueled by his junk bonds, strengthened companies, purged them of excess. Not everyone loved junk bonds, however. In June 1985, Mickie Siebert testified before the Senate Banking Committee and told them that in her opinion, junk bonds should carry a warning label the same way that cigarettes did: "Hazardous to your financial health." In response, Fred Joseph, the chief executive of Drexel Burnham Lambert, sent Mickie a letter telling her that she "didn't know what [she] was talking about."

Phyllis Strong, who at Lehman had escaped the Hartford insurance men and was now working on media deals, had been promoted from analyst to associate. Ordinarily, she would have been expected to leave for business school after her two years in the analyst program, and then return to Wall Street on the associate track. But it was 1985, the market was exploding, and "they needed bodies more than they needed people going in and out." When she'd started at Lehman, anything from a $50 million deal to a $500 million deal was considered big, seriously big, but three years later the deals were ten times as much. Junior people—analysts and early associates—were in demand because they were the ones who did the number crunching, running the computer programs and the financial analysis: what might a merger look like if the profits were 2 percent or 5 percent or 7 percent? Myriad possibilities, all now being fed into computers. There were so many variables to configure that it required all hands on deck. When her department was doing a deal for Westinghouse Cable, the partners and executives would meet at 3 p.m. and then the underlings, Phyllis included, would get their marching orders. They worked through the night to put out an entire booklet examining the various scenarios based on a host of variables in play, then went home, slept, and returned the next day to do it all over again.

Phyllis noticed that while the *Animal House* antics had always been there and were nothing new, now they were seen as evidence of how hard you were working: if you played hard, it implied you worked hard. The screaming, cursing, and throwing of things came from a sense of your own privilege, a belief that you had passed through "these golden gates" and had a right to act out. The perks were set up to bolster the myth of enormous profits being a product of long hours; if you worked past 8 p.m., you were automatically eligible to get a free dinner and black car service home. (As Westina Matthews's uncle, civil rights activist Bill Berry, assured her when she was feeling bashful about using the perks—the cars were there to encourage you to work later into the night, and not using the fancy dining rooms would make *them* uncomfortable, as if she were judging how they lived.)

It was clear to Phyllis that "there was a premium put on looking like you were working hard." Or, as historian Steve Fraser sees it, starting with the Reagan years, "Wall Street came to be widely admired not just as an avenue to wealth, but as a school of life, open to all, rewarding innovation, tough-mindedness, and studious attention to the inexorable laws of the free market. Reservations about its darker side were muted if not entirely silenced." Sometimes Phyllis and her friends would go to one of the dance clubs and then return to Lehman to pull an all-nighter. It was a showy move. Everyone was just a few years out of college, and dinner breaks, food containers strewn across desks, were like a Wall Street simulacrum of the college cafeterias they had all frequented until just recently. The discussions barely differed from those they'd had in college, and certainly no one seemed to address the implications of what they were doing as they helped facilitate one M&A deal after another.

Phyllis only began to seriously consider the fallout when she was in a meeting for a cable-company merger that her Lehman team was setting up. Discussion centered on how to merge this company, how best to pull money out of it to service the debt that had been placed on it via junk bonds. Prior to 1982, the thinking was that a good company CEO did their best to keep their company debt-free. But now debt was seen as "smart" because interest payments on certain kinds of debt were tax deductible.

Phyllis was sitting next to the Lehman VP, the second in command after the partner on the deal, and together they were going over

WHAT GOES UP MUST COME DOWN

the annual report of the target company. They needed to make cuts, he said. He pointed Phyllis to the page with a footnote about pensions and indicated that these were traditionally overfunded, so she could pull the money out from there. No one in the room was thinking, or perhaps allowing themselves to think, or maybe they didn't even care, that there were actual people behind these annual reports, buried there within the small print in the footnote section on pensions. It made her pause.

She found herself thinking how she and her colleagues were now making life-and-death decisions, playing God. Before, corporations had looked to investment banks when they needed financing by selling their stock in order to feed capital back into their companies. Now, investment banks eyed corporations not as partners in growing the economy but as "assets to be sold off for a profit." Companies, seeing the writing on the wall, had to fend off takeovers, resorting to short-term thinking instead of long-term planning, with employees an afterthought at best.

Phyllis felt it "was a winner-take-all feeling. A reverence for the markets, the belief that they would settle everything." There was also, from what Phyllis could see, a lot of entitlement parading around, creating an atmosphere in which real ability easily went unrecognized while showmanship was rewarded. Often it was those with an overblown sense of their skill set who took credit for the windfalls.

Phyllis would often look at her expensive Swiss watch, the one she'd impulsively bought at duty-free in the Geneva airport, and feel the weight of her "golden handcuff." The watch increasingly came to represent her dawning realization, however clichéd, that money could not in fact buy happiness. Every time her team closed a deal with one of their entertainment and media clients, she wanted to follow them out to Hollywood and never look back. It was a heady game she played, making deals with 20th Century Fox, pitching to Disney, orchestrating the sale of cable companies and broadcasting outlets, but the truth was that she wasn't building anything. She was pulling it all apart. Her team's job was to merge businesses, and whatever parts of them were failing to generate profit, to surgically remove. In 1986, Phyllis Strong wrangled her wrist free, put the watch in a drawer, and left Wall Street for good.

———

BUT ELISA ANCONA, FOR ONE, *WANTED* THE GOLDEN HANDCUFFS. IN high school, working at Key Food and wearing clothes sewn by her Basque immigrant mother, Elisa looked ahead to when she would own a BMW of her own, the car that the wealthy families drove. When some of the high school kids got in her face and tried to fight her, she'd laugh—summers in Basque territory had toughened her up: shootings, beatings, hiding under parked cars, watching carefully for anyone wearing red and yellow, Basque's independence colors. Her father worked in construction, a foreman on the Twin Towers, and he had mastered concrete sculpture on the side, winning awards for his work. Her mother had found a job in a factory sewing suits and designer dresses for Saks Fifth Avenue, bringing home $90 a week. Elisa had a very different number to which she aspired: $1 million.

But with yuppies roaming Manhattan like hungry coyotes, what had once seemed rich was now tagged as merely "comfortable." As a student at Pace University in 1982, Elisa flipped through the career center listings for part-time work arranged in a large binder sitting out on a table. She stopped randomly at Gabelli & Company, who were looking for a "Girl Friday." She got the job and was put to work filing away clients' stock-market portfolios: Marsha Mason, *The Goodbye Girl* star, and then wife of Neil Simon . . . Lillian Vernon, entrepreneur and philanthropist. As she looked at their stock holdings, it dawned on her: the goal post had shifted. A million dollars was peanuts now!

Money manager Mario Gabelli, or "Super Mario" as he was

called by some, had about $300 million worth of portfolio accounts. His investment strategy since the 1970s had been to identify companies whose stock was selling at far less than their asset value, and now here he was, in the midst of a crazed mergers and buyouts frenzy, reaping the rewards. In 1984, he put out a client report he named, tongue-in-cheek, "Rest in Peace," an ode to all the companies acquired or bought out, in which he and his clients held stock. He sarcastically asked his readers to "share his 'grief.' " Gabelli was, like Elisa, from the outer boroughs, the Bronx, and every day was like a street fight. He would look at his employees, chomping on his cigar like it was a pacifier, and single one out for a verbal thrashing. Elisa had an advantage, at least at the beginning, and it was not their shared working-class roots or both being the children of immigrants, but rather her name, which was also Gabelli's daughter's. He could not bring himself to bellow *"ELISA!!!"*

Elisa was a quick learner, and when she graduated from Pace University in 1986, after having worked as the Girl Friday throughout college, Mario Gabelli offered her a full-time job for $35,000 plus bonus. By then, Gabelli & Company had various departments going—the trading room, the Gamco Investors Group, arbitrage, retail, mutual funds. The support staff were largely women, and the only woman in venture capital, a feminist who smoked cigars, stood out like a sore thumb, a lone wolf. Thirty-five thousand dollars plus a bonus for a twenty-two-year-old in 1986 was damn good, and Elisa was happy to have it, but there was a lot she had to put up with for that money. She came to understand that Gabelli was a "demanding perfectionist." Elisa had a theory that as you attained this level of power, you also developed an ego to match, and you let go of the filters that others still possessed. Money bought freedom from accountability. "You think you have the right to speak to people in a particular way." Managing billions of dollars now, different products, different investors, "the ego gets skewed, and people are willing

to kiss your ring." For Gabelli, she said, it was normal to say to someone: "Go fuck yourself. Go stand by that wall and be a fly."

Elisa learned to anticipate her boss's next move before he asked
her to do something. She had to be one step ahead, always. She knew
that if she stuck it out for a year or two, she could get a job anywhere.
The job Gabelli offered her was as an assistant to his chain smoking, puffy-sleeved secretary Roseanne (buying a little of whatever
Gabelli was buying, Roseanne would eventually buy an apartment
with her husband, a plumber, in Trump Tower). Mario Gabelli sat at
a huge cherrywood desk, chomping that cigar, and would scream his
requests at Roseanne because that is how they communicated, just as
no one at the office passed anything to anyone but instead tossed it.

Roseanne decided she would communicate with Elisa, *her* under-
ling, in the same way she was treated by Gabelli. She screamed her
orders at Elisa; she tossed envelopes and memos into her cubicle as if
she were feeding the sea lions at the Central Park Zoo. One day, Elisa
had had enough. While Roseanne was gone, she loosened the screws
at the bottom of her spring chair. When Roseanne returned and sat
down, she went flying. Elisa walked over and, looking down at Roseanne sprawled on the floor, said, "If you ever speak to me again the
way he speaks to you. . . ." And then she offered Roseanne her hand
and helped her up. From that day, Roseanne was "sweet as pie," and
they became partners in the workplace.

Mario Gabelli had noticed that when Elisa was asked to record
shares bought or sold, she was thorough. This was nothing to scoff
at—every brokerage firm, and every floor broker at the NYSE, was
perpetually terrified of finding themselves with errors in the recorded
sale. Gabelli promoted her to assistant in the trading room, where she
was given all his client portfolios to manually enter trades and check
them over. She soon had it down to an error-free science. Every Monday morning at 9:15 a.m., Gabelli would show up with a long list of

trades and Elisa had fifteen minutes in which to write up a stack of orders that was inches high.

The trading room was like Mario Gabelli amplified. Every other word was "fuck." One time, he asked her for some portfolios and then called to have his Jaguar brought around to the front. As he was leaving, Elisa started running after him with the portfolios in her arms, down eleven flights of stairs, and out onto the street trying to catch up. He was already sitting in the back of the Jaguar, and when he saw her, he lowered his window. She hoisted the portfolios and threw them at him: "When you ask for something, you wait for it!" When she got back up to the office, the phones were ringing off the hook, one after another. It was Gabelli trying to find her. When she finally picked up, he said, "Thank you," and then hung up.

Elisa's best friend in the office was Maria, who spoke Spanish, which Elisa spoke, too, in addition to Catalan. Altogether there were four "street kids," as she referred to herself and Maria and the other two, none of whom had been born with silver spoons in their mouths. All spoke Spanish, which they used to their advantage and amusement. A favorite pastime was to pass by the desk of one of the silver spoons, the *gilipollas*, the assholes, who treated them "like garbage," and say things in Spanish that no one except the four of them could understand. But there were also other ways of getting back at the *gilipollas*. They all wore expensive Brooks Brothers ties, and the "street kids" liked to punch holes in the bottom of the paper cups, so when the *gilipollas* poured a cup of coffee, their ties were wrecked.

Gabelli sat opposite Elisa on the trading desk, with a shoulder rest attached to his phone to alleviate neck cramps. When "he was pissed off, he'd fling it at the board," and she would have to duck as it sailed through the air. One day, she arrived decked out in full football gear. He took one look and started laughing. Point taken.

The one time he truly got Elisa, however, he wasn't even aware.

The previous night she'd gone to Delmonico's with a team from Shearson. She eventually called her mother—she was still living at home—because it was 4 a.m. and everything was spinning. She managed to get home, shower, dress, and board the B train back, her pores still reeking of alcohol. On the trading desk, she found a Big Mac waiting for her, and everyone was laughing. As luck would have it, Gabelli, who never showed up in the office on a Friday, happened to be there. He called her into his office, along with one of the department heads. Elisa's head was pounding, and holding a notebook in her shaky hands, she tried to keep up as he rattled off his orders that he wanted her to trade on a million-dollar account. But the words all seemed to float past her. Done, he sent them out of his office, and Elisa turned to the department head who shrugged and then headed off to do another line of coke before going back to their office. Elisa turned for help to Irene, one of the traders.

"Just buy the usual stock," Irene advised. She was right—it was practically impossible *not* to make money in the market in the 1980s.

DOREEN MOGAVERO WAS ON THE FLOOR OF THE NYSE, WORKING FOR one of Jolyne's heroes, who many believed possessed a crystal ball. Ivan Boesky had a reputation as someone who barely slept, worked impossible hours, and juggled multiple calls and conversations at once. It was no secret that a vital element to being a skilled arbitrageur was the acquisition of information. But the use of material nonpublic information (MNPI) was, according to the Securities Exchange Commission, illegal, offering an unfair advantage: it was insider trading. The SEC, Wall Street's oversight body, had remained fairly lax about policing, but now there were whispers on the Street that Boesky's "arbitrage gains were ill-gotten," so much so that when Drexel Burnham Lambert's executives learned that Michael Milken, their superstar, planned to raise $640 million for Boesky, they were not happy.

Some worried that with Boesky inevitably betting on LBOs that Milken would most likely be helping to put into play, it would be too tempting for Milken to share information with Boesky. Sharing of information often meant walking a fine line but one that you had to see clearly. All research on Wall Street is about having an edge on others through information and data that others might not possess. The SEC's thinking was that one could build a mosaic of clues gleaned, of bits and pieces of information and data, and make an educated guess as to whether a company might be a potential takeover target. But anything more than that was illegal. This was what worried Drexel Burnham Lambert's executives, but Michael Milken could not be dissuaded. Now happily ensconced in his offices under the California sunshine, he ignored what they were saying back in New York.

Every morning, up since 5 a.m. and having already watched and read the news, Doreen Mogavero came in to work from Staten Island with her husband, Arcky. As money was surging through Wall Street, so too was it surging globally, and she had to keep up with the overseas market news. Arriving at the NYSE, Doreen would go upstairs to the Luncheon Club to have breakfast with other brokers, all talking about their previous day's orders so that by the time she was ready to walk out onto the floor, she had a much better idea of what might lay ahead. Once at her booth, she talked to her clerks, who'd already been there for some time. While she'd had breakfast, gauging the markets, the clerks had been calling clients, getting a feel for what they were thinking at their end. Now they relayed that information to Doreen, who went out to the specialist posts to get a pre-opening look into the stocks her clients were after that day. If there was a large stock order, she would ease in once the bell rang, get a sense of its movement, not go all in: "We were the original algorithms . . ." The display board with brokers' badge numbers summoning them back to their booths had disappeared, and now it was beepers instead. And no longer did Doreen have to call a squad to get a message to her clerk out in the booth; now there were islands of yellow phones with which to communicate.

It was the decade of deals. Working for Boesky meant that Doreen's stock orders were substantial. If he wanted to amass a position, he bought millions of shares (not the norm back then), and she was smack in the middle of it. When she went out onto the floor, everyone knew it was likely to be big. She had her calculator, but there was one guy on the floor who didn't bother with one: he could do the sums faster in his head. "If you need that, forget it," he once said coming up behind Doreen, and, to her shock, tossed away her calculator.

The market was so hot, and the deals so persistent, no one dared leave the floor. Restaurants delivered, and a broker who was feeling particularly flush from a deal might order in hundreds of White Castle burgers or towers of boxed pizzas to share. Ostentation was applauded. There was the well-known story of how Boesky, who routinely appeared on magazine covers and television spots, arrived with his wife at the New York restaurant Café des Artistes for a dinner with an up-and-coming young arbitrageur, John Mulheren, and his wife. Boesky, looking over the menu, announced to the waiter that he would first have one of "every entrée" and then decide what he wanted. The dishes were wheeled in, and Boesky stood up, fork in hand, and took a bite of each before declaring the winner. The remaining seven were sent back to the kitchen.

At Mitch Jennings's request, Jolyne Caruso was sitting in on risk arbitrage meetings, taking notes on the mergers and acquisitions under discussion, and calling Bear Stearns clients who had takeover stock in their portfolios and might be willing to make a trade. Every afternoon at 2 p.m., in her mid-twenties and newly married (now Jolyne Caruso-FitzGerald), she got on the trading room's squawk box. She would come up to the mic at the center of the room and wait while an announcement was put out to all the branches—San Francisco, Boston, Chicago: "We're starting the 2 p.m. sales call."

She could feel the power standing at that microphone as she got "on the horn," and reported the day's rundown: "We increased our position in Pillsbury, we decreased our position in TransAmerica . . ."

After about a year, as the popularity of her 2 p.m. call grew, Mitch suggested she do the same but in written form—a monthly newsletter for investors, especially for portfolio managers like Patricia Chadwick. Patricia was now finding what was inside her portfolios to be ever more complicated because if she had, for example, Pillsbury stock in there, and Pillsbury got taken over, the acquiring company did not always pay cash. More often, they paid a package made up of cash mixed in with junk bonds that added up to the value of the acquisition price. Someone now had to guide investors on what to do with these. That became Jolyne's job; to help others manage the junk bonds, to help them decide when to sell them. Those who read Jolyne's report would then be more likely to trade their junk bonds through Bear Stearns—which is exactly what happened, helping to grow Bear Stearns's risk arbitrage junk bond trading desk into one of the largest on Wall Street.

Janet Tiebout, at Goldman Sachs, whose ex-husband had told her she was too old to date at thirty-two, had arrived on Wall Street at the very tail end of the 1970s—when Vietnam vets still dominated the hardscrabble trading floors. If you had served your country, you were considered fit for the job. But by the mid-1980s, in some sectors, more specialized people were needed in this newly computerized, rapid-trade decade. A different kind of person was installed at the desks, someone who, Janet noted, was "less human," "less random," and certainly not someone driven by a "whimsical approach" to trading. Risk needed to be better managed, and stock picking could not come down to having "a feeling."

Thus, a new breed appeared on Wall Street: the math wizard, the quantitative analyst, the "quant," who could run the increasingly complex algorithms, combining technology and high-level mathematics. In many ways, it was Lew Ranieri's securitization that had first beckoned the quants to Wall Street. To make the mortgage-backed securities more engaging for institutional funds, Ranieri had come up with yet another kind of bond: the collateralized mortgage obligation, the CMO, which chopped up the baskets of mortgages into various "tranches" from which portfolio managers like Patricia Chadwick could pick and choose, depending on their needs. But these were so complex—or, as Ranieri proclaimed, "mortgages are math"—that his team needed to be plucked not from the Salomon Brothers back office, as he himself had been, but from top-level MBA programs and mathematics departments.

And while the quants were rarely women, women were now arriving on Wall Street in droves because every division inside every investment bank and brokerage house was exploding exponentially, and when they needed people to fill the seats, they couldn't afford to be quite so discriminating—in both senses of the word. In the 1970s, there had been so few women in finance that no one, Janet felt, really cared that she was sitting there, but now they started to care because women were suddenly everywhere: "Wall Street made Madison Avenue"—Mad Ave, with its notoriously Mad Men—"look like church."

In 1982, Ivan Boesky's star had momentarily dimmed after he experienced a significant loss on a deal with Gulf Oil that fell through. After that, he was in search of a workaround in the same way that Donald Trump had found a loophole after Mayor Ed Koch had refused to give him the 421-a tax abatement for Trump Towers. Boesky needed to find a way to avert risk going forward. He found it, just as the New York office of Drexel Burnham Lambert had feared, with Michael Milken. The two began to run a clandestine tab of their profits and losses. Milken would "park" Boesky's money, hiding it from view, so that Boesky could keep his cards hidden during the complex game of M&A. Milken and Boesky were not exactly the first to park money even though it clearly went against the SEC's full-disclosure rules. But Rudy Giuliani, the U.S. attorney for Manhattan's Southern District, basking in the glow of his recent wins pursuing New York's top mafia families, was sniffing about for his next target. He turned his sights on the Junk Bond King—Milken.

Getting to Milken required other dominoes to fall: Giuliani first went after Dennis Levine, in the New York office of Drexel, for insider training. Levine in turn offered up Ivan Boesky, and Boesky, cornered, also agreed to cooperate. On November 14, 1986—a day forever known on Wall Street as "Boesky Day"—the SEC chairman called a press conference. Boesky would pay a $100 million fine for insider trading and be barred from the American securities industry following an eighteen-month phase-out period.

Wall Street went on high alert. Most suspected that "Ivan the Terrible," as Boesky had long been called, was handing over names. One of the ruling kings had become a snitch. The TV show *Dynasty* remained fully in step with the times, having incorporated the character of arbitrageur and junk bond specialist Dirk Maurier into the storyline from 1983 to 1987.

For Doreen, the shock of Boesky's indictment was compounded by her mother's diagnosis of late-stage pancreatic cancer. The day her mother was diagnosed, Doreen got up at three in the morning, unable to sleep, and told Arcky she was going to drive in to work: "I have got to get out of here. I just have to go." Ivan, well known for barely sleeping, was already at the office when she arrived at 4:30 a.m. He was in his phase-out months, granted permission by the SEC to wind down operations. He came out of his office to ask what she was doing there.

Crying, she said: "My God, my mother's so sick . . . She's got three weeks to live."

Boesky didn't say a word. He went into the kitchen and returned with a cup of tea that he placed in front of her.

That Boesky was even available to make tea for Doreen, that he was

given eighteen months to unfurl himself from Wall Street, was an outrage to many. Some believed that the SEC chairman, a former investment
banker, was so fixated on liquidity—the vast movements of capital in
and out of the markets at which Boesky excelled—that he held a grudg-
ing respect for Boesky and had dragged his feet on the investigation.

Louise Jones, a great believer in liquidity herself, felt only disgust.
She didn't care that Boesky made tea for Doreen: "You don't have to
be evil to be a thief." Her disgust shifted to outrage when everyone
came to understand that the SEC had in fact gifted Boesky with time
before publicly announcing his plea bargain, meaning that he had
known of his own demise ahead of everyone else, and could trade on
this insider knowledge. The irony was staggering.

But even Boesky Day had not dampened the buying spree. The
following year, 1987, saw a fifth year of a thriving bull market, and
while there had been some blips here and there, the market was
already up 35 percent from the beginning of the year, and it didn't
seem to matter to anyone that interest rates were rising.

But by August of 1987, there were some who were starting to feel
a touch nervous about this long streak of good luck and favorable
winds. At least one Wall Street CEO had started to question the new
buildings going up all over the Financial District and the flush brokerage firms anointing their lobbies with mahogany and marble as if they
were indestructible, as if the lessons of the past didn't apply to them.

Then, on October 12, Elaine Garzarelli, the wild child of Wall
Street, a market strategist at Shearson Lehman, went on CNN and
warned that a repeat of the 1929 financial crash was just around the
corner. Elaine was known for her television appearances, including
Rukeyser's Wall $treet Week, of course, as well as for her disdain
for conservative clothes, preferring "short skirts and spiked heels,"
which she accessorized with "10 pairs of color contacts." In her early
days on Wall Street, in her twenties and thirties, she had worked a
minimum of twelve-hour days, finding stress relief and after-hours

aerobic exercise in New York City's nightclubs, which she went to at least three times a week, leaving the office at 11 p.m. and the club at 2 a.m. Her office at Lehman was decorated with autographed photos of the rocker Joan Jett and pop star Cyndi Lauper, and Lauper had signed hers with a clever rewording of her hit song: "*Elaine, Girls just wanna have funds.*" Elaine was sometimes derided for being a "media hound," and disliked by some women on Wall Street for her flamboyant style, which they felt was not helping women.

Elaine had started at Drexel Burnham Lambert during the 1970s, and had no doubt that the women's movement had helped catapult her to VP even as she still felt like "a kid." In her view, 1980s sexism was worse, however. Or maybe it was that she had risen to a position that made her more of a threat? Her strategy for dealing with all of it was to stroke the men's egos, she said, because "I don't care if they steal my ideas, as long as the market goes up when I want it to go up and down when I want it to go down. But they always like to be important in their own meetings." She was rumored to make an annual salary of $1.6 million, but her idea of financial independence was, in her words, to have enough so that she could "fall in love with whomever, like Cher."

Earlier that year, Shearson Lehman had awarded the thirty-six-year-old "financial wizard," listed as "the foremost quantitative analyst" by *Institutional Investor* magazine for the four previous years, her own fund of $440 million, called Sector Analysis.

During the contract negotiations around the fund, a Lehman colleague insisted that there be a clause to protect the firm should Elaine abandon it to get married (not that she hadn't already done marriage—twice in fact—but neither of her husbands, she said, had been able to handle her success, one apparently lobbing a copy of the *Wall Street Journal* at her face). She refused to sign any contract with such a clause. She got the fund nonetheless, but even so, she had to do the heavy lifting of bringing in major clients: "I had to take each and every one of these guys out to dinner, and just keep explaining and explaining and *explaining* what I was doing." Fifty thousand investors eventually joined her new fund, but barely a month after launching it, she took a good look at her indicators and pulled much of the money out of the market.

On Tuesday, October 12, 1987, Elaine was sure enough about her predictions that she agreed to go on CNN's *Moneyline* with Lou Dobbs even as she worried that "Lehman's going to kill me." She didn't sugarcoat her financial forecast: "It's going to collapse," she said on camera.

On Thursday, October 15, Barbara Byrne (formerly Moakler), who had had to learn how to pronounce "elite" at Mount Holyoke, was delivering her first baby. After she had broken up with her fake Goldman Sachs "boyfriend," the man she pretended had bought her the white-amber mink, she had started dating the very real Tom Byrne, a stock futures index trader and son of a former governor of New Jersey. They had met at a Williams College party in the city. Barbara had stepped over to the right side of the tracks to claim her place, and when the wedding announcement came out in the *New York Times* in 1985, it was noted that Barbara Ann Moakler, "a senior vice president in the investment banking division of Shearson Lehman Brothers in New York," was also a member of the Junior League of New York. The wedding was held on the grounds of Mount Holyoke. The week before the wedding in 1985, Lehman had her pull two all-nighters for a deal they were working on: "It was like for sport."

Now she was in labor, lying in her hospital bed in the maternity ward, when her husband told the doctor that the markets were most likely going to crash soon, which sent him rushing out to sell his stock while Barbara lay there unattended: "I'm having a baby!"

Friday, October 16, looked even worse. On the floor of the NYSE, some traders were shouting: "Buy 'em, buy 'em, we've hit rock bottom!" Louise Jones thought otherwise. She thought they should hold their horses; in her opinion, it was too early to call it. That Friday afternoon, the CEO of Drexel Burnham Lambert picked up Ace Greenberg, the CEO of Bear Stearns, to go bow hunting (one of Greenberg's many hobbies). They turned to each other and agreed Monday was going to be a disaster, and then said no more of it. There wasn't much they could do, except brace themselves. That weekend, Jim Cramer, running the hedge fund Cramer & Co., and his fiancée, the trader Karen Backfisch, were attending the wedding of Silda Wall and Eliot Spitzer—later dubbed the "Sheriff of Wall Street" until his fall from grace when he was found cavorting with prostitutes. Karen had already convinced Cramer to pull out of the market a week or so earlier, and now she, like Elaine Garzarelli, was predicting its collapse on Monday.

On Monday, October 19, Doreen, who was an NYSE floor official, part of the floor structure that ensured checks and balances, could feel the tension rise as they neared the 9:30 a.m. opening bell. Some had been hoping to see a turnaround, but already that morning, Asia was down, Europe was down. Louise Jones and Mike Cassidy had done their morning market call, and they hadn't minced words. It was going to be bad. The specialists were holding lots of stock from Friday's frenzied sell-off so that the moment the morning bell rang, everything was up for sale. A fire sale. The relatively new computer trading programs hit go. The DOT (designated order turnaround) electronic trading system—for smaller orders relayed straight to a specialist—was not based on market valuation but on market movement, and suddenly the market was moving at accelerated speed in a steep downward trajectory.

Louise was in the thick of it. There was no 24/7 information flow, no TV screens, no round-the-clock news to rely on. She had only the digital ticker tape, and screens with a simple quote system: IBM, where to buy, where to sell, for how much. It all came down to instinct. Louise could hear the panic around her. Monday's sell-off was fast and furious, worse than Friday's. Don Marron, Paine Webber's chairman who championed women like Margo Alexander and

Mary Farrell, was also on the floor, and what he could see, "looking in the eyes and faces of the people trading," was that they "were really scared, petrified." It didn't help that "the guys on the front lines were young," and "it was something they'd never seen before . . ." They only knew a climate in which markets went up, up, and up.

As a floor trader there were only two things that Louise could do for her clients: buy or sell. When she was selling, the best she could do was to sell before the other guys did, which meant she had to have muscle in the crowd. She had to shout louder because it came down to whom the specialist, as well as the other traders in the crowd, could hear. If you heard someone bid, you physically grabbed them and didn't let go. When she was buying, she stepped back. She had to decide: would she buy a little and then wait for the price to fall again, and buy a little more, or would she just wait and try to figure out when to go full in, when the stock hit rock bottom? She let the energy of the floor speak to her; a seasoned broker could hear the markets, but even so, right now it was hard to concentrate with all the noise and the visceral panic.

Across trading rooms at various firms, the phones were ringing off the hook, and no one was willing to go near them. It was better to pretend you didn't hear them ring. It was impossible to know whether the listed stock quotes were accurate from one minute to the next, so what could you tell the frantic customer? By 3 p.m., the market was down 300 points, but then the gas pedal really sank to the floor, and within an hour, the market had dropped another 200 points. There were rumors going around that Fidelity was putting up barricades to stop investors from storming the building.

Elaine Garzarelli was at home watching the crash play out on TV when she started to have heart palpitations. She knew *her* fund was not careening downward because she had already scaled back, hedged her bets the week before, and yet her heart would not stop racing. She called her cousin, a nurse, who was sure Elaine was having a heart attack, and who, much to Elaine's embarrassment, called an ambulance. When the paramedics arrived, they told Elaine she was having an anxiety attack. Her clients had been calling all day, some in tears about the money they'd lost elsewhere.

Mickie Siebert was in her office at Siebert Financial on the second floor of 444 Madison Avenue watching stocks plummet. She had never seen anything like it, and the only calm she could find was in looking out her window onto the street below. It was a beautiful New York fall day, and she watched people go about their lives: "They weren't running around going nuts; they were eating hot dogs." It gave her some comfort.

When the closing bell finally rang, the market had dropped 508 points, down 22.6 percent (and two days later worse—35 percent). Afterward, they called it "Black Monday."

Reading the Black Monday headlines on the floor of the New York Stock Exchange, 1987.

Everyone was spent, drained, yet almost no one at the NYSE went home that night, staying on the floor to match trades because the trading volume had been so excruciatingly high. Harry's, Wall Street's favorite bar and restaurant, also stayed open all night. When her fund's results came out after the markets closed, Elaine Garzarelli went out with friends to her favorite Japanese restaurant to celebrate, but she was one of a rare few. Louise and Mike Cassidy had made a huge amount of money that day, paid as they were on commissions for doing a trade, whether buy or sell, but that didn't mean they were pleased. A scared market and gun-shy investors were what they feared. It was not good for business. Mary Farrell, now in the investment strategy group at Paine Webber, had watched in disbelief as the market fell and traders were trading but the ticker tape was running sometimes as much as three hours behind. The next day her team instructed their brokers: "cautious, be cautious."

Barbara Byrne brought her baby home and thought to herself that it was a good thing she had something to do now.

She had managed to wrangle one of the first maternity leaves on Wall Street. Official policy was six weeks of "disability leave" for the transgression of having a baby, but she had pointed out to her boss that a fellow male banker had just gone on a client junket and come down with hepatitis, and so far, he'd been out on disability for three months. "So, he ate some bad shellfish, turned yellow, and you've given him three months? And I'm producing a future taxpayer . . . it seems to me I should get the same as he did." Her boss grudgingly agreed ("for you we'll do this"), not realizing he was setting a precedent, that there would be many more pregnant women asking for maternity leave.

On Tuesday morning, determined not to make the same mistakes made after the 1929 crash, Alan Greenspan, who had only just become head of the Federal Reserve, got on TV to announce that the federal government would immediately begin to pump money into the system, make capital available as quickly as possible, and create liquidity in the markets. At noon, corporations started to announce stock buyback programs. The markets slowly began to move again. Even so, even as the direst of predictions about the fallout from Black Monday eventually failed to materialize and experts agreed it had been a market correction more than anything else, Doreen watched as small, family-owned specialist units left the floor, no longer willing to risk their money in a volatile trading environment egged on by the new electronic trading. For a while, Elaine Garzarelli, who had walked away from Black Monday a winner, would be the Cassandra of Wall Street.

Three years earlier the media had trumpeted the reign of the yuppie, but now after Black Monday, they gleefully posted the yuppies' death notices. One NBC News analyst renamed them "puppies" as in "poor urban professionals." Elizabeth Kolbert, in the *New York Times*, poked fun at the "young stockbrokers too poor or shaken to order radicchio and warm goat cheese salads at their favorite track-lighted restaurants." Jokes made the rounds: What's the difference between a yuppie and a pigeon? A pigeon can still make a deposit on a BMW.

In December, less than two months later, Oliver Stone's much-awaited film, *Wall Street*, arrived in theaters. Stone had intended the film as a critique of everything that the Street had become during the 1980s. The year before, when Ivan Boesky was still king, he'd given the commencement speech at the University of California's business school. Grinning widely, he assured Berkeley students—until recently better known for radicalism than capitalism—that "greed is alright, by the way. I want you to know that. I think greed is healthy. You can be greedy and still feel good about yourself." They applauded wildly, as if they had been pardoned by the pope. In the film *Wall Street*, the protagonist Gordon Gekko—based at least in part on Doreen's boss, Boesky—announces, "Greed, for lack of a better word, is good!"

Despite Oliver Stone's intentions to make Gekko into a villain, or an antihero at best, filmgoers eagerly read the film as a guide on how to succeed on Wall Street: Black Monday had done little to dampen the enthusiasm for the market and its get-rich-quick allure. In fact, the film became "a cult phenomenon on business school campuses." A banker who joined Wall Street around the same time as the film came out noticed "a proliferation of suspenders, slicked-back hair and Sun Tzu's *The Art of War*" (Gekko's favorite book) on the trading floor.

14

R.E.S.P.E.C.T.

Not one woman was indicted in the insider-trading scandal that brought down Boesky and, soon after, Michael Milken, and got Drexel Burnham Lambert tagged by Giuliani as a "racketeering enterprise." Statistically, there should have been at least one woman. But much like the men-only clubs of the past, much like the Harvard Business School's informal study groups, insider trading was about creating networks of trust and brotherhood, and women—still—were not included. In the men's locker room at New York's Vertical Club an insider trading ring calling itself the "yuppie five" would exchange information, sometimes for no reward other than being one of the boys. As the *New York Times* pointed out, this tradition of keeping women out had kept women out of jail. But it also kept them out of M&As, LBOs, and arbitrage, which were all based on acquiring information, being let into the inner circle.

Milken and Boesky were now both serving time in prison, and Drexel Burnham Lambert had gone bankrupt, but there was some good news: the women of the New York Stock Exchange were finally getting a bathroom at the Luncheon Club. The lack of ladies' rooms

at the NYSE had long been a running joke, and early on, Mickie Siebert's friends liked to send her dollhouse-sized toilets and chamber
pots. When, much later, one of the men's bathrooms on the exchange
floor was finally converted into a women's bathroom, it took some
time before men stopped barging in, not having read the new sign
on the door.

Twenty years after Mickie had bought her seat, however, there
was still no ladies' room near the Luncheon Club on the seventh floor
of the NYSE (women had to go one flight down), and Mickie Siebert
along with all the other women, paying members of the exchange
and the club, had had enough. Mickie threatened the Board of Governors that if they did not install one, she would have a port-a-potty
brought in. They relented. It turned out to be an easy fix, exactly as
Mickie had said. All they had to do was rip out a telephone booth
and repurpose a section of the men's room. To think it took so long.

Janet Tiebout at Goldman Sachs, who'd had to watch Valentine roses arrive for her ex-husband, was thriving, but her clock was
ticking. The men she wanted to date were more interested in young,
"beautiful and sexy" women than those in their thirties working
twelve-hour-plus days and looking the worse for it. How even to date
when you were at your desk all day and often into the night? There
was video dating, but it was a clunky process that meant signing up
with an agency to go through books of profiles, asking to see someone's VCR recording, and watching as they sat awkwardly in front
of a camera saying too little or too much. She was feeling "tired and
old," drinking too much, and overweight.

Just before Black Monday, she'd sent out a company memo saying she was leaving. Unable to bring herself to tell the truth—"I was
leaving because I was terrified that I'd never get married and have
kids"—she said she was leaving to open a marina with her father.

Yet almost as soon as she'd left, she reconnected with Jeff Hanson, also at Goldman Sachs, whom she'd previously ignored, and by

April 1988, they were married. Her first child, a daughter, was born in October of that year. Janet Tiebout (now Hanson) had done what feminist Mary Kay Blakely advised against: she had gone from working full-time to parenting full-time. Now seven months pregnant with her second child, and with a toddler at home, Janet wrote despairingly in her diary: "I'm sitting here paying bills, doing absolutely ZERO that is fulfilling or satisfying and wishing that I could close my eyes and make it all go away." The next day: "I'm sitting here staring out my window wondering what I'm going to do with myself. . . . I'll probably start watching soap operas and drinking martinis at 2 o'clock in the afternoon. The boredom is excruciating."

But the boredom also pushed her to imagine what she'd really like to be doing. She wanted to start a coaching consultancy for women on Wall Street. She wrote to a male friend at Goldman Sachs, Jon Corzine, who would become the CFO the following year, where she hoped she might begin developing her idea: "Women need help in how to handle a dual-career marriage, maternity leave, time management, and getting and staying ahead . . . In the last three years, I have seen women opt to leave the firm rather than try to articulate their problems to management in a way that makes professional sense . . . Regrettably, this is because women find it extremely difficult to 'connect' with their (male) managers." Janet believed that there were two languages spoken on Wall Street: one by women and the other by men, and as a manager, she'd learned both fluently. She could now be that crucial translator.

Two months later, however, her son was born, and her consultancy plans were put on hold as she was hurtled back into postpartum depression.

Barbara (Moakler) Byrne was having a much easier time of it as a mother. After she'd had her first child just days before Black Monday (she would have three more in quick succession), she put a support system in place. She and her husband moved to Princeton, New Jersey, where her mother-in-law and sister-in-law lived, and could help in a pinch. Just six months after Black Monday, the markets recovering and a nanny hired, Barbara was again on the Street. She had started as an energy investment banker when she first talked her way from Mobil to Lehman, and she was now specializing in "IPO carveouts and split-offs, and various ways of monetizing businesses."

In 1988, she went to call on Burlington Northern in Seattle, a huge conglomerate whose executives, she'd heard, were not feeling much love toward Shearson Lehman. She was scheduled to make her pitch alongside one of the senior partners, but at the last minute he was unable to make it, and Barbara, still only a senior vice president—a step up from an associate but not yet a managing director—was on her own. She flew out to Seattle, only an associate with her. The pitch idea had been to split the IPO, to carve out the energy business from the railroad business. (This had yet to be done simultaneously.) What Barbara did not know was that Burlington Northern had already decided to do a split and had retained Morgan Stanley to do it, except that Morgan Stanley had pitched the split differently—an IPO for the railroad business but leaving the energy business intact.

Tom O'Leary, in charge of the energy subsidiary, welcomed Barbara to headquarters and let her go through her entire pitch before telling her they'd already retained Morgan Stanley.

But Barbara had done her research to figure out how best to approach him. "Mr. O'Leary, has anyone else come out here and pitched this to you? Has anyone else come out here?"

No, they hadn't, he admitted. And, yes, doing an IPO of the energy business instead of the railroad business sounded like a better plan.

"Then why wouldn't you allow us to come in as a joint road runner on this particular transaction that you're considering with Morgan Stanley?" she asked.

O'Leary shook his head and started in about how he hated Lehman for something that had happened in the past.

She tried again: "Yeah, well, that's why I'm here. It's me and my associate, there's the two of us . . . Don't you realize how really upset they will be when they realize that you're giving *me* the IPO? That I am getting it? Not them. Do you think the boys in the band would have been here if they thought there was a 500-million-dollar IPO, and a multimillion-dollar spin-off?"

"You're absolutely right."

"Success is the best revenge! Your success and my success!"

When Barbara and her associate walked out of the building, deal in hand, they were giddy—Lehman was now going to share the deal with Morgan Stanley. She returned to the New York office and announced it: "Look, we're going to be doing an IPO, it's going to be the energy company, and we're going to be joint bookrunning manager on a $500 million deal."

"You couldn't have heard that right."

"Oh, yeah, I heard that right."

That year Barbara generated $57 million in revenue. The deal was monumental for her; she was put forward for managing director. She later heard from one of her advocates that when someone in the meeting objected, others turned to him and said, "You've never produced so much but we named you managing director!" Barbara was only thirty-four years old. By the end of the 1980s, even as 40 percent of jobs at Wall Street's ten largest securities firms were held by women, they represented only 4 percent of partners or managing directors. Now she was one of the 4 percent.

What the Burlington deal had taught Barbara was that you don't get if you don't ask. It made her realize that she could *ask* for business. At Bear Stearns, Jolyne Caruso (now Caruso-FitzGerald), had Mitch Jennings, Beth Dater's husband, looking out for her, but even so, she too had had to learn to ask for what was hers. She prided herself on not being a "militant" feminist, but at the same time, she found she cried a lot in the early years. When she was twenty-six years old, and

Bear Stearns put out the list of new associate directors, her name was
not on it, even as a guy, one year younger and with less to show for his
time, was on it. She cried that night and the next day went to see her
boss to ask why. It was almost as if they'd forgotten about her. Her
boss corrected the mistake, and the following week, Jolyne's name
appeared in the *Wall Street Journal* as an associate director. But it
would never have happened if she had not spoken up.

Barbara had long noticed that the men at Lehman, as elsewhere,
did not hesitate to offer themselves up for a promotion even if they did
not yet have the necessary skills. Women, in contrast, thought they
not only had to have the skills but they needed to have perfected them.
And if women knew their worth, and were unabashed in saying so,
that too had its pitfalls. Patricia Chadwick, the former Feeneyite, was
universally feared. When in 1985 Mitch asked Jolyne to take over the
account for Chancellor Capital Management, a prestigious money-
management firm attached to Citibank, he explained the problem: the
portfolio manager there, who essentially ran the enormous Boeing
pension plan money, was a client of Bear Stearns. But they were not
getting enough business from her. She had chewed up Mitch's salesmen, one-by-one, and spat them out. Mitch needed to get her over
to their side, to start running her trades through them, and he was
sending Jolyne in.

Oh my God, Jolyne thought to herself. *That's Patricia Chadwick.*

Out loud she said: "Oh, I would love to cover Chancellor."

But the fact was that Patricia was roundly known as "the witch
of Wall Street."

Patricia did not know that then, but she knew she was exacting.
She expected people to step up, to do their homework, to be prepared
when they pitched her stocks and bonds. She would have said that
the female top players were always seen as aggressive, starting with
Mickie Siebert, the Wall Street legend. One night, as Patricia was
walking home from Citibank, she stopped in at a beauty salon to

get her nails done, and as she settled back in the pedicure chair, she suddenly saw that right across from her was Mickie. Mickie had once told the *New York Times,* "I'm probably the only girl who walks into a beauty shop reading Missile and Space Daily." But now she was asleep, out like a light, "snoring." "Well," thought Patricia, "I'm in her presence."

Jolyne approached Patricia gingerly: "God help you if you did not have all the facts, all your research in order . . . intelligent, quick, articulate when you called her. Because she was impatient, she wanted the story right away, and it better be right." Once Jolyne understood what Patricia needed, what she demanded, she passed on Bear Stearns's best research to her—which stocks to buy, which stocks were being downgraded. She fought for Patricia to get shares of IPOs. In return, Patricia started executing her trades through the firm, helping make Jolyne the "golden girl" of sales; at barely thirty years old, Jolyne was made a managing director.

———

RONALD REAGAN, NOW OUT OF OFFICE, TOOK MIKHAIL GORBACHEV— also recently out of a job after the fall of communism—for a visit to the NYSE. It was 1992: two former Cold War rivals on a field trip together. Gorbachev was shown an enormous Fabergé urn, given to the Stock Exchange by Tsar Nicholas II in the early 1900s to commemorate the listing of Imperial bonds (which, following the Russian Revolution, became worthless). Gorbachev, admiring the urn that still today sits in the Board Room, quipped that he'd like to have it back. An NYSE board member, quick on his feet, replied: "I'll give you the urn if you redeem your railroad . . . bonds."

It was the early 1990s, and commuters were now more likely to reach for a minidisc player than a first-generation Walkman. 1980s power suits were giving way to 1990s Donna Karan silhouettes—simple lines, soft fabrics, flowy feminine luxury. The designer Marc Jacobs, talking to the *Los Angeles Times* about his collection for spring 1993, said: "The '80s was Nancy Reagan and 'Dynasty,' huge shoulders, nasty little suits, dress for success, hard-edge, hard-core, mean, aggressive clothes." Twenty-nine-year-old Jacobs admitted he had voted for the very first time in the recent presidential election, and he'd been rewarded with a "more liberal-thinking president, a less structured-looking First Lady." The Clintons had just moved into the White House.

The seeming calm with the end of the Cold War was temporarily interrupted on February 26, 1993, when a bomb was detonated in an underground garage below the World Trade Center. Marlene Jupiter looked up and asked if anyone else had felt the building shake (the DLJ offices were a few blocks away from the Twin Towers, at 140 Broadway). Someone smirked and called her hysterical.

———

CHANGE AND TRANSFORMATION ARE NOT ALWAYS SYNONYMOUS, especially for women, as historian Judith Bennett has noted. Change always takes place, but that does not mean that transformation necessarily follows. Change does not guarantee transformation. When in 1988, Margo Alexander, director of research at Paine Webber, was promoted to co-head of Research, Sales, and Trading alongside established trader Charlie Milligan, she received a chilly reception from the traders. It was finally a woman on the trading desk who explained the problem to her: the traders would not even tell their wives they were now reporting to a woman; in fact, trading desks at other firms were making fun of them, calling them up and saying, "Hey, how do you like working for a girrrl?!" After that, Margo worked hard on winning them over, buying rounds of after-work drinks.

In 1989, Alice Jarcho had returned to Wall Street. With her son now three years old, fighting back a working mother's guilt, she took a job with Michael "Mike" Steinhardt at his hedge fund, Steinhardt Partners. Hedge funds were about to explode in number, and his was one of the first, but already hedge funds were, Alice knew, "sexy money." The concept behind a hedge fund had been around since 1949, when Alfred Winslow Jones, a sociologist and economics writer, came up with a way to invest that involved risk but balanced it out. The idea was that while most investors only bought stocks that would generate profits as the shares went up in value (also called "going long"), a hedge fund would also "short" stocks of companies thought to be overvalued, profiting if those shares dropped in price. They were "hedging" their bets.

Alice had personally known Mike Steinhardt for years, and she knew he was notoriously tough to work for, but she also knew that she would make a ton of money, seven figures easily. She assured herself that despite his reputation, they had an established relationship. She started at Steinhardt Partners in April 1989. From April until early January, Alice was "his darling," but as soon as he had paid her (hedge funds pay employees after the end of the year), their relationship became transactional: "He owned me," "I was his indentured servant," and everything changed.

It was not easy. He would randomly scream at people, he would run into a room as if he were about to physically assault them, he would fire people whom he had recently hired, who had just moved their lives and families to New York. (Allegations of sexual harassment would come much later.) His stock-in-trade, Alice came to believe, was the humiliation of others, including herself. He wanted to degrade you, he wanted to make you feel degraded, she felt. In the three years she worked for him, she cried more "than I cried my entire life . . ." She also earned more in those three years than she had in the entire preceding years on Wall Street.

When the office politics of it all became too much for everyone, Steinhardt hired a psychologist for the office. Alice warned the psychologist that he, too, would end up on the chopping block, but he scoffed, which made it that much more interesting when Steinhardt fired him in the company gym while they all listened in because they were wired to one another.

Steinhardt went to his own therapist twice a week, and when Alice asked him what that therapist thought of his temper, he replied: "I've never told him."

One day, Alice was called into Steinhardt's office, and he let loose on her. She started to cry, fled for the ladies' room, and then he started to run after her, shouting, "I'm so sorry. I love you, and I don't want to hurt you!"

"It was like being a battered woman," she said.

Hedge-fund guys, Alice concluded, could get away with anything because these were their own private firms—they were accountable to no one.

In 1992, Margo Alexander's co-department head at Paine Webber, Charlie Milligan, left and the firm's CFO took Milligan's place. But he demanded that Margo be demoted so that she would now report to him instead of the company president. He got what he asked for and Margo felt "humiliated" and "embarrassed." She considered leaving, but when she assessed the situation, she decided she had invested too much of her life in the company. She stayed, even as she licked her wounds.

That same year, 1992, Jolyne was being headhunted by JP Morgan, and it was hard for an "Italian girl from Long Island" to turn down a white-shoe firm. Bear Stearns and Mitch Jennings counteroffered—more money, better accounts—but it was too little too late. "It took me quitting for Mitch to say we'll groom you to run the business." She had always wanted to run something, and now JP Morgan was offering her that. But there was a caveat. She was already an MD, but she would have to come in as a VP and then go through a grueling first year to work her way back up to MD. Why? she asked.

"We don't hire people in as MDs." Except they did; after her, Jolyne watched countless people be brought in on the MD level.

By 1993, Alice, still working for Steinhardt, had had enough. She felt—no, she knew—that she had sold her soul. She had made the ultimate Faustian deal. She had become that person who tolerates the intolerable for a buck. One time Steinhardt screamed at her what he considered to be the worst insult of all: "You don't love money!"

And she realized that, yes, he was right.

As for insults, she could insult herself better than anyone. She'd taken to calling herself "the S&M whore." Taking punishment for money.

She finally walked out after four years. Money could mean just so much. There was also self-respect. Alice Jarcho left Wall Street for good.

———

ELISA ANCONA, WHO HAD ONCE DREAMED THAT A MILLION DOLLARS would mean being rich, only to realize that it was peanuts for many, was finding Gabelli & Co. ever more inhospitable after seven years there. Mario Gabelli had a rule that no employee could take off two weeks in a row, "because he didn't believe in fun," and two weeks straight sounded like you were having a good time. But in 1990 Elisa was getting married and she wanted to go to Hawaii for her honeymoon. Gabelli eventually let her go, but he punished her for it when she returned. When he'd go looking for her, he'd scream through the offices: "Where's the asshole?!" Having the name "Elisa" could no longer protect her. One day she too had had enough. Elisa stood up and screamed: "Go to hell!"

Elisa, like Alice, found a job at a hedge fund: Porter Felleman. It was a three-person operation with two hedge fund managers—Alex Porter and John Felleman—and Grace Lonergan, their secretary. Porter had worked for Alfred Wilson Jones back in 1967, the man credited with inventing the hedge fund. Porter was six-foot-two, a former wrestler and football player, an avid reader and writer. Porter was a Southerner in the best sense of the word, exuding charm from his very pores. Women would fall all over him. His partner, John Felleman, was a sweet man who conducted much of his business out of the Blarney Stone pub on Forty-First Street and Park Avenue. Grace, the secretary, was a Grateful Dead groupie. Elisa soon got the name "Bulldog" because she'd clamp down on things and not let go. But unlike at Gabelli, where fun was frowned upon, at Porter Felleman, work-life balance was the company credo.

They had been in business for about twenty years when Elisa arrived, and had an impressive record of outperforming the S&P 500, but hedge funds were still a relatively secretive corner of the investment world, largely unregulated, which also made it a sort of Wild West for those in the know. There were a handful of hedge funds with enormous assets, such as Tiger Management, started by Porter's fellow North Carolinian Julian Robertson, but in the early 1990s, most hedge funds were small, even tiny, like Porter Felleman. Elisa was twenty-six years old and was making $98,500 a year. Gifts would come streaming into the office sent by brokers wanting to do business: the signature blue Tiffany boxes, VIP concert tickets, impossible-to-get restaurant reservations, front-row basketball seats.

But then suddenly everything fell apart when Felleman died of liver damage, and Porter's mother, a driving-Miss-Daisy rarefied Southern lady in her nineties, died soon after. Porter, grief-stricken, took a sharp turn in what had been a relatively staid life until then. Elisa would go into his office and find a thin coating of white powder across every surface, which she suspected was cocaine. He would call Elisa out of the blue from somewhere and tell her: *Wire 25k to this car dealership in North Carolina because I just bought this twenty-two-year-old girl a red Mustang.* Margaret, the office's new Girl Friday, had to write checks to Porter's "girlfriends," and she and

Elisa couldn't help but wonder what these girls were doing for the $1,000, $5,000, let alone the $10,000 checks. Sometimes they would show up at the office—tall and stunning—to ask Porter for his American Express card, and he would grandly send them off on shopping sprees. One girl bought herself a $10,000 boa, which really got under Elisa's skin. In part because "what do you do with a ten-thousand-dollar boa?" but also because it seemed she, Elisa, was having to do a heck of a lot more for a $10,000 raise.

Unlike the large brokerage houses, which were utilizing more and more (even if clunky) technology to systemize trading, hedge funds in the 1990s were largely operating on telephone calls and pen and paper. Within this throwback environment, Elisa was herself a throwback to the she-wolves of the 1960s and 1970s who took the circuitous path onto and through Wall Street. Elisa was, for all intents and purposes, the trader, the office manager, the head of compliance, and the entire back office. She would oversee the trades sent in from the partners, meaning she was on the phone with brokers, not only telling them what to sell and for how much but strategizing the best way forward. She then had to make sure the orders were executed correctly, and at the end of the day, she faxed pages of handwritten trade blotters, her view of the day's business, to the prime broker (the firm's central custodian of the portfolio). Back in the next morning, she'd be poring over reports to make sure all the trades were booked properly and then she'd begin a new day of buying and selling stocks. Now, on top of all that, she was taking care of Porter, picking up after him, covering for him.

As the popularity of hedge funds soared over the decade, Porter Felleman was doing better than ever, but instead of Elisa's role being expanded, she was increasingly marginalized. Instead of promoting her to trader, Porter brought in a trader with a Harvard MBA. The partners' compensations grew into the millions of dollars, whereas Elisa was still fighting for those $10,000 raises. She had had enough. If she had been of Alice Jarcho's generation, Elisa, a graduate of Pace University who started off as a Girl Friday for Gabelli, might well have moved up through the ranks. But that pathway was now largely blocked by the influx of MBAs and Ivy League graduates coming to Wall Street. These types of credentials were now mandatory, and Elisa didn't have them.

The only space that remained a meritocracy of sorts, and not dependent on fancy colleges and graduate degrees, was the trading floor—whether a firm's trading floor or a stock-exchange floor. In May 1989, Mike Cassidy had finally promoted Louise from clerk to floor broker, making her an official member of the NYSE. She was twenty-four years old; the youngest woman to become an NYSE member while the exchange was still a private membership. Her assigned badge number was "18," which in the Hebrew alphabet means "life." (Over the years, she would receive countless necklaces with the life sign as gifts—"easily fifty"—as well as a steady stream of offers to buy the number from her. Floor brokers, like gamblers, had an obsession with lucky numbers and lucky objects.)

As Louise and Cassidy grew the firm, they started to cut out the middlemen and work directly with institutional accounts, increasing the size of their commissions considerably. It turned Louise into a heavy hitter on the floor, alongside Doreen and several other women, including Gail Pankey, in 1985 the first Black woman to become a member. Everyone had something they were known for that gave them an advantage; in Doreen's case, it was her piercing voice, for Louise, it was her height. Louise, at five-foot-eight, had a good three inches on Mike Cassidy and many other men on the floor.

In 1995 Goldman Sachs approached Louise: they wanted her to run their trading floor. She couldn't believe it. She agreed to speak with them, to start talks, but she was so unfamiliar with corporate culture that by the time she was sitting in her fifth interview making small talk, she couldn't take it anymore.

"What are you guys offering me? I don't even know what it is," she said straight out.

The answer was a seven-figure package flush with perks.

When she told Cassidy she was leaving for Goldman Sachs, he turned pale and said they needed to talk.

After closing, he walked her over to 60 Wall Street, where they sat down in the atrium. Cassidy always carried restaurant peppermint candies in his pocket, the cheap red-and-white striped kind offered in a bowl on the way out of diners. He reached into his pocket and started throwing them across the table at her, each candy another part of his counteroffer. One peppermint candy after another skidded across the table at her: how about a raise? Another went flying at her, along with another proposition. She kept saying no as the candies landed. Finally, he threw his last peppermint: "I'll give you half the company."

"But I don't even know what that means!"

She didn't. What was Cassidy even worth? They had built up the company together from the time she was first "pork-chopping" for him, picking up the ringing phone in his booth when he was out on the floor, but she'd never been able to take a look at the books.

Now he told her for the first time just how much the company was worth.

Hearing the number, she "got pissed." This entire time she had been underpaid.

To make amends, he offered to rename the firm Jones, Cassidy— with her name going first. But she didn't need that. Now that she knew she wouldn't be taking a pay cut by turning down Goldman Sachs, she accepted his offer.

In that moment, inside the atrium, she became a multimillionaire.

It wasn't just that Cassidy had handed over half the company and

Louise Jones on the floor of the exchange.

changed its name, but as a partner Louise now had a different kind of clout out there on the trading floor.

Not only was the NYSE still then a closed private membership (in 2006 it would go public), it was a "fiefdom." She could ask for favors, she could ask for charitable donations. She could ask, and she would get. It was the power and respect that spoke to her—"the money was just the gravy."

Every year, on July 17, Louise gathered her friends and went out to the phone booth on Columbus Avenue and Eighty-Eighth Street where she'd been found, swaddled, a newborn abandoned. She brought Champagne to celebrate her "birthday." She had long since stopped imagining that every blond woman who walked onto the subway might, just might, be her biological mother. She had hoped she would at least find Pedro Martinez, the man who'd found her and brought her to the police station, "but try looking up a 'Pedro Martinez' on Manhattan's Upper West Side during this time and you might get ten thousand of them." She had become a board member of the New York Foundling Hospital, the only foundling to ever sit on the board. But her own origins were still a mystery. The telephone booth remained the most tangible fact of her birth.

Doreen Mogavero had taken a hard fall. One of the last people to leave Ivan F. Boesky & Company, literally closing the windows behind her, it had not been easy. She had lost her job, and now no one was hiring. She was getting some offers here and there, but the salaries were a pittance. She didn't know whether it was because the recovery from Black Monday was still taking time or if she had become a pariah, tainted by Boesky in the same way she had once been anointed by him, or if it was because she was a woman on the floor. She returned to working for a two-dollar broker, almost as if she were starting over again. But that was going nowhere and after a while she knew the only way forward was to start her own floor firm.

She began to ask around, trying to solicit advice from the men she'd known for years who ran their own floor businesses, trading for themselves or a select group of clients. How should she start? What was the best way of going about it? What were the tricks of the trade?

Even though Doreen had been working an exchange floor since 1975, first the Amex, then the New York Futures Exchange, and finally the NYSE, she was taken aback by their reluctance to offer help. Instead of encouraging her, they did what they could to dissuade her.

"Why do you want to do that?" they said.

"It's so much paperwork for you. It's going to be a lot of time away from home."

Doreen, having worked as a floor clerk for many years, knew one thing: she had to find the best clerk she could so she'd be freed up to go out on the floor. She interviewed countless applicants, and many of the men said the very same thing to her: "Don't worry. I'll take care of everything." She scratched off their names the minute they uttered those words.

She finally interviewed Jennifer Lee, a former trading assistant at First Boston who'd just had a baby and whose husband was a specialist on the floor. The two women were around the same age and shared the same mindset. They went out to dinner and agreed: "What the hell? Might as well." Doreen leased a seat on the NYSE, and Mogavero, Lee & Co. was born on May 1, 1989—the very same day of the month that she had first started on the American Stock Exchange in 1975.

The consensus on the floor was that she and Jennifer would never pull in enough business to make it. They both had experience as clerks and Doreen as a floor broker, but neither had sales experience—how were they going to find clients? But the two of them got on the phones and started calling everyone they could think of, asking for orders. It was finally a veteran trader, "Tubby" Burnham of Drexel Burnham, who rang them up and said that if they "were brave enough to start the firm, he was brave enough to give us an order."

As Mogavero, Lee grew, they hired Joy Benfante as their back-office manager. When Joy asked for a computer, Doreen protested: "What do you need a computer for? I've been doing everything without one for years." Joy had to drag Doreen, who loved her paper and pencil as much as she loved the floor, kicking and screaming into the computer age.

———

DOREEN WAS NOT THE ONLY WHO HAD TO FACE THE FACT THAT A new age was dawning predicated on emerging technologies. In 1993, NYSE chairman Dick Grasso decided to open up the floor to television viewers, to demystify Wall Street. He struck a deal with CNBC, and a pretty young reporter, Maria Bartiromo, just twenty-seven, arrived on the floor of the NYSE.

Grasso called Louise Jones in and said he needed her help: "There's a young lady coming and she's going to do something that's

Maria Bartiromo on
the NYSE floor in front
of one of the yellow
telephone banks.

never been done before. She's going to report the news from the floor
as it's happening. I want you to show her how you do your morning
market call, how you get your information."

"So she's taking my job?" Louise quipped.

She was not exactly thrilled as they all watched a "little Sophia
Loren" suddenly materialize. Some men were rattled to see a woman
in full makeup when the women on the floor typically sported a more
disheveled look as they dashed around, taking and executing orders.
Louise considered herself lucky if she even had time to pull her hair
back in a scrunchy.

But while some men were flirting with Maria, others were trying
to intimidate her, jostling her to get out of the way when they needed

to get to a trading post fast. Mike Robbins, a well-known independent floor trader who refused to utter the names of his famous clients and referred to them by code numbers instead, was furious with the exposure that Maria was bringing to the floor, yelling that he didn't want her around. Maria would often walk around the entire stock exchange if it meant not having to pass him.

Even as she was dubbed the "money honey," she grew on Louise. She was a quick learner, and ambitious, and Louise observed that she "knew how to throw a softball but make it look like a hardball." Her family owned the Rex Manor Catering Hall in Dyker Heights (also Maria Marsala's hometown), and in that sense, Maria Bartiromo was very much a creature of the NYSE floor, an "outer-borough girl" trying to make it in the finance world.

The look of the trading floor was changing. Doreen promoted Jennifer to broker and hired Debbie Raymond as their new clerk, making them an all-woman team; and when in 1994 they finally made the move from leasing to buying their own seat, Mogavero, Lee officially became the first and only women-run NYSE-member firm. Doreen hadn't set out to do that, but along the way she'd tapped into the most underutilized source of talent that there was: women.

Now thriving, Mogavero, Lee subleased a room in Doreen's accountant's offices and when Doreen found herself unexpectedly pregnant, she installed a playpen, and in addition to her other work, Joy was put in charge of morning childcare, learning how to diaper a baby. When Joy tired of climbing over the playpen to get to her desk, they moved their offices to a studio apartment at 55 Wall Street. Next came a two-bedroom place on 25 Broad Street, right across from the NYSE, and then finally a three-bedroom apartment in the same building. As the number of employees grew, as well as the office square footage, so too did the number of children. In the three-bedroom iteration of Mogavero, Lee, one bedroom was con-

Mogavero, Lee, the first and only women-run NYSE-member firm, on the
NYSE balcony.

figured into an office for Doreen and Jennifer, another was made
into the back office, where Joy took charge, and the remainder of
the apartment was arranged as just that—an apartment, with the
third bedroom available for overnight stays in the city or emergency
accommodations for sick children home from school. You brought
your child in to work with you, put them to bed, and got on with
your work.

The "office" was filled with toys and bassinets, and everyone took
care of everyone's children. As a press profile of the firm observed,
"Mogavero, Lee has instilled motherhood into its very culture."
Without thinking much about it, they had also set up an informal
job-sharing system. If someone needed to be at home with their children, the office took care of her tasks. There were no set vacation
days; if you wanted a vacation, you took one, no questions asked,
and everyone covered for you. At its height, between 1998 and 2000,
Mogavero, Lee would have twenty-one employees.

In May 1998, Mickie Siebert gave the commencement speech at her alma mater, now called Case Western Reserve University. She recalled how in the 1950s she had dropped out and left for New York in her beat-up Studebaker. Just as Beth Dater felt the Vomit Comet had taught her how to approach work, so the Studebaker had taught Mickie how to approach life: "That darned car door would never open right—it would always stick. I'd pull it, I'd cajole it, I'd shake it, I'd even plead with it. There were times I swore at it. Finally, I learned, I just had to kick it. And you know what? That is the real lesson that old Studebaker taught me. When a door is hard to open, and if nothing else works, sometimes you just have to rear back and kick it open."

Two years earlier—she continued—she'd seen on the "broad tape" (Dow Jones & Co.'s streaming business news and information) that Calvin Grigsby had resigned abruptly from his firm, the largest Black-owned firm in the municipal bond business, and one of the largest altogether, which "underwrote more than all the other women- and minority-owned firms put together." She called the two remaining partners, Suzanne Shank and Napoleon Brandford, and proposed they create Siebert Brandford Shank, a municipal bond-underwriting operation. The following year, they underwrote ("ran the books and priced the deal") $250 million for Detroit Water. And just recently, they'd underwritten $200 million for the State of California, "and under us was Bear Stearns and Morgan Guarantee," the very same "bank that wouldn't make me the loan for the seat was under us for underwriting—and that's important."

But for others, maintaining one's status on the Street as a woman was a precarious proposition. A year after Maria Bartiromo appeared on the floor for CNBC in 1993, becoming a star, Elaine Garzarelli, the Cassandra of Wall Street who had accurately predicted Black Monday, was fired from Lehman. Her mutual fund was not doing well, and her fortune-telling was no longer accurate, everyone said. She had been arrested in the Hamptons on a DUI. Her bullish take on the market—"Stock Market Correction Is Over"—appeared one day before Katherine Hensel, Lehman's chief stock analyst, posted: "Market Is Up But the Coast Is Not Clear; It's Time to Raise More Cash." Garzarelli was becoming a hindrance rather than a help, and she was fired almost seven years to the day on which she'd made her prediction about Black Monday on Lou Dobbs's *Moneyline*. The talk on the Street was that with a salary of over a million dollars, she was making too many mistakes. She'd become more of a risk than an asset.

Yet as any woman on Wall Street knew, mistakes and bad predictions, when made by men, were easily forgiven and forgotten. The *Washington Post* noted in the same year, 1994, "For all the attention paid to Michael Milken and greed on Wall Street in the 1980s, the surprising fact is that the real mountain of money has been piling up in the 1990s." In fact, those working on Wall Street now had "nearly three times the compensation earned in the same period in the 1980s." As for Garzarelli's salary, was it too much or was it too much for a woman?

Two years later, another female Wall Street soothsayer, Abby Joseph Cohen, who had famously continued to live in Queens, where she grew up, taking a commuter bus to work each day, would be passed over for partner at Goldman Sachs even as she had called the bull market of the mid-1990s, making significant money for those who had listened to her advice. Many on the Street were outraged when she was passed over, including her friend Patricia Chadwick, who considered "not trading with Goldman after that." The following year, in 1997, even *Vanity Fair* included Abby Joseph Cohen among spring's hottest items, alongside the Lexus LX 50 and the Gucci thong. In 1998, she finally made partner, but she, too, would eventually be called out for being overly bullish and failing to predict the 2008 financial crash.

15

B*tch!

Marianne Spraggins had taken time off from Wall Street to help her old friend David Dinkins run for New York mayor against Rudy Giuliani. Dinkins won, and on January 1, 1990, he became the city's first Black mayor, and Marianne, who'd parlayed her contacts to build up the campaign coffers, was even more of a hot commodity. Approached by Lewis Glucksman, who was now at Smith Barney, he asked her if she'd join the municipal finance department as its managing director, making her the first Black female MD on Wall Street.

But the culture at Smith Barney was starkly different from Salomon Brothers, and even as she came in as MD, she soon found that "these awful men were not going to respond to my authority . . . I can see their faces even now." Even the secretary got in on it, expecting Marianne to report her whereabouts. In Marianne's view, there was no team, no teamwork, no collaboration, there was only the persistent attitude of "Who's this bitch?"

In 1992, Marianne was profiled by *Black Enterprise* magazine, with a photograph of her perched on a desk at Smith Barney wear-

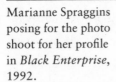

Marianne Spraggins
posing for the photo
shoot for her profile
in *Black Enterprise*,
1992.

ing one of her signature standout brightly colored suits, in this case
a flame-orange jacket and skirt offset by a cascade of gold necklaces
mixed in with one single strand of oh-so-Wall-Street pearls. Wall
Street is "still a very macho environment," she told *Black Enterprise*.
"In the work environment being black was usually an issue. But on
Wall Street being a woman became a critical concern." She knew
she could never be privy to the locker-room conversations—"where
whatever little magic between men happens," she quipped. Her strategy was to ensure that there was always a man in that locker room
who was on her side and "looking out for my interests."

But being Black on Wall Street was in itself no easy task, especially without Spraggins's clout. Cin Fabré, coming to Wall Street
in the 1990s, observed that at the firm where she worked, "ninety
percent of the cold callers . . . were Black or Latinx" and were routinely blocked from taking the Series 7 exam to become brokers, even
as it was dangled before them. The segregation was so intense that
cold callers "were not allowed to initiate conversations with their

brokers. We weren't even allowed to stray to the brokers' side of the room . . . brokers walked on the left side of the hallway and cold callers and assistants on the right." (This continued into the 2000s, where Lola West observed it up close at Merrill Lynch: Black men and women were hired, sent to a two-to-three-day introductory symposium, and then found themselves with no one willing to show them the ropes, no senior team interested in taking them in. All that was left was to do cold calling—"Black calling" as Lola referred to it. Up to five hundred calls a day. There was no chance anyone could pull in the million-dollar clients demanded of them, and they were out the door two years later, but the firm could point to a record of hiring Black employees.)

SHORTLY BEFORE JOLYNE CARUSO-FITZGERALD LEFT BEAR STEARNS for JP Morgan, she had hired a young saleswoman on the institutional equities desk. Maureen Sherry came to her by way of Drexel Burnham Lambert, which had collapsed in 1990 following Michael Milken's indictment. Maureen had graduated from Cornell University in 1986 with significant college loans to pay off, but when she tried for a job on Wall Street, the campus recruiters found her cluelessness laughable. She moved to New York, into a "hovel," a fifth-floor walk-up on Thirty-Ninth Street, and took a "terrible, terrible job" at the department store, Lord & Taylor. A six-foot-tall blond triathlete, she also joined a swim team, which happened to have a lot of bankers on it, including an institutional salesman at Drexel, managing a significant portfolio, who hired her as his secretary-assistant.

He turned out to be "so lazy" and "hated going to meetings," where he sent Maureen instead. It was "the most incredible gift" for her—even as she didn't understand half of what people said, but "I can read and research and I figured it out, but it took a long time." Once it was clear she was more than capable, her boss had her call his clients because "he would just love to take vacation." He was a single guy in New York, with a serious social schedule, and Maureen was making his life that much easier. All this put her in good stead when Drexel Burnham Lambert collapsed, and she landed at Bear Stearns on the sales desk next to Jolyne on the trading floor, with Bear Stearns CEO, Ace Greenberg, seated close by. Ace was a legend—as the *Wall Street Journal* described: "Working in shirt sleeves and sometimes wearing a dark visor, Alan Greenberg sits on a dais in the clamorous trading room at Bear, Stearns & Co. He is grabbing at telephones, barking instructions to traders or dressing down a subordinate whose trading may be straying from the securities firm's current strategy. . . . The balding, muscular-looking, poker-faced Mr. Greenberg seems the very epitome of a shrewd pit boss riding herd on his team."

Maria Marsala had had a taste of this herself. One day she picked up the phone and there was a man shouting at her that she was fired. She had no idea what she'd done. When she asked her immediate boss, he started to laugh. It had been Ace Greenberg on the phone, and while she wasn't really fired, "we're going to have to put the bells on the phone now." The phone lines, a hundred and twenty of them, silently flashed when a call was coming in, and Maria had missed one. The punishment for a missed call was to turn on the bells. It was both loud and humiliating, and the punishment lasted for a week.

Ace generally liked to make a point. When he read about a secretary who'd snitched on her boss's illegal practices to an investigating committee, he tracked her down and hired her because she "had the guts to turn in her boss—I love it." When Alice Jarcho was Larry Tisch's trader, she had called up Ace to complain about one of his traders who'd made a fool out of her. Ace responded: "What's the guy's name? I want to give him a promotion."

Maureen Sherry's first impression of the trading floor was that it was enormous, like an "entire street on Park Avenue," "turrets laid out like a grid"—stacked with screens, including Bloomberg terminals (Michael Bloomberg's invention after he was fired from Salomon Brothers) that had supplanted the former Quotrons. It was a mini city of digital information. (Maria Marsala marveled that there was even a fix-it guy on standby because so many traders threw their phones at the turrets.) A dais across the back of the trading floor was where the most senior people sat, Ace in the center, beside him his assistant, and on either side the heads of the various departments: risk arbitrage, convertible bonds, and so on. From the dais, like "fingers" stretching out, sat the traders for each department. Ace "had a trading mentality" and he liked to hear what was going on in each trading department, and this way he could; he was in the very thick of it.

The digital ticker tape wound around the room, ceiling-level, but now it seemed largely "decorative" because the same information was right there on the screens. The temperature was set at a cold 60 degrees Fahrenheit to keep everyone awake (leading to countless remarks from male traders in this era of nonpadded bras: "Cold?!"). Clocks adjusted to various time zones were spaced out across the walls for the international traders. It was impossible to see out the windows because they'd been darkened to remove the glare that might make the screens unreadable, if only for a few critical seconds. Besides, it was money and not the rising and setting of the sun that determined the day's cycle.

There was no privacy, no way to keep secrets, which in turn bred "overfamiliarity," destroyed boundaries. There were barely any cell phones then, and every call was right there at the desk, overheard: every deal, every marital squabble, every infidelity. In the words of a female hedge-fund trader on a similar floor: "If I had to call the beauty salon for an emergency bikini-wax appointment . . . it was awkward." Almost everyone stood, seldom sat, which only amplified the shouting, the screaming. "It was sort of like a nightclub with the energy and the noise." But Maureen didn't mind the noise. In fact, she thrived on it; it allowed her mind to better focus.

The floor's energy fell in line with Ace's well-documented aversion to anything or anyone Ivy League, and when someone showed up with an MBA, he was known to say: "*I won't hold it against you.*" Although he did. Antics were celebrated, high-fived, adding to the frat-boy culture. Inflatable sex dolls flew through the air, men punching at them to keep them aloft, floating over Maureen's head. Sometimes the men danced with them, which made her laugh. Strippers popping out of cakes was routine.

If a man made a significant trade, other traders tackled him to the ground and chopped off his designer tie—usually a "beautiful, three-hundred-dollar Hermès"—and pinned it to the wall like a hunting trophy. If a woman did a huge trade, a stuffed beaver was brought out and thrown onto her desk as a sign of her win. New traders went through a hazing period. A young trader in training might suddenly be told everyone was in the mood for a Philly cheese steak, from Philly, and he would have to run to Penn Station, grab an Amtrak to Philadelphia, and return with hundreds of Philly steaks in time for lunch. From the moment he hightailed it out of there, someone would start the timer, and if the trainee was back by lunchtime, he was rewarded with cheers and backslaps and a little more acceptance.

Bear Stearns was also managing some of Donald Trump's money, and Trump would love to come visit to see how his money was doing. What he didn't like was that he first had to sign in at the security desk, and even after they'd given him directions on where to go, he'd often be back at the desk, lost. During a trip to Asia, Bear Stearns senior executives decided they would hire models, whom they named "geisha girls," to lead visitors from the security desk to their destination. Trump, now taken to his destination by two long-legged beauties on either side of him, loved it. "They were literally escorting him." When female executives eventually complained, the geisha girls were instructed to cover up and show less flesh, but it was only when *Business Week* wrote about it that the scheme was brought to an end.

Jolyne thought Maureen Sherry "so smart and so talented," but "she was not out there." She was "timid . . . very soft-spoken," a hard worker who "didn't shake the bushes." But in fact Maureen was taking it all in. She sometimes felt sorry for the young men who arrived with fancy college degrees, unknowingly having entered a frat house of a workplace, and now they had to adjust, fast, or else be ridiculed forever. She could see their initial hesitation, and then their gradual realization that this was the only entry point into the boys' club. Besides, if she and the other women had to adjust, why shouldn't they too? At one point, she sat near a man who would greet his young assistant: "You know you're in every wet dream I have . . . Good morning!" You had to grow a thick skin, which Maureen quickly did. She learned to wait until their antics and comments were out of the way, like children who needed to wind down from a tantrum, and then with a smile on her face, she'd say: "Are you finished? Can we talk now?"

Jolyne had prided herself on being able to take it, and Maureen was no different in that. They were referred to as "team players," anointed with male approval, and "like members of a dysfunctional family, we kept our secrets to ourselves."

Maureen's desk was close to where Ace Greenberg was seated, and if he was heading home and had his driver waiting outside, and if Maureen was also packing up to leave, he would offer her a ride home, the driver dropping him off first and then continuing to Maureen's apartment now on the Upper West Side. Here she was, a twenty-seven-year-old woman in the back of the limousine next to the firm's CEO who was asking for her opinion about clients and deals. In part it was this antiestablishment atmosphere at Bear Stearns that helped get her promoted quickly. At twenty-eight, she was made a managing director, something that would never have happened so soon at a firm like Goldman Sachs, where rules were rules and hierarchies were sacred.

It was soon after Jolyne had first hired her that Maureen met Steven Klinsky, a partner at an investment firm. She was walking down Sixty-Eighth Street on a rainy night, sobbing because she had just broken up with her boyfriend. Klinsky was in a cab going down Second Avenue when he saw her. Intrigued, he jumped out, ran after her, and tried to talk to her, walking alongside her from one block to the next. Still crying, she tried to lose this freak, and finally gave him her name and place of work so he'd leave her alone. Starting the next day, a steady stream of flowers and letters began to arrive daily until she finally agreed to a date. They were married six years later, in 1995. Maureen was pregnant with her first child soon after, followed by another, and another, and finally a fourth. Like Barbara Byrne.

And with each pregnancy, Bear Stearns considered her good as gone. The first time she returned from maternity leave, she found a "curly-haired stranger sitting at my desk, his feet propped on a cardboard box with my client account list packed inside." When she got up from her desk to pump breast milk in the nurse's office, the male traders made mooing sounds at her. One even took up the dare to take a slug of her breast milk that she stored in the communal office fridge. Yet she and a few of the other women who were mothers dared not display photos of their children, as if it were "a dirty secret" that they had this other life, even as the men's desks were littered with pictures of their progeny, proof of their virility. *Their* wives, for the most part, stayed at home because a trader's salary made that possible.

But even as Maureen had to wrestle back her desk chair each time she returned from maternity leave, Bear Stearns management liked nothing more than to parade around a very pregnant Maureen Sherry, this beautiful MD and ferocious institutional saleswoman. She was presented as visible proof of how good the firm was to its female executives. Maureen felt a pang of guilt because the young women who attended the college talks and roundtables and interview sessions where she was brought in to play her role were being fooled on some level. Even as she loved her job, she felt she was there to sell them a lie. At the same time, sometimes she was caught off guard by how much more these young women expected when compared to her and Jolyne: unlike the two of them, *they* did not feel grateful to be "allowed" to have both work and children. Once, Maureen was interviewing a smart new graduate from Wharton who asked her point-blank: "How do the women who work here find this environment? Tell me the truth."

Maureen was startled. She was unused to confiding in other women, more accustomed to keeping everything close to the chest. She laughed off the question with an anecdote about her first day on Wall Street when she opened a pizza box and the pepperoni slices had been swapped out for condoms.

Maureen thought it was funny.

The young woman stared at her, horrified.

Maureen was offering her a six-figure salary—*so what does the pizza matter?* she couldn't help but think to herself. (There had been a time, at the beginning, when she told herself she was staying long enough to pay off her college loans but, like Phyllis, she "definitely got sucked into what they call the golden handcuffs.")

That woman she interviewed accepted the job offer, but just five years later, she left Bear Stearns after suing and settling. Maureen could only imagine what had been that final straw.

Maureen was fully aware that men didn't pay the price of their transgressions with their careers, ever. They paid the price with a check. There was one man, a repeat offender, who liked to grope women. He would come up behind them, put his hands out, and grab their breasts. Short and unattractive, he'd say to the other guys, "I'm going in!"—because the most pressing question in the trading room was whether a woman's breasts were real or fake. He was constantly having to pay out enormous checks, but he kept his job because the firm liked the money he brought in. Eventually he was told he'd have to start paying out with his own personal checks, instead of the company's checks. "It was a very expensive habit," Maureen marveled; she knew of one payout that "got close to a million dollars."

It was especially hard, she believed, on the most ambitious women because when faced with this kind of atmosphere, which had barely improved over the years, "what are your options?" You had to play along, or not let it get to you. Or you could go even further. If there was a "hot deal," and the stock was going to soar on an IPO, it was "very subjective on who'd get the stock." One woman she knew, for example, had a relationship with a man in syndicate, who decided on stock distribution. Her clients would inevitably get large amounts. It was not so very different really from what Alice Jarcho had witnessed decades earlier: male brokers trying to date the female assistants on institutional trading desks, hoping to land a sale. Just the tables were turned, but sex was still the currency.

Moreover, the language for sexual harassment still barely existed. It was not really a part of the vernacular until Anita Hill testified in 1991 at the Clarence Thomas hearings for his nomination to the Supreme Court, and she was forced to describe his countless suggestive remarks and acts. At Paine Webber, Mary Farrell and her Investment Strategy Group closed the door and pretended to have a long strategy session while they watched the hearings together.

Wall Street, sensing it might be called out for similar bad actors in its midst, went on the defensive. The month after the Thomas hearings, Merrill Lynch put out a letter stating that it would "not tolerate any form of sexual harassment," and Morgan Stanley, Bear Stearns, Salomon Brothers, and First Boston made a lot of noise about equality and their determination to wipe out sexism.

But when in 1993 a new mutual fund called the Women's Equity Mutual Fund was rolled out, with a promise to invest only in women-friendly companies, almost immediately the phones were ringing with women from these companies telling vivid stories of discrimination.

That same year, in 1993, Ace Greenberg was replaced by Jimmy Cayne as CEO of Bear Stearns. Cayne liked to put out his cigars in an ashtray he'd received from the FWA, the Financial Women's Association. Sometime later, the head of Legal came up with an idea to invite Bear Stearns's female employees from all over the country who held the rank of VP and above to small, intimate lunches with Jimmy Cayne to discuss their experiences—"women's issues" was how it was phrased.

When it was Maureen's turn for lunch with a group of other executive women, she went in guns blazing. She wanted to talk about how some man was always sitting in her chair whenever she returned from maternity leave (not that it was actual maternity; it was classified as unpaid leave). There was another top-ranked woman, from Boston, who covered huge accounts and was just as annoyed: one of her male colleagues had set up a major golf outing for their clients. She loved to golf but when she arrived with her clubs, she found he'd scheduled it at a men-only club. She couldn't do anything but leave—if she made "a stink," she'd only look bad in front of her clients.

The women arrived at the meeting pumped up, but when they entered, they saw the room was miked and there was a woman from HR—always a woman who would throw the others under the bus, Maureen observed—ready to take notes. The meeting inevitably turned into "a total kumbaya moment." Only the woman from Boston tried to tell the story of the golf outing. Cayne promptly evaluated her complaint: "That sounds like that's your problem," he said. It certainly wasn't his, none of it, which he made clear by taking calls throughout and leaving the room whenever he felt like it.

Maureen was fuming. But why was she surprised, she asked herself. Bear Stearns was still reimbursing employees who took clients to topless bars. The real rub was that the men came off as the good-time guys who took the clients to golf clubs and naughty strip bars, and when it was time to make a deal, they were the ones the clients called, while Maureen and the other women were "doing all the frickin' work behind the scenes," while "the fun guy" got to be "the senior on the account."

But through their silence, the women at the lunch were also complicit, acting as "a cheerleader in that moment when they should have let this all out." Instead of complaints, well-grounded complaints, it was: "I just want to thank you, Jimmy, for this opportunity . . . it's changed my life." The minute he left and the woman from HR had packed up her things, they turned to one another: "Can you believe this shit?!"

The women of Beth Dater's generation, the ones still standing, felt they shared in Wall Street's legacy, and were wedded to the silences. But Maureen's generation was not much better; one of Maureen's friends, who had made a fortune as a pre-IPO partner at Goldman Sachs, liked to say she'd never experienced any harassment or discrimination even as Maureen's husband had worked there at the time and had seen it differently. But we are the lucky ones, they told themselves and each other. Unlike Beth's generation, they were "allowed" to have both work and family, never mind that they had to hide the photographic evidence.

You could be called many things, but for Barbara Byrne at Lehman, the worst was the accusation women often lobbed at one another: "Who does she think she is, that bitch?" Barbara had a friend, around fifty years old and with a long career on Wall Street, who was suddenly informed by Lehman's HR department that there were complaints about how she was coming off: she was aggressive, hard to get along with, essentially "a bitch." They had taken the matter into their own hands and hired her a behavior coach without asking.

Barbara tried to intervene. "She's not difficult," she insisted to

HR. "She's driven, she's focused, she's unbelievably good at what she does."

"Well, you're being difficult right now," they responded.

"Why?" Barbara asked. "Because I just spoke to you in this tone of voice? And if John here spoke to you in this way . . . ?"

"Barbara, that's not how we do things around here," they huffed.

Her friend, involuntarily assigned behavior coaching, was at the end of her tether and asked Barbara for advice. Barbara told her she'd need to leave: "Because you're never going to get yourself out from this particular person."

Shortly after, her friend called with terrific news: one of her clients, a major firm, wanted to hire her as the head of their M&A corporate strategy.

Barbara burst out laughing. It was karma. "You need to take that job!"

"I'm going to tell these guys to go fuck themselves," her friend said.

"No, you're not!" Barbara, ever the strategist, insisted, instructing her friend to play the long game. "You're going to go in to the head and say to him, 'I just want to thank you so much for all the wonderful opportunities that you've given me. The coach that you provided me with sort of helped me figure out how to present a more agreeable style.' (Like any of these guys are agreeable, are you kidding me, with their paunches out to here . . .) And just say, 'Ya know, I've just received an offer to go become the EVP head of M&A corporate strategy . . .' (And this is going to be a client they'd just die for. . . .) 'And I so look forward to you guys calling on me. And, oh, by the way, I know that technically I'm not allowed to receive my deferred stocks since I'm leaving, but it would be tremendously valuable to me, and it would make me think incredibly well of you guys if you were to give it to me.'"

"I'm not sure I can do this!" her friend said.

"Yes, you can. You're going to get an Oscar."

She did as Barbara told her, and got the stock, because as Barbara predicted, "these men are very gullible."

Six months later, she called up Barbara and told her that she was about to do a big M&A deal and she was bringing in Goldman Sachs instead of Lehman.

"Good for you! And when they call you up—'Why did you not give it to us!'—that's when you can tell them, 'You guys were incredibly naïve. After what you did to me, and what you said you were going to do, and after you put a coach in place, and all these things, you actually believe that I would trust you to be my advisor in mergers and acquisitions? I wish you the best, but you're not going to have it with me. Good luck. . . .' Boom! Hit him with it, boom!"

That was Barbara's way. Let him now have to explain to his boss why "he has no call on one of the leading companies in the industry that he makes his living off." That would teach him.

———

IN EARLY JANUARY 1994, AFTER HAVING BEEN FEATURED IN THE October 1992 issue of *Black Enterprise* magazine as the first Black female MD, Marianne Spraggins resigned from Smith Barney. The reasons given in the press were vague and the timing seemed inopportune; in a matter of weeks, the firm would be handing out year-end bonuses. Clearly, something had happened.

What had happened was that Marianne had filed a complaint against Smith Barney and entered arbitration behind closed doors. On Wall Street, that was one's only recourse: any grievance, any accusation, had to be dealt with through mandatory arbitration. Almost everyone who worked on Wall Street had to sign away their right to prove their case in a court of law and instead try to find justice and compensation through arbitration.

But if Wall Street's arbitration track record was anything to go by, Marianne's claim that "she had been humiliated and discriminated against because she was black and a woman" would probably have had little traction. But, Marianne had always been careful to surround herself with heavyweights from outside the finance world who could step in if it came to that. Now it had. Reverend Jesse Jackson, at the time a powerful figure in American politics, showed up at Smith Barney for an impromptu visit that was intentionally under the radar. But he was making a point: this time I come without the press, next time it'll be different. Reverend Al Sharpton, another major player in Black community politics, also came to visit, and even as he sat outside the closed-door meeting about Marianne, the fact that he was there showed the firm "what we might be facing if we didn't settle this in a way that everybody walked away feeling good about it." Smith Barney settled with Marianne Spraggins for $1.35 million and a signed NDA (a non-disclosure agreement).

One of the scant public references to what had happened was a short piece in *The Bond Buyer*, where one "anonymous friend" of Marianne was cited as saying they believed the complaint was centered around compensation, Marianne's grievance being that "she wasn't compensated at a level she should have been compensated at, based upon her perception of what others did at Smith Barney." But unnamed "former colleagues and friends" suggested that "clearly, other issues were involved." Based on interviews done with Michael Lissack, Marianne's former colleague at Smith Barney, by journalist Susan Antilla, who has long focused on discrimination on Wall Street, it turned out Spraggins was "mocked for her race and her aggressiveness." Employees referred to her as the N-word, and "a top manager speculated about the size of Marianne Spraggins's penis."

Marianne put out an innocuous official statement, as required: "After 14 years on Wall Street, I am looking forward to pursuing a long held interest in capital formation in the African American community." Smith Barney's official statement was that there had never been any allegations of racial and/or sexual discrimination.

In 1994, just nine months after Marianne received her settlement, Pamela Martens wrote to Smith Barney's COO Jamie Dimon to ask that he review "a systemic problem of sexual harassment, sexual discrimination and lewd conduct." It had been going on for at least ten years. When in 1984 Pamela first arrived at the Garden City, Long Island, branch of Shearson Lehman, soon to be Smith Barney, fifty-two-year-old Nicholas Cuneo, the branch manager, resented having to hire women, believing they belonged at home with the kids. He informed female employees they were going to be paid less than the men while also having to hew to a dress code of short skirts and no pantsuits.

On Cuneo's watch, there were three-martini lunches and a basement room known as the Boom-Boom Room, which was even listed under "B" in the company directory. The Boom-Boom Room was the purview of the men, of lap dances and booze. Cuneo proudly proclaimed his branch to be "the biggest whorehouse in Garden City."

A year after she sent her letter, Pamela was fired, seen as a troublemaker, and in 1996, she took Smith Barney to court. Among her many allegations was Cuneo's use of the term "slits and tits" to denote women, and his telling a female broker that she was a "jewish [sic] bitch" who "should be hit by a bus." Other women followed Pamela in accusing Smith Barney of sexual harassment and misogynistic hiring practices. Eventually twenty-three Smith Barney women, joined by two thousand others, filed a class-action suit against the firm; it was the only way to bring a complaint to a court of law rather than keeping it in closed-door arbitration. Smith Barney was forced to pay $150 million in settlements.

Women from other brokerage firms, including Merrill Lynch and Morgan Stanley, followed, also filing class-action suits against their respective firms. Wall Street answered its critics by posting "photographs of smiling female employees" on their websites and "sponsoring" one "feel-good networking event for women" after another.

In 1998, Marlene Jupiter was also forced to take DLJ, the firm where she had worked on the options desk for sixteen years, to arbitration. She had first started to feel uncomfortable in the late 1980s, at the time of the insider-trading scandals. At the rowdy block trading desk, a trader had pinned up Jesse Jackson's infamous utterance that New York was "Hymietown" and each time another indicted Wall Streeter turned out to be Jewish, the trader added the press announcement to his wall. Marlene stayed silent, quietly commiserating with the other Jewish employee, a man who was the liaison between block trading and investment banking. Then there were the "jokes" aimed at the lone Black trader on the block trading desk, such as one referencing a system of New York–based sleepaway camps for underprivileged kids: "Where's your kid going to summer camp? The Fresh Air Fund?"

Things got worse when a former hedge-fund trader was hired in as a VP. Astute when it came to office politics, seemingly allergic to outspoken single women, let alone those who were Jewish (or that's certainly what Marlene concluded), he gradually rallied everyone to his side and against Marlene. His antipathy and bullying only got worse when, in 1991, Marlene tapped into a great lead through her alma mater, Cornell University, and suddenly began making millions for the firm, and was profiled in the press as a Wall Street heavy hitter.

In the office, she was ridiculed for being a feminist, for being a Jew. A new male hire, a graduate of Notre Dame brought in to drum up business with Irish American hedge funds, would sing, "*I am woman, hear me roar!*" whenever she gave her opinion on a trade. Sometimes he switched it up and sang the dreidel song at her. When she arrived late at work after a breakfast meeting, they'd ask if she'd had a late night out at a "dyke" bar. When she cut her hair short in a popular style, she was greeted by a block trader, a former friend who'd since joined the "wolf pack," as Marlene now thought of them, with "Nice haircut, dyke." During Fleet Week, the lead wolf announced to everyone that if she were the only woman on a navy ship, even with hundred-dollar bills pasted to her chest, there'd be no takers.

Marlene tried various avenues, pleading with her boss, her former mentor, to intervene, but he refused and increasingly seemed to be enjoying the show. Human Resources offered a sympathetic ear but made sure not to keep a written record of what was happening. Eventually, there was nothing left for Marlene to do but walk away from a job that was lucrative and that she had once loved. She would have quietly licked her wounds, like countless other Wall Street women, but soon after, she was up for a dream job with the Royal Bank of Canada. The position was hers, with only background checks left to do. The bank called DLJ to check on her references and when someone went in search of her old boss, the man who had bullied her relentlessly, the leader of the wolf pack, grabbed the phone and told them that Marlene was lazy, incompetent, and couldn't sell anything for the life of her.

The job offer was retracted, and Marlene had no choice now but to seek compensation, to clear her name. But she wasn't able to take DLJ to court, of course. As of 1972, those who worked in the securities industry signed away their right to bring a claim to court. Instead, a panel of three arbitrators decided your fate; in 1992, it was estimated that the majority of the New York arbitrators—specifically 89 percent of the 726 active arbitrators—were "white men, averaging sixty years of age."

The closed-door proceedings, held in a room at the New York Stock Exchange, began in January 1998. The three-person arbitration panel she was assigned was chaired by a female attorney, and the other two panelists were men; one an arbitrator for corporations (which almost guaranteed he would side with DLJ) and the other a retired floor broker for Merrill Lynch. Marlene, so stressed she was unable to eat, was down to about one hundred pounds. Marlene's lawyers presented their evidence. She had been at the firm for sixteen years, she had won the "Super Achiever" award in 1995. Even so, she was never made a principal and when she asked why, she'd been told she had to bring in twice as much to be considered; not ten but twenty million. Yet this was not the case for everyone, and her lawyers argued it was in fact subtle retaliation for how she had called out the antisemitism, the racism, and the gender discrimination at the trading desk. They recounted many stories of each, bringing in witnesses where they could.

The DLJ legal team counter-argued, presenting Marlene as the instigator in the office bullying. They made claims such as that Marlene had boasted having "gone through" the entire hockey team at college. An Asian American desk assistant, who was repeatedly called a "gook," and the other Jew at the trading desk with whom Marlene had once commiserated, came in to swear that there was no racism or antisemitism. The daily abuse that Marlene had experienced was cast as healthy ribbing, an expression of competition between Marlene and the wolf-pack leader. The defamation charge—that he had sabotaged her job offer from the Royal Bank of Canada—was the most difficult to prove because the headhunter, for his own self-preservation, was unwilling to testify.

On June 12, 1998, six months and twenty-seven sessions later, it was over, and now the three panelists had to decide on the legitimacy of Marlene's claims. Five weeks later, on July 20, the decision came in. The two men on the panel, Stephen H. Busch and Nicholas D. Zigo, both sided with DLJ. In their joint statement, they wrote: "In order to succeed Claimant must demonstrate by a preponderance of the evidence that she was discriminated against because of her gender or religion and that conditions in her workplace were so egregious, ongoing, pervasive and intolerable that she had no other choice but to leave." But as they saw it, "there were three isolated and offensive" incidents only, which took place "three or more years prior to the time Claimant left DLJ's employ, but only one was directed specifically at Claimant." Moreover, they believed each incident "was dealt with firmly and promptly by Respondent," and that overall "DLJ did not countenance discrimination, and such isolated incidents do not constitute religious or gender discrimination."

As to the abuse Marlene had endured, the two men felt that she "was occasionally teased by some of her colleagues, but we found most of the teasing was general in nature and not directed towards her in particular . . . In fact, the testimony showed that Claimant herself engaged in the same sort of occasional teasing towards others." While Marlene had testified to being put into an untenable position and eventually having to leave DLJ to escape the toxicity, the male arbitration panelists saw her departure as instead based on "a reduction of her productivity," because in 1994 she had made $850,000, whereas in 1995, her earnings had fallen to $720,000. Marlene lost her case.

Carol Weir, who chaired the panel, voted in Marlene's favor. In her dissenting opinion, she noted that while Marlene felt herself to be in a "hostile" environment, the arbitration rules required that "a sexually objectionable environment must be both objectively and subjectively offensive." Marlene's claim of a "hostile" environment was *not* subjective, she wrote, and she and her lawyers had clearly demonstrated this to be the case. From what Carol Weir had heard, it was clear that, "Donaldson, Lufkin & Jenrette did in fact discriminate against Marlene Jupiter, subjecting her to continual ridicule and denigration." It was clear that she was hounded out rather than leaving of her own volition because "it defies common sense to believe that any reasonable person would leave such an economically beneficial situation unless the working conditions had become too painful to endure."

If Marlene Jupiter had been able to take her case to a court of law, witnesses would have been forced to show up and reporters would have had access to the proceedings. But she could not.

———

IT WAS AFTER A COMPANY GET-TOGETHER THAT MAUREEN SHERRY and some other women from Bear Stearns decided to go out for drinks. Over cocktails, they found themselves sharing stories, comparing notes. That first informal drinks session in 1993 turned into more get-togethers—regular dinners every two months if they could find a date that worked. They shared information, what they called "survival hints": always stay in full view on the trading floor when working with a notorious groper; there's that guy who has mistresses hidden away everywhere, and if you travel with him to make a pitch, be prepared to do it alone while he entertains one of his lady friends. They started to call themselves the Glass Ceiling Club.

But Maureen had the worrying sense that perhaps it was too little, too late. The Glass Ceiling Club members agreed to start calling things out, to give a name to the discrimination and transgressions in the same way that Anita Hill had. But more often than not, their efforts backfired because they'd "drawn a line in the sand," but a line that hadn't been there before, and now they were suddenly pointing to it.

They were also facing off against a culture that they themselves were fully steeped in. Maureen had started to notice that she only valued the careers that came with that same high compensation, and to correlate a lower salary with "less worth." It was only when her children started school, and she saw just how hard their low-paid teachers worked, that she had to reassess. Her kids' teachers were getting a fraction of what someone on Wall Street made even as "you could come into my job every day and be, whatever, hungover, tired, and you could get through your day and be kind of productive." To everyone around her, as well as to her, money and profit were the end-all, the bottom line; it excused behavior, erased transgressions.

At the same time, gender-based pay inequity continued, never having disappeared from the time when Mickie Siebert found herself hopscotching from firm to firm, trying to secure an equal salary, until she gave up and founded her own firm. Compensation was usually shrouded in mystery, but Maureen had a friend "who had all the spreadsheets." She also had a friend who was a compensation consultant at Morgan Stanley, and who was able to look up the salaries of the men there doing comparable work and with the same accounts as Maureen at Bear Stearns. Her friend estimated that Maureen was being compensated at least 30 percent below the "male salary," and her pay discrepancy only widened once she'd started having children. The compensation consultant referred to it as the "female discount."

But Maureen also learned that if you were willing to have some "knock-down, drag-out fights," "they sort of respected you more and compensated you more." At the same time, even as she did that, she hated sitting there "fighting over money because the numbers" were "so stupid," so ridiculously high anyway. Numbers her kids' teachers could only dream of if they were to win the lottery.

Pay inequity in the bonus culture of the 1990s was especially fickle. In 1996, Jacki Zehner was made partner at Goldman Sachs— the youngest woman and the first female trader to do so. Once partner, she made sure she sat in on compensation meetings, where she found the conversation often went like this: "Oh, Joe is such a great guy, what do you have him down for? No, that doesn't seem enough. He's great. OK, next, Susan. Who's Susan? What does she do? I dunno." Jacki was there to step in and tell them who "Susan" was and to advocate for her bonus.

Janet Hanson, who had left Goldman Sachs and now had two children, had since started a firm with her husband. Janet described leaving Goldman Sachs after fourteen years "like stepping off a cliff," even though she had eventually landed on her feet. But she had not given up on the idea of helping women navigate Wall Street. On November 17, 1997, she invited thirty of her favorite former colleagues from Goldman Sachs to the Water Club on the East River for the "first GS women's reunion." Her sister made T-shirts for the occasion: a woman standing on a ladder nailing an *s* to "85 Broad." It was a play on Goldman Sachs' address—85 Broad Street. Janet had just created *85 Broads*.

The idea behind 85 Broads was that women did not network enough, or else found themselves isolated in the office, or else had taken time off for children and now, "with applesauce stains" on their shirts, they felt "embarrassed about no longer being considered a heavy hitter," not knowing how to get back into the game. They needed one another.

Later, sending out thank-you notes to everyone, Janet added a copy of Darla Moore's response to a recent controversy. Moore, president of Rainwater Inc, had recently appeared on the cover of *Fortune* magazine with the headline "The Toughest Babe in Business." Some women had felt offended by the magazine describing her as a "babe," but Moore had insisted she didn't mind, and that the objections were trivial: "You know what I think is one of the world's biggest wastes of time for a woman? Networking with other females. Where is that going to get you if men are the ones with all the power? Every single one of my mentors has been male. At no time have I ever encountered a woman who would have been a smart choice to help pull me up the ladder, to give me the tools and power needed to make a difference." Janet jokingly told the 85 Broads members that they should all send Darla Moore a note: "Hey Babe! Good luck finding another babe to have lunch with!" When the *New York Times* profiled 85 Broads, membership jumped to a thousand, and then continued to grow exponentially when Janet opened it up to all Wall Street women.

16

Ground Zero

By the end of the 1990s, Louise Jones and Mike Cassidy had forty employees on the floor of the NYSE, making Cassidy, Jones & Co. the exchange's largest floor firm. It was then that Louise got a call from NYSE chairman Dick Grasso. He needed her help on a pilot program to shift trading to the decimal system, away from the fractions that had been the language of trading ever since the start of the NYSE. They would first test it out on ten stocks.

She hung up and thought: "*Oh, shit, I'm out of business!*" The system of trading in pieces of eight had been in use for nearly four hundred years, derived from Spanish investors who in the 1600s divided their gold doubloons (coins) into halves, quarters, and eighths so they could count them out quickly on their fingers (eight fingers—minus the thumbs). Eighths were the language of trading, and now those 8 increments were going to go to 100 increments: the more she thought about it, "how do you physically now write I bought 100 shares at 101 and a penny?" She knew that this was more than a mere adjustment in the mental math. It was part of the long and incremental decline of commissions, which began on May-

day when Doreen had stepped onto the Amex floor. Commissions
had steadily dropped since, even to less than a penny on some electronic exchanges. The fees that had bankrolled brokers, as well as
the whole superstructure that supported them, was fast disappearing. Not just that, but the new electronic trading had increasingly
cut out the intermediary, the specialist, by allowing trades to be
completed without them.

Louise called Grasso back: "We can't do this. . . . We're going
to look like idiots to NASDAQ. We have no real good handheld
technology."

He agreed and told her to put together a committee to find the
right handhelds into which the floor brokers could input the new
increments. It was the only way this was going to work.

She put together a committee and invited companies to come
up with a handheld for punching in the trades in "rapid fire" and
then sending them over to the booths. They settled on one from a
company called SunGard Global. Once that was done, Louise finally
paused and realized she was exhausted. She had been at this since
she was a teenager. These days, she could barely stay awake during
her days off—she would fall asleep in the midst of a conversation.
SunGard Global, she thought, would do well to buy Cassidy, Jones,
to combine their handhelds with a thriving floor business. She convinced them to buy Cassidy, Jones, and then further talked them into
buying another two floor firms so that they had close to a hundred
employees on the NYSE. But she herself was done, and as soon as she
could, she handed over the reins and left.

If for twenty years her mind had been focused on catching the
dollars raining down on her, now she switched her focus to a new
goal: children. It was fortuitous that as she was getting into a cab, a
friend's wife popped out of it and handed her the Vogue magazine
fall issue: "Look at this! Designer genes." Inside was an article with
a list of the world's best sperm banks.

Louise signed on with one and began to scour its donor profiles. She had never thought about a person's voice, even as her job on the floor was all about voices, but suddenly she realized how important it was for her. She would find a profile she liked, ask to listen to his recording . . . and discard him. She was, quite literally, waiting until the right voice spoke to her.

She had made friends with a woman at the sperm bank, who called Louise one day to say a new donor had come in and, "Oh my God, he's gorgeous!" He was a medical school student. Louise knew she had to act fast. She had been worrying that once she had her children with the help of a sperm bank, they'd end up with hundreds of half-siblings out there in the world. She didn't think she wanted that for them. Like other Wall Street women, Louise saw money as a way to buy security, not luxury. To ease her worries.

"I'm putting in a bid right now."

She placed a bid on it, meaning any forthcoming sperm collected was automatically hers.

When she heard his voice finally, it was perfect: "Deep, masculine, and he was saying such wonderful things like 'Whoever you are out there, I hope it all works out for you.'"

Louise ended up paying for seventy-six vials in all, each worth thousands of dollars, but she didn't care. She had used her money to buy what she needed for herself. The first of her two children, a daughter, was born on July 25, 2001.

———

JANET HANSON, WHO HAD FOUNDED 85 BROADS, WAS STAYING OVER-night in the city. She had been invited to join the board of a corporate campaign to help fund select entrepreneurial business plans. The winners were going to be announced the next day, on September 11, at the Tribeca Grand Hotel. As the board members gathered for drinks in the lobby of the hotel before heading off to dinner at the City Hall restaurant, they looked out at the lightning and thunder that was lighting up the sky and agreed that it "looked and sounded fake—like the kind you'd see and hear in a 1950s horror movie." But the next morning was a stunner of a day, with crystal-clear blue skies, as if all the dirt had been wiped clean by the downpour the night before.

Louise Jones was holding her newborn daughter when she looked out of her kitchen windows and saw the first tower hit. Her hormones were still raging after having given birth just five weeks earlier, she most definitely had baby brain fog, and as she watched, she couldn't piece together what she was seeing. She stared at the burning inferno and couldn't understand it. The news was on—she still had to listen to the financial news, she couldn't wean herself off the markets so quickly—and then she heard ambulances. She thought she was seeing people jumping from the tower. It still wasn't registering. Then she heard that the Pentagon had been hit, and all she could think was that that was impossible, because the airspace around it was protected, impenetrable. And that's the moment she started to panic.

At the same time, her apartment building began to broadcast an announcement: everyone had to get out . . . now! It was an evacuation.

She was wearing boxer shorts, a nursing top, "with tits out to here." She grabbed her baby, she left her keys. Outside, someone ushered her into Stuyvesant High School, Marlene Jupiter's former high school, saying there was a bomb shelter inside, but then just as quickly, everyone was told to evacuate the school. There was now nothing left to do but run north.

Phyllis Strong had long ago left Wall Street for Hollywood, but her friend and former roommate, Joanne Lipman, was still at the *Wall Street Journal*, now a deputy managing editor and one of the highest-ranked women at the newspaper. Her daughter was turning twelve the next day and had asked for refrigerator magnets for her school locker. Joanne had stopped in at the Lechters Housewares store in the concourse of the World Trade Center and found two magnets: one a violin that played a tune (her daughter was taking violin lessons) and another a flip phone. She'd bumped into a friend, Joe Dizney, the *Wall Street Journal*'s design director, and he'd walked with her to the store so they could chat about the newspaper's visual redesign that they'd been planning for months. As they approached the cash register, two security guards were shepherding people out toward the Church Street exit. The cashier wanted to leave, too, but Joanne insisted that she ring up the magnets. The receipt read 8:55 a.m.—it was nine minutes after the first plane had hit the North Tower, directly above Lechters.

When they emerged from the concourse out onto the street, they were stunned, disoriented. It had been a perfect morning when they'd gone inside, but now it seemed to be snowing dark, metallic flakes that pinged off Joanne's "sunglasses perched on top of my head." She stood there, in her high heels, trying to take in the meaning of the pieces of paper, the "blank financial order forms," that were "wafting through the air." Cars had been abandoned, one "crushed by a giant chunk of concrete." People were moving, shouting to one another, but everything was "muffled" as if "in slow motion." The two of them tried to make their way to the *WSJ* offices right across from the World Trade Center. Liberty Street was on fire, with airline seats in the street, and "human carnage, raw and red, was splattered thickly across the pavement and the sidewalks." They needed to look where they were stepping but also tried not to look. When they got to the West Side Highway, they went out of their way to avoid the headless corpse that someone had tried to cover, but failed, with a "restaurant napkin." At that moment, the second plane flew over them.

Louise was now racing up the West Side Highway, shoeless, and it felt like a bad dream. She held her daughter "in a football hold," better to keep a grip on her. She looked behind her and all she could see was an enormous cloud of dust and debris coming at them and all she could think was, "You fucking asshole, how could you bring a child into this world right now?"

"I became a mother that moment."

She had only recently moved into her apartment, a block away from the World Trade Center. She'd made friends with a woman she'd met in the laundry room, and as she ran alongside others up the West Side Highway, she recognized the woman's husband. He was running with their children. She asked if she could run with him. He had a gym bag on him, and he handed it to her; inside were men's sneakers, "giant clown sneakers," but she was glad to have them. There was also a shirt inside that she pulled over her tank top.

They ran from Chambers Street up to Houston and, exhausted, they stopped for a moment at the piers, where there was some shelter and they could take a breather. As Louise stood there, resting, a woman kept coming up to her saying that she must be tired, and that she would take her baby to hold for her. "No, thank you, it's OK," Louise replied. But the woman wouldn't let up, and the third time she approached, Louise started screaming at her. She was in no doubt the woman was angling to take her baby amidst the chaos.

She moved on and found herself in someone's apartment in Greenwich Village. Most cell service was out, but the apartment had a fax machine, and people were using it to contact family to let them know they were alive. That night she stayed in someone's Pilates studio in Manhattan, lying on an exercise mat with her newborn while fighter jets passed over throughout the night. The explosions and sirens made it sound like they were in the middle of a war zone.

September 11 was Maria Bartiromo's birthday, and as usual she was broadcasting live from the floor of the New York Stock Exchange. The morning was perfect, and her assistant was waiting for her with a bouquet of flowers. They saw the first plane hit on the television screens, and then Maria's boss called and told her to go outside and call into the studio with live coverage. She went out onto Broadway, where hundreds had gathered looking at the towers one block over. Those who had cell phones still working were lending them out for others to call their families. It was then that the second plane crashed into the second tower. Next to her someone said, "Oh my God, the world will never be the same." Then the buildings collapsed, and she was, like everyone else, running for her life. Smoke, paper, and debris were whirling in the air, getting into her eyes, and it was impossible to see.

She tried to get back into the NYSE but the doors were locked, and so instead she tried the doors of the New York Life Building across the street. Inside was a woman "crying, crying uncontrollably." Maria was wearing a burgundy on-air suit and black patent-leather shoes, both now covered in "white soot and smoke." She went back outside and again tried the doors of the exchange and this time a security guard caught sight of her, opened the doors, and pulled her in.

Doreen Mogavero was desperate to find Jennifer, her business partner and friend. She knew she was coming in from New Jersey, which meant that her train was right under that tower. Since 1993, when a bomb had gone off in a parking garage under one of the towers, almost everyone had an emergency plan in place. Some had agreed to meet at Trinity Church, some at the ferry. Doreen's and Jennifer's plan was to meet in the lobby of their three-bedroom office at 25 Broad Street. But Jennifer wasn't there, and the National Guard had arrived and were shutting down the streets.

When Jennifer eventually showed up, the second tower fell, and outside—looking out from the windows of their office—it was now pitch-black. They made their way down to the lobby, packed with people who'd been wandering the dark streets. Doreen said to the doorman on duty that she hadn't realized the building had emergency metal shutters that came down over the doors and windows. They didn't, he said, it just looked that way because there was zero visibility. Outside, they could hear cars crashing into one another.

Smoke was starting to seep in from under the front doors of 25 Broad, and Doreen and Jennifer directed everyone into the stairwell, which was fireproof. As they crowded in, a man came sauntering down the stairs—the elevators were no longer working—and asked what was going on. Shocked, they told him.

"But I can see daylight from my apartment."

He was on the back end of the building, where it was like a different world.

Without missing a beat, Doreen and Jennifer, both daughters of military fathers, commandeered his apartment and led everyone up there, where they put people to work filling containers with water, wetting towels, putting together first-aid supplies. They told everyone to go use the bathroom while there was still water. The man had a landline that was working because he was on the side of Broadway that continued to have working telephone lines, and Doreen called her husband, Arcky, who was in Brooklyn at their son's school. "Listen," he said, "I want you to get out of there . . . The television says lower Manhattan could potentially blow up from gas lines. They're all cut."

Doreen called Jennifer over. "We gotta get out of here."

They announced to everyone that they were leaving. They took the wet towels, and almost everyone decided to follow them out. But when they all got down to the lobby again, the National Guard wouldn't let them out of the building. Doreen said: "Listen to me. This is still America, you better open this door. I'm outta here." They left, including two NYU students who were now in their group, and started to walk toward the Brooklyn Bridge. But by the time they got there, it was closed down because there were too many people on it. They continued toward the Manhattan Bridge, trying to hitchhike to Brooklyn, Jennifer's feet bleeding because she wasn't wearing sneakers until someone eventually gave her a pair from their backpack. Doreen was just grateful that she'd sent a very pregnant Joy home the day before because she looked like she'd give birth any minute, and she'd specifically barred her from coming in that Tuesday.

They had been walking for hours, waving down cars that just kept going, until finally a plumbing contractor stopped his truck, and Doreen's childhood friend Marilyn, who worked at the firm and who had never had an athletic bone in her body, who had never run more than ten feet in one go, vaulted into the truck. "How the hell did you . . . ?!" Doreen asked in astonishment. It was a brief moment of comic relief.

Westina Matthews, her closet full of St. John's suits, was one of the people on the Brooklyn Bridge. She had been on the thirty-third floor of the South Tower sitting in the executive dining room, hosting a breakfast for four women who'd won a place on the New York Women's Forum's most-prominent list. She was starting to get annoyed because she kept pressing the button for service and no one was coming around with the coffee carafe. When the waiter finally appeared, his hands were shaking. A security guard then popped his head in and said to get out immediately. A plane had hit the North Tower. "Would they like to take the elevator?"

Heck no, Westina said.

She couldn't believe it when the four other women said they'd go to the ladies' room first, but Westina was not about to wait. She headed straight to the stairwell and ran down the thirty-three flights. When she got to the street and turned around, she saw men jumping from windows, their ties flying up in the air. She ran, like everyone else, and made it to the Brooklyn Bridge, where she teamed up with a group of Black teenage boys, and together they ran, dodging people, hoping to make it across the bridge before it got closed.

Lehman's employees, like Barbara Byrne, sitting at their desks at the World Financial Center, across from the towers, could see everything. Some were on the phone with their counterparts at Cantor Fitzgerald: "Your building is on fire."

———

THE NEXT DAY, MARY FARRELL APPEARED ON BOTH CNN AND CNBC. She told the viewers that this was a country that had been born of a revolution, had survived the Civil War, financial panics, economic depressions and recessions, and the market would survive terrorism too.

Jolyne was living in Manhasset on Long Island, where she had bought her first house when she was still in her twenties. It was a New York City suburb with a significant number of Wall Streeters, especially from among the hardest-hit firms, Cantor Fitzgerald, Sandler O'Neill, and Fred Alger. They all knew one another; they would all catch the same 5:44 a.m. train into the city. Now when she boarded, the train was half-empty, and the funerals were nonstop.

After Marlene Jupiter's arbitration trial was over in 1998, she was taking a stroll near the Staten Island Ferry and saw a golden cockapoo running around, lost. People had gathered, deciding what to do about the stray, and when someone worried out loud that it would be taken to a kill shelter, she offered to take it home with her. She named him Justice because she liked to say that she had "finally found justice." Justice opened up a whole new life for her: morning coffees sitting outside, midday walks around Battery Park with a group of other dog owners. On Tuesday, September 11, Marlene had been on the last PATH train out to New Jersey for a meeting. It was not until Thursday, two days later, that she was even allowed back into Manhattan. She and other desperate pet owners had now gathered near Battery Park and were waiting anxiously for their lottery numbers to give them a turn in a small van that would shuttle them back to their apartments to rescue their pets. Marlene was seldom lucky and so she couldn't believe it when she drew a number that would get her into the first convoy back into the Gateway Plaza apartment complex.

Sitting in the back of the van with seven others, all holding hands and praying, they made their way slowly into Battery Park. Marlene looked out the window to see abandoned shoes, mud, blown-out glass, and smoke everywhere. The electricity was out, and the parks police who accompanied them led the way with flashlights as together they climbed the thirty-four flights to her apartment. When she opened the door, Justice was nowhere to be found. Her adrenaline was pumping, and she thought she might be sick. But then they heard a scratching; in the chaos and noise, Justice had trapped himself in the bedroom. He darted out and ran desperately to the toilet bowl to drink. She had made it in the nick of time; she later learned three days was the maximum he could have survived without water.

After 9/11, Joanne Lipman—caught out wearing heels that day—purchased a pair of "fleeing sneakers" and kept them stashed in her office. Most of the other women did too.

The New York Stock Exchange opened again on Monday, September 17. Doreen had had to abandon her car in Manhattan the previous Tuesday, but now she was on the first ferry back with her husband. Standing at the bow, they moved slowly through the water toward Manhattan, and watched in stunned silence; it was still dark outside, but with the electricity finally back on, the city was again lit up so that now they could see the smoke still billowing up, moving like apparitions amongst the skyscrapers.

Maria Bartiromo arrived back that day too. The birthday flowers that her assistant had given her on Tuesday morning had turned black, and the exchange, just like all of lower Manhattan, stank of smoke and chemicals. Up in the gallery to ring the opening bell was NYSE chairman Dick Grasso, who had been doing all-nighters on the floor. Next to him was Mayor Rudy Giuliani, who had brought down Boesky and Milken and turned his win on Wall Street into a successful mayoral run, on his second try defeating Mayor Dinkins, Marianne Spraggins's friend and candidate. Next to them stood firefighters and police officers and traders. Doreen looked around at her friends on the floor and realized they were the last generation that could get the markets up and running, if push came to shove, with just paper and pencil. The younger set only knew computers and handhelds. It was the end of an era.

EVERYTHING SEEMED SOLID, ETERNAL, INDOMITABLE, UNTIL IT WAS
not. The dotcom bubble had burst in 2000, the markets plunged
in 2002 after the WTC attacks, and then came the Great Financial
Crisis of 2008. Lehman Brothers and Bear Stearns imploded, as did
other banks and financial institutions, while the rest were bailed out
by American taxpayers. A major cause for the financial crash was the
mortgage bubble, fueled by subprime mortgages. Lew Ranieri had
invented the mortgage-backed security, which over time had changed
its form like a mutant creature, but Ranieri still worried that he was
the original "Dr. Frankenstein."

But it wasn't just subprime mortgages.

Harvard Business School professor and Barnard College President Debora Spar wrote in a 2009 *Washington Post* op-ed, "I like
men. My husband is one, as are my two sons. I have spent most of my
career surrounded by men, and I have no major complaints. But as
the financial debacle unfolds, I can't help noticing that all the perpe-
trators of the greatest economic mess in eight decades are, well, men.
Specifically, they are rich, white, middle-aged guys, same as the ones
who brought us Watergate in the 1970s, the Teapot Dome scandal
in the 1920s and, presumably, the fall of Rome." The same question
was brought up at the Davos Conference in Switzerland a month later.
One panel moderator asked if things would look better had it been
Lehman Sisters instead of Lehman Brothers.

The question was serious yet fleeting. One senior finance guy
at Davos immediately quipped: "Probably not—women would never
have come up with all those sophisticated tools." As high-level Wall
Streeters lost their jobs in the fallout that followed, there seemed to
be a certain glee as the few women on top were dislodged. When the
female CFO of Lehman Brothers stepped down, along with countless
male executives, she was attacked as having been "fluffy," and "more

focused on fashion than on finance." The CFO of Morgan Stanley, once called "the most powerful woman on Wall Street," was forced out, and her male colleagues joked that "it was worth the billions in dollars of losses Morgan incurred last year, just to have her gone."

These days, some former Wall Street women focus on what they call "financial feminism." They quote Gloria Steinem's 2003 statement that "we'll never solve the feminization of power until we solve the masculinity of wealth." In other words, women will never have equal political power until the creation of wealth ceases to be synonymous with men and masculinity. The idea behind financial feminism is for women to reorder society's values through mindful investment and wealth accruement.

The idea echoes the convictions of Wilma Soss, who after World War II was on a mission to show Corporate America that women were major investors in their companies; and to show women that in being stockholders, they had the power to make change.

When Wilma Soss was rallying women and promoting women's investing power, she was still addressing a tiny minority of American women—largely the inheritors of generational wealth. Today's financial feminism is geared to many more women who, if only through a pension fund, can ostensibly make change. But Wall Street was built for men, and fundamentally, it remains an old boys' club.

Electronic trading eventually made floor trading on the NYSE a thing of the past. Doreen's paper and pencil are no more. The exchange exists but is a shadow of its former self. Power has shifted from trading desks to investment banking, hedge funds, and especially private equity firms—tellingly, in 2022, women were only 12 percent of managing directors and 16 percent of principals and partners at private equity firms. Fewer than 1 in 10 of those who sit on the investment committees where private equity investment decisions are made are women. Women's perspectives, in other words, are usually missing in decisions that have long-term effects for us all. Women of color fare the worst; while all women start to fall off the conveyor belt from "entry level to the C-suite," Black, Latina, and Asian women see an 80 percent fall.

In March 2017, a small bronze statue of a girl wearing sneakers, sporting a ponytail, with her hands on her hips, superhero-style, was commissioned by a large asset-management company, State Street Global Advisors. Called the "Fearless Girl," the statue came with a plaque that read, "Know the power of women in leadership. SHE makes a difference." State Street Global Advisors claimed to want to promote female empowerment alongside one of its funds that had the ticker abbreviation SHE. But soon after, the firm was forced to settle claims of gender and racial discrimination. The firm has also taken the statue's creator to court, trying to wrestle the copyright from her.

The four-foot Fearless Girl was initially placed opposite the

The *Fearless Girl* facing the NYSE: Broken Glass Ceiling installation in honor of International Women's Day, 2021.

famous Charging Bull that has become the visual symbol of Wall
Street, and which stands at the north end of Bowling Green Park,
drawing vast crowds. She was looking at the Charging Bull head-on,
as if staring him down.

Although criticized by some as "fake corporate feminism" and
"corporate advertising masquerading as art," the small statue became
an immediate crowd-pleaser. Maybe too much so for Arturo Di
Modica, the Charging Bull's creator, who argued that the corporate-
sponsored Fearless Girl was debasing his art. At his insistence, in
November 2018, she was removed and relocated. She is now in front
of the NYSE, where she stands by herself, no longer staring down the
bull. The anxiety over the Fearless Girl, commissioned by a firm claim-
ing to want to promote women's empowerment, the Charging Bull's
creator's indignation over her arrival, and her final location standing
alone, shunted aside, encapsulates perfectly—if unintentionally—the
story of so many She-Wolves of Wall Street.

Postscript

MARGO ALEXANDER found she had to put her idealism on hold while she was on Wall Street, but now, retired, she focuses on getting Democratic Party female candidates elected.

ELISA ANCONA finally bought herself the BMW she had dreamed of owning one day, the same car that the rich girls at her high school had. She drove it back to her house in Brooklyn, but the rear-wheel-drive car couldn't make it up the small hill to her driveway. Appalled, she shipped it out to her summer house in Catalonia, where it is still going strong after twenty-one years, preferring European terrain.

At BARBARA BYRNE's retirement party at MoMA, everyone took turns sharing stories and laughing over "Barbarisms" ("the client is always right, especially when you're wrong" . . . "stay on your horse"). Her husband then got up and revealed to her former colleagues at Lehman that she had never had a boyfriend at Goldman Sachs who bought her the mink coat. She had made it up to keep them on their toes—as they deserved.

In January 2007, **JOLYNE CARUSO-FITZGERALD** finally took three years off. Her son was ten and her daughter eight, and she realized she didn't know the name of their pediatrician. Her husband, a lawyer turned stay-at-home dad after their first child was born in 1995, took away her BlackBerry and sent her away for a week to the Miraval spa. She has now worked in every aspect of finance, including leading a hedge fund and starting her own firm. Her most recent job was in wealth management, which she believes will be the last holdout for human, non-AI interaction "because rich people want to know what the other rich people are doing."

PATRICIA CHADWICK had not told anyone but her husband about growing up in the Cambridge Catholic sect, but after her retirement, she published a memoir, *Little Sister*, in which she laid it all out.

In 2004, **BETH DATER** and her husband, Mitch Jennings, joined Wall Street's Secret Society—Kappa Beta Phi, its motto "Dum vivamus edimus et biberimus," Latin for "While we live, we eat and drink." It was fun and games: cocktails, dress-ups, and comedy skits. But in 2008, Mitch had a massive stroke following the unexpected collapse of Bear Stearns. Beth has been his caretaker ever since.

MARY FARRELL now sits on so many boards that her children joke she still works full-time.

JANET HANSON eventually sold 85 Broads, by then 30,000 members strong, to Sallie Krawcheck.

NINA HAYES plays the stock market and still dreams of the vodka gimlets at Delmonico's.

In 2003, **LILLIAN HOBSON**, now Lillian Lincoln Lambert, was shocked to receive a letter from the Harvard Business School that she was to be honored with one of that year's Harvard Alumni Achievement Awards. They offered her a table for eight guests; she convinced HBS to turn it into three tables of eight for all her family and friends. Up onstage with a group of white male executives also receiving the award, Lillian felt nervous. But when the first question came—"Who motivated you the most?"—she was the first to answer. Memories of HBS came rushing back, and she knew to jump in, speak first, be strong. Her answer was: my mother and Professor Fitzhugh.

What bothers **ALICE JARCHO** is that "younger women do not think that what we went through has anything to do with their current life . . . You want to have seventeen parties before you get married, when we got married with little flowers in our [hair]? Okay. . . . All right! But not to acknowledge—even acknowledge what we went through?" But she is also the first to say, "I had a great career. I had a lot of fun. I made more money than I deserved. . . . How lucky was I to be there at that point in time?"

With DNA testing, **LOUISE JONES** finally found out about her biological mother: she'd been a student at Barnard College, fluent in five languages. The man who got her pregnant was much older, a highly decorated military officer. By the time Louise traced her DNA, both had passed away.

MARLENE JUPITER, always an incurable romantic, finally found not only "Justice" but her soul mate, her true love. Their first date was at a party for the Black National Republican Council at the Boathouse restaurant in Central Park.

MARIA MARSALA calls herself a recovering Wall Street executive.

WESTINA MATHEWS is now a public speaker and author of books about faith, healing, and Black sisterhood. She still has her St. John's suits hanging in her closet.

In 2011, **DOREEN MOGAVERO** approached the NYSE governing board about reopening a ninety-year-old institution: the Member's Smoke Shop. Originally opened in the 1920s at 20 Broad Street, Morris Raskin, a floor broker, later moved it to the 12 Broad Street entrance of the NYSE. Once meant for floor traders buying cigars and cigarettes, Doreen cleaned up the shuttered store and restocked it with candy bars, sodas, and aspirin, and hired family members to work there. She closed the store when her husband retired; its last day was December 22, 2017. The NYSE has since torn it down.

After leaving Wall Street, **PRISCILLA RABB** worked in various capacities for the executive branch of the U.S. government, and later for Motorola and IBM. She can attest to the fact that none of these workplaces were oases of equality.

MAUREEN SHERRY's memoir about her life at Bear Stearns, called *The Glass Ceiling Club*, was about to hit the bookshelves when it was suddenly pulled; she turned it instead into a successful novel—*Opening Belle*—which she could claim was "fiction."

MURIEL SIEBERT acquired a Chihuahua named Monster Girl. When Mickie set up her offices on the seventeenth floor of the Lipstick Building in New York, the same floor where Ponzi-scheme conman Bernie Madoff had his office, Monster Girl would bark inexplicably every time they walked past. Mickie, the college dropout with nineteen honorary degrees, died in 2013, leaving $100,000 for the care of Monster Girl. Most of her $48 million, however, went to her non-profit foundation, which focuses on both financial literacy and the humane care of animals "especially those owned by the elderly who are financially challenged."

MARIANNE SPRAGGINS turned her real estate hobby into a full-time profession. Now when she sees corporate skyscrapers, she says "they look like prisons to me." When asked what she'd like to be remembered for, she said as "somebody who stood up to power."

PHYLLIS STRONG became a television writer and screenwriter, exactly as she had wanted all along. She still has her "golden hand-cuff" somewhere in a drawer, although she's not sure the Swiss watch works anymore.

Acknowledgments

*S*he-Wolves in many ways takes over where my previous book, *The Barbizon*, winds down. In the 1960s, the Barbizon's female residents began to reject living in this famous women-only sanctuary on New York's Upper East Side, and I wanted to see where they were going instead. It turns out some were heading to Wall Street, opting for apartment shares and independence even as New York City was turning grim and graffitied. Curiosity always leads the way into my next book project, and while I initially knew little about Wall Street, the women I interviewed over the following two years, whether they ended up on these pages or not, were remarkably kind and patient as they told me their stories while explaining their world. I cannot thank them enough. I hope I did good by them.

I am especially grateful to the women who are the central "characters" in *She-Wolves*, many of whom instinctively understood even before I came along that records need to be kept, testimonies made and preserved, especially when it comes to women's lives. Some had already recorded oral histories with the New-York Historical Society and the HistoryMakers Digital Archive, while others had put pen to paper to write down their experiences in the form of memoirs, recollections, and even a novel. I am grateful to them all for speaking with me, especially when Wall Street is a place of many secrets.

There were others too who helped me tell the story of a bygone Wall Street: Peter Asch at the New York Stock Exchange Archives was supportive from beginning to end of this project (as was Samantha Citarella). Tim Mahoney, Heather Oswald, and Melissa Murphy at Harvard's Baker Library Special Collections and Archives dug out documents from the business school's past. Crystal Toscano and Mariam Touba at the New-York Historical Society's Patricia D. Klingenstein Library helped me access the oral history archive, Remembering Wall Street, 1950–1980, made in partnership with the Narrative Trust. Many of those interviews were conducted by the Narrative Trust's cofounder, Melanie Shorin, who met with me over Zoom to discuss this world she knew well. Xan Parker, codirector of the 2003 documentary *Risk/Reward*, and I spent an afternoon together talking women on Wall Street. She was generous with her contacts and enthusiasm.

While researching *She-Wolves*, there were very few books to lean on; memoirs abound but most are very circumscribed or pitched as financial self-help. None of them conjure up the world that I have tried to depict here. A rare find therefore was a recent PhD dissertation by historian Dylan Gottlieb about the yuppie-fication of New York, and although his dissertation was blocked to readers, he sent me a copy. I am delighted that it is forthcoming with Harvard University Press, titled *Yuppies: Wall Street and the Remaking of New York*. Susan Antilla, a seasoned journalist, longtime women's advocate, and author of *Tales from the Boom-Boom Room*, generously offered article references and smart thoughts.

I wish to thank the Jane Rosenthal Heimerdinger Fund of Vassar College for funding parts of this research and my Vassar colleagues for their ongoing support. Steve Taylor was my IT guru, as always.

I also thank my two Vassar student research assistants—Keira Seyd and Tiffany Kuo—who took care of website upkeep, library book pickups, Instagram tutorials, and so much more. The New York Public Library's Center for Research in the Humanities gave me space to finish up *She-Wolves*. The whole crew at W. W. Norton have been wonderful. I feel fortunate to have my brilliant agent, Gillian MacKenzie (along with co-agent Liz Rudnick), by my side. I remain grateful to my late film and TV agent, Shari Smiley.

While I was writing the first draft of this book, my sister, Kamilla Hurley, died unexpectedly. An Ivy League graduate who went on to a prestigious B-School, she started on a trajectory familiar to many of the 1980s arrivals on Wall Street, but eventually opted for family over finance. I think of her all the time. My husband, Zoltan Markus, and our daughter, Zsofi Markus, have been my incredible support throughout, as they always are, helping not only me but my parents, Halina and Pavel Bren. My friends have been no less vital. And so I also want to thank you, my dear friends (you know who you are!), for being there. In particular, my Wesleyan "gang" (if aging college friends can be called a gang)—we are always there for one another, whether it be for celebrations, funerals, milestones, or the mundane. Here's to the quiet joy of the mundane!

Notes

PROLOGUE

2 "rich, white, middle-aged men" . . . "You will never see": "Paul Tudor Jones comments on the lack of female traders," Video, 6:53, *Washington Post*, May 23, 2013.

CHAPTER 1: JAMMING A FOOT IN THE DOOR

3 "Glamour stocks" with futuristic names: Kenneth Silber, "The Go-Go Sixties," *Think Advisor*, April 1, 2008.

3 "From the days of street-sweeping skirts": Shirley Willett, "1960s: Hemlines and the Stock Market!" *Fashion Solutions Blog*, October 27, 2006.

4 The one-bedroom apartment she shared: Interview with Alice Jarcho, conducted by Melanie Shorin with Christine Doudna of the Narrative Trust, December 14, 2016, and May 24, 2017, *Remembering Wall Street, 1950–1980*, The Bonnie and Richard Reiss Wall Street Oral History Archive, New-York Historical Society, Transcript, 10.

4 a card-carrying Communist: Interview with Alice Jarcho, NYHS, Transcript, 3, 5.

4 She did not play canasta: Interview with Alice Jarcho, NYHS, Transcript, 4.

4 "came often": Interview with Alice Jarcho, NYHS, Transcript, 6.

5 "A feminist I am not": Terry Robards, "Partner in Hirsch Is Scheduled to Be 2d Woman on Big Board," *New York Times*, May 21, 1970, 55.

5 Alice agreed: Interview with Alice Jarcho, NYHS, Transcript, 14.

6 they refused to pay: Interview with Alice Jarcho, NYHS, Transcript, 15.

6 "overthrowing the government": Interview with Alice Jarcho, NYHS, Transcript, 18.

7 "slam on the desk": Interview with Alice Jarcho, NYHS, Transcript, 17.

7 "a maniac" . . . "a screamer": Author's interview with Alice Jarcho, New York City, September 19, 2021.

8 "bragged about the size": Interview with Alice Jarcho, NYHS, Transcript, 20.

8 Just as Alice appraised: Author's interview with Alice Jarcho (2021). Also: Interview with Alice Jarcho, NYHS, Transcript, 20.

8 "a new toy, a shiny new object": Author's interview with Alice Jarcho (2021).

8 **choking her with a curtain rod:** Author's interview with Alice Jarcho (2021).

8 **navigate dysfunction:** My thanks to Kathy Abizaid, who came up with the idea of "navigating dysfunction" during a discussion we had about the early women on Wall Street.

9 **"Blond Bomb":** As quoted in Dana Wechsler Linden, "The Class of '65," *Forbes*, July 4, 1994, 92.

10 **In the first year of that experiment:** Judith Spofford Gibson, "Bridging the Charles: The First Women Graduates of the Harvard Business School, 1960–1965," PhD dissertation, Drew University, Caspersen School of Graduate Studies, 2009, 8. [Gibson herself ended up graduating in 1965 with the "first women" of Harvard Business School, but as one of the Radcliffe Program transfers.]

10 **"I taught the same material":** Gibson, "Bridging the Charles," 204–205.

10 **"guinea pigs":** Gibson, "Bridging the Charles," 203.

10 **"we didn't need Gloria Steinem":** Gibson, "Bridging the Charles," 204–205.

11 **In 1961, 95 percent:** Gibson, "Bridging the Charles," 166.

11 **"A woman who is determined":** Gibson, "Bridging the Charles," 168.

11 **"flatly repellent":** "Women at the Top," *Newsweek*, June 27, 1966, 77.

11 **Another professor asked a married woman:** Gibson, "Bridging the Charles," 223–224.

12 **Presented with two to three case studies:** Lillian Lincoln Lambert, *The Road to Someplace Better: From the Segregated South to Harvard Business School and Beyond* (New Jersey: Wiley & Sons, 2010), 94.

12 **Jane Lack walked into class:** Gibson, "Bridging the Charles," 225.

12 **"some of them were nice":** Gibson, "Bridging the Charles," 235.

12 **On Fridays, students received:** Delivery times for the WAC varied over the years. The chute cut-off was anywhere from 5 p.m. to 9 p.m., with allowances given to those living off campus—but not the women at the Radcliffe Graduate Center.

13 **A 1955 *Fortune* article described:** Julie Marie Still, *A History of the Corporate Wife, 1900–1990*, MA thesis (University of Richmond, 1994), 50.

13 **"the wife he left behind":** Still, *Corporate Wife*, 56.

13 **"highly adaptable":** Still, *Corporate Wife*, 59.

14 **Guidelines for executive wives:** Still, *Corporate Wife*, 59.

14 **a 1957 survey of 4,000 executive wives:** Still, *Corporate Wife*, 62–63.

14 **In one case, a man lost:** Still, *Corporate Wife*, 64.

14 **When the cab dropped her off:** Finally in 1969, four out of the fifty women attending would move into a dorm on the HBS campus. It would be another four years before female students were finally fully integrated into the MBA program, with dorms of their own on the other—the "right"—side of the Charles River.

14 **"nondescript brick building":** Lambert, *Road to Someplace Better*, 87.

15 **"Why am I here?":** Lambert, *Road to Someplace Better*, 88.

15 **"I was in Harvard, but not of it":** Lambert, *Road to Someplace Better*, 87.

16 **Growing up, Lillian wore:** Lambert, *Road to Someplace Better*, 29.

16 **"outside of the segregation system":** Heather Dunhill, "Entrepreneur Lillian Lambert on Being the First Black Woman to Graduate from Harvard Business School," (Part of the series Listening to Diverse Voices) *Sarasota*, May 10, 2022.

17 **"Indeed, even if I'd wanted it":** Lambert, *Road to Someplace Better*, 78.

17 **"Why not Harvard?":** Lambert, *Road to Someplace Better*, 80.

17 **"symbolized the Great Divide":** Lambert, *Road to Someplace Better*, 89.

18 **Harvard students called:** Lambert, *Road to Someplace Better*, 90.

18 **"black leather miniskirt":** Patricia Chadwick, *Little Sister: A Memoir* (New York: Post Hill Press, 2019), 246.

18 "Hippies, unkempt and unwashed": Chadwick, *Little Sister*, 258.

18 "their gray flannel suits": Lambert, *Road to Someplace Better*, 90.

18 "as if he were running": Lambert, *Road to Someplace Better*, 93.

19 "Never before": Lambert, *Road to Someplace Better*, 95.

19 "pissed off": Lambert, *Road to Someplace Better*, 95.

19 "the Temptations": Lambert, *Road to Someplace Better*, 95–6.

19 Sometimes Nancy Pelz: Author's interview with Lillian Lambert, Zoom, June 7, 2022.

19 "To think that these women": Lambert, *Road to Someplace Better*, 98.

20 "paltry—$57 a week": Garry Emmons, "Down the Memory Chute: WAC, WOC, and Doing the Write Thing," Harvard Business School Website/Alumni, September 1, 2006, https://www.alumni.hbs.edu/stories/Pages/story-bulletin .aspx?num=292/.

20 "I have no idea": Interview with Ambassador John Loeb, conducted by Melanie Shorin of the Narrative Trust, April 22, 2016, *Remembering Wall Street, 1950– 1980*, The Bonnie and Richard Reiss Wall Street Oral History Archive, New-York Historical Society, New York.

20 "significantly older": Bobbi Clarke, "Analyze This," Harvard Business School Website/Alumni, September 1, 2006, https://www.alumni.hbs.edu/stories/Pages/ story-bulletin.aspx?num=292/.

20 In fact, WAC reader applications: Emmons, "Down the Memory Chute."

21 looking "cool": Author's interview with Priscilla Rabb, Zoom, September 21, 2021. All subsequent references to Priscilla Rabb are from this interview.

CHAPTER 2: BREACHING A WALL

23 In 1792: Steven Fraser, historian of Wall Street, believes the Buttonwood story was most probably a myth but that the core idea, that some kind of self-regulation and coordination was created and cemented within the Wall Street Community during the 1790s, remains valid.

24 "The Tontine coffee-house": John Lambert, *Travels Through Lower Canada, and the United States of North America, in the Years 1806, 1807, 1808*, Vol. 2 (London: Printed for Richard Phillips, 1810), 156–157.

25 "a prophecy of the future": Sheri J. Caplan, *Petticoats and Pinstripes: Portraits of Women in Wall Street's History* (New York: Praeger, 2013), 37.

25 "These two ladies": Caplan, *Petticoats and Pinstripes*, 38.

25 "The Witch of Wall Street": Caplan, *Petticoats and Pinstripes*, 45.

26 "greatest miser": Caplan, *Petticoats and Pinstripes*, 52.

26 litigious, penny-pinching, and fashion-challenged: Jason Zweig, "Business Headlines, 1889: Female Speculators Rattle Wall Street Traditions," *Wall Street Journal* (online), July 7, 2014.

26 "private bank": Caplan, *Petticoats and Pinstripes*, 51.

26 "a masculine instinct for finance": Caplan, *Petticoats and Pinstripes*, 51.

26 Mary opened a ladies-only exchange: George Rabb, "Ladies of the Ticker: Pioneering Women Stockbrokers from the 1889s to the 1920s," Museum of American Finance, Summer 2017, *Financial History* 21, https://www.moaf.org/ publications-collections/financial-history-magazine/122/_res/id=Attachments/ index=0/Ladies%20of%20the%20Ticker.pdf

27 "the Petticoat Line": Caplan, *Petticoats and Pinstripes*, 67.

27 "turned out as so many mannequins": Eunice Fuller Barnard, "Ladies of the Ticker," *The North American Review* 227 (January 1, 1929): 405.

28 "than all the noisy suffrage campaigns": Eunice Fuller Barnard, "Women in Wall Street Wielding a New Power," *New York Times*, June 23, 1929, XX15.

28 "the men's board rooms": Barnard, "Women in Wall Street."

28 "responsibility, character and citizenship": "Woman Seeks a Seat on Stock Exchange: Would Upset Male-Membership Tradition," *New York Times*, January 14, 1927, 1.

28 "banksters": Melissa S. Fisher, *Wall Street Women* (Durham, NC: Duke University Press, 2012), 32.

29 In 1933, the Glass-Steagall Act: Fisher, *Wall Street Women*, 32.

29 overturned until 1999, although: "The Long Demise of Glass-Steagall," The Wall Street Fix, *Frontline*, PBS, May 8, 2003.

29 "first woman to appear": "Exchange Tradition to Go As Woman Gets Floor Job," *New York Times*, April 28, 1943, 31.

29 "a barrage of boos, catcalls,": "Din Like Dodger Ball Game Sounds as Girl Takes Up Job on Exchange," *New York Times*, April 29, 1943, 24.

29 "Helen the Second": "Helen 2D at Exchange," *New York Times*, June 2, 1943, 33.

30 "French blue": "Stock Exchange to Make 36 Young Women 'Quote Girls' and 'Carrier Pages' on Floor," *New York Times*, July 11, 1943, S7.

31 "women can handle the money": Lucy Greenbaum, "Wall Street: Man's World," *New York Times*, May 13, 1945, 11.

31 "The market failed to react": Greenbaum, "Wall Street: Man's World."

31 The young page's cry: Janice M. Traflet and Robert E. Wright, *Fearless: Wilma Soss and America's Forgotten Investor Movement* (Fort Lauderdale, FL: All Seasons Press, 2023), 17.

31 Anson-Jones chain, where all the dresses: "New Downtown Shop Has Youthful Styles," *New York Times*, February 17, 1948, 29.

31 "Men make the big money": Gloria Emerson, "Retail Shops Vital to Life of Wall Street," *New York Times*, August 5, 1959, 18.

31 "first group floods this store": Emerson, "Retail Shops Vital."

31 "Wall Street has always been": Greenbaum, "Wall Street: Man's World."

32 If you found yourself in: Fred Whittemore, in Eric J. Weiner, *What Goes Up: The Uncensored History of Modern Wall Street as Told by the Bankers, Brokers, CEOs, and Scoundrels Who Made It Happen* (New York: Back Bay Books, 2005), 30.

32 "economic suffragette": Traflet and Wright, *Fearless*, 13.

32 "Federation of Woman Shareholders in American Business": "Topics of the Day in Wall Street," *New York Times*, May 6, 1947, 41. Her name was incorrectly reported as Willa Soss.

32 "a late Victorian costume": Michael Norman, "Wilma Porter Soss, 86, A Gadfly at Stock Meetings of Companies," *New York Times*, October 16, 1986, B20.

32 "considerable and increasing": C. J. Sinclair Armstrong, "Today's Capital Markets and the Work of the Securities and Exchange Commission," Speech given by the commissioner of the Securities and Exchange Commission, before the Calvin Bullock Forum, NYC, May 23, 1955, page 9, Commission Speeches and Public Statements Archive, 1955, U.S. Securities and Exchange Commission, https://www.sec.gov/news/speech/1955/052355armstrong.pdf/.

32 "an ash-blond interior decorator": A. H. Raskin, "Stock Market as the 'Little Man' Sees It; Clients in a Broker's Office Tell Why and How They Buy," *New York Times*, March 20, 1955, 8.

33 "customer's women": Arturo Gonzalez and Janeann Gonzalez, "Where No

Woman Reaches the Summit," *New York Times Magazine*, August 17, 1958, SM34.

33 **Little is known about her:** "Five African American Women Pioneers in U.S. Finance," Columbia University Press Blog, March 20, 2019.

33 **had "crammed":** "Woman Passes NY Stock Exchange Exam," *Jet*, May 7, 1953, 18.

33 **In 1957, Special Markets,:** Gary S. Bell, *In the Black: A History of African Americans on Wall Street* (New Jersey: Wiley & Sons, 2002), 50–51.

34 **placing advertisements:** Traflet and Wright, *Fearless*, 26–7.

34 **before traveling the country:** NYSE Women's History Timeline (Archives 2021), Slide 14. NYSE Archives, NJ.

36 **"their word is enough":** Oscar Rudolf, dir., *The Lady and the Stock Exchange*, Paramount Pictures, NYSE, 1962.

36 **"The exchange insists":** Rudolf, *Lady and the Stock Exchange*.

36 **"No woman has ever seriously applied.":** Gonzalez and Gonzalez, "Where No Woman Reaches the Summit."

37 **"genial, fraternal, man-to-man":** Gonzalez and Gonzalez, "Where No Woman Reaches the Summit."

37 **"for long reading, maybe":** "The 'Voice' of the Exchange," *The Exchange* 23, no. 11, November 1962, NYSE Archive, NJ.

37 **"had a God-given voice":** Richard Phalon, *Forbes Greatest Investing Stories* (New York: Wiley & Sons, 2001), 176.

38 **"sea of men":** Muriel Siebert (with Aimee Lee Ball), *Changing the Rules: Adventures of a Wall Street Maverick* (New York: The Free Press, 2002), 2.

38 **"Welcome to the NYSE":** Caplan, *Petticoats and Pinstripes*, 136.

38 **He observed as the limousines:** Martin Mayer, *Wall Street: Men and Money* (New York: Collier Books, 1955), 24.

39 **"the coffee men":** Lucie Levine, "Roasteries and Refineries: The History of Sugar and Coffee in NYC," https://www.6sqft.com/roasteries-and-refineries-the-history-of-sugar-and-coffee-in-nyc/.

39 **With setbacks on tall buildings:** Mayer, *Wall Street*, 16.

39 **"brick bas-reliefs,":** Mayer, *Wall Street*, 17.

39 **"or in smaller amounts":** Alec Benn, *The Unseen Wall Street of 1969–1975: And Its Significance for Today* (Westport, CT: Quorum Books, 2000), 11.

39 **In the 1950s, the telephone was:** Mayer, *Wall Street*, 22.

40 **"hideaway beds":** Mayer, *Wall Street*, 23.

40 **"pension funds, mutual funds":** Siebert, *Changing the Rules*, 6.

40 **"seeing a pattern in those numbers":** Siebert, *Changing the Rules*, 6.

41 **"saddled":** Siebert, *Changing the Rules*, 8.

41 **But a man by the name of Benjamin Graham:** John Steele Gordon, *The Great Game: The Emergence of Wall Street as a World Power: 1653–2000* (New York: Simon & Schuster, 2000), 255–258.

42 **"I was with the geeks":** Fisher, *Wall Street Women*, 39.

42 **By 1966, there were around sixty women:** Fisher, *Wall Street Women*, 40.

42 **"a pert, attractive brunette":** Vartanig G. Vartan, "She Enjoys Being a Stock-Market Analyst," *New York Times*, February 6, 1964, 37.

42 **insisting that the "mystery":** Donald Regan, quoted in Weiner, *What Goes Up*, 15.

42 **By 1960, Merrill Lynch's firm:** Gordon, *Great Game*, 254.

42 **"the thundering herd":** Gordon, *Great Game*, 255.

42 **"153 offices and more than":** Vartan, "She Enjoys Being a Stock-Market Analyst."

43 "Why are you here?": Judith Spofford Gibson, "Bridging the Charles: The First Women Graduates of the Harvard Business School, 1960–1965," PhD dissertation, Drew University, Caspersen School of Graduate Studies, 2009, 244.

43 but only for kicks: Gibson, "Bridging the Charles," 242.

44 "at least when I go shopping": Dana Wechsler Linden, "The Class of '65," Forbes, July 4, 1994, 93.

44 "the experiment": Gibson, "Bridging the Charles," 243.

44 "You don't understand": Gibson, "Bridging the Charles," 241.

44 only just hired a woman: Linden, "The Class of '65," 93.

44 She was finally hired: Gibson, "Bridging the Charles," 256.

44 "been promised romantically": Laurie P. Cohen, William Power, and Michael Siconolfi, "Wall Street Women: Financial Firms Act to Curb Office Sexism, with Mixed Results," Wall Street Journal, November 5, 1991, A1.

45 "long client list": Patricia Chadwick, Little Sister: A Memoir (New York: Post Hill Press, 2019), 277.

45 "in the pitch black": Chadwick, Little Sister, 277.

CHAPTER 3: MICKIE AND THE GUNSLINGERS

47 By the 1950s, a Jewish broker might: Joe Nocera, in Eric J. Weiner, What Goes Up: The Uncensored History of Modern Wall Street as Told by the Bankers, Brokers, CEOs, and Scoundrels Who Made It Happen (New York: Back Bay Books, 2005), 22.

47 Wall Street investment banks and brokerage houses: For more on this, see Stephen Birmingham, "Our Crowd": The Great Jewish Families of New York (New York: Harper & Row, 1967; Syracuse: Syracuse University Press, 1996).

47 "should go to Lehman Brothers": Robert Bernhard, in Weiner, What Goes Up, 40.

48 "white-shoe" of course: Fred Whittemore, in Weiner, What Goes Up, 32.

48 "mahogany walls": Winthrop Smith Jr., in Weiner, What Goes Up, 16.

48 "the course for corporate": Weiner, What Goes Up, 27.

48 "nebulous half-mile-square": Arturo Gonzalez and Janeann Gonzalez, "Where No Woman Reaches the Summit," New York Times Magazine, August 17, 1958, SM34.

48 "a single phone call": Jack Hyland, in Weiner, What Goes Up, 28.

49 "It really was": Joe Nocera, in Weiner, What Goes Up, 29.

49 At the Stock Exchange Club: Martin Mayer, Wall Street: Men and Money (New York: Collier Books, 1955), 25–26.

49 "broad stairs, old tables": Mayer, Wall Street, 26.

49 "What the food lacks": Mayer, Wall Street, 26.

50 "like the rest of": Muriel Siebert (with Aimee Lee Ball), Changing the Rules: Adventures of a Wall Street Maverick (New York: The Free Press, 2002), 11.

50 Even earlier, Isabel Benham: Tracy Alloway, "Isabel Benham, Wall Street's first female partner," Financial Times, June 14, 2013.

51 A male colleague doing: Siebert, Changing the Rules, 13.

51 "piled chest-high": Quoting historian Vincent Cannato: "Today in NYC History: The Great Garbage Strike of 1968," UntappedNewYork.

51 (Once the ticker tape itself became): John Steele Gordon, The Great Game: The Emergence of Wall Street as a World Power: 1653–2000 (New York: Simon & Schuster, 2000), 268–269.

52 **"Hardly anything else on"**: John Brooks, *The Go-Go Years: The Drama and Crashing Finale of Wall Street's Bullish 60s* (New York: Wiley, 1991), 210.

53 **"radiates total cool"**: As quoted in "From the Go-Go Years to YOLO," *Stray Reflections*, September 21, 2021, https://stray-reflections.com/article/205/ From_the_GoGo_Years_to_YOLO.

54 **They managed to bring:** Author's interview with Lillian Lambert, Zoom, June 7, 2022.

54 **They next lobbied:** Heather Dunhill, "Entrepreneur Lillian Lambert on Being the First Black Woman to Graduate from Harvard Business School," (Part of the series Listening to Diverse Voices) *Sarasota*, May 10, 2022.

54 **"Don't be ridiculous"**: Siebert, *Changing the Rules*, 29.

55 **"Can I buy a seat"**: Sheri J. Caplan, *Petticoats and Pinstripes: Portraits of Women in Wall Street's History* (New York: Praeger, 2013), 138.

55 **One of them later said:** Caplan, *Petticoats and Pinstripes*, 139.

56 **"Jan Eddins got her loan"**: June Kronholz, "Bars to Borrowing: Women Complain That New Equal Credit Law Is Applied Unevenly, Enforced Haphazardly," *Wall Street Journal*, January 21, 1977, 32.

56 **Eventually Chase Manhattan Bank:** Muriel Siebert, in Weiner, *What Goes Up*, 115.

56 **"the most expensive piece"**: Muriel F. Siebert, in Martin Mayer (photographs by Cornell Capa), *New Breed on Wall Street: The Young Men Who Make the Money GO* (New York: Macmillan, 1969), 98.

56 **Mickie took her badge:** Siebert, *Changing the Rules*, 4.

56 **Sometimes she fantasized:** Siebert, *Changing the Rules*, 4.

56 **"Now the Girls Want"**: Roslyn Lacks, "Muriel Siebert: Playing the Numbers on Wall Street," in Maxine Gold, ed., *Women Making History: Conversations with Fifteen New Yorkers* (New York City Commission on the Status of Women, 1985), 104.

57 **When in 1969 pranks:** Terry Robards, "Exchange's Talcum Throwers Are Advised to Take a Powder," *New York Times*, June 10, 1969, 67.

57 **"bubbly and"**: Vartanig G. Vartan, "First New York Exchange Seat for Woman Sought by Analyst," *New York Times*, December 9, 1967, 1.

57 **"five feet four inches"**: Vartanig G. Vartan, "Miss Siebert's Memorable Day," *New York Times*, January 1, 1968, 23.

58 **"a token"**: "Wall Street & The Role of Women," *The Takeaway*, WNYC, September 9, 2013.

58 **"the petite blonde"**: Vartan, "First New York Exchange Seat."

58 **But when she submitted:** Caplan, *Petticoats and Pinstripes*, 139.

58 **"masculine air"**: Mayer, *Wall Street*, 32.

58 **"could afford to pay"**: Siebert, in Mayer, *New Breed*, 98.

59 **Most of the 1,366:** Alec Benn, *The Unseen Wall Street of 1969–1975: And Its Significance for Today* (Westport, CT: Quorum Books, 2000), 1.

59 **In 1952, 6.5 million:** Benn, *Unseen Wall Street*, 12.

59 **"value of shares"**: Benn, *Unseen Wall Street*, 14.

60 **At one firm:** Interview with Bernadette Bartels Murphy, conducted by Karen A. Frankel of the Narrative Trust, October 30, 2014, *Remembering Wall Street, 1950–1980*, The Bonnie and Richard Reiss Wall Street Oral History Archive, New-York Historical Society, Transcript, 34.

60 **"were like deck officers"**: Benn, *Unseen Wall Street*, 15.

60 **"spoke with broad a's"**: Benn, *Unseen Wall Street*, 16.

60 **In 1965, the NYSE had predicted:** Gary S. Bell, *In the Black: A History of African Americans on Wall Street* (New Jersey: Wiley & Sons, 2002), 92.

61 **That is when a boutique:** William D. Cohan, "When Bankers Started Playing with Other People's Money," *The Atlantic*, February 18, 2017, https://www.theatlantic .com/business/archive/2017/02/how-wall-street-went-public/517419/.

61 **"Old men screaming":** Dan Lufkin, in Weiner, *What Goes Up*, 123.

61 **At the dinner:** Benn, *Unseen Wall Street*, 7.

61 **The Associated Press compared:** Benn, *Unseen Wall Street*, 7–8.

62 **In 1971, Merrill Lynch:** Gordon, *Great Game*, 270.

62 **A 1960s study:** Peter Kihss, "Study Finds Wall St. Lawyers Practice 'Creative Conformity,'" *New York Times*, April 18, 1964, 57.

CHAPTER 4: W.I.T.C.H. ON WALL STREET

63 **"click-click-clack-click":** Martin Mayer, *Wall Street: Men and Money* (New York: Collier Books, 1955), 32.

64 **Over five thousand men:** Arturo Gonzalez and Janeann Gonzalez, "Where No Woman Reaches the Summit," *New York Times Magazine*, August 17, 1958, SM34.

65 **"These people in Wall Street":** Leonard Sloane, "Boom and Bust on Wall Street," *New York Magazine*, October 14, 1968 [1 (28)], 33.

65 **"destruction of passivity":** As stated by WITCH, quoted in: Marian Jones, "Women's International Terrorist Conspiracy from Hell: What to Know," *Teen Vogue*, October 28, 2021, https://www.teenvogue.com/story/womens-international -terrorist-conspiracy-from-hell.

66 **"Beware of the curse":** Jones, "Women's International Terrorist Conspiracy from Hell."

66 **"the epicenter of corporate America's":** Jones, "Women's International Terrorist Conspiracy from Hell."

66 **"a paper-maché":** Jones, "Women's International Terrorist Conspiracy from Hell."

66 **"a symbol of patriarchal":** As quoted in Jones, "Women's International Terrorist Conspiracy from Hell."

67 **"What would corporate America":** Lillian Lincoln Lambert, *The Road to Someplace Better: From the Segregated South to Harvard Business School and Beyond* (New Jersey: Wiley & Sons, 2010), 124.

67 **"*Left HBS eager*":** Lambert, *Road to Someplace Better*, 124.

68 **"Maybe, maybe, hmm":** Berkeley Haas; Dean's Speaker Series; November 5, 2018, https://www.youtube.com/watch?v=sQh-w4LyCSg. Also: Author's interview with Margo Alexander, New York City, December 8, 2021.

68 **Lillian's mother arrived:** Author's interview with Lillian Lambert, Zoom, June 7, 2022.

68 **first three Black stockbrokers:** Gary S. Bell, *In the Black: A History of African Americans on Wall Street* (New Jersey: Wiley & Sons, 2002), 45.

68 **George King, one of:** Bell, *In the Black*, 47.

69 **"who likes to cook chicken":** Vartanig G. Vartan, "A Girlhood Dream Is Realized: Negro Woman Now Selling Stocks for Big-Board Firm," *New York Times*, February 5, 1965, 39.

69 **Married to an architect:** Vartan, "Girlhood Dream."

70 **"not a bedroom war":** Linda Charlton, "Women March Down Fifth in Equality Drive," *New York Times*, August 27, 1970, 1.

70 **"the most visible symbol"**: Marilyn Bender, "Women's Lib Bearish in Wall Street," *New York Times*, October 11, 1970, 147.

70 **"I just had lunch"**: Terry Robards, "Market Place," *New York Times*, August 27, 1970, 63.

71 **"from rare vice president"**: Bender, "Women's Lib Bearish."

71 **"from their male sovereigns"**: Bender, "Women's Lib Bearish."

71 **"In the long run"**: Bender, "Women's Lib Bearish."

71 **"afford inflammatory"**: Bender, "Women's Lib Bearish."

71 **"If I ever thought"**: Bender, "Women's Lib Bearish."

72 **"Wall Street's stag atmosphere"**: Bender, "Women's Lib Bearish."

72 **"turn the tables"**: Quoted from Susan Brownmiller's memoir, *In Our Time*, in Nina Renata Aron, "Sexually Charged 'Ogle-Ins' Allowed 1970s Feminists to Humiliate Catcalling Men," *Timeline*, April 6, 2018, https://timeline.com/ogle -ins-allowed-women-to-teach-catcallers-a-lesson-691a5eaa3a37.

72 **"I just looove"**: Footage included in Mary Dore, dir., *She's Beautiful When She's Angry,* Music Box Films, 2014.

73 **"sauntered up"**: Quoted from Susan Brownmiller's memoir, *In Our Time*, in Aron, "Sexually Charged 'Ogle-Ins.' "

73 **A group of women**: Interview with Beth Dater, conducted by Melanie Shorin of the Narrative Trust, February 10, 2015, *Remembering Wall Street, 1950–1980*, The Bonnie and Richard Reiss Wall Street Oral History Archive, New-York Historical Society, Transcript, 24–25.

CHAPTER 5: RUKEYSER'S ELVES

75 **"the arcane world"**: Thomas Goldwasser, "Wall Street Week Becomes a Blue Chip," *Washington Post*, June 15, 1981, WB24.

75 **"snowy Edwardian hairdo"**: Maggie Mahar, *Bull!: A History of the Boom and Bust, 1982–2004* (New York: Harper Business, Reprint edition 2004), 310.

76 **"best and gaudiest"**: James Grant, "Louis Rukeyser, Television Host, Dies at 73," *New York Times*, May 3, 2006, B8.

76 **"Indomitably hopping"**: Goldwasser, "Wall Street Week Becomes a Blue Chip."

76 **"lunges across"**: John Brooks, "Onward and Upward with Wall Street," *The New Yorker*, Vol. 59, November 14, 1983, 114.

77 **"Fridays at 8:30"**: Grant, "Louis Rukeyser."

77 **"There sure is news"**: As quoted in Brooks, "Onward and Upward."

77 **"Wall Street Wake"**: Brooks, "Onward and Upward."

78 **"anti-semantic"**: Brooks, "Onward and Upward."

78 **"not previously noted"**: Grant, "Louis Rukeyser."

79 **"Is this an emergency"**: Julia Montgomery Walsh, with Anne Conover Carson, *Risks and Rewards: A Memoir* (McLean, Virginia: EPM Publications, Inc.), 23.

79 **"Like so many women"**: Walsh, *Risks and Rewards*, 49.

80 **"the dust and dirt"**: Walsh, *Risks and Rewards*, 78.

80 **"like any dutiful"**: Walsh, *Risks and Rewards*, 81.

80 **"I have delightful"**: Walsh, *Risks and Rewards*, 95.

81 **"the comfortable apartment"**: Walsh, *Risks and Rewards*, 96.

81 **"at 39 I faced"**: Walsh, *Risks and Rewards*, 96.

82 **"emotionally insecure"**: Walsh, *Risks and Rewards*, 97.

82 **"smelled the salt"**: Interview with Bernadette Bartels Murphy, conducted by Karen A. Frankel of the Narrative Trust, October 30, 2014, *Remembering Wall Street, 1950–1980*, The Bonnie and Richard Reiss Wall Street Oral History Archive,

New-York Historical Society, Transcript, 2. [NB: The transcript incorrectly has "of the harbor."]

83 **"a big cork board"**: Interview with Bernadette Bartels Murphy, NYHS, Transcript, 5.

83 **"There has got"**: Sue Herera, *Women of the Street* (New York: Wiley & Sons, 1997), 143.

84 **"selling for three"**: Peter Low, in Eric J. Weiner, *What Goes Up: The Uncensored History of Modern Wall Street as Told by the Bankers, Brokers, CEOs, and Scoundrels Who Made It Happen* (New York: Back Bay Books, 2005), 278.

84 **"Ron, they killed our"**: Interview with Bernadette Bartels Murphy, NYHS, Transcript, 12.

84 **"Ah, here she comes"**: Interview with Bernadette Bartels Murphy, NYHS, Transcript, 6.

84 **"You are young"**: Interview with Bernadette Bartels Murphy, NYHS, Transcript, 21.

84 **"Oh, you are not being"**: Interview with Bernadette Bartels Murphy, NYHS, Transcript, 23.

85 **A friend of hers**: Interview with Bernadette Bartels Murphy, NYHS, Transcript, 48.

85 **It was originally called:** Jane Boutwell, "The Talk of the Town: Financial Women," *The New Yorker*, September 6, 1976, 22.

85 **"We had no one"**: Margot Witty, "Financial Women and Children," *Working Woman*, September 1981, 78.

85 **They would tell:** Interview with Bernadette Bartels Murphy, NYHS, Transcript, 9.

85 **it was still using non-pressurized DC-4s:** Philip James Tiemeyer, "Manhood Up in the Air: Gender, Sexuality, Corporate Culture, and the Law in Twentieth Century America," Dissertation, UT Austin, May 2007, footnote 42.

86 **The Vomit Comet left:** Interview with Beth Dater, conducted by Melanie Shorin of the Narrative Trust, February 10, 2015, *Remembering Wall Street, 1950–1980*, The Bonnie and Richard Reiss Wall Street Oral History Archive, New-York Historical Society, Transcript, 15.

86 **Actress Joan Crawford:** Interview with Beth Dater, NYHS, Transcript, 17.

86 **Almost always a group from:** Interview with Beth Dater, NYHS, Transcript, 15.

86 **Not only was the rent:** Interview with Beth Dater, NYHS, Transcript, 18.

87 **Then one day, the agency:** Interview with Beth Dater, NYHS, Transcript, 19–20.

87 **"You seem like a"**: Interview with Beth Dater, NYHS, Transcript, 20.

87 **"very, very temperamental"**: Interview with Beth Dater, NYHS, Transcript, 21.

87 **He fired her:** Author's interview with Beth Dater, Zoom, August 25, 2021.

87 **"trading big accounts"**: Interview with Beth Dater, NYHS, Transcript, 23.

88 **"it could not be"**: Interview with Beth Dater, NYHS, Transcript, 23.

88 **"it was that in-between"**: Interview with Beth Dater, NYHS, Transcript, 19.

88 **"Jolly"**: "Darley Talbot Randall," obituary, Solimne Funeral Homes, https://www.tributearchive.com/obituaries/21953785/darley-talbot-randall/.

88 **"Well, give it a try"**: Interview with Beth Dater, NYHS, Transcript, 25.

88 **"miracle"**: Interview with Beth Dater, NYHS, Transcript, 45.

89 **"Hey, look what you've"**: Interview with Bernadette Bartels Murphy, NYHS, Transcript, 10.

89 **"Why do so many pension funds"**: Display Ad 98, *Wall Street Journal*, October 14, 1965, 24.

89 **"Ideas are a dime"**: Display Ad 96, *Wall Street Journal*, March 18, 1969, 23.

CHAPTER 6: ZERO POINTS FOR "INTELLIGENCE"

91 **"buy blue-chip stocks"**: Email correspondence between author and Nina Hayes, January 20, 2022.

92 **She checked in to**: For more on the history of the hotel and its residents, see Paulina Bren, *The Barbizon: The Hotel That Set Women Free* (New York: Simon & Schuster, 2021).

92 **"a total environment"**: "Foreword, Mayor John V. Lindsay," in *The Report of the New York City Commission on Human Rights: Women's Role in Contemporary Society*, ed. Eleanor Holmes Norton (New York: Avon Books, 1972), 17.

93 **"wicked, rich women"**: "Dr. Margaret Mead—Women's Rights: A Cultural Dilemma," in Norton, *Women's Role in Contemporary Society*, 175.

93 **"even fewer of those"**: Mr. Roger David, representing Merrill Lynch, in Norton, *Women's Role in Contemporary Society*, 277.

93 **"Why wouldn't more"**: David, in Norton, *Women's Role in Contemporary Society*, 283.

93 **"would become an occupational"**: David, in Norton, *Women's Role in Contemporary Society*, 283.

94 **"ambitious secretaries"**: Marilyn Bender, "Women's Lib Bearish in Wall Street," *New York Times*, October 11, 1970.

94 **"Financial analysis is"**: Bender, "Women's Lib Bearish in Wall Street."

94 **In December 1970**: Lisa Cronin Wohl, "What's So Rare as a Woman on Wall Street?" *Ms. Magazine*, June 1973, 83.

94 **"What's a nice girl"**: Memo: To: The Women of the Class of 1971; From: Robin Wigger, Class of 1970; Subject: Life at H.B.S., 1971. Harvard Business School, Baker Library, Archives.

94 **"whether there were any"**: Wigger, Memo: To: The Women of the Class of 1971.

95 **"about women's work"**: Ilene Lang, "Women at HBS: A Woman's View," *Harbus News*, February 10, 1972.

96 **"When you fight"**: As quoted in Christine Sgarlata Chung, "From Lily Bart to the Boom-Boom Room: How Wall Street's Social and Cultural Response to Women Has Shaped Securities Regulation," *Harvard Journal of Law & Gender* 33 (2010): 226.

96 **"what interests you most"**: Susan Antilla, *Tales from the Boom-Boom Room: The Landmark Legal Battles that Exposed Wall Street's Shocking Culture of Sexual Harassment* (New York: Harper Business, 2003), 7.

96 **Although by all accounts**: Wellesley Alumnae Achievement Awards 1980, Helen Bohen O'Bannon '61, https://www.wellesley.edu/alumnae/awards/achievement awards/allrecipients/helen-bohen-o-bannon-61/.

96 **"Let's get Priscilla"**: Author's interview with Priscilla Rabb, Zoom, September 21, 2021.

97 **"turned to stone"**: Author's interview with Priscilla Rabb (2021).

98 **"anonymous handmaiden"**: John Brooks, "Onward and Upward with Wall Street," *The New Yorker*, Vol. 59, November 14, 1983.

98 **"For some reason her presence"**: Brooks, "Onward and Upward."

99 **(out of approximately 205,000 brokers)**: SEC 1973: 39th Annual Report of the U.S. Securities and Exchange Commission for the Fiscal Year Ended June 30th, page 54: "During the fiscal year, the number of registered representatives and principals (these categories include all partners, officers, traders, salesmen and other persons employed by or affiliated with member firms in capacities which require

registration) increased by 7,125 to 205,028 as of June 30, 1973. This increase
reflects the net result of 28,203 initial registrations, 27,466 re-registrations and
48,544 terminations of registration during the year." https://www.sec.gov/about/
annual_report/1973.pdf/.

99 **"some advanced studies"**: On *Wall $treet Week*, Rukeyser did not generally name
the place of employment of his guests or panelists. But in 1971, Mimi Green had
been hired to join the Institutional Marketing Department at Brukenfeld, Mitchell
& Co. (Display Ad 109, *Wall Street Journal*, November 3, 1971, 28.). By 1974, she
was a stockbroker at Hayden Stone. ("Mimi Green Is Wed to T. C. Dillenberg,"
New York Times, August 30, 1974, 16.)

99 **"Tell him it's Mimi"**: "Women on the Street," *Wall $treet Week with Louis
Rukeyser*, air date February 2, 1973, American Archives of Public Broadcasting.

100 **"shocked at"**: Robert Metz, "Market Place: Broker Assesses a Broker's Role,"
New York Times, April 26, 1972, 58.

100 **"to attract more female customers"**: "Dent Asks Caution on Recession: People
and Business," *New York Times*, December 17, 1974, 57.

100 **"are no longer"**: "Business Bulletin," *Wall Street Journal*, January 16, 1975, 1.

100 **Just a few months later**: Display Ad 173, *New York Times*, June 3, 1975, 29.

100 **"thundering around"**: Interview with Beth Dater, conducted by Melanie Shorin of
the Narrative Trust, February 10, 2015, *Remembering Wall Street, 1950–1980*,
The Bonnie and Richard Reiss Wall Street Oral History Archive, New-York Historical Society, 29.

100 **When Rukeyser approached Gannett**: C. Kim Goodwin would later be the first
Black female panelist to appear on the show, but by then it was broadcast on
CNBC.

101 **"I just want to tell"**: Interview with Beth Dater, NYHS, Transcript, 48.

101 **Beth was invited**: Interview with Beth Dater, NYHS, Transcript, 36.

101 **"We think this"**: Interview with Beth Dater, NYHS, Transcript, 37.

101 **A member of**: Interview with Beth Dater, NYHS, Transcript, 38.

101 **Even as she fully**: Interview with Beth Dater, NYHS, Transcript, 35.

102 **"Sure, there were women"**: Interview with Alice Jarcho, conducted by Melanie
Shorin with Christine Doudna of the Narrative Trust, December 14, 2016, and
May 24, 2017, *Remembering Wall Street, 1950–1980*, The Bonnie and Richard
Reiss Wall Street Oral History Archive, New-York Historical Society, Transcript,
65.

102 **She had learned something**: Antilla, *Tales from the Boom-Boom Room*, 7.

102 **Helen's drawn-out legal battle**: "Merrill Lynch Will Pay $1.9 Million in Bias
Suits," *New York Times*, June 5, 1976, 1.

102 **which in 1972 was**: June Kronholz, "Lagging Behind: Though More Women
Work, Job Equality Fails to Materialize Most are Still Concentrated in Low-Level
Positions; Recession Was a Setback Less Rank and More File Lagging Behind:
More Women Go to Work but in Low-Level Jobs," *Wall Street Journal*, July 6,
1976, 1.

102 **As part of that separate settlement**: Susan Antilla, "Stark Lessons from Wall
Street's #MeToo Moment," *The Intercept*, October 7, 2019, https://theintercept
.com/2019/10/07/metoo-wall-street-sexual-harassment-arbitration/.

103 **In addition, women and minorities**: *New York Times*, "Merrill Lynch Will Pay
$1.9 Million in Bias Suits."

103 **"spinach pâté"**: Jane Boutwell, "The Talk of the Town: Financial Women," *The
New Yorker*, September 6, 1976, 23.

104 **"the tabletops"**: NYC LGBT Historic Sites Project; Pompier Restaurant/Tenth

of Always/Bonnie & Clyde, https://www.nyclgbtsites.org/site/tenth-of-always
-bonnie-clyde/.

104 **When the partners at Epstein:** Email correspondence between author and Nina Hayes, September 9, 2021.

105 **In 1973, Nixon's bear market:** John Steele Gordon, *The Great Game: The Emergence of Wall Street as a World Power: 1653–2000* (New York: Simon & Schuster, 2000), 272–273.

CHAPTER 7: "DRESS FOR SUCCESS"

109 **"bellbottoms, a neat shirt":** John Brooks, *The Go-Go Years: The Drama and Crashing Finale of Wall Street's Bullish 60s* (New York: Wiley, 1991), 201.

109 **"just businessmen making a buck":** Brooks, *Go-Go Years*, 203.

109 **"right in Trinity churchyard":** Brooks, *Go-Go Years*, 202.

109 **"young office girls on pills":** Brooks, *Go-Go Years*, 203.

109 **"white-collar pill party":** Nicolas Rasmussen, *On Speed: From Benzedrine to Adderall* (New York: New York University Press, 2008), 174.

109 **The drug scene was commonplace:** Brooks, *Go-Go Years*, 210.

110 **Peter Cohen, who ten years later:** Interview with Alice Jarcho, conducted by Melanie Shorin with Christine Doudna of the Narrative Trust, December 14, 2016, and May 24, 2017, *Remembering Wall Street, 1950–1980*, The Bonnie and Richard Reiss Wall Street Oral History Archive, New-York Historical Society, Transcript, 32. (Ms. Jarcho incorrectly names Cogan rather than Weill as Cohen's boss at the time.)

110 **"Corned Beef With Lettuce":** Marshall Cogan, in Eric J. Weiner, *What Goes Up: The Uncensored History of Modern Wall Street as Told by the Bankers, Brokers, CEOs, and Scoundrels Who Made It Happen* (New York: Back Bay Books, 2005), 134–135.

111 **One unattractive but:** Interview with Alice Jarcho, NYHS, Transcript, 25.

111 **The annual Christmas Party:** Author's interview with Alice Jarcho (2021). Also: Interview with Alice Jarcho, NYHS, Transcript, 26.

111 **With an undergraduate degree:** Cogan, in Weiner, *What Goes Up*, 83.

111 **and neither Goldman Sachs nor:** Judith Ramsey Ehrlich, in Weiner, *What Goes Up*, 84.

111 **"a hell of a salesman":** Roger Berlind, in Weiner, *What Goes Up*, 86.

111 **"the personification of":** Author's interview with Alice Jarcho (2021).

112 **"like Julia Roberts":** Interview with Alice Jarcho, NYHS, Transcript, 27.

112 **"taken over by a bunch":** Sandy Weill, in Weiner, *What Goes Up*, 142.

112 **"smarter than we were":** Wick Simmons, in Weiner, *What Goes Up*, 143.

113 **an investing god:** Author's interview with Alice Jarcho (2021). (In Interview with Alice Jarcho, NYHS, Ms. Jarcho is more vague about who introduced her to the idea of applying for the job with Tisch. She does not credit Cogan with giving her the idea and encouraging her but instead an institutional trader whom she knew. Transcript, 34)

113 **"shaking":** Author's interview with Alice Jarcho (2021).

113 **"liked bargains":** Interview with Alice Jarcho, NYHS, Transcript, 34.

113 **"How much":** Author's interview with Alice Jarcho (2021). Also: Interview with Alice Jarcho, NYHS, Transcript, 43.

113 **"cheap":** Author's interview with Alice Jarcho (2021). (In Interview with Alice Jarcho, NYHS, Ms. Jarcho tells it slightly differently—she does not get the raise.)

114 **But Larry's stinginess:** Author's interview with Alice Jarcho (2021).

114 **spoke luridly about his sex life.:** Interview with Alice Jarcho, NYHS, Transcript, 36. Also: Author's interview with Alice Jarcho (2021).

114 **In 1989, his fiftieth birthday:** Martha Sherrill, "Abuzz About a Million Dollar Bash," *Washington Post*, August 16, 1989, D1.

114 **hers served on a plastic plate:** Interview with Alice Jarcho, NYHS, Transcript, 38.

114 **"And which are you?!":** Author's interview with Alice Jarcho (2021).

114 **"act like a man":** Author's interview with Alice Jarcho (2021).

114 **"I had a reputation":** Interview with Alice Jarcho, NYHS, Transcript, 40.

115 **"cramped studio apartments":** Melissa S. Fisher, *Wall Street Women* (Durham, NC: Duke University Press, 2012), 13–14.

116 **"Schulder . . . does not fit":** Terry Robards, "Woman, 36, at Top in Brokerage House," *New York Times*, March 23, 1969, 3.

116 **"Today hundreds of thousands":** John T. Molloy, *The Woman's Dress for Success Book* (New York: Warner Books, 1978), 22.

116 **"business uniform":** Molloy, *Dress for Success*, 34.

116 **"nothing morally wrong":** Molloy, *Dress for Success*, 27.

117 **"imitation man look":** Molloy, *Dress for Success*, 28.

117 **"lightweight":** Molloy, *Dress for Success*, 18.

117 **"despite the rhetoric":** Molloy, *Dress for Success*, 21.

117 **"OK. So you've made it":** Florence Graves, "The Art of Luring a Man," *New York Times Magazine*, November 26, 1978, SM214.

117 **"Molloy seeks to":** Deborah Sue Yaeger, "Women are What They Wear (in the Office)," *Wall Street Journal*, March 3, 1978, 8.

117 **"pumps, gold or":** Graves, "Art of Luring a Man."

118 **"if two women":** Judy Klemesrud, "Behind the Best Sellers: John T. Molloy," *New York Times*, March 12, 1978, BR12.

118 **"hotel employees":** Molloy, *Dress for Success*, 33.

118 **"three of the best":** Molloy, *Dress for Success*, 34.

118 **"smile more":** Marilyn Loden, "Why I Invented the Glass Ceiling Phrase," *100 Women*, BBC News, December 13, 2017, https://www.bbc.com/news/world-42026266.

119 **identify her socio-economic status:** Graves, "Art of Luring a Man."

119 **hired Lillian Hobson in 1971:** Author's interview with Lillian Lincoln Lambert, Zoom, June 7, 2022.

119 **"an anomaly":** Lillian Lincoln Lambert, *The Road to Someplace Better: From the Segregated South to Harvard Business School and Beyond* (New Jersey: Wiley & Sons, 2010), 138.

120 **"could relate it to":** Lambert, *Road to Someplace Better*, 138.

CHAPTER 8: THE PINTO DECADE

121 **they singled out the hippies:** Joshua B. Freeman, "Construction Workers, Manliness, and the 1970 Pro-War Demonstrations," *Journal of Social History* 26, no. 4 (Summer 1993): 736.

122 **"by their advantages:":** David Gelman et al., "How Men Are Changing," *Newsweek*, January 16, 1978, 52.

122 **"Typically, they would endorse":** Mirra Komarovsky quoted in Gelman et al., "How Men Are Changing," 59–60.

122 **"I don't think":** Bob Amore quoted in Gelman et al., "How Men Are Changing," 60.

123 **"Uncle Sam, traitor":** As quoted in Victoria Ludas, "American Manpower: Work

and Masculinity in the 1970s," MA thesis, Graduate Center, City University of New York, 2011, 62.

123 **the 1963 Equal Pay Act:** U.S. Equal Employment Opportunity Commission "Timeline of Important EEOC Events," https://www.eeoc.gov/youth/timeline -important-eeoc-events.

123 **"great leap forward":** June Kronholz, "Lagging Behind: Though More Women Work, Job Equality Fails to Materialize Most Are Still Concentrated in Low-Level Positions," *Wall Street Journal*, July 6, 1976, 1.

123 **"More women":** Kronholz, "Lagging Behind," 1.

123 **The Labor Department reported:** Kronholz, "Lagging Behind," 2.

124 **"stopped rampaging":** Terry Robards, "Go-Go Fund Managers Mostly Gone," *New York Times*, February 12, 1973, 39.

124 **While Mickie Siebert's:** John Steele Gordon, *The Great Game: The Emergence of Wall Street as a World Power: 1653–2000* (New York: Simon & Schuster, 2000), 274.

124 **"Hello from the gutters":** "From the Archives: Jimmy Breslin, the Son of Sam, and New York Tabloid Wars," *Columbia Journalism Review* (March 20, 2017), https://www.cjr.org/from_the_archives/jimmy_breslin_new_york_daily_news .php.

124 **In 1978 the director of compliance:** Frank J. Prial, "BUSINESS PEOPLE: They're Capitalizing on Capital Experience, Defense for Wall Street Women, Poignant Exit for Richard Burow, He's President, But of What?" *New York Times*, June 21, 1978, D2.

125 **"Stuffed":** Author's interview with Maria Marsala, Zoom, August 1, 2022.

125 **"Stop that!":** Author's interview with Maria Marsala (2022).

126 **how to hire cheap talent:** Author's interview with Mary Farrell, Zoom, August 24, 2021.

126 **"he said/she said":** Author's interview with Mary Farrell (2021).

127 **Mary arrived to work:** Author's interview with Mary Farrell (2021).

127 **"nerdy but prestigious":** Marlene Jupiter, *Dancing with Snakes*, Unpublished manuscript, 6 (I would like to thank Ms. Jupiter for her generosity in sharing her manuscript, a memoir of her experiences on Wall Street, and allowing me to quote from it).

128 **"Welcome to Wall Street!":** Jupiter, *Dancing with Snakes*, 12.

128 **Marlene as the "new girl":** Jupiter, *Dancing with Snakes*, 14.

129 **tableside backgammon boards:** Aaron Goldfarb, "Backgammon's Secret Celebrity Society," *Punch*, July 9, 2021, https://punchdrink.com/articles/history-of -backgammons-secret-celebrity-society/.

130 **"involved with a best friend of his":** Interview with Alice Jarcho, conducted by Melanie Shorin with Christine Doudna of the Narrative Trust, December 14, 2016, and May 24, 2017, *Remembering Wall Street, 1950–1980*, The Bonnie and Richard Reiss Wall Street Oral History Archive, New-York Historical Society, Transcript, 27.

130 **everyone assumed she was sleeping with *him*:** Author's interview with Alice Jarcho, New York City, September 19, 2021. Also: Interview with Alice Jarcho, NYHS, Transcript, 35, 39.

130 **And then there were the targeted lies:** Interview with Alice Jarcho, NYHS, Transcript, 35.

130 **"charm":** Author's interview with Alice Jarcho (2021).

130 **"very iconoclastic":** Interview with Alice Jarcho, NYHS, Transcript, 44.

130 **"Are you crazy?":** Interview with Alice Jarcho, NYHS, Transcript, 44.

131 **But Alice had a crush:** Author's interview with Alice Jarcho (2021).

131 **But Gus Levy:** Author's interview with Alice Jarcho (2021).

131 **"a roar that sounds":** Vartanig G. Vartan, "The New York Stock Exchange: An Amalgam of Coolness and Excitement," *New York Times*, January 22, 1964, 50.

132 **"pocket-sized radio receivers":** "Beeps Join Waggles on Trading Floor," *New York Times*, August 11, 1971, 49.

133 **"pink, yellow":** Vartan, "New York Stock Exchange."

133 **"soft-drink lids":** Sonny Kleinfield, *The Traders* (Greenville, SC: Traders Press, 1993 [Reprint from 1983]), 1.

133 **There was so much paper:** Patricia O'Toole, "A Day in the Life of the New York Stock Exchange," *Savvy*, August 1981, 36.

133 **moved using a thumbwheel:** O'Toole, "A Day in the Life," 37.

133 **"Three-eighths for a thousand":** Kleinfield, *Traders*, 13.

133 **One ritual was so stress-inducing:** Interview with Doreen Mogavero, conducted by Christine Doudna of the Narrative Trust, October 25, 2016, *Remembering Wall Street, 1950–1980*, The Bonnie and Richard Reiss Wall Street Oral History Archive, New-York Historical Society, Transcript, 44.

134 **Only later did she learn:** Interview with Alice Jarcho, NYHS, Transcript, 46.

134 **"on [her] ass":** Author's interview with Alice Jarcho (2021). (In Interview with Alice Jarcho, NYHS, Transcript, 49. Here Ms. Jarcho notes only "a daughter.")

134 **"I have all the fears":** Leonard Sloane, "New Floor Trader Ends a Tradition at Big Board," *New York Times*, November 1, 1976, 77.

134 **always referred to herself:** Author's interview with Alice Jarcho (2021).

135 **"a snob":** Author's interview with Alice Jarcho (2021).

135 **The attacks on Alice:** Interview with Alice Jarcho, NYHS, Transcript, 49–50.

135 **"Oh, you must have your":** Author's interview with Alice Jarcho (2021).

136 **"There were women with":** Interview with Alice Jarcho, NYHS, Transcript, 57–58.

137 **"You're not understanding":** Author's interview with Alice Jarcho (2021).

137 **"pure Teddy Roosevelt":** O'Toole, "A Day in the Life," 36.

137 **"a lone black man":** Gary S. Bell, *In the Black: A History of African Americans on Wall Street* (New Jersey: Wiley & Sons, 2002), 71.

137 **"When are you":** Author's interview with Alice Jarcho (2021).

CHAPTER 9: FLOOR QUEENS AND AN ARB KING

139 **had admitted its first two women:** Vartanig G. Vartan, "First New York Exchange Seat for Woman Sought by Analyst," *New York Times*, December 9, 1967.

139 **"Mayday":** Gary S. Bell, *In the Black: A History of African Americans on Wall Street* (New Jersey: Wiley & Sons, 2002), 108.

140 **"I am concerned":** As quoted in Alec Benn, *The Unseen Wall Street of 1969–1975: And Its Significance for Today* (Westport, CT: Quorum Books, 2000), 127.

140 **"financial Camelot":** Bell, *In the Black*, 94.

141 **Others weren't smiling:** Roslyn Lacks, "Muriel Siebert: Playing the Numbers on Wall Street," in Maxine Gold, ed., *Women Making History: Conversations with Fifteen New Yorkers* (New York City Commission on the Status of Women, 1985), 105.

141 **The fixed rate commission:** Dylan Gottlieb, "Yuppies: Young Urban Professionals and the Making of Postindustrial New York," PhD dissertation, Princeton University, 2020, 39. I would like to thank Dylan Gottlieb for his generosity in

sharing his PhD dissertation with me. His dissertation is now a forthcoming book with Harvard University Press.

141 **Her father had died:** Interview with Doreen Mogavero, conducted by Christine Doudna of the Narrative Trust, October 25, 2016, *Remembering Wall Street, 1950–1980*, The Bonnie and Richard Reiss Wall Street Oral History Archive, New-York Historical Society, Transcript, 7.

141 **"husky traders":** Sonny Kleinfield, *The Traders* (Greenville, SC: Traders Press, 1993 [Reprint from 1983]), 52.

142 **He had been hiding them:** Interview with Doreen Mogavero, NYHS, Transcript, 5–6.

142 **possibly as a department-store buyer:** Interview with Doreen Mogavero, NYHS, Transcript, 12.

142 **"into which traders":** Kleinfield, *Traders*, 51.

143 **The American Stock Exchange was for her:** Interview with Doreen Mogavero, NYHS, Transcript, 13.

143 **Almost everyone found it:** Interview with Doreen Mogavero, NYHS, Transcript, 51–52.

144 **Doreen accessorized:** Author's interview with Doreen Mogavero, New York City, September 16, 2021.

144 **Doreen secretly hoped:** Interview with Doreen Mogavero, NYHS, Transcript, 14.

144 **buying a membership for $52,000:** Douglas W. Cray, "People in Business: Big Board, Amex Each Adding a Woman as Trading Members," *New York Times*, March 10, 1977, 57.

144 **Ace Greenberg took a shine to him:** Jenny Lee LaVertu, "The Women of Jeffrey Epstein," *Medium*, August 15, 2019, https://medium.com/@jennyleelavertu/the-women-of-jeffrey-epstein-f76ae6801ffa.

144 **Doreen was still living at home:** Author's interview with Doreen Mogavero (New York City, 2021).

144 **Opened in 1972:** Frank J. Prial, "Years of Feeding Wall Street Meet Abrupt End at Harry's," *New York Times*, November 1, 2003, B4.

145 **a small hammer:** Kleinfield, *Traders*, 53.

145 **After she'd finished her breakfast:** Interview with Doreen Mogavero, NYHS, Transcript, 20.

145 **Doreen found an apartment:** Interview with Doreen Mogavero, NYHS, Transcript, 19.

145 **Her best friend lived:** Author's interview with Doreen Mogavero (New York City, 2021).

145 **Having untethered herself:** Interview with Doreen Mogavero, NYHS, Transcript, 25.

146 **"an extremely, extremely nice man":** Interview with Doreen Mogavero, NYHS, Transcript, 28.

147 **It was a total culture shock:** Interview with Doreen Mogavero, NYHS, Transcript, 30–31.

147 **"where traders cluster[ed]":** Anne Mackay-Smith, "Women Are Facing Hostility and Hazing As a Few Break into Commodity," *The Wall Street Journal*, January 22, 1982, 33.

147 **She was just twenty-four:** Interview with Doreen Mogavero, NYHS, Transcript, 31.

148 **"Get me a quote on IBM":** Interview with Doreen Mogavero, NYHS, Transcript, 54.

149 **solo flying:** Lacks, "Muriel Siebert," 102.

149 **"It gives me great"**: Lacks, "Muriel Siebert," 104.

150 **"Oh, that was nice"**: Interview with Doreen Mogavero, NYHS, Transcript, 35. Further details: Author's Interview with Doreen Mogavero (2021).

150 **"I felt like I could breathe"**: Author's interviews with Louise Jones, New Jersey, April 28 and June 28, 2022. Please note that *all* references to Louise Jones are based on the author's interviews.

153 **"People were screaming"**: Patricia O'Toole, "A Day in the Life of the New York Stock Exchange," *Savvy*, August 1981, 34.

155 **a floor trader in his late forties**: My interviewees who worked on an exchange floor tended to use the terms "floor broker" and "floor trader" indiscriminately and interchangeably. In theory, those who executed orders for brokerage house clients were called "commission brokers," those who helped commission brokers execute orders (for any firm) were called "two-dollar brokers," and those who traded their own accounts were called "floor traders." See Kleinfield, *Traders*, 11.

CHAPTER 10: POWER PLAY

159 **"What's an eee-light?"**: Author's interview with Barbara Byrne, Zoom, August 17, 2021.

160 **"a journeyman's school"**: Author's interview with Barbara Byrne (2021).

160 **"How much money do you think"**: Author's interview with Barbara Byrne (2021).

162 **"Jacquard typewriters"**: Author's interview with Barbara Byrne (2021).

162 **"Look, Barbara, this is market data"**: Author's interview with Barbara Byrne (2021).

163 **"they would call you names"**: Johnny Wu, "Career Advice from an Investment Banking Legend, Shattering the Glass Ceiling," with Barbara Byrne, Former Vice Chairman of Investment Banking, Barclays and Lehman Brothers, AAAIM High (Podcast), August 4, 2021, Episode 26.

163 **as he puffed on his own cigar**: Author's interview with Barbara Byrne (2021).

163 **"I don't understand"**: Author's interview with Barbara Byrne (2021).

164 **"You're quiet"**: Wu, "Career Advice from an Investment Banking Legend."

164 **"Do you agree with this?!"**: Wu, "Career Advice from an Investment Banking Legend." Also: Author's interview with Barbara Byrne (2021).

164 **"So is there anything positive"**: Wu, "Career Advice from an Investment Banking Legend."

164 **"Do you really think I'm"**: Author's interview with Barbara Byrne (2021). Also: Wu, "Career Advice from an Investment Banking Legend."

164 **"so ridiculously tacky"**: Author's interview with Barbara Byrne (2021).

165 **"Oh, and by the way"**: Author's interview with Barbara Byrne (2021).

165 **favorite television show**: Ms. Byrne refers to the television show *1L* (as in first year of law school). Presumably, she meant *The Paper Chase*. Author's interview with Barbara Byrne (2021).

165 **"Ladies' Day"**: Brenda Feigen, *Not One of the Boys: Living Life as a Feminist* (New York: Knopf, 2000), 5.

165 **But it wasn't just about**: Author's interview with Barbara Byrne (2021).

165 **("which is true"!)**: Author's interview with Cali Cole, Zoom, August 20, 2021.

165 **The daughter of a prominent lawyer**: Marianne Camille Spraggins, interviewed by Julieanna L. Richardson at New York, NY, with videographer Matthew Hickey on October 20, 2013, *HistoryMakers*, Tape 2.

167 **Marianne now had a law degree**: Spraggins, *HistoryMakers*, Tape 1

167 **"a very suave . . . mysterious"**: Spraggins, *HistoryMakers*, Tape 2.

167 **Deak had in fact worked as an operative:** "Was CIA Financier-Turned Wall Street Banker Assassinated by the Bearded Bag Lady? New Evidence May Solve Mystery of 1985 Shooting," *Daily Mail*, December 9, 2012, https://www.dailymail.co.uk/news/article-2245682/Nicholas-Deak-Colleague-questions-murder-CIA-financier-killed-homeless-woman.html.

167 **Deak represented a level of power:** Author's interview with Marianne Camille Spraggins, New York City, June 11, 2022.

167 **"understood political power":** Spraggins, *HistoryMakers*, Tape 2.

168 **"but that wasn't the driving force":** Spraggins, *HistoryMakers*, Tape 2.

168 **Alice in Wonderland:** Spraggins, *HistoryMakers*, Tape 2.

168 **"brutal for Black people":** Spraggins, *HistoryMakers*: Tape 2.

168 **"I called up every single":** David J. Dent, "Taking Their Seats on The Street: Blacks Have Made It on Wall Street to a Point. Now They're Asking, 'What's Next?,'" *New York Times*, February 23, 1997, 127.

169 **"Oh, how long have you":** Spraggins, *HistoryMakers*, Tape 4.

169 **"very bankerly":** Spraggins, *HistoryMakers*, Tape 2.

170 **"false front":** Author's interview with Marianne Camille Spraggins (2022).

170 **"Average":** Author's interview with Marianne Camille Spraggins (2022).

170 **"If you believe you are":** Lisa Rawson, "Second Generation Alumnus Returns to Teach," *Equitas*, November 1977, 9.

170 **"had no idea":** Author's interview with Marianne Camille Spraggins (2022).

170 **"I don't see anyone here":** Author's interview with Marianne Camille Spraggins (2022).

170 **On Friday, they told her:** Marianne Spraggins's various interviews across time offer up different dates as her starting point on Wall Street. In "Taking Their Seats on The Street," the article cites her starting year as 1978. In Audrey Edwards, "Marianne Spraggins: Doing the Count," *Essence*, August 1993, Spraggins speaks of the early 1980s as when she started. In an extensive oral history interview for *HistoryMakers*, as well as an interview with the author, Spraggins is less specific but seems to suggest 1980–81.

170 **"beauty contests":** Author's interview with Marianne Camille Spraggins (2022).

171 **"little yellow tie thing":** Author's interview with Marianne Camille Spraggins (2022).

171 **"So this is who I am":** Spraggins, *HistoryMakers*, Tape 3.

171 **Now there were three Black trainees left:** Author's interview with Marianne Camille Spraggins (2022).

172 **"like Hester Prynne":** Spraggins, *HistoryMakers*, Tape 3.

172 **"a fatal error":** Author's interview with Marianne Camille Spraggins (2022).

172 **"Marianne, I can't believe you didn't":** Author's interview with Marianne Camille Spraggins (2022).

173 **"uncouth, ill-bred":** Author's interview with Marianne Camille Spraggins (2022).

173 **She had been reduced:** Author's interview with Marianne Camille Spraggins (2022).

173 **"steel-blue eyes, like a beetle":** Author's interview with Marianne Camille Spraggins (2022).

174 **The man then looked up:** Author's interview with Marianne Camille Spraggins (2022).

174 **"Let me tell you one thing":** Spraggins, *HistoryMakers*, Tape 3.

174 **"up there":** Spraggins, *HistoryMakers*, Tape 3.

174 **"carried out feet first":** Author's interview with Marianne Camille Spraggins (2022).

175 "one day, somebody": Spraggins, *HistoryMakers*, Tape 3.

175 "ready to bite the ass off a bear": Michael Lewis, *Liar's Poker: Rising Through the Wreckage of Wall Street* (New York: W. W. Norton, 1989), 22.

175 "I was in the class": Spraggins, *HistoryMakers*, Tape 3.

176 He would be known for coining: "25 People to Blame for the Financial Crisis," *Time*, https://content.time.com/time/specials/packages/completelist/0,29569, 1877351,00.html.

176 "uncouth": Edward Morris, *Wall Streeters: The Creators and Corruptors of American Finance* (New York: Columbia Business School Publishing, 2015), 252.

176 "the firm's Biggest Swinging Dicks": Lewis, *Liar's Poker*, 95.

176 "baddest dudes": Lewis, *Liar's Poker*, 95.

177 Outstanding mortgage loans were: Lewis, *Liar's Poker*, 104.

177 "women have it": Author's interview with Marianne Camille Spraggins (2022).

177 "So I knew I was on to something": Spraggins, *HistoryMakers*, Tape 3.

179 made $150 million for Salomon Brothers: Lewis, *Liar's Poker*, 135.

179 "We are pioneers": Hearing Before the Subcommittee on Labor-Management Relations of the Committee on Education and Labor House of Representatives on H.R. 1179 and H.R. 4243, 119.

179 "I would love to say": Hearing Before the Subcommittee on Labor-Management Relations of the Committee on Education and Labor House of Representatives on H.R. 1179 and H.R. 4243, 121.

179 "now trading about $15 billion": Hearing Before the Subcommittee on Labor-Management Relations of the Committee on Education and Labor House of Representatives on H.R. 1179 and H.R. 4243, 122.

179 totaled $500 million: This is actually what the interviewer asks Marianne—to confirm that she brought in $500 million. Marianne says she does not remember but trusts it's true. Spraggins, *HistoryMakers*, Tape 3.

179 the worst of it was: Author's interview with Marianne Camille Spraggins (2022).

179 "twofers": Keith L. Alexander, "Minority Women Feel Racism, Sexism Are Blocking the Path to Management," *Wall Street Journal*, July 25, 1990, B1.

179 "And that's a direct order!": Author's interview with Marianne Camille Spraggins (2022).

179 "always did whatever": Author's interview with Marianne Camille Spraggins (2022).

180 "There are people who know": Author's interview with Marianne Camille Spraggins (2022).

180 "known as the city's most": Mimi Sheraton, "Restaurants; Palace Revisited; New in Midtown," *New York Times*, November 20, 1981, C22.

180 "because we're going to break them!": Author's interview with Marianne Camille Spraggins (2022).

CHAPTER 11: YUPPIEDOM

181 "came glittering down": John Duka, "A New Opulence Triumphs in Capital," *New York Times*, January 22, 1981, C1.

182 "All of the women here": Duka, "New Opulence."

182 household debt: Paul Krugman, "Reagan Did It," op-ed, *New York Times*, May 31, 2009, 21.

183 "I wore granny dresses": As quoted in Gil Troy, *Morning in America: How Ronald Reagan Invented the 1980s* (Princeton: Princeton University Press, 2007), 56.

183 "Dawn of a Bull Market": James Grant, in Eric J. Weiner, *What Goes Up: The*

Uncensored History of Modern Wall Street as Told by the Bankers, Brokers, CEOs, and Scoundrels Who Made It Happen (New York: Back Bay Books, 2005), 270.

183 **He even did the unthinkable:** Author's interview with Patricia Chadwick, Greenwich, CT, December 4, 2021.

183 **Five days later, on August 17:** Gary Silverman, " 'Shock the Market': Wall Street's Original 'Dr Doom' Tells Fed to Toughen Up," *Financial Times*, August 17, 2022, https://www.ft.com/content/47d407c1-2353-4068-90a7-27a9f901f051.

183 **By August 20:** Jason DeSena Trennert, "Remembering the Reagan Bull Market," *Wall Street Journal*, August 13, 2009, A15.

184 **MTV arrived in August 1981:** For more on the Cold War cues played on MTV in the 1980s, see Tom Nichols, "I Want My Mutually Assured Destruction," *The Atlantic*, May 8, 2021, https://www.theatlantic.com/ideas/archive/2021/05/my-mtv-cold-war-retrospective/618812/.

184 **Suddenly New York was the place:** Matthew Galkin, dir., *Empires of New York*, Fairhaven Films, 2020, Episodes 1 and 2.

184 **When, in October 1981:** Dylan Gottlieb, "Yuppies: Young Urban Professionals and the Making of Postindustrial New York," PhD dissertation, Princeton University, 2020, 65–66.

185 **"The M.B.A degree is":** Warren Kalbacker, "Playboy Interview: Louis Rukeyser," *Playboy*, April 1987, 53.

185 **In 1971, women:** Gottlieb, "Yuppies," 68.

185 **"At cocktail parties":** As quoted in Gottlieb, "Yuppies," 40.

186 **"a means of creating":** Michael Lewis, *Liar's Poker: Rising Through the Wreckage of Wall Street* (New York: W. W. Norton, 1989), 43–44.

186 **She had never wanted a fur coat:** Author's interview with Mary Farrell, Zoom, August 24, 2021.

186 **"a herd mentality":** Gottlieb, "Yuppies," 56.

186 **"No, no, no":** Gottlieb, "Yuppies," 23.

186 **In 1986, over 30 percent:** James B. Stewart, "Taking the Dare," *The New Yorker*, July 26, 1993, 35.

186 **Phyllis Strong, Yale class of 1983:** Author's interview with Phyllis Strong, Zoom, September 14, 2021. All subsequent references to Phyllis Strong are from this interview.

188 **"because I open my boss's mail":** Julie Salamon, "Working Women Grill Major Banks in Noon Mock Trial," *Wall Street Journal*, August 27, 1980, 21.

188 **"if someone gave me an order":** Commencement DB, Muriel Siebert at Case Western Reserve University (1998), https://whatrocks.github.io/commencement-db/1998-muriel-siebert-case-western-reserve-university/.

190 **"If you want the job":** Joanne Lipman, "The Mismeasure of Woman," Op-Ed, *New York Times*, October 23, 2009, 21.

190 **She'd landed a:** Author's interview with Joanne Lipman, Zoom, July 26, 2021.

190 **"Valley of the Dolls":** Lipman, "Mismeasure of Woman."

191 **"curse like truck drivers":** Lipman, "Mismeasure of Woman."

191 **In 1984, LGBT Stanford alumni:** The interviewee did not want to give her name: interview on Zoom, November 21, 2022.

191 **The question of whether:** Annette Friskopp and Sharon Silverstein, *Straight Jobs, Gay Lives: Gay and Lesbian Professionals, the Harvard Business School, and the American Workplace* (New York: Scribner, 1995), 350.

191 **Gay culture largely identified:** Friskopp and Silverstein, *Straight Jobs, Gay Lives*, 364–366.

191 **"My generation of professional"**: Lipman, "Mismeasure of Woman."

191 **"Being an analyst"**: Author's interview with Barbara Byrne, Zoom, August 17, 2021.

192 **Beth Dater, now a partner**: Interview with Beth Dater, conducted by Melanie Shorin of the Narrative Trust, February 10, 2015, *Remembering Wall Street, 1950–1980*, The Bonnie and Richard Reiss Wall Street Oral History Archive, New-York Historical Society, 41.

192 **"was putting linebacker"**: Marlen Komar, "The Evolution of the Female Power Suit," *Bustle*, April 14, 2016, https://www.bustle.com/articles/152069-the -evolution-of-the-female-power-suit-what-it-means-photos.

193 **"You can go to Ford"**: Author's interview with Westina Matthews, Zoom, August 20, 2021.

193 **could not abide**: Interview with Beth Dater, NYHS, Transcript, 49.

194 **"limousines lined up"**: Trip Gabriel, "For Those Who Lived It, the Surf Club Lives On," *New York Times*, March 16, 1997, 49.

194 **In 1970 almost 73,000**: "NYC in Chaos," Blackout/Image Gallery, PBS/*American Experience*, https://www.pbs.org/wgbh/americanexperience/features/blackout -gallery/.

194 **Typical then was a 1973**: Gottlieb, "Yuppies," 62.

195 **"contrary to popular rumor"**: Gottlieb, "Yuppies," 62.

195 **"one of the most highly-favored"**: Gottlieb, "Yuppies," 63.

195 **On a weekend morning**: Gottlieb, "Yuppies," 63.

196 **"a little showy"**: Michael Beschloss, "Historysource: The Ad That Helped Reagan Sell Good Times to an Uncertain Nation," *New York Times* (online), May 7, 2016, https://www.nytimes.com/2016/05/08/business/the-ad-that-helped-reagan -sell-good-times-to-an-uncertain-nation.html?partner=bloomberg.

196 **"a year-long tan"**: Marlene Jupiter, *Dancing with Snakes*, unpublished manuscript, 35.

196 **and at 2 p.m.**: Author's interview with Marlene Jupiter, Zoom, June 17, 2022.

196 **"entire room would look"**: Jupiter, *Dancing with Snakes*, 40.

197 **"For the first time in decades"**: Merida Welles, "Wall Street by Night," *New York Times*, January 1, 1984, Section 3, page 4.

197 **Like Phyllis and Joanne**: Jupiter, *Dancing with Snakes*, 46.

197 **"if you were blowing up"**: Interview with Beth Dater, NYHS, Transcript, 45.

198 **drank Champagne served by maids**: "The 50 Most Influential Reality TV Seasons of All Time," *Time*, August 4, 2022, https://time.com/collection/reality-tv-most -influential-seasons/.

198 **"a subculture in which cocaine"**: Peter Kerr, "15 Employees of Wall Street Firms Are Arrested on Cocaine Charges," *New York Times*, April 17, 1987, 1.

199 **"barely looking up"**: "The Year of the Yuppie," *Newsweek*, December 31, 1984, 14.

199 **"a couple so far ahead"**: *Newsweek*, "Year of the Yuppie," 16.

200 **"In the eighties"**: Barbara Ehrenreich, *Fear of Falling: The Inner Life of the Middle Class* (New York: Pantheon, 1989), 200.

200 **"driving the bears back"**: Rudy Abramson, "President Gives Bullish Wall St. Pep Talk," *Los Angeles Times*, March 29, 1985, 26.

203 **they'd have to build**: See: Muriel Siebert (with Aimee Lee Ball), *Changing the Rules: Adventures of a Wall Street Maverick* (New York: The Free Press, 2002), 39. Also, Muriel Siebert, in Weiner, *What Goes Up*, 114. Siebert writes that for two years she did not know that there was even a bathroom near the trading floor. Finally, a broker took pity on her and led her to the bathrooms built for the female pages hired during the Korean War. This has proven difficult to confirm, but it

seems the ones she referred to are the ones that still remain with the door sign: Female Clerks Rest Room. For more, see The Good Men Project, "The New York Stock Exchange Really Needs to Move the Women's Restroom," *Jezebel*, August 2, 2012. To view photographs of how hard it is still to find the bathrooms, see: The Good Feed Blog Editors, "NYSE's 'Moving the Needle' Might Have to Start with 'Moving the Bathroom'," *Forbes*, August 2, 2012, https://www.forbes.com/sites/goodmenproject/2012/08/02/266/?sh=674fdadc4c32.

CHAPTER 12: MAMMA MIA!

205 **"a tough world"**: Author's interview with Barbara Byrne, Zoom, August 17, 2021.

205 **"If anyone ever hears"**: Author's interview with Barbara Byrne (2021).

206 **"smoke signal"**: Maria Marsala, Guest Columnist: "A Woman Who Survived Wall Street's 'Liquid Lunches' and 'Boom, Boom Rooms' of the 1970s and 1980s Weighs in on the Ken Fisher Sexism Fracas," RIABiz, March 2, 2020, https://riabiz.com/a/2020/3/5/a-woman-who-survived-wall-streets-liquid-lunches-and-boom-boom-rooms-of-the-1970s-and-1980s-weighs-in-on-the-ken-fisher-sexism-fracas.

206 **"Not only do we have"**: Author's interview with Alice Jarcho, New York City, September 19, 2021.

207 **"I'm not going to look"**: Author's interview with Alice Jarcho (2021).

207 **"You think you're going to"**: Author's interview with Alice Jarcho (2021).

207 **"some polyester people"**: Jane Gross, "Against the Odds: A Woman's Ascent on Wall Street," *New York Times Magazine*, January 6, 1985, 1.

208 **"intoxicating"**: Author's interview with Alice Jarcho (2021).

209 **"I'm not going to pay"**: Gross, "Against the Odds."

210 **"The over-30 mother"**: Mary Kay Blakely, "Executive Mothers: A Cautionary Tale," *Working Woman*, August 1983, 70.

210 **"If I can't give"**: Dena Kleiman, "Many Young Women Now Say They'd Pick Family over Career," *New York Times*, December 28, 1980, 1.

210 **"mothers should either"**: Kleiman, "Many Young Women."

210 **A recent Gallup poll**: Gross, "Against the Odds."

211 **She had graduated from Columbia**: Author's interview with Janet Hanson, Hastings-On-Hudson, NY, November 23, 2021.

211 **"the dogs"**: Author's interview with Janet Hanson (2021).

211 **having already paid her dues**: D. Murali, "Books: Mistreatment in the Money Den," *The Hindu*, May 31, 2011, https://www.thehindu.com/books/mistreatment-in-the-money-den/article2065756.ece.

211 **"amusing"**: Janet Hanson, *More Than 85 Broads: Women Making Career Choices, Taking Risks, and Defining Success on Their Own Terms* (New York: McGraw-Hill, 2006), 1–2.

212 **"Thirty years ago"**: Peter Davis, "The $100,000 a Year Woman," *Esquire*, June 1984, 72.

212 **"The single men I meet"**: Davis, "$100,000 a Year Woman," 72.

212 **"I didn't know if"**: Davis, "$100,000 a Year Woman," 82.

212 **she allowed the reporter**: Author's interview with Lisa Wolfson, Zoom, May 4, 2023.

213 **"You begin to feel"**: Davis, "$100,000 a Year Woman," 73.

213 **"the high forehead"**: Davis, "$100,000 a Year Woman," 73.

213 **"avuncular crush on her"**: Davis, "$100,000 a Year Woman," 81.

214 **"Now just think"**: Davis, "$100,000 a Year Woman," 81.

214 **"men have these profound"**: Davis, "$100,000 a Year Woman," 82.

214 **"I'm still enough of a"**: Davis, "$100,000 a Year Woman," 86.

214 **"dressed in suits"**: Margot Witty, "Financial Women and Children," *Working Woman*, September 1981, 77.

215 **"have disposable diapers"**: Witty, "Financial Women and Children," 77.

215 **"How much"**: Witty, "Financial Women and Children," 78.

216 **"It was an eye-opener"**: Author's interview with Mary Farrell, Zoom, August 24, 2021.

216 **"hooked on the stock market"**: Witty, "Financial Women and Children," 78.

216 **with women who didn't question:** Author's interview with Mary Farrell (2021).

216 **"a downtown Junior League"**: Melissa Suzanne Fisher, "Wall Street Women: Engendering Global Finance in the Manhattan Landscape," *City & Society* 22, no. 2 (December 2010): 268–269.

216 **purposefully choosing the august Federal Hall:** Fisher, "Wall Street Women," 262.

217 **It was clear to them all:** Author's interview with Ellen Sills-Levy, Zoom, April 27, 2023.

217 **"analyzing for two"**: John Brooks, "Onward and Upward with Wall Street," *The New Yorker*, Vol. 59, November 14, 1983.

217 **What surprised her:** Author's interview with Mary Farrell (2021).

217 **Well into the late 1990s:** Elizabeth Holder and Xan Parker, dirs. *Risk/Reward,* Organic Pictures, 2003.

217 **"probably the most prominent"**: Author's interview with Mary Farrell (2021).

217 **Margo had started out:** Author's interview with Margo Alexander, New York City, December 8, 2021.

218 **quietly left her name off:** Author's interview with Mary Farrell (2021).

218 **Paine Webber noticed that:** Author's interview with Margo Alexander (2021).

218 **It further helped:** Author's interview with Margo Alexander (2021).

218 **"whether I would have"**: Scott McMurray, "Goldman, Sachs Moves to Reassure Stanford Candidates," *Wall Street Journal*, February 4, 1985, 14.

218 **"go to the end of"**: As quoted in McMurray, "Goldman, Sachs Moves."

218 **he "wouldn't fit in"**: McMurray, "Goldman, Sachs Moves."

218 **Antidiscriminatory Underground:** Muriel Siebert (with Aimee Lee Ball), *Changing the Rules: Adventures of a Wall Street Maverick* (New York: The Free Press, 2002), 210.

218 **"they tended to look for"**: Siebert, *Changing the Rules,* 210.

218 **"moment of introspection"**: Author's interview with Janet Hanson (2021).

219 **Women were found more often:** Author's interview with Janet Hanson (2021).

219 **"That was it"**: Interview with Alice Jarcho, conducted by Melanie Shorin with Christine Doudna of the Narrative Trust, December 14, 2016, and May 24, 2017, *Remembering Wall Street, 1950–1980,* The Bonnie and Richard Reiss Wall Street Oral History Archive, New-York Historical Society, Transcript, 62.

219 **"One of them was"**: Interview with Alice Jarcho, NYHS, Transcript, 61.

219 **The numbers couldn't lie:** Author's interview with Alice Jarcho (2021).

220 **"the Lehman guys wouldn't"**: Interview with Alice Jarcho, NYHS, Transcript, 63.

220 **"the five phases of grief"**: Interview with Alice Jarcho, NYHS, Transcript, 64.

CHAPTER 13: WHAT GOES UP MUST COME DOWN

221 **"an ill-fitting toupee"**: Edward Morris, *Wall Streeters: The Creators and Corruptors of American Finance* (New York: Columbia Business School Publishing, 2015), 226–227.

221 **The return was alluring:** Dylan Gottlieb, "Yuppies: Young Urban Professionals and the Making of Postindustrial New York," PhD dissertation, Princeton University, 2020, 41.

222 **Milken's department:** Morris, *Wall Streeters*, 234.

222 **According to his tax returns:** Morris, *Wall Streeters*, 235.

222 **When for his thirty-eighth birthday:** Morris, *Wall Streeters*, 252.

222 **"In 1975, the total value":** Gottlieb, "Yuppies," 42.

223 **"many U.S. corporate managements":** Warren Kalbacker, "Playboy Interview: Louis Rukeyser," *Playboy*, April 1987, 60.

223 **wanting to be a young Barbara Walters:** Author's interview with Jolyne Caruso-FitzGerald, New York City, June 1, 2022.

224 **"commission shop":** Author's interview with Jolyne Caruso-FitzGerald, New York City, September 30, 2021.

224 **"like walking into a bar":** Author's interview with Jolyne Caruso-FitzGerald (2021).

224 **"jammed with":** Tim Carrington, "Tough Pit Boss: Alan Greenberg Leads Bear Stearns Traders In the Big-Block Game Intense, Poker-Faced Chief, Who 'Loves Small Losses,' Also Diversifies the Firm," *Wall Street Journal*, January 18, 1982, 1.

225 **including former NY Rangers:** Author's interview with Jolyne Caruso-FitzGerald (2022).

225 **"very fit, handsome":** Author's interview with Jolyne Caruso-FitzGerald (2022).

225 **"whip-smart":** Author's interview with Jolyne Caruso-FitzGerald (2022).

226 **"big deal kings":** Author's interview with Jolyne Caruso-FitzGerald (2022).

226 **"schlep":** Author's interview with Jolyne Caruso-FitzGerald (2022).

226 **"I loved going to work":** Author's interview with Jolyne Caruso-FitzGerald (2022).

226 **"plopped down":** Author's interview with Jolyne Caruso-FitzGerald (2022).

227 **"Hazardous to your":** Muriel Siebert (with Aimee Lee Ball), *Changing the Rules: Adventures of a Wall Street Maverick* (New York: The Free Press, 2002), 162.

227 **"they needed bodies":** Author's interview with Phyllis Strong (2021).

228 **As Westina Matthews' uncle:** Author's interview with Westina Matthews (2021).

228 **"there was a premium":** Author's interview with Phyllis Strong (2021).

228 **"Wall Street came to be":** Steve Fraser, "Toward a Cultural History of Wall Street," *Raritan* 22, no. 3 (2003): 4.

228 **"smart":** Jonathon Peterson, "Junk Bonds: a Financial Revolution That Failed Wall Street: The Economic Highfliers of the 1980s' Growing Economy Are a Peril in the Downturn of the '90s," *Los Angeles Times*, November 22, 1990, 1.

229 **"assets to be sold":** Gottlieb, "Yuppies," 42.

229 **"was a winner-take-all feeling":** Author's interview with Phyllis Strong (2021).

231 **"share his 'grief'":** Anise C. Wallace, "Investing; Cashing on the Merger Madness," *New York Times*, July 8, 1984, Section 3, 10.

231 **"demanding perfectionist":** Author's interview with Elisa Ancona, New York City, September 7, 2021.

232 **Roseanne would eventually:** Author's interview with Elisa Ancona (2021).

232 **"If you ever speak to":** Author's interview with Elisa Ancona (2021).

233 **"When you ask for something":** Author's interview with Elisa Ancona (2021).

233 **"street kids":** Author's interview with Elisa Ancona (2021).

233 **"he was pissed off":** Author's interview with Elisa Ancona (2021).

234 **"arbitrage gains were ill-gotten":** Morris, *Wall Streeters*, 240.

235 **"We were the original algorithms":** Interview with Doreen Mogavero, conducted by Christine Doudna of the Narrative Trust, October 25, 2016, *Remembering*

Wall Street, 1950–1980, The Bonnie and Richard Reiss Wall Street Oral History Archive, New-York Historical Society, Transcript, 57.

236 **"If you need that"**: Interview with Doreen Mogavero, NYHS, Transcript, 85.

236 **White Castle burgers or**: Interview with Doreen Mogavero, NYHS, Transcript, 63.

236 **"every entrée"**: James B. Stewart, *Den of Thieves* (New York: Touchstone, 1992), 96.

236 **"We're starting the 2 p.m."**: Author's interview with Jolyne Caruso-FitzGerald (2022).

237 **"less human"**: Author's interview with Janet Hanson, Hastings-On-Hudson, NY, November 23, 2021.

238 **"mortgages are math"**: Morris, *Wall Streeters*, 258.

238 **"Wall Street made"**: Author's interview with Janet Hanson (2021).

239 **junk-bond specialist Dirk Maurier**: Michael W. Miller, "Coming Attractions: Wall Street's Stock Soars in the Movies," *Wall Street Journal*, February 18, 1987, 1.

239 **"I have got to"**: Interview with Doreen Mogavero, NYHS, Transcript, 47.

239 **"My God, my mother's"**: Interview with Doreen Mogavero, NYHS, Transcript, 48.

240 **with mahogany and marble**: Joseph Grano, in Eric J. Weiner, *What Goes Up: The Uncensored History of Modern Wall Street as Told by the Bankers, Brokers, CEOs, and Scoundrels Who Made It Happen* (New York: Back Bay Books, 2005), 280.

240 **"short skirts and spiked heels"**: Susan Antilla, "The Hottest Woman on Wall Street," *Working Woman*, August 1991, 51.

240 **In her early days on Wall Street**: Sheri J. Caplan, *Petticoats and Pinstripes: Portraits of Women in Wall Street's History* (New York: Praeger, 2013), 152.

241 **"*Elaine, Girls just wanna have funds*"**: Antilla, "Hottest Woman on Wall Street," 51.

241 **"media hound"**: Antilla, "Hottest Woman on Wall Street," 50.

241 **"a kid"**: Sandra McElwaine, "Cosmo Talks to Elaine Garzarelli: Wall-Street Wizard," *Cosmopolitan*, August 1988, 158.

241 **"fall in love"**: McElwaine, "Cosmo Talks to Elaine Garzarelli," 158.

241 **"financial wizard"**: McElwaine, "Cosmo Talks to Elaine Garzarelli," 158.

241 **already done marriage**: Caplan, *Petticoats and Pinstripes*, 153.

241 **She refused to sign**: Antilla, "Hottest Woman on Wall Street," 51.

241 **"I had to take each"**: Caplan, *Petticoats and Pinstripes*, 153.

242 **"Lehman's going to"**: Sue Herera, *Women of the Street* (New York: Wiley & Sons, 1997), 154.

242 **"a senior vice president"**: "Brendan Thomas Byrne Jr. Marries Barbara Moakler at Mount Holyoke," *New York Times*, September 29, 1985, 69.

242 **"It was like for sport"**: Author's interview with Barbara Byrne, Zoom, August 17, 2021.

242 **"I'm having a baby!"**: Author's interview with Barbara Byrne (2021).

243 **That Friday afternoon**: "Remembering Black Monday: Fred Joseph," *CNN Money*, https://money.cnn.com/galleries/2007/fortune/0709/gallery.black_monday.fortune/6.html.

243 **Karen had already convinced**: "Remembering Black Monday: Jim Cramer," *CNN Money*, https://money.cnn.com/galleries/2007/fortune/0709/gallery.black_monday.fortune/5.html.

244 **"looking in the eyes"**: Donald Marron, in Weiner, *What Goes Up*, 285.

244 **There were rumors**: Michael Labranche, in Weiner, *What Goes Up*, 288.

245 **When the paramedics arrived:** "Remembering Black Monday: Elaine Garzarelli," *CNN Money*, https://money.cnn.com/galleries/2007/fortune/0709/gallery.black_monday.fortune/2.html.

245 **"They weren't running around":** "Remembering Black Monday: Muriel Siebert," *CNN Money*, https://money.cnn.com/galleries/2007/fortune/0709/gallery.black_monday.fortune/7.html.

245 **the market had dropped:** Federal Reserve History. Time Period: The Great Moderation/ Stock Market Crash of 1987, https://www.federalreservehistory.org/essays/great-moderation.

246 **staying on the floor:** Author's interview with Doreen Mogavero, New York City, September 16, 2021.

246 **stayed open all night:** Tim Arango and Julie Creswell, "End of an Era on Wall Street: Goodbye to All That," *New York Times*, October 4, 2008, https://www.nytimes.com/2008/10/05/business/05era.html/.

246 **to her favorite Japanese restaurant:** *CNN Money*, "Remembering Black Monday: Elaine Garzarelli."

246 **"cautious, be cautious":** Author's interview with Mary Farrell, Zoom, August 24, 2021.

246 **"So, he ate some bad":** Author's interview with Barbara Byrne (2021).

247 **Doreen watched as:** Interview with Doreen Mogavero, NYHS, Transcript, 66.

247 **"puppies":** Gottlieb, "Yuppies," 85.

247 **A pigeon can still:** Siebert, *Changing the Rules*, 171.

247 **"greed is alright":** Quoted extensively. Here see: Bob Greene, "A $100 Million Idea: Use Greed for Good," *Chicago Tribune*, December 15, 1986, D1.

248 **"a cult phenomenon":** Ken Moelis, a former UBS banker and "one of Wall Street's best-known dealmakers" in Francesco Guerrrera, "How 'Wall Street' Changed Wall Street," *Financial Times*, September 24, 2010, https://www.ft.com/content/7e55442a-c76a-11df-aeb1-00144feab49a.

248 **"a proliferation of suspenders":** Guerrrera, "How 'Wall Street' Changed Wall Street."

CHAPTER 14: R.E.S.P.E.C.T.

249 **"racketeering enterprise":** Edward Morris, *Wall Streeters: The Creators and Corruptors of American Finance* (New York: Columbia Business School Publishing, 2015), 245.

249 **"yuppie five":** Lois L. Evans and Heather H. Evans, "Why Women Are Outsiders to Insider Trading," *New York Times*, February 21, 1987, 27.

250 **men stopped barging in:** Author's email correspondence with Doreen Mogavero, September 25, 2023.

250 **All they had to do:** Interview with Doreen Mogavero, conducted by Christine Doudna of the Narrative Trust, October 25, 2016, *Remembering Wall Street, 1950–1980*, The Bonnie and Richard Reiss Wall Street Oral History Archive, New-York Historical Society, Transcript, 62–63.

250 **"beautiful and sexy":** Janet Hanson, *More Than 85 Broads: Women Making Career Choices, Taking Risks, and Defining Success on Their Own Terms* (New York: McGraw-Hill, 2006), 2.

250 **"tired and old":** Hanson, *More Than 85 Broads*, 2.

250 **"I was leaving because":** Hanson, *More Than 85 Broads*, 2.

251 **"I'm sitting here":** Hanson, *More Than 85 Broads*, 4.

251 **"Women need help":** Hanson, *More Than 85 Broads*, 5.

252 **"IPO carve-outs"**: Author's interview with Barbara Byrne, Zoom, August 17, 2021.

252 **"Mr. O'Leary, has anyone"**: Johnny Wu, "Career Advice from an Investment Banking Legend, Shattering the Glass Ceiling," with Barbara Byrne, Former Vice Chairman of Investment Banking, Barclays and Lehman Brothers, AAAIM High (Podcast), August 4, 2021, Episode 26.

253 **"You've never produced"**: Wu, "Career Advice from an Investment Banking Legend."

253 **represented only 4 percent of**: Laurie P. Cohen, William Power and Michael Siconolfi, "Wall Street Women: Financial Firms Act to Curb Office Sexism, with Mixed Results," *Wall Street Journal*, November 5, 1991, A1.

253 **It made her realize**: Wu, "Career Advice from an Investment Banking Legend."

253 **"militant"**: Author's interview with Jolyne Caruso-FitzGerald, New York City, September 30, 2021.

254 **"Oh, I would love to"**: Author's interview with Jolyne Caruso-FitzGerald, New York City, June 1, 2022. (Ms. Chadwick mentions this, too, in her memoir.)

255 **"I'm probably the only"**: Vartanig G. Vartan, "Miss Siebert's Memorable Day," *New York Times*, January 1, 1968, 23.

255 **"I'm in her presence"**: Author's interview with Patricia Chadwick, Greenwich, CT, December 4, 2021.

255 **"God help you"**: Author's interview with Jolyne Caruso-FitzGerald (2022).

255 **"golden girl"**: Author's interview with Jolyne Caruso-FitzGerald (2022).

255 **"I'll give you"**: Michael Kaplan, "How the macho NYSE Trader Became an Endangered Species," *New York Post*, February 15, 2020, https://nypost.com/2020/02/15/how-the-macho-nyse-trader-became-an-endangered-species/.

256 **"The '80s was"**: Mary Rourke, "Slouching into the '90s," *Los Angeles Times*, November 13, 1992, 1.

256 **Someone smirked**: Author's interview with Marlene Jupiter, Zoom, June 17, 2022.

256 **Change and transformation**: Judith Bennett, *History Matters: Patriarchy and the Challenge of Feminism* (Philadelphia: University of Pennsylvania Press, 2007).

256 **"Hey, how do you like"**: Author's interview with Margo Alexander, New York City, December 8, 2021.

257 **"sexy money"**: Interview with Alice Jarcho, conducted by Melanie Shorin with Christine Doudna of the Narrative Trust, December 14, 2016, and May 24, 2017, *Remembering Wall Street, 1950–1980*, The Bonnie and Richard Reiss Wall Street Oral History Archive, New-York Historical Society, Transcript, 67.

257 **"his darling"**: Author's interview with Alice Jarcho, New York City, September 19, 2021.

257 **He would randomly**: Interview with Alice Jarcho, NYHS, Transcript, 67.

257 **Allegations of sexual**: Sharon Otterman and Hannah Dreyfus, "Michael Steinhardt, a Leader in Jewish Philanthropy, Is Accused of a Pattern of Sexual Harassment," *New York Times*, March 21, 2019, https://www.nytimes.com/2019/03/21/nyregion/michael-steinhardt-sexual-harassment.html.

257 **His stock-in-trade**: Author's interview with Alice Jarcho (2021).

257 **"than I cried my entire"**: Interview with Alice Jarcho, NYHS, Transcript, 67.

257 **When the office politics**: Author's interview with Alice Jarcho (2021). Also: Interview with Alice Jarcho, NYHS, Transcript, 68.

258 **"I've never told him"**: Author's interview with Alice Jarcho (2021).

258 **"I'm so sorry"**: Author's interview with Alice Jarcho (2021).

258 **Charlie Milligan, left**: Author's interview with Margo Alexander (2021). Also:

Kurt Eichenwald, "COMPANY NEWS; 'A New Paine Webber,'" *New York Times*, July 15, 1992, D1.

258 **"humiliated":** Author's interview with Margo Alexander (2021).

258 **"Italian girl from Long Island":** Author's interview with Jolyne Caruso-FitzGerald (2022).

258 **"We don't hire":** Author's interview with Jolyne Caruso-FitzGerald (2021).

259 **"You don't love money!":** Interview with Alice Jarcho, NYHS, Transcript, 68.

259 **"the S&M whore":** Interview with Alice Jarcho, NYHS, Transcript, 67. Also: Author's interview with Alice Jarcho (2021).

259 **"because he didn't believe":** Author's interview with Elisa Ancona, New York City, September 7, 2021.

259 **Porter had worked for:** Obituary: A. Alex Porter, Dignity Memorial, https://www.dignitymemorial.com/obituaries/charlotte-nc/a-porter-5939469/.

260 **"Bulldog":** Author's interview with Elisa Ancona (2021).

260 **"*Wire 25k to*":** Author's interview with Elisa Ancona (2021).

265 **She was getting some offers:** Interview with Doreen Mogavero, NYHS, Transcript, 68.

265 **"Why do you want":** Interview with Doreen Mogavero, NYHS, Transcript, 70.

265 **"Don't worry":** Interview with Doreen Mogavero, NYHS, Transcript, 70.

266 **"What the hell?":** Interview with Doreen Mogavero, NYHS, Transcript, 70.

266 **Doreen leased a seat:** Interview with Doreen Mogavero, NYHS, Transcript, 49.

266 **It was finally a veteran:** Interview with Doreen Mogavero, NYHS, Transcript, 49.

266 **"were brave enough":** "The Climb: Doreen Mogavero," as told to Suzanne McGee, *Forbes*, November 14, 2008, https://www.forbes.com/2008/11/06/056.html?sh=26d6c5c71d97/.

266 **"What do you need a":** Author's interview with Doreen Mogavero, Zoom, October 26, 2021.

268 **Mike Robbins:** Lulu Chiang, "Bartiromo—An Eyewitness to History," CNBC, September 13, 2013, https://www.cnbc.com/2010/08/04/bartiromoan-eyewitness-to-history.html/.

268 **underutilized source of talent:** Interview with Doreen Mogavero, NYHS, Transcript, 70.

268 **she installed a playpen:** *Investment Dealers' Digest,* "Building a Legacy on the Floor."

268 **When Joy tired of climbing:** Interview with Doreen Mogavero, NYHS, Transcript, 71. Also: Author's interview with Doreen Mogavero (Zoom, 2021).

269 **"Mogavero, Lee has instilled motherhood":** *Investment Dealers' Digest,* "Building a Legacy on the Floor."

269 **an informal job-sharing system:** Interview with Doreen Mogavero, NYHS, Transcript, 72. Also: Author's interview with Doreen Mogavero (Zoom, 2021).

269 **At its height:** *Forbes,* "The Climb: Doreen Mogavero."

270 **"That darned car door":** Commencement DB, Muriel Siebert at Case Western Reserve University, 1998, https://whatrocks.github.io/commencement-db/1998-muriel-siebert-case-western-reserve-university/.

270 **Calvin Grigsby had resigned:** He was indicted on charges of money laundering, wire fraud, and bribery, but acquitted of all charges in 1999.

270 **"underwrote more than":** Creative Investment Research, Grigsby Brandford, Associated Press, Wednesday, October 2, 1996, https://www.creativeinvest.com/grigsbybrandford.html/.

270 **"and under us was"**: Muriel Siebert at Case Western Reserve University, 1998.

271 **"Stock Market Correction Is Over"**: David E. Kalish, "Lehman Fires Garzarelli, Famous Wall Street Soothsayer, *Associated Press*, October 27, 1994, https://apnews.com/article/a1ff32bc09164907c57b1ac5c039ac65.

271 **"For all the attention"**: Brett D. Fromson, "The Golden Years; Wall Street's '90s Prosperity Makes the Go-Go '80s Look Small-Time," *Washington Post*, July 3, 1994, H01.

271 **"not trading with Goldman"**: Author's interview with Patricia Chadwick (2021).

271 **spring's hottest items**: Albert B. Crenshaw, "Cohen Named Partner at Goldman Sachs," *Washington Post*, October 21, 1998, C10.

CHAPTER 15: B*TCH!

273 **first Black female MD:** Author's interview with Marianne Camille Spraggins, New York City, June 11, 2022.

273 **"these awful men":** Author's interview with Marianne Camille Spraggins (2022).

273 **"Who's this bitch?":** Author's interview with Marianne Camille Spraggins (2022).

274 **"still a very macho":** "Cover Story: 25 Hottest Blacks on Wall Street; Marianne Spraggins, A Powerhouse Banker," *Black Enterprise*, October 1992, 90.

274 **"ninety percent of":** Cin Fabré, *Wolf Hustle: A Black Woman on Wall Street* (New York: Henry Holt & Company, 2022), 144.

274 **"were not allowed to initiate":** Fabré, *Wolf Hustle*, 147

275 **"Black calling":** Author's interview with Lola West, San Francisco, July 27, 2021. Lola West joined Merrill Lynch as a financial advisor in 2000, when she was already in her early fifties. Thanks to her previous career in event planning, she had a substantial Rolodex of potential clients, and was treated with respect accordingly. What she observed took place from 2000 to 2009.

275 **"hovel":** Author's interview with Maureen Sherry, Zoom, September 28, 2021.

275 **"so lazy":** Author's interview with Maureen Sherry (2021).

276 **"Working in shirt sleeves":** Tim Carrington, "Tough Pit Boss: Alan Greenberg Leads Bear Stearns Traders In the Big-Block Game Intense, Poker-Faced Chief, Who 'Loves Small Losses,' Also Diversifies the Firm," *Wall Street Journal*, January 18, 1982.

276 **"we're going to have to":** Author's interview with Maria Marsala, Zoom, August 1, 2022.

276 **"had the guts":** Michael Siconolfi, "Bear Stearns Prospers Hiring Daring Traders That Rival Firms Shun: It Lets Them Make Big Bets, But Sharp-Eyed 'Ferrets' Watch Their Every Move Grilled at the 'Cold-Sweat,'" *Wall Street Journal*, November 11, 1993, A1.

276 **"What's the guy's name?":** Interview with Alice Jarcho, conducted by Melanie Shorin with Christine Doudna of the Narrative Trust, December 14, 2016, and May 24, 2017, *Remembering Wall Street, 1950–1980*, The Bonnie and Richard Reiss Wall Street Oral History Archive, New-York Historical Society, Transcript, 41.

276 **"entire street on Park Avenue":** Author's interview with Maureen Sherry (2021).

277 **"Cold?!":** Author's interview with Jolyne Caruso-FitzGerald, June 1, 2022.

277 **"overfamiliarity":** Author's interview with Maureen Sherry (2021).

277 **"If I had to call":** Dominique Mielle, *Damsel in Distressed: My Life in the Golden Age of Hedge Funds* (New York: Post Hill Press, 2021), 17.

277 **"It was sort of like":** Author's interview with Maureen Sherry (2021).

278 **"*I won't hold it*":** Author's interview with Maureen Sherry (2021).

278 **"beautiful, three-hundred-dollar"**: Author's interview with Maureen Sherry (2021).

278 **back at the desk, lost**: Author's interview with Maureen Sherry (2021).

278 **"geisha girls"**: Siconolfi, "Bear Stearns Prospers."

278 **"They were literally"**: Author's interview with Maureen Sherry (2021).

278 **When female executives**: Siconolfi, "Bear Stearns Prospers."

279 **but it was only**: Author's interview with Maureen Sherry (2021).

279 **"timid . . . very soft-spoken"**: Author's interview with Jolyne Caruso-Fitzgerald (2022).

279 **"You know you're in"**: Author's interview with Maureen Sherry (2021).

279 **"team players"**: Maureen Sherry, "Op-Ed: A Colleague Drank My Breast Milk and Other Wall Street Tales," *New York Times*, January 23, 2016.

280 **She was walking down**: Lois Smith Brady, "Wedding: Vows, Maureen Sherry and Steve Klinsky," *New York Times*, April 30, 1995, 15.

280 **"curly-haired stranger"**: Sherry, "A Colleague Drank My Breast Milk."

280 **One even took**: Sherry, "A Colleague Drank My Breast Milk."

280 **"a dirty secret"**: Author's interview with Maureen Sherry (2021).

281 **"How do the women"**: Sherry, "A Colleague Drank My Breast Milk."

281 **She laughed off**: Jane Wollman Rusoff, "Condom Pizza and Breast Milk Shots: True Stories From a Woman on Wall St.," *Think Advisor*, April 12, 2016, https://www.thinkadvisor.com/2016/04/12/condom-pizza-and-breast-milk-shots-true-stories-from-a-woman-on-wall-st/.

281 **"definitely got sucked into"**: Author's interview with Maureen Sherry (2021).

281 **They paid the price**: Author's interview with Maureen Sherry (2021).

281 **"I'm going in!"**: Author's interview with Maureen Sherry (2021). Also: Sherry, "A Colleague Drank My Breast Milk."

282 **"It was a very expensive"**: Author's interview with Maureen Sherry (2021).

282 **"what are your options?"**: Author's interview with Maureen Sherry (2021).

282 **"not tolerate any"**: Laurie P. Cohen, William Power and Michael Siconolfi, "Wall Street Women: Financial Firms Act to Curb Office Sexism, with Mixed Results," *Wall Street Journal*, November 5, 1991, A1.

283 **almost immediately the phones**: Susan Antilla, "COMPANY NEWS; New 'Woman Friendly' Fund Hits Its First Glitch," *New York Times*, October 7, 1993, D5.

283 **Cayne liked to put out**: Kate Kelly, *Street Fighters: The Last 72 Hours of Bear Stearns, the Toughest Firm on Wall Street* (New York: Portfolio, 2010), 26.

283 **"women's issues"**: Author's interview with Maureen Sherry (2021).

283 **"a stink"**: Author's interview with Maureen Sherry (2021).

283 **"a total kumbaya moment"**: Author's interview with Maureen Sherry (2021).

284 **"doing all the frickin' work"**: Author's interview with Maureen Sherry (2021).

284 **"Can you believe this shit?!"**: Author's interview with Maureen Sherry (2021).

284 **"Who does she"**: Author's interview with Barbara Byrne, Zoom, August 17, 2021.

284 **"She's not difficult"**: Author's interview with Barbara Byrne (2021).

286 **"he has no call"**: Author's interview with Barbara Byrne (2021).

287 **"she had been humiliated"**: Barry Meier, "Bias Suits Against Wall St. Firms," *New York Times*, November 21, 1996, D4.

287 **"what we might be facing"**: From private testimony given in another case by James Boshart, managing director of the capital markets division, in Susan Antilla, *Tales from the Boom-Boom Room: The Landmark Legal Battles that Exposed Wall Street's Shocking Culture of Sexual Harassment* (New York: Harper Business, 2003), 120.

287 **"anonymous friend"**: Charles Gasparino, "Smith Barney Banker Leaves After Dispute over Compensation, Ex-Associates Say," *The Bond Buyer*, January 10, 1994, 1.

287 **Employees referred to her**: Antilla, *Tales from the Boom-Boom Room*, 95.

287 **"After 14 years on"**: Gasparino, "Smith Barney Banker Leaves."

288 **"a systemic problem of"**: Susan Antilla, "Stark Lessons from Wall Street's #MeToo Moment," *The Intercept*, October 7, 2019, https://theintercept.com/2019/10/07/metoo-wall-street-sexual-harassment-arbitration/.

288 **"the biggest whorehouse"**: Martens in fact included this in her 1994 letter to Jamie Dimon. See Antilla, *Tales from the Boom-Boom Room*, 115.

288 **"slits and tits"**: As quoted in Christine Sgarlata Chung, "From Lily Bart to the Boom-Boom Room: How Wall Street's Social and Cultural Response to Women Has Shaped Securities Regulation," *Harvard Journal of Law & Gender* 33 (2010): 228.

288 **$150 million in settlements**: Susan Antilla, "Decades after 'Boom-Boom Room' Suit, Bias Persists for Women," *New York Times*, May 22, 2016, https://www.nytimes.com/2016/05/23/business/dealbook/decades-after-boom-boom-room-suit-bias-persists-for-women.html.

289 **"photographs of smiling"**: Susan Antilla, "How Wall Street Keeps Outrageous Gender Bias Quiet 20 Years After the Boom-Boom Room," *The Street*, June 4, 2016, https://susanantilla.com/how-wall-street-keeps-outrageous-gender-bias-quiet-20-years-after-the-boom-boom-room/.

289 **At the rowdy block trading desk**: Marlene Jupiter, *Dancing with Snakes*, unpublished manuscript, 68.

289 **"Where's your kid going"**: Author's interview with Marlene Jupiter, Zoom, June 17, 2022.

290 **"Nice haircut, dyke"**: Jupiter, *Dancing with Snakes*, 126.

290 **During Fleet Week:** "Sexual Misconduct at Work, Again," Episode 1 (13m 9s), *Retro Report on PBS*, Video, https://www.pbs.org/video/retro-report-on-pbs-season-1-episode-1-sexual-misconduct-work-again-full-report/.

290 **grabbed the phone:** Author's interview with Marlene Jupiter (2022). This was corroborated by one of her colleagues: see Antilla, "Stark Lessons from Wall Street's #MeToo Moment."

290 **in 1992, it was estimated:** *Retro Report on PBS*, "Sexual Misconduct at Work, Again," Episode 1.

291 **"In order to succeed Claimant":** FINRA Database; 1997–006473-Award-NYSE–19980720: New York Stock Exchange in the Matter of Arbitration Between Marlene Jupiter v Donaldson, Lufkin & Jenrette Securities Corporation and Donaldson, Lufkin & Jenrette, Inc. Date Filed: 04/14/1997; First Scheduled: 10/22/1997; Decided: 07/20/1998

292 **"a sexually objectionable environment":** New York Stock Exchange in the Matter of Arbitration Between Marlene Jupiter v Donaldson, Lufkin & Jenrette Securities Corporation and Donaldson, Lufkin & Jenrette, Inc.

293 **"survival hints":** Julie Creswell and Tiffany Hsu, "Women's Whisper Network Raises Its Voice," *New York Times*, November 5, 2017, BU1.

293 **"drawn a line in the sand":** Author's interview with Maureen Sherry (2021).

293 **"less worth":** Author's interview with Maureen Sherry (2021).

294 **"who had all the spreadsheets":** Author's interview with Maureen Sherry (2021).

294 **"knock-down, drag-out fights":** Author's interview with Maureen Sherry (2021).

294 **In 1996, Jacki Zehner:** Author's interview with Jacki Zehner, Zoom, June 2, 2022.

294 **"Oh, Joe is such a"**: Author's interview with Jacki Zehner (2022).

294 **"like stepping off a cliff"**: Reed Abelson, "Just for Women: A Corporate Alumni Network Just for Women," *New York Times*, October 27, 1999, C1.

295 **"with applesauce stains"**: Abelson, "Corporate Alumni Network."

295 **"You know what I think"**: Janet Hanson writes about this in Janet Hanson, *More Than 85 Broads: Women Making Career Choices, Taking Risks, and Defining Success on Their Own Terms* (New York: McGraw-Hill, 2006). I have not been able to find Moore's published response that Hanson cites.

295 **"Hey Babe!"**: Hanson, *More Than 85 Broads*, 10.

CHAPTER 16: GROUND ZERO

300 **"looked and sounded fake"**: Janet Hanson, *More Than 85 Broads: Women Making Career Choices, Taking Risks, and Defining Success on Their Own Terms* (New York: McGraw-Hill, 2006), 12.

301 **"sunglasses perched"**: Roy J. Harris Jr., "Book Excerpt: As 9/11 Turns 20, 'September Twelfth' Looks at the Wall Street Journal's Pulitzer-Winning Coverage," *Poytner*, September 9, 2021, https://www.poynter.org/business-work/2021/book -excerpt-as-9-11-turns-20-september-twelfth-looks-at-the-wall-street-journals -pulitzer-winning-coverage/.

303 **"Oh my God, the world"**: Lulu Chiang, "Bartiromo—An Eyewitness to History," CNBC, September 13, 2013, https://www.cnbc.com/2010/08/04/bartiromoan -eyewitness-to-history.html.

303 **"crying, crying uncontrollably"**: Chiang, "Eyewitness to History."

303 **Doreen's and Jennifer's plan**: Author's interview with Doreen Mogavero (New York City, 2021).

303 **Doreen said to the doorman**: Author's interview with Doreen Mogavero (New York City, 2021).

304 **"I can see daylight from my apartment"**: Author's interview with Doreen Mogavero (New York City, 2021).

304 **"Listen"**: Author's interview with Doreen Mogavero (New York City, 2021).

304 **"Listen to me"**: Author's interview with Doreen Mogavero (New York City, 2021).

305 **"How the hell did you . . . ?!"** Author's interview with Doreen Mogavero (New York City, 2021).

305 **The next day, Mary Farrell**: Author's interview with Mary Farrell, Zoom, August 24, 2021.

307 **"fleeing sneakers"**: Harris Jr., "Book Excerpt: As 9/11 Turns 20."

307 **The birthday flowers**: Chiang, "An Eyewitness to History."

307 **with just paper and pencil**: Author's interview with Doreen Mogavero (New York City, 2021).

308 **"Dr. Frankenstein"**: Edward Morris, *Wall Streeters: The Creators and Corruptors of American Finance* (New York: Columbia Business School Publishing, 2015), 251.

308 **"I like men"**: Debora Spar, "An Economic Crash Women Might Have Helped Avert," *Washington Post*, January 4, 2009, https://www.washingtonpost.com/ wp-dyn/content/article/2009/01/02/AR2009010202099.html.

308 **"Probably not—"**: Katrin Bennhold, "Where Would We Be If Women Ran Wall Street?" *International Herald Tribune*, February 2, 2009, http://www.theloudest duck.com/mediapdf/IHT%20article_01.2009.pdf/.

308 **"fluffy"**: Carol Hymowitz, "Wall Street's Woman Problem," *The Wall Street Journal*, June 26, 2008, Eastern Edition, 0.

309 **"we'll never solve"**: Shawn T. Taylor, "For Steinem, Women Should Mean Business," *Chicago Tribune*, April 30, 2003, 6.1

309 **In other words:** For example, Jacki Zehner, a former Goldman Sachs partner, founded ShePlace. Jessica Robinson founded Moxie Future. Sallie Krawchek bought 85 Broads and turned it into Ellevest, a digital financial advisor for women.

309 **The idea behind:** LinkedIn Seminar with Jack Zehner, special guest Jessica Robinson, July 14, 2021.

309 **tellingly, in 2022:** Corinne Post, "Private Equity Manages $10 Trillion with Few Women Decision Makers," *Forbes*, November 8, 2022, https://www.forbes.com/sites/corinnepost/2022/11/08/pe-manages-10-trillion-but-is-failing-its-diversity-equation-we-should-all-be-concerned/.

310 **"entry level to the C-suite"**: Kweilin Ellingrud, Alexis Krivkovich, Marie-Claude Nadeau, and Jill Zucker, "Closing the Gender and Race Gaps in North American Financial Services," McKinsey & Company, October 21, 2021, https://www.mckinsey.com/industries/financial-services/our-insights/closing-the-gender-and-race-gaps-in-north-american-financial-services.

310 **The firm has also taken:** Sheelah Kolhatkar, "The Ongoing Saga of the 'Fearless Girl' Statue," *New Yorker*, January 7, 2022, https://www.newyorker.com/business/currency/the-ongoing-saga-of-the-fearless-girl-statue.

POSTSCRIPT

315 **"younger women do not"**: Interview with Alice Jarcho, conducted by Melanie Shorin with Christine Doudna of the Narrative Trust, December 14, 2016, and May 24, 2017, *Remembering Wall Street, 1950–1980*, The Bonnie and Richard Reiss Wall Street Oral History Archive, New-York Historical Society, Transcript, 70.

317 **"somebody who stood up to power"**: Marianne Camille Spraggins, interviewed by Julieanna L. Richardson at New York, NY, with videographer Matthew Hickey on October 20, 2013, *HistoryMakers*, Tape 5.

Image Credits

Index